# Meredith's
# COMPLETE
# Book *of*
# Bible Lists

D0062481

# ABOUT THE AUTHOR

JOEL L. MEREDITH's many years of experience in writing technical manuals for the electronics industry has provided excellent background from which to draw in preparing the information for this book. His personal, in-depth study of the Bible, his careful research in related materials, and his meticulous attention to detail are rounded out by a wry humor—all combining to produce enjoyable and educational reference works. He and his wife live in Roanoke, Texas.

# Meredith's
# COMPLETE
# Book *of*
# Bible Lists

## A One-of-a-Kind
## *Collection of Bible Facts*

# Joel L. Meredith

BETHANY HOUSE PUBLISHERS

*Minneapolis, Minnesota*

*Meredith's Complete Book of Bible Lists*
Copyright © 1980, 1983, 2009
Joel L. Meredith

Originally published in two volumes: *Meredith's Book of Bible Lists* and *Meredith's Second Book of Bible Lists*

The 2009 edition has been edited and updated.

Cover Design by Dan Pitts

Published by Bethany House Publishers
11400 Hampshire Avenue South
Minneapolis, Minnesota 55438

Bethany House Publishers is a division of
Baker Publishing Group, Grand Rapids, Michigan.

Printed in the United States of America

**Library of Congress Cataloging-in-Publication Data**

Meredith, J. L. (Joel L.)
    Meredith's complete book of Bible lists: a one-of-a-kind collection of Bible facts / J.L. Meredith.
        p.   cm.
    "Originally published in two volumes: Meredith's book of Bible lists and Meredith's second book of Bible lists"—T.p. verso.
    Includes bibliographical references.
    ISBN 978-0-7642-0339-8 (pbk. : alk. paper)
    1. Bible indexes.  I. Title.  II. Title: Complete book of Bible lists.

BS432.M39      2009
220.02'16—dc22
                                                                    2008044237

This book is dedicated to my wife, Lorraine Meredith,
and to my mother, Barbara O'Keeffe.

# ACKNOWLEDGMENTS

I wish to pay tribute to the following people for their invaluable help in the preparation and publication of this book.

To my wife, Lorraine, I owe much thanks for her many hours of typing and proofreading. I owe her even more thanks perhaps for her encouragement and her continuous support both as a wife and as a prayer warrior. Her many suggestions for lists were also very helpful.

I want to especially thank the editorial staff at Bethany House for all their work on the book. They also provided me with many ideas for lists, and were so kind and patient with me.

I want to thank the numerous people who wrote to me with suggestions for new lists.

I met a man in Dallas, Texas, who told me he had given my first book, *Meredith's Book of Bible Lists*, to his son, and it turned his son's life around. That sort of news makes it all worthwhile!

# CONTENTS

## FOUR: SUPERNATURAL EVENTS

## FIVE: WORD POWER

## TWELVE: SIN

## THIRTEEN: LIES

## FOURTEEN: MIRACLE WORKERS AND THEIR DEEDS

## FIFTEEN: NUMBERS

## SIXTEEN: FLORA AND FAUNA

## SEVENTEEN: NAMES

## EIGHTEEN: BIBLE TREASURES

## NINETEEN: SHIPS AND OTHER FLOATING OBJECTS

# TWENTY-TWO: DWELLINGS

# TWENTY-THREE: JUST FOR LOOKS

# TWENTY-FOUR: EAT AND DRINK

# THIRTY-TWO: WORK AS UNTO THE LORD

# THIRTY-THREE: MONEY

# THIRTY-FOUR: PEOPLE TO PEOPLE

# THIRTY-FIVE: THE ANIMAL WORLD

# PREFACE

The purpose of *Meredith's Complete Book of Bible Lists* is to entertain, interest, fascinate, stimulate, and most of all, educate. Many people have complained that the Bible is dull reading and that they can't get past all the "begats" (e.g., "Abraham begat Isaac," etc.). Here's a fresh and informative look at some of the interesting and helpful portions of the Scriptures, showing that the Bible is anything but a dull book. And if this book gets the reader back into *The Book*, its real purpose will have been fulfilled.

Some people have complained that the Bible (and religion in general) has too many "thou shalt nots." While *Meredith's Complete Book of Bible Lists* does include some negatives, you will realize from a quick perusal of the Contents pages that the greater weight of Christianity and the Bible is on the positive side—what God has done and is doing for His creation. There are more than four hundred fifty promises from the Bible listed in this book, with special attention paid to conditions for acquiring those promises.

Bible references quoted are from the King James Version, with a few exceptions where the *New International Version* is used or the *New King James Version* is used. Some Scripture quotes are paraphrased by the compiler in the interest of condensing longer passages.

The compiler's preparation for this project includes a thorough familiarity with the Bible; he has read the Old and New Testaments numerous times. His hope is that you will enjoy reading *Meredith's Complete Book of Bible Lists* as much as he enjoyed putting it together.

# 1

# COMMANDMENTS

Laws form the foundation of civilized society. One of the wonders of history is that so much was summed up in the list known as the Ten Commandments. When Jesus lived on the earth, He taught what He called the *two greatest commandments* and in so doing produced an even more concise statement. In the final analysis, governing man's attitude and behavior toward God and his fellow human beings can be summed up in one word—*love*.

Though this truth is found also in the Old Testament, when Jesus came more than two thousand years ago, He further revealed the nature of God: a God who is a Judge and yet a Father, a King and yet a Savior. We are able to find as many as two hundred fifty New Testament commandments. These do not replace the Ten Commandments of the Old Testament, but are a more detailed, further unfolding of God's expectations for the way people should live. Included here is a list of Old Testament laws with Jesus' commentary and application of them.

You will also find Jesus' exhortation to the unconverted, His commandments concerning human relationships, fifty ways to please God, the apostles' exhortations about how to treat others, warnings about other spirits, principles for good family relationships, and guidelines for church leaders.

## 1. The Ten Commandments

1. Thou shalt have no other gods before me (Exodus 20:3).
2. Thou shalt not make unto thee any graven image (Exodus 20:4–5).
3. Thou shalt not take the name of the Lord thy God in vain (Exodus 20:7).
4. Remember the sabbath day, to keep it holy (Exodus 20:8–11).
5. Honour thy father and thy mother (Exodus 20:12).
6. Thou shalt not kill (Exodus 20:13).
7. Thou shalt not commit adultery (Exodus 20:14).
8. Thou shalt not steal (Exodus 20:15).
9. Thou shalt not bear false witness against thy neighbour (Exodus 20:16).
10. Thou shalt not covet . . . any thing that is thy neighbour's (Exodus 20:17).

## 2. The Two Greatest Commandments and the New Commandment

1. Thou shalt love the Lord thy God with all thy heart, and with all thy soul, and with all thy mind (Matthew 22:36–38).
2. Thou shalt love thy neighbour as thyself (Matthew 22:39).
3. A new commandment I give unto you, that ye love one another; as I have loved you, that ye also love one another. By this shall all men know that ye are my disciples, if ye have love one to another (John 13:34–35).

## 3. The Ten Commandments as They Appear in the New Testament

1. According to Jesus
   A. Matthew 19:17–19
      1. Thou shalt do no murder.
      2. Thou shalt not commit adultery.
      3. Thou shalt not steal.
      4. Thou shalt not bear false witness.

     5. Honour thy father and thy mother.

     6. Thou shalt love thy neighbour as thyself.

  B. Mark 10:19

     1. Do not commit adultery.

     2. Do not kill.

     3. Do not steal.

     4. Do not bear false witness.

     5. Defraud not.

     6. Honour thy father and mother.

  C. Luke 18:20

     1. Do not commit adultery.

     2. Do not kill.

     3. Do not steal.

     4. Do not bear false witness.

     5. Honour thy father and thy mother.

2. According to Paul

Romans 13:9

     1. Thou shalt not commit adultery.

     2. Thou shalt not kill.

     3. Thou shalt not steal.

     4. Thou shalt not bear false witness.

     5. Thou shalt not covet.

     6. Thou shalt love thy neighbour as thyself.

## 4. Jesus' Interpretation of Old Testament Law

1. Thou shalt not kill: But I say unto you, that whosoever is angry with his brother without a cause shall be in danger of the judgment (Matthew 5:21–22).

2. Thou shalt not commit adultery: But I say unto you, that whosoever looketh on a woman to lust after her hath committed adultery with her already in his heart (Matthew 5:27–28).

3. Whosoever shall put away his wife, let him give her a writing of divorcement: But I say unto you, that whosoever shall put away his wife, saving for the cause of fornication, causeth her to

commit adultery: and whosoever shall marry her that is divorced committeth adultery (Matthew 5:31–32).

4. Thou shalt not forswear thyself, but shalt perform unto the Lord thy oaths: But I say unto you, Swear not at all (Matthew 5:33–34).

5. An eye for an eye, and a tooth for a tooth: But I say unto you, that ye resist not evil: but whosoever shall smite thee on thy right cheek, turn to him the other also (Matthew 5:38–39).

6. Thou shalt love thy neighbour, and hate thine enemy: But I say unto you, Love your enemies (Matthew 5:43–44).

7. Be ye therefore perfect, even as your Father which is in heaven is perfect (Matthew 5:48).

8. Whatsoever ye would that men should do to you, do ye even so to them: for this is the law and the prophets (Matthew 7:12).

9. Why do thy disciples transgress the tradition of the elders? for they wash not their hands when they eat bread. . . . And he called the multitude, and said unto them, Hear, and understand: Not that which goeth into the mouth defileth a man; but that which cometh out of the mouth, this defileth a man (Matthew 15:2, 10–11).

10. Moses because of the hardness of your hearts suffered you to put away your wives: but from the beginning it was not so. And I say unto you, Whosoever shall put away his wife, except it be for fornication, and shall marry another, committeth adultery: and whoso marrieth her which is put away doth commit adultery (Matthew 19:8–9).

11. Moses suffered to write a bill of divorcement, and to put her away. Jesus answered and said unto them, For the hardness of your heart he wrote you this precept. But from the beginning of the creation God made them male and female. . . . What therefore God hath joined together, let not man put asunder (Mark 10:4–6, 9).

12. Why do ye that which is not lawful to do on the sabbath days? . . . And he said unto them, that the Son of man is Lord also of the sabbath. . . . I will ask you one thing; Is it lawful on the sabbath days to do good, or to do evil? to save life, or to destroy it? (Luke 6:2, 5, 9).

13. Is it lawful to heal on the sabbath day? And he took him, and healed him (Luke 14:3–4).

14. Moses wrote unto us, If any man's brother die, having a wife, and he die without children, that his brother should take his wife, and raise up seed unto his brother. . . . Jesus answering said unto them, The children of this world marry, and are given in marriage (Luke 20:28, 34).

15. The Jews persecuted Jesus, and sought to slay him, because he had done these things on the sabbath day. But Jesus answered them, My Father worketh hitherto, and I work (John 5:16–17).

16. Do not think that I will accuse you to the Father: there is one that accuseth you, even Moses, in whom ye trust. For had ye believed Moses, ye would have believed me: for he wrote of me. But if ye believe not his writings, how shall ye believe my words? (John 5:45–47).

17. Did not Moses give you the law, and yet none of you keepeth the law? Why go ye about to kill me? (John 7:19).

18. Master, this woman was taken in adultery, in the very act. Now Moses in the law commanded us, that such should be stoned: but what sayest thou? . . . When they continued asking him, he lifted up himself, and said unto them, He that is without sin among you, let him first cast a stone at her (John 8:4–5, 7).

19. It is written in your law, that the testimony of two men is true. I am one that bears witness of myself, and the Father that sent me beareth witness of me (John 8:17–18).

20. We know that God spake unto Moses: as for this fellow, we know not from whence he is. The man answered and said unto them, Why herein is a marvelous thing, that ye know not from whence he is, and yet he hath opened mine eyes. . . . If this man were not of God, he could do nothing. . . . And they cast him out. Jesus heard that they had cast him out; and when he had found him, he said unto him, Dost thou believe on the Son of God? . . . Thou hast both seen him, and he it is that talketh with thee (John 9:29–30, 33–35, 37).

21. For a good work we stone thee not; but for blasphemy; and because that thou, being a man, makest thyself God. Jesus answered them, Is it not written in your law, I said, Ye are gods? If he called them gods, unto whom the word of God came, and the scripture cannot be broken; say ye of him, whom the Father hath sanctified,

and sent into the world, Thou blasphemest; because I said, I am the Son of God? (John 10:33–36).

22. I know that he shall rise again in the resurrection at the last day. Jesus said unto her, I am the resurrection, and the life (John 11:24–25).

23. We have heard out of the law that Christ abideth for ever: and how sayest thou, The Son of Man must be lifted up? who is this Son of man? Then Jesus said unto them, Yet a little while is the light with you. Walk while ye have the light, lest darkness come upon you (John 12:34–35).

24. We have a law, and by our law he ought to die, because he made himself the Son of God. . . . Then said Pilate unto him, Speakest thou not unto me? knowest thou not that I have power to crucify thee, and have power to release thee? Jesus answered, Thou couldest have no power at all against me, except it were given thee from above: therefore he that delivered me unto thee hath the greater sin (John 19:7–11).

## 5. The Four Commandments for Gentile Converts

1. Abstain from meats offered to idols (Acts 15:29).

2. Abstain from blood (Acts 15:29).

3. Abstain from things strangled (Acts 15:29).

4. Abstain from fornication (Acts 15:29).

## 6. Exhortations to the Unconverted From the Gospel of Matthew

1. Bring forth fruits meet for repentance (Matthew 3:8).

2. Every tree which bringeth not forth good fruit is hewn down, and cast into the fire (Matthew 3:10; 7:19).

3. He will burn up the chaff with unquenchable fire (Matthew 3:12).

4. Repent: for the kingdom of heaven is at hand (Matthew 4:17).

5. Except your righteousness shall exceed the righteousness of the scribes and Pharisees, ye shall in no case enter into the kingdom of heaven (Matthew 5:20).

6. It is profitable for thee that one of thy members should perish, and not that thy whole body should be cast into hell (Matthew 5:29).

7. No man can serve two masters, for either he will hate the one, and love the other; or else he will hold to the one, and despise the other. Ye cannot serve God and mammon (Matthew 6:24).

8. Enter ye in at the strait gate: for wide is the gate, and broad is the way, that leadeth to destruction, and many there be which go in thereat: because strait is the gate and narrow is the way, which leadeth unto life and few there be that find it (Matthew 7:13–14).

9. Not every one that saith unto me, Lord, Lord, shall enter into the kingdom of heaven; but, he that doeth the will of my Father which is in heaven (Matthew 7:21).

10. Then will I profess unto them, I never knew you: depart from me, ye that work iniquity (Matthew 7:23).

11. Every one that heareth these sayings of mine, and doeth them not, shall be likened unto a foolish man, which built his house upon the sand (Matthew 7:26).

12. Many shall come from the east and west, and shall sit down with Abraham, and Isaac, and Jacob, in the kingdom of heaven. But the children of the kingdom shall be cast out into outer darkness: there shall be weeping and gnashing of teeth (Matthew 8:11–12).

13. Follow me; and let the dead bury their dead (Matthew 8:22).

14. That ye may know that the Son of man hath power on earth to forgive sins, (then saith he to the sick of the palsy,) Arise, take up thy bed, and go unto thine house (Matthew 9:6).

15. I am not come to call the righteous, but sinners to repentance (Matthew 9:13).

16. Fear not them which kill the body, but are not able to kill the soul: but rather fear him which is able to destroy both soul and body in hell (Matthew 10:28).

17. Whosoever shall confess me before men, him will I confess also before my Father which is in heaven. But whosoever shall deny me before men, him will I also deny before my Father which is in heaven (Matthew 10:32–33).

18. He that taketh not his cross, and followeth after me, is not worthy

of me. He that findeth his life shall lose it: and he that loseth his life for my sake shall find it (Matthew 10:38–39).

19. If the mighty works, which were done in you, had been done in Tyre and Sidon, they would have repented long ago in sackcloth and ashes (Matthew 11:21).

20. He that is not with me is against me; and he that gathereth not with me scattereth abroad (Matthew 12:30).

21. How can ye, being evil, speak good things? for out of the abundance of the heart the mouth speaketh (Matthew 12:34).

22. Every idle word that men shall speak, they shall give account thereof in the day of judgment. For by thy words thou shalt be justified, and by thy words thou shalt be condemned (Matthew 12:36–37).

23. In the time of harvest I will say to the reapers, Gather ye together first the tares, and bind them in bundles to burn them: but gather the wheat into my barn (Matthew 13:30).

24. The Son of man shall send forth his angels, and they shall gather out of his kingdom all things that offend, and them which do iniquity; and shall cast them into a furnace of fire: there shall be wailing and gnashing of teeth (Matthew 13:41–42).

25. So shall it be at the end of the world: the angels shall come forth, and sever the wicked from among the just, and shall cast them into the furnace of fire (Matthew 13:49–50).

26. This people draweth nigh unto me with their mouth, and honoureth me with their lips; but their heart is far from me (Matthew 15:8).

27. Every plant which my heavenly Father hath not planted, shall be rooted up (Matthew 15:13).

28. If the blind lead the blind, both shall fall into the ditch (Matthew 15:14).

29. Those things which proceed out of the mouth come forth from the heart: and they defile the man. For out of the heart proceed evil thoughts, murders, adulteries, fornications, thefts, false witness, blasphemies: these are the things which defile a man (Matthew 15:18–20).

30. I am not sent but unto the lost sheep of the house of Israel (Matthew 15:24).

31. If any man will come after me, let him deny himself, and take up his cross, and follow me. For whosoever will save his life shall lose it: and whosoever will lose his life for my sake shall find it. For what is a man profited, if he shall gain the whole world, and lose his own soul? (Matthew 16:24–26).

32. Except ye be converted, and become as little children, ye shall not enter into the kingdom of heaven (Matthew 18:3).

33. It is better for thee to enter into life halt or maimed, rather than having two hands or two feet to be cast into everlasting fire. . . . It is better for thee to enter into life with one eye, rather than having two eyes to be cast into hell fire (Matthew 18:8–9).

34. The Son of man is come to save that which was lost (Matthew 18:11).

35. It is not the will of your Father which is in heaven, that one of these little ones should perish (Matthew 18:14).

36. If thou wilt be perfect, go and sell that thou hast, and give to the poor, and thou shalt have treasure in heaven: and come and follow me (Matthew 19:21).

37. It is easier for a camel to go through the eye of a needle, than for a rich man to enter into the kingdom of God (Matthew 19:24).

38. Every one that hath forsaken houses, or brethren, or sisters, or father, or mother, or wife, or children, or lands, for my name's sake, shall receive an hundredfold, and shall inherit everlasting life (Matthew 19:29).

39. The publicans and the harlots go into the kingdom of God before you. For John came unto you in the way of righteousness, and ye believed him not: but, the publicans and the harlots believed him: and ye, when ye had seen it, repented not afterward, that ye might believe him (Matthew 21:31–32).

40. Whosoever shall fall on this stone shall be broken: but on whomsoever it shall fall, it will grind him to powder (Matthew 21:44).

41. Friend, how camest thou in hither not having a wedding garment? And he was speechless. Then said the king to the servants, Bind him hand and foot, and take him away, and cast him into outer darkness (Matthew 22:12–13).

42. Render therefore unto Caesar the things which are Caesar's; and unto God the things that are God's (Matthew 22:21).

43. Ye shut up the kingdom of heaven against men: for ye neither go in yourselves, neither suffer ye them that are entering to go in. . . . Ye devour widows' houses, and for a pretense make long prayer: therefore ye shall receive the greater damnation. . . . Ye compass sea and land to make one proselyte, and when he is made, ye make him twofold more the child of hell than yourselves (Matthew 23:13–15).

44. Ye pay tithe of mint and anise and cummin, and have omitted the weightier matters of the law, judgment, mercy, and faith: these ought ye to have done, and not to leave the other undone (Matthew 23:23).

45. Ye make clean the outside of the cup and of the platter, but within they are full of extortion and excess. . . . Cleanse first that which is within the cup and platter, that the outside of them may be clean also (Matthew 23:25–26).

46. Ye are like unto whited sepulchres, which indeed appear beautiful outward, but are within full of dead men's bones, and of all unclean- ness. Even so ye also outwardly appear righteous unto men, but within ye are full of hypocrisy and iniquity (Matthew 23:27–28).

47. Ye be witnesses unto yourselves, that ye are the children of them which killed the prophets (Matthew 23:31).

48. Ye serpents, ye generation of vipers, how can ye escape the dam- nation of hell? (Matthew 23:33).

49. He that shall endure unto the end, the same shall be saved (Matthew 24:13).

50. Watch therefore, for ye know neither the day nor the hour wherein the Son of man cometh (Matthew 25:13).

51. Cast ye the unprofitable servant into outer darkness: there shall be weeping and gnashing of teeth (Matthew 25:30).

52. Depart from me, ye cursed, into everlasting fire, prepared for the devil and his angels (Matthew 25:41).

53. These shall go away into everlasting punishment: but the righ- teous into life eternal (Matthew 25:46).

54. This is my blood of the new testament, which is shed for many for the remission of sins (Matthew 26:28).

55. All they that take the sword shall perish with the sword (Matthew 26:52).

## 7. *Fifty Ways to Please God*

1. It becometh us to fulfill all righteousness (Matthew 3:15).

2. Man shall not live by bread alone, but by every word that proceedeth out of the mouth of God (Matthew 4:4).

3. Thou shalt worship the Lord thy God, and him only shalt thou serve (Matthew 4:10).

4. Seek ye first the kingdom of God, and his righteousness (Matthew 6:33).

5. Pray that the Lord of the harvest will send forth labourers into his harvest (Matthew 9:38).

6. Ye must be born again (John 3:7).

7. Worship God in spirit and in truth (John 4:24).

8. Repent and be baptized (Acts 2:38).

9. Obey God rather than man (Acts 5:29).

10. Reckon yourselves to be dead indeed unto sin, but alive unto God through Jesus Christ our Lord (Romans 6:11).

11. Present your bodies a living sacrifice unto God (Romans 12:1).

12. Glorify God in your body, and in your spirit (1 Corinthians 6:20).

13. Desire spiritual gifts (1 Corinthians 14:1).

14. Stand fast in the faith (1 Corinthians 16:13).

15. Do not grieve the Holy Spirit of God (Ephesians 4:30).

16. Be filled with the Spirit (Ephesians 5:18).

17. Pray in the Spirit (Ephesians 6:18).

18. Rejoice in the Lord (Philippians 3:1).

19. Set your affection on things above, where Christ sits at the right hand of God, and not on things on earth (Colossians 3:1–2).

20. Let the peace of God rule in your heart (Colossians 3:15).

21. Let the word of Christ dwell in you richly in all wisdom (Colossians 3:16).

22. Whatsoever ye do in word or deed, do all in the name of the Lord Jesus, giving thanks to God and the Father by him (Colossians 3:17).

23. Pray without ceasing (1 Thessalonians 5:17).

24. In everything give thanks (1 Thessalonians 5:18).

25. Do not neglect your spiritual gift (1 Timothy 4:14).

26. Lay hold on eternal life (1 Timothy 6:12).

27. Be not ashamed of the testimony of our Lord (2 Timothy 1:8).

28. Labour to enter into the rest of the people of God (Hebrews 4:11).

29. Hold fast to your profession of faith without wavering (Hebrews 10:23).

30. The just shall live by faith (Hebrews 10:38).

31. But without faith it is impossible to please him: for he that cometh to God must believe that he is, and that he is a rewarder of them that diligently seek him (Hebrews 11:6).

32. Despise not thou the chastening of the Lord, for whom the Lord loveth he chasteneth, and scourgeth every son whom he receiveth (Hebrews 12:5–6).

33. Make straight paths for your feet (Hebrews 12:13).

34. Refuse not him that speaketh (Hebrews 12:25).

35. Offer the sacrifice of praise to God continually, that is, the fruit of our lips giving thanks to his name (Hebrews 13:15).

36. Receive with meekness the engrafted word, which is able to save your souls (James 1:21).

37. Submit yourselves to God (James 4:7).

38. Is any among you afflicted? Let him pray (James 5:13).

39. Is any merry? Let him sing psalms (James 5:13).

40. Fear God (1 Peter 2:17).

41. Sanctify the Lord God in your heart (1 Peter 3:15).

42. Commit the keeping of [your soul] to God in well doing (1 Peter 4:19).

43. Casting all your care upon him, for he careth for you (1 Peter 5:7).

44. Looking for and hasting unto the coming of the day of God (2 Peter 3:12).

45. Believe on the name of the Son of God; that ye may know that ye have eternal life (1 John 5:13).

46. Build up yourselves on your most holy faith, praying in the Holy Ghost (Jude 20).

47. Keep yourselves in the love of God (Jude 21).

48. Remember from whence thou art fallen, and repent, and do the first works (Revelation 2:5).

49. Fear God, and give glory to him (Revelation 14:7).

50. Worship him that made heaven, and earth, and sea, and the fountains of waters (Revelation 14:7).

## 8. *Jesus' Commandments and Comments Concerning Relationships*

1. I will make you fishers of men (Matthew 4:19).

2. Blessed are the peacemakers: for they shall be called the children of God (Matthew 5:9).

3. Blessed are ye, when men shall revile you, and persecute you, and shall say all manner of evil against you falsely, for my sake (Matthew 5:11).

4. Ye are the light of the world (Matthew 5:14).

5. Let your light so shine before men, that they may see your good works, and glorify your Father (Matthew 5:16).

6. Be reconciled to thy brother, and then come and offer thy gift (Matthew 5:24).

7. Agree with thine adversary quickly, while thou art in the way with him (Matthew 5:25).

8. If any man will sue thee at the law, and take away thy coat, let him have thy cloak also (Matthew 5:40).

9. Whosoever shall compel thee to go a mile, go with him twain (Matthew 5:41).

10. Give to him that asketh thee, and from him that would borrow of thee turn not thou away (Matthew 5:42).

11. If ye love them which love you, what reward have ye? do not even the publicans the same? And if ye salute your brethren only, what do ye more than others? do not even the publicans so? (Matthew 5:46–47).

12. When thou doest thine alms, do not sound a trumpet before thee (Matthew 6:2).

13. When thou prayest, thou shalt not be as the hypocrites are: for they love to pray standing in the synagogues and in the corners of the streets, that they may be seen of men (Matthew 6:5).

14. If ye forgive men their trespasses, your heavenly Father will also forgive you (Matthew 6:14).

15. When ye fast, be not, as the hypocrites, of a sad countenance: for they disfigure their faces, that they may appear unto men to fast (Matthew 6:16).

16. Judge not, that ye be not judged (Matthew 7:1).

17. Thou hypocrite, first cast out the beam out of thine own eye; and then thou shalt see clearly to cast out the mote out of thy brother's eye (Matthew 7:5).

18. Give not that which is holy unto the dogs, neither cast ye your pearls before swine, lest they trample them under their feet, and turn again and rend you (Matthew 7:6).

19. Whatsoever ye would that men should do to you, do ye even so to them: for this is the law and the prophets (Matthew 7:12).

20. By their fruits ye shall know them (Matthew 7:20).

21. Go thy way, show thyself to the priest, and offer the gift that Moses commanded, for a testimony unto them (Matthew 8:4).

22. Follow me; and let the dead bury their dead (Matthew 8:22).

23. They said unto his disciples, Why eateth your Master with publicans and sinners? But when Jesus heard that, he said unto them, They that be whole need not a physician, but they that are sick (Matthew 9:11–12).

24. Pray ye therefore the Lord of the harvest, that he will send forth labourers into his harvest (Matthew 9:38).

25. Go rather to the lost sheep of the house of Israel. And as ye go, preach (Matthew 10:6–7).

26. Heal the sick, cleanse the lepers, raise the dead, cast out devils: freely ye have received, freely give (Matthew 10:8).

27. Whosoever shall not receive you, nor hear your words, when ye depart out of that house or city, shake off the dust of your feet (Matthew 10:14).

28. I send you forth as sheep in the midst of wolves: be ye therefore wise as serpents, and harmless as doves (Matthew 10:16).

29. But beware of men: for they will deliver you up. . . . When they deliver you up, take no thought how or what ye shall speak: for it shall be given you in that same hour what ye shall speak (Matthew 10:17, 19).

30. Ye shall be hated of all men for my name's sake: but he that endureth to the end shall be saved (Matthew 10:22).

31. Fear not them which kill the body, but are not able to kill the soul: but rather fear him which is able to destroy both soul and body in hell (Matthew 10:28).

32. Whosoever therefore shall confess me before men, him will I confess also before my Father which is in heaven (Matthew 10:32).

33. He that loveth father or mother more than me is not worthy of me (Matthew 10:37).

34. He that receiveth you receiveth me (Matthew 10:40).

35. Whosoever shall give to drink unto one of these little ones a cup of cold water only in the name of a disciple, verily I say unto you, he shall in no wise lose his reward (Matthew 10:42).

36. Give ye them to eat (Matthew 14:16).

37. Whoso shall receive one such little child in my name receiveth me (Matthew 18:5).

38. Whoso shall offend one of these little ones which believe in me, it were better that a millstone were hanged about his neck, and that he were drowned in the depth of the sea (Matthew 18:6).

39. If thy brother shall trespass against thee, go and tell him his fault

between thee and him alone: if he shall hear thee, thou hast gained thy brother. But if he will not hear thee, then take with thee one or two more, that in the mouth of two or three witnesses every word may be established. And if he shall neglect to hear them, tell it to the church: but if he neglect to hear the church, let him be unto thee as a heathen man and a publican (Matthew 18:15–17).

40. If two of you shall agree on earth as touching anything that they shall ask, it shall be done for them of my Father which is in heaven (Matthew 18:19).

41. Lord, how oft shall my brother sin against me, and I forgive him? till seven times? Jesus saith unto him, I say not unto thee, Until seven times: but, Until seventy times seven (Matthew 18:21–22).

42. His lord was wroth, and delivered him to the tormentors, till he should pay all that was due unto him. So likewise shall my heavenly Father do also unto you, if ye from your hearts forgive not every one his brother their trespasses (Matthew 18:34–35).

43. All men cannot receive this saying, save they to whom it is given. For there are some eunuchs, which were so born from their mother's womb: and there are some eunuchs, which were made eunuchs of men: and there be eunuchs for the kingdom of heaven's sake. He that is able to receive it, let him receive it (Matthew 19:11–12).

44. Suffer little children, and forbid them not, to come unto me: for of such is the kingdom of heaven (Matthew 19:14–15).

45. Every one that hath forsaken houses, or brethren, or sisters, or father, or mother, or wife, or children, or lands, for my name's sake, shall receive an hundredfold, and shall inherit everlasting life (Matthew 19:29).

46. Whosoever will be chief among you, let him be your servant: even as the Son of man came not to be ministered unto, but to minister, and to give his life a ransom for many (Matthew 20:27–28).

47. Render unto Caesar the things which are Caesar's; and unto God the things that are God's (Matthew 22:21).

48. In the resurrection they neither marry, nor are given in marriage, but are as the angels of God in heaven (Matthew 22:30).

49. Thou shalt love thy neighbour as thyself (Matthew 22:39).

50. Whosoever shall exalt himself shall be abased; and he that shall humble himself shall be exalted (Matthew 23:12).

51. Two shall be in the field; the one shall be taken, and the other left. Two women shall be grinding at the mill; the one shall be taken, and the other left (Matthew 24:40–41).

52. Inasmuch as ye have done it unto one of the least of these my brethren, ye have done it unto me (Matthew 25:40).

53. Put up again thy sword into his place: for all they that take the sword shall perish with the sword (Matthew 26:52).

54. Go tell my brethren that they go into Galilee, and there shall they see me (Matthew 28:10).

55. Go ye therefore, and teach all nations, baptizing them in the name of the Father, and of the Son, and of the Holy Ghost: teaching them to observe all things whatsoever I have commanded you (Matthew 28:19–20).

56. Go home to thy friends, and tell them how great things the Lord hath done for thee, and hath had compassion on thee (Mark 5:19).

57. A prophet is not without honour, but in his own country, and among his own kin, and in his own house (Mark 6:4).

58. Master, we saw one casting out devils in thy name, and he followeth not us: and we forbade him, because he followeth not us. But Jesus said, Forbid him not: for there is no man which shall do a miracle in my name, that can lightly speak evil of me (Mark 9:38–39).

59. Sell whatsoever thou hast, and give to the poor (Mark 10:21).

60. Beware of the scribes, which love to go in long clothing, and love salutations in the marketplaces, and the chief seats in the synagogues, and the uppermost rooms at feasts: which devour widows' houses, and for a pretense make long prayers: these shall receive greater damnation (Mark 12:38–40).

61. When Simon Peter saw it, he fell down at Jesus' knees, saying, Depart from me; for I am a sinful man, O Lord. . . . And Jesus said unto Simon, Fear not; from henceforth thou shalt catch men (Luke 5:8–10).

62. I will ask you one thing; Is it lawful on the sabbath days to do good, or to do evil? to save life, or to destroy it? (Luke 6:9).

63. Woe unto you, when all men shall speak well of you! for so did their fathers to the false prophets (Luke 6:26).

64. Love your enemies, do good to them which hate you, bless them that curse you, and pray for them which despitefully use you (Luke 6:27–28).

65. If ye lend to them of whom ye hope to receive, what thank have ye? for sinners also lend to sinners, to receive as much again. But love ye your enemies, and do good, and lend, hoping for nothing again; and your reward shall be great, and ye shall be the children of the Highest: for he is kind unto the unthankful and to the evil (Luke 6:34–35).

66. Be ye therefore merciful, as your Father also is merciful (Luke 6:36).

67. Give, and it shall be given unto you; good measure, pressed down, and shaken together, and running over, shall men give into your bosom. For with the same measure that ye mete withal it shall be measured to you again (Luke 6:38).

68. Seest thou this woman? I entered into thine house, thou gavest me no water for my feet: but she hath washed my feet with tears, and wiped them with the hairs of her head. Thou gavest me no kiss: but this woman since the time I came in hath not ceased to kiss my feet. My head with oil thou didst not anoint: but this woman hath anointed my feet with ointment. Wherefore I say unto thee, Her sins, which are many, are forgiven (Luke 7:44–47).

69. Which now of these three, thinkest thou, was neighbour unto him that fell among the thieves? And he said, He that showed mercy on him. Then Jesus said unto him, Go, and do thou likewise (Luke 10:36–37).

70. Take heed, and beware of covetousness: for a man's life consisteth not in the abundance of the things which he possesseth (Luke 12:15).

71. When thou art bidden of any man to a wedding, sit not down in the highest room; lest a more honourable man than thou be bidden of him; and he that bade thee and him come and say to thee, Give this man place; and thou begin with shame to take the lowest room. But when thou art bidden, go and sit down in

the lowest room; that when he that bade thee cometh, he may say unto thee, Friend, go up higher (Luke 14:8–10).

72. When thou makest a feast, call the poor, the maimed, the lame, the blind: and thou shalt be blessed; for they cannot recompense thee: for thou shalt be recompensed at the resurrection of the just (Luke 14:13–14).

73. Son, thou art ever with me, and all that I have is thine. It was meet that we should make merry, and be glad: for this thy brother was dead, and is alive again; and was lost, and is found (Luke 15:31–32).

74. If thy brother trespass against thee, rebuke him; and if he repent, forgive him (Luke 17:3).

75. Whether is greater, he that sitteth at meat, or he that serveth? is not he that sitteth at meat? but I am among you as he that serveth (Luke 22:27).

76. If I then, your Lord and Master, have washed your feet; ye also ought to wash one another's feet (John 13:14).

77. By this shall all men know that ye are my disciples, if ye have love one to another (John 13:35).

78. Greater love hath no man than this, that a man lay down his life for his friends. Ye are my friends, if ye do whatsoever I command you (John 15:13–14).

79. Whose soever sins ye remit, they are remitted unto them: and whose soever sins ye retain, they are retained (John 20:23).

80. Jesus saith to Simon Peter, Simon, son of Jonas, lovest thou me more than these? He saith unto him, Yea, Lord; thou knowest that I love thee. He saith unto him, Feed my lambs (John 21:15).

## 9. Guidelines From the Early Church Concerning Relationships

1. Thou, Lord, which knowest the hearts of all men, show whether of these two thou hast chosen, that he may take part of this ministry and apostleship. . . . And they gave forth their lots; and the lot fell upon Matthias; and he was numbered with the eleven apostles (Acts 1:24–26).

2. All that believed were together, and had all things common; and

sold their possessions and goods, and parted them to all men, as every man had need (Acts 2:44–45).

3. Silver and gold have I none; but such as I have give I thee; In the name of Jesus Christ of Nazareth rise up and walk (Acts 3:6).

4. And the multitude of them that believed were of one heart and of one soul: neither said any of them that aught of the things which he possessed was his own; but they had all things common. . . . Neither was there any among them that lacked: for as many as were possessors of lands or houses sold them, and brought the price of the things that were sold, and laid them down at the apostles' feet: and distribution was made unto every man according as he had need (Acts 4:32, 34–35).

5. Their widows were neglected in the daily ministration. Then the twelve called the multitude of the disciples unto them, and said, It is not reason that we should leave the word of God, and serve tables. Wherefore, brethren, look ye out among you seven men of honest report, full of the Holy Ghost and wisdom, whom we may appoint over this business (Acts 6:1–3).

6. He kneeled down, and cried with a loud voice, Lord, lay not this sin to their charge. And when he had said this, he fell asleep (Acts 7:60).

7. What God hath cleansed, that call not thou common (Acts 10:15).

8. Ye know how that it is an unlawful thing for a man that is a Jew to keep company, or come unto one of another nation; but God hath showed me that I should not call any man common or unclean (Acts 10:28).

9. Of a truth I perceive that God is no respecter of persons: but in every nation he that feareth him, and worketh righteousness, is accepted with him (Acts 10:34–35).

10. Can any man forbid water, that these should not be baptized, which have received the Holy Ghost as well as we? And he commanded them to be baptized in the name of the Lord (Acts 10:47–48).

11. As God gave them the like gift as he did unto us, who believed on the Lord Jesus Christ; what was I, that I could withstand God? (Acts 11:17).

12. When they were come, and had gathered the church together, they rehearsed all that God had done with them and how he had opened the door of faith unto the Gentiles (Acts 14:27).

13. My sentence is, that we trouble not them, which from among the Gentiles are turned to God: but that we write unto them [what God and the church require] (Acts 15:19–20).

14. When they had read, they rejoiced for the consolation. And Judas and Silas, being prophets also themselves, exhorted the brethren with many words and confirmed them (Acts 15:31–32).

15. Let us go again and visit our brethren in every city where we have preached the word of the Lord, and see how they do (Acts 15:36).

16. They spake unto him the word of the Lord, and to all that were in his house, and he took them the same hour of that night, and washed their stripes; and was baptized, he and all his, straightway (Acts 16:32–33).

17. I kept back nothing that was profitable unto you, but have showed you, and have taught you publicly, and from house to house (Acts 20:20).

18. I have showed you all things, how that so labouring ye ought to support the weak, and to remember the words of the Lord Jesus, how he said, It is more blessed to give than to receive (Acts 20:35).

19. Then said Paul unto him, God shall smite thee, thou whited wall: for sittest thou to judge me after the law, and commandest me to be smitten contrary to the law? And they that stood by said, Revilest thou God's high priest? Then said Paul, I wist not, brethren, that he was the high priest: for it is written, Thou shalt not speak evil of the ruler of thy people (Acts 23:3–5).

20. Paul besought them all to take meat, saying, This is the fourteenth day that ye have tarried and continued fasting, having taken nothing. Wherefore I pray you to take some meat: for this is for your health: for there shall not a hair fall from the head of any of you (Acts 27:33–34).

21. Paul dwelt two whole years in his own hired house, and received all that came in unto him (Acts 28:30).

## 10. Paul's Examples and Exhortations About How to Treat Others

1. I thank my God through Jesus Christ for you all, that your faith is spoken of throughout the whole world. For God is my witness, whom I serve with my spirit in the gospel of his Son, that without ceasing I make mention of you always in my prayers (Romans 1:8–9).

2. Thou art inexcusable, O man, whosoever thou art that judgest: for wherein thou judgest another, thou condemnest thyself; for thou that judgest doest the same things (Romans 2:1).

3. Thou therefore which teachest another, teachest thou not thyself? (Romans 2:21).

4. I could wish that myself were accursed from Christ for my brethren, my kinsmen according to the flesh (Romans 9:3).

5. Brethren, my heart's desire and prayer to God for Israel is, that they might be saved (Romans 10:1).

6. If some of the branches be broken off, and thou, being a wild olive tree, wert grafted in among them, and with them partakest of the root and the fatness of the olive tree; boast not against the branches (Romans 11:17–18).

7. Be kindly affectioned one to another with brotherly love; in honour preferring one another (Romans 12:10).

8. Distributing to the necessity of the saints; given to hospitality. Bless them which persecute you: bless, and curse not. Rejoice with them that do rejoice, and weep with them that weep. Be of the same mind one toward another. Mind not high things, but condescend to men of low estate. Be not wise in your own conceits. Recompense to no man evil for evil. Provide things honest in the sight of all men. If it be possible, as much as lieth in you, live peaceably with all men. Dearly beloved, avenge not yourselves, but rather give place unto wrath: for it is written, Vengeance is mine; I will repay, saith the Lord. Therefore if thine enemy hunger, feed him; if he thirst, give him drink: for in so doing thou shalt heap coals of fire on his head (Romans 12:13–20).

9. Let every soul be subject unto the higher powers. For there is no power but of God: the powers that be are ordained of God. Whosoever therefore resisteth the power, resisteth the ordinance

of God: and they that resist shall receive to themselves damnation (Romans 13:1–2).

10. Pay ye tribute also: for they are God's ministers, attending continually upon this very thing. Render therefore to all their dues: tribute to whom tribute is due; custom to whom custom; fear to whom fear; honour to whom honour (Romans 13:6–7).

11. Owe no man any thing, but to love one another: for he that loveth another hath fulfilled the law (Romans 13:8).

12. If there be any other commandment, it is briefly comprehended in this saying, namely, Thou shalt love thy neighbour as thyself. Love worketh no ill to his neighbour: therefore love is the fulfilling of the law (Romans 13:9–10).

13. Him that is weak in the faith receive ye, but not to doubtful disputations. For one believeth that he may eat all things: another, who is weak, eateth herbs. Let not him that eateth despise him that eateth not; and let not him which eateth not judge him that eateth: for God hath received him (Romans 14:1–2).

14. Who art thou that judgest another man's servant? to his own master he standeth or falleth (Romans 14:4).

15. Why dost thou judge thy brother? or why dost thou set at nought thy brother? for we shall all stand before the judgment seat of Christ (Romans 14:10).

16. Let us not therefore judge one another any more: but judge this rather, that no man put a stumblingblock or an occasion to fall in his brother's way (Romans 14:13).

17. If thy brother be grieved with thy meat, now walkest thou not charitably. Destroy not him with thy meat, for whom Christ died (Romans 14:15).

18. Let us therefore follow after the things which make for peace, and things wherewith one may edify another. . . . It is good neither to eat flesh, nor to drink wine, nor any thing whereby thy brother stumbleth, or is offended, or is made weak (Romans 14:19, 21).

19. We then that are strong ought to bear the infirmities of the weak, and not to please ourselves. Let every one of us please his neighbour for his good to edification. For even Christ pleased not himself (Romans 15:1–3).

20. The God of patience and consolation grant you to be like-minded one toward another according to Christ Jesus: that ye may with one mind and one mouth glorify God, even the Father of our Lord Jesus Christ. Wherefore receive ye one another, as Christ also received us to the glory of God (Romans 15:5–7).

21. I have strived to preach the gospel, not where Christ was named, lest I should build upon another man's foundation (Romans 15:20).

22. Receive her in the Lord, as becometh saints, and ye assist her in whatsoever business she hath need of you: for she hath been a succourer of many, and of myself also (Romans 16:2).

23. Greet Priscilla and Aquila my helpers in Christ Jesus: who have for my life laid down their own necks (Romans 16:3–4).

24. Greet Mary, who bestowed much labour on us. . . . Salute Urbane, our helper in Christ. . . . Salute Tryphaena and Tryphosa, who labour in the Lord. Salute the beloved Persis, which laboured much in the Lord (Romans 16:6, 9, 12).

25. Salute one another with a holy kiss (Romans 16:16).

26. Mark them which cause divisions and offenses contrary to the doctrine which ye have learned; and avoid them (Romans 16:17).

27. I beseech you, brethren, by the name of our Lord Jesus Christ, that ye all speak the same thing, and that there be no divisions among you; but that ye be perfectly joined together in the same mind and in the same judgment (1 Corinthians 1:10).

28. Ye are yet carnal: for whereas there is among you envying, strife, and divisions, are ye not carnal, and walk as men? For while one saith, I am of Paul; and another, I am of Apollos; are ye not carnal? (1 Corinthians 3:3–4).

29. We are labourers together with God (1 Corinthians 3:9).

30. We both hunger, and thirst, and are naked, and are buffeted, and have no certain dwelling place; and labour, working with our own hands: being reviled, we bless, being persecuted, we suffer it: being defamed, we entreat (1 Corinthians 4:11–13).

31. Concerning him that hath so done this deed [fornication], in the name of the Lord Jesus Christ, when ye are gathered together, and my spirit, with the power of our Lord Jesus Christ, to deliver such

an one unto Satan for the destruction of the flesh, that the spirit may be saved in the day of the Lord Jesus (1 Corinthians 5:4–5).

32. I wrote unto you in an epistle not to company with fornicators: yet not altogether with the fornicators of this world, or with the covetous, or extortioners, or with idolaters; for then must ye needs go out of the world. But now I have written unto you not to keep company, if any man that is called a brother be a fornicator, or covetous, or an idolater, or a railer, or a drunkard, or an extortioner; with such a one, no, not to eat. For what have I to do to judge them also that are without? do not ye judge them that are within? But them that are without God judgeth. Therefore put away from among yourselves that wicked person (1 Corinthians 5:9–13).

33. Dare any of you, having a matter against another, go to law before the unjust, and not before the saints? Do ye not know that the saints shall judge the world? and if the world shall be judged by you, are ye unworthy to judge the smallest matters? Know ye not that we shall judge angels? how much more things that pertain to this life? (1 Corinthians 6:1–3).

34. Now therefore there is utterly a fault among you, because ye go to law one with another. Why do ye not rather take wrong? why do ye not rather suffer yourselves to be defrauded? (1 Corinthians 6:7).

35. Take heed lest by any means this liberty of yours become a stumblingblock to them that are weak (1 Corinthians 8:9).

36. If meat make my brother to offend, I will eat no flesh while the world standeth, lest I make my brother to offend (1 Corinthians 8:13).

37. Let no man seek his own, but every man another's wealth (1 Corinthians 10:24).

38. If any of them that believe not bid you to a feast, and ye be disposed to go; whatsoever is set before you, eat, asking no question for conscience sake. But if any man say unto you, This is offered in sacrifice unto idols, eat not for his sake that showed it (1 Corinthians 10:27–28).

39. Give none offense, neither to the Jews, nor to the Gentiles, nor to the church of God: even as I please all men in all things, not seeking mine own profit, but the profit of many, that they may be saved (1 Corinthians 10:32–33).

40. The body is not one member, but many. If the foot shall say, Because I am not the hand, I am not of the body; is it therefore not of the body?. . . But now hath God set the members every one of them in the body, as it hath pleased him (1 Corinthians 12:14–15, 18).

41. There should be no schism in the body; but that the members should have the same care one for another. And whether one member suffer, all the members suffer with it; or one member be honoured, all the members rejoice with it (1 Corinthians 12:25–26).

42. Though I bestow all my goods to feed the poor, and though I give my body to be burned, and have not charity, it profiteth me nothing (1 Corinthians 13:3).

43. Concerning the collection for the saints, as I have given order to the churches of Galatia, even so do ye. Upon the first day of the week let every one of you lay by him in store, as God hath prospered him (1 Corinthians 16:1–2).

44. Submit yourselves unto such, and to every one that helpeth with us, and laboureth (1 Corinthians 16:16).

45. We faint not; but have renounced the hidden things of dishonesty, not walking in craftiness, nor handling the word of God deceitfully; but by manifestation of the truth commending ourselves to every man's conscience in the sight of God (2 Corinthians 4:1–2).

46. Giving no offense in any thing, that the ministry be not blamed (2 Corinthians 6:3).

47. Providing for honest things, not only in the sight of the Lord, but also in the sight of men (2 Corinthians 8:21).

48. Every man according as he purposeth in his heart, so let him give; not grudgingly, or of necessity: for God loveth a cheerful giver (2 Corinthians 9:7).

49. Do ye look on things after the outward appearance? (2 Corinthians 10:7).

50. They would that we should remember the poor; the same which I also was forward to do (Galatians 2:10).

51. There is neither Jew nor Greek, there is neither bond nor free, there is neither male nor female: for ye are all one in Christ Jesus (Galatians 3:28).

52. If ye bite and devour one another, take heed that ye be not consumed one of another (Galatians 5:15).

53. Let us not be desirous of vain glory, provoking one another, envying one another (Galatians 5:26).

54. If a man be overtaken in a fault, ye which are spiritual, restore such an one in the spirit of meekness; considering thyself, lest thou also be tempted. Bear ye one another's burdens, and so fulfil the law of Christ (Galatians 6:1–2).

55. As we have therefore opportunity, let us do good unto all men, especially unto them who are of the household of faith (Galatians 6:10).

56. Walk worthy of the vocation wherewith ye are called, with all lowliness and meekness, with long-suffering, forbearing one another in love; endeavoring to keep the unity of the Spirit in the bond of peace (Ephesians 4:1–3).

57. Putting away lying, speak every man truth with his neighbour: for we are members one of another. Be ye angry, and sin not: let not the sun go down upon your wrath (Ephesians 4:25–26).

58. Let him that stole steal no more: but rather let him labour, working with his hands the thing which is good, that he may have to give to him that needeth. Let no corrupt communication proceed out of your mouth, but that which is good to the use of edifying, that it may minister grace unto the hearers (Ephesians 4:28–29).

59. Be ye kind one to another, tenderhearted, forgiving one another, even as God for Christ's sake hath forgiven you (Ephesians 4:32).

60. Servants, be obedient to them that are your masters according to the flesh, with singleness of your heart, as unto Christ; not with eyeservice, as menpleasers; but as the servants of Christ, doing the will of God from the heart; with good will doing service, as to the Lord, and not to men (Ephesians 6:5–7).

61. Ye masters, do the same things unto them, forbearing threatening: knowing that your Master also is in heaven (Ephesians 6:9).

62. Stand fast in one spirit, with one mind striving together for the faith of the gospel; and in nothing terrified by your adversaries (Philippians 1:27–28).

63. Let nothing be done through strife or vainglory; but in lowliness of mind let each esteem other better than themselves. Look not every man on his own things, but every man also on the things of others (Philippians 2:3–4).

64. Beware lest any man spoil you through philosophy and vain deceit, after the tradition of men, after the rudiments of the world, and not after Christ (Colossians 2:8).

65. Lie not one to another, seeing that ye have put off the old man with his deeds. . . . Forbearing one another, and forgiving one another, if any man have a quarrel against any: even as Christ forgave you, so also do ye (Colossians 3:9, 13).

66. No man go beyond and defraud his brother in any matter: because that the Lord is the avenger of all such, as we also have fore-warned you and testified (1 Thessalonians 4:6).

67. We exhort you, brethren, warn them that are unruly, comfort the feebleminded, support the weak, be patient toward all men. See that none render evil for evil unto any man; but ever follow that which is good, both among yourselves, and to all men (1 Thessalonians 5:14–15).

68. If any man obey not our word by this epistle, note that man, and have no company with him, that he may be ashamed. Yet count him not as an enemy, but admonish him as a brother (2 Thessalonians 3:14–15).

69. Let no man despise thy youth; but be thou an example of the believers, in word, in conversation, in charity, in spirit, in faith, in purity (1 Timothy 4:12).

70. Rebuke not an elder, but entreat him as a father; and the younger men as brethren; the elder women as mothers; the younger as sisters, with all purity. Honour widows that are widows indeed (1 Timothy 5:1–3).

71. Them that sin rebuke before all, that others also may fear. I charge thee before God, and the Lord Jesus Christ, and the elect angels, that thou observe these things without preferring one before another, doing nothing by partiality. Lay hands suddenly on no man, neither be partaker of other men's sins: keep thyself pure (1 Timothy 5:20–22).

72. Charge them that are rich in this world, that they be not high-

minded, nor trust in uncertain riches, but in the living God, who giveth us richly all things to enjoy; that they do good, that they be rich in good works, ready to distribute, willing to communicate; laying up in store for themselves a good foundation against the time to come, that they may lay hold on eternal life (1 Timothy 6:17–19).

73. The servant of the Lord must not strive; but be gentle unto all men, apt to teach, patient, in meekness instructing those that oppose themselves; if God peradventure will give them repentance to the acknowledging of the truth (2 Timothy 2:24–25).

74. A man that is an heretic after the first and second admonition reject; knowing that he that is such is subverted, and sinneth, being condemned of himself (Titus 3:10–11).

## 11. *Exhortations From Other Apostles About How to Treat Others*

1. Pure religion and undefiled before God and the Father is this: to visit the fatherless and the widows in their affliction, and to keep himself unspotted from the world (James 1:27).

2. If ye have respect to persons, ye commit sin, and are convinced of the law as transgressors (James 2:9).

3. If a brother or sister be naked and destitute of daily food, and one of you say unto them, Depart in peace, be ye warmed and filled; notwithstanding ye give them not those things which are needful to the body; what doth it profit? (James 2:15–16).

4. Ye adulterers and adulteresses, know ye not that the friendship of the world is enmity with God? Whosoever therefore will be a friend of the world is the enemy of God (James 4:4).

5. Speak not evil one of another, brethren. He that speaketh evil of his brother and judgeth his brother, speaketh evil of the law, and judgeth the law (James 4:11).

6. Grudge not one against another, brethren, lest ye be condemned: behold, the judge standeth before the door (James 5:9).

7. Is any sick among you? let him call for the elders of the church; and let them pray over him, anointing him with oil in the name of the Lord (James 5:14).

8. Confess your faults one to another, and pray for one another, that ye may be healed (James 5:16).

9. Seeing ye have purified your souls in obeying the truth through the Spirit unto unfeigned love of the brethren, see that ye love one another with a pure heart fervently (1 Peter 1:22).

10. Having your conversation honest among the Gentiles: that, whereas they speak against you as evildoers, they may by your good works, which they shall behold, glorify God in the day of visitation. Submit yourselves to every ordinance of man for the Lord's sake: whether it be to the king, as supreme: or unto governors, as unto them that are sent by him for the punishment of evildoers, and for the praise of them that do well (1 Peter 2:12–14).

11. Honour all men. Love the brotherhood. Fear God. Honour the king (1 Peter 2:17).

12. Servants, be subject to your masters with all fear; not only to the good and gentle, but also the froward. For this is thankworthy, if a man for conscience toward God endure grief, suffering wrongfully. For what glory is it, if, when ye be buffeted for your faults, ye shall take it patiently? but if, when ye do well, and suffer for it, ye take it patiently, this is acceptable with God (1 Peter 2:18–20).

13. Be ye all of one mind, having compassion one of another, love as brethren, be pitiful, be courteous: not rendering evil for evil, or railing for railing: but contrariwise blessing; knowing that ye are thereunto called, that ye should inherit a blessing (1 Peter 3:8–9).

14. If ye suffer for righteousness' sake, happy are ye: and be not afraid of their terror, neither be troubled; but sanctify the Lord God in your hearts: and be ready always to give an answer to every man that asketh you a reason of the hope that is in you with meekness and fear (1 Peter 3:14–15).

15. Above all things have fervent charity among yourselves: for charity shall cover a multitude of sins. Use hospitality one to another without grudging. As every man hath received the gift, even so minister the same one to another, as good stewards of the manifold grace of God (1 Peter 4:8–10).

16. Greet ye one another with a kiss of charity (1 Peter 5:14).

17. Add to your faith virtue; and to virtue knowledge; and to

knowledge temperance; and to temperance patience; and to patience godliness; and to godliness brotherly kindness; and to brotherly kindness charity (2 Peter 1:5–7).

18. He that saith he is in the light, and hateth his brother, is in darkness even until now. He that loveth his brother abideth in the light, and there is none occasion of stumbling in him. But he that hateth his brother is in darkness, and walketh in darkness, and knoweth not whither he goeth, because that darkness hath blinded his eyes (1 John 2:9–11).

19. This is the message that ye heard from the beginning, that we should love one another (1 John 3:11).

20. We know that we have passed from death unto life, because we love the brethren. He that loveth not his brother abideth in death. Whosoever hateth his brother is a murderer: and ye know that no murderer hath eternal life abiding in him. Hereby perceive we the love of God, because he laid down his life for us: and we ought to lay down our lives for the brethren. But whoso hath this world's good, and seeth his brother have need, and shutteth up his bowels of compassion from him, how dwelleth the love of God in him? My little children, let us not love in word, neither in tongue; but in deed and in truth (1 John 3:14–18).

21. This is his commandment: that we should believe on the name of his Son Jesus Christ, and love one another, as he gave us commandment (1 John 3:23).

22. Beloved, let us love one another: for love is of God; and every one that loveth is born of God, and knoweth God. He that loveth not knoweth not God; for God is love (1 John 4:7–8).

23. If God so loved us, we ought also to love one another. No man hath seen God at any time. If we love one another, God dwelleth in us, and his love is perfected in us (1 John 4:11–12).

24. If a man say, I love God, and hateth his brother, he is a liar: for he that loveth not his brother whom he hath seen, how can he love God whom he hath not seen? And this commandment have we from him: that he who loveth God love his brother also (1 John 4:20–21).

25. If any man see his brother sin a sin which is not unto death, he shall ask, and he shall give him life for them that sin not unto

death. There is a sin unto death: I do not say that he shall pray for it (1 John 5:16).

26. I beseech thee, lady, not as though I wrote a new commandment unto thee, but that which we had from the beginning, that we love one another. And this is love: that we walk after his commandments (2 John 5–6).

27. If there come any unto you, and bring not this doctrine, receive him not into your house, neither bid him Godspeed; for he that biddeth him Godspeed is partaker of his evil deeds (2 John 10–11).

28. Keep yourselves in the love of God, looking for the mercy of our Lord Jesus Christ unto eternal life. And of some have compassion, making a difference: and others save with fear, pulling them out of the fire; hating even the garment spotted by the flesh (Jude 21–23).

29. I know thy works, and thy labour, and thy patience, and how thou canst not bear them which are evil: and thou hast tried them which say they are apostles, and are not, and hast found them liars (Revelation 2:2).

## 12. *Eight Warnings Concerning Evil Spirits*

1. When the unclean spirit is gone out of a man, he walketh through dry places, seeking rest, and findeth none. Then he saith, I will return into my house from whence I came out; and when he is come, he findeth it empty, swept, and garnished. Then goeth he, and taketh with himself seven other spirits more wicked than himself, and they enter in and dwell there: and the last state of that man is worse than the first (Matthew 12:43–45).

2. Neither give place to the devil (Ephesians 4:27).

3. Put on the whole armour of God, that ye may be able to stand against the wiles of the devil (Ephesians 6:11).

4. Resist the devil, and he will flee from you (James 4:7).

5. Be sober, be vigilant; because your adversary the devil, as a roaring lion, walketh about, seeking whom he may devour: whom resist, steadfast in the faith (1 Peter 5:8–9).

6. Believe not every spirit, but try the spirits whether they are of God: because many false prophets are gone out into the world. Hereby

know ye the Spirit of God: Every spirit that confesseth that Jesus Christ is come in the flesh is of God: and every spirit that confesseth not that Jesus Christ is come in the flesh is not of God: and this is that spirit of antichrist, whereof ye have heard that it should come; and even now already is it in the world (1 John 4:1–3).

7. If any man worship the beast and his image, and receive his mark in his forehead, or in his hand, the same shall drink of the wine of the wrath of God, which is poured out without mixture into the cup of his indignation; and he shall be tormented with fire and brimstone in the presence of the holy angels, and in the presence of the Lamb: and the smoke of their torment ascendeth up for ever and ever: and they have no rest day nor night, who worship the beast and his image, and whosoever receiveth the mark of his name (Revelation 14:9–11).

8. They are the spirits of devils, working miracles, which go forth unto the kings of the earth and of the whole world, to gather them to the battle of that great day of God Almighty (Revelation 16:14).

## 13. Principles for Good Family Relationships

1. Let every man have his own wife, and let every women have her own husband. Let the husband render unto the wife due benevolence: and likewise also the wife unto the husband. The wife hath not power of her own body, but the husband: and likewise also the husband hath not power of his own body, but the wife. Defraud ye not one the other, except it be with consent for a time, that ye may give yourselves to fasting and prayer; and come together again, that Satan tempt you not for your incontinency (1 Corinthians 7:2–5).

2. Unto the married I command, yet not I, but the Lord, Let not the wife depart from her husband: but and if she depart, let her remain unmarried, or be reconciled to her husband: and let not the husband put away his wife. . . . And the woman which hath an husband that believeth not, and if he be pleased to dwell with her, let her not leave him. For the unbelieving husband is sanctified by the wife, and the unbelieving wife is sanctified by the husband: else were your children unclean; but now are they holy. But if the unbelieving depart, let him depart. A brother or

a sister is not under bondage in such cases: but God hath called us to peace (1 Corinthians 7:10–15).

3. I would have you know, that the head of every man is Christ; and the head of the woman is the man; and the head of Christ is God (1 Corinthians 11:3).

4. Be ye not unequally yoked together with unbelievers: for what fellowship hath righteousness with unrighteousness: and what communion hath light with darkness? (2 Corinthians 6:14).

5. The children ought not to lay up for the parents, but the parents for the children (2 Corinthians 12:14).

6. Children, obey your parents in the Lord: for this is right. Honour thy father and mother; which is the first commandment with promise; that it may be well with thee, and thou mayest live long on the earth. And, ye fathers, provoke not your children to wrath: but bring them up in the nurture and admonition of the Lord (Ephesians 6:1–4).

7. Wives, submit yourselves unto your own husband, as it is fit in the Lord. Husbands, love your wives, and be not bitter against them. Children, obey your parents in all things: for this is well-pleasing unto the Lord. Fathers, provoke not your children to anger, lest they be discouraged (Colossians 3:18–21).

8. If any provide not for his own, and specially for those of his own house, he hath denied the faith, and is worse than an infidel (1 Timothy 5:8).

9. I will therefore that the younger women marry, bear children, guide the house, give none occasion to the adversary to speak reproachfully (1 Timothy 5:14).

10. Ye wives, be in subjection to your own husbands; that, if any obey not the word, they also may without the word be won by the conversation of the wives; while they behold your chaste conversation coupled with fear. Whose adorning let it not be that outward adorning of plaiting the hair, and of wearing of gold, or of putting on of apparel; but let it be the hidden man of the heart, in that which is not corruptible, even the ornament of a meek and quiet spirit, which is in the sight of God of great price. For after this manner in the old time the holy women also, who trusted in God, adorned themselves, being in subjection unto

their own husbands: even as Sarah obeyed Abraham calling him lord: whose daughters ye are, as long as ye do well, and are not afraid with any amazement. Likewise, ye husbands, dwell with them according to knowledge, giving honour unto the wife, as unto the weaker vessel, and as being heirs together of the grace of life; that your prayers be not hindered (1 Peter 3:1–7).

## 14. Guidelines for Church Leaders

1. Look ye out among you seven men of honest report, full of the Holy Ghost and wisdom, whom we may appoint over this business. But we will give ourselves continually to prayer, and to the ministry of the word (Acts 6:3–4).

2. If a man desire the office of a bishop, he desireth a good work. A bishop then must be blameless, the husband of one wife, vigilant, sober, of good behaviour, given to hospitality, apt to teach; not given to wine, no striker, not greedy of filthy lucre; but patient, not a brawler, not covetous; one that ruleth well his own house, having his children in subjection with all gravity; (for if a man know not how to rule his own house, how shall he take charge of the church of God?) Not a novice, lest being lifted up with pride he fall into the condemnation of the devil. Moreover he must have a good report of them which are without; lest he fall into the reproach and snare of the devil (1 Timothy 3:1–7).

3. Likewise must the deacons be grave, not doubletongued, not given to much wine, not greedy of filthy lucre; holding the mystery of the faith in a pure conscience. And let these also first be proved; then let them use the office of a deacon, being found blameless. Even so must their wives be grave, not slanderers, sober, faithful in all things. Let the deacons be the husbands of one wife, ruling their children and their own houses well. For they that have used the office of a deacon well purchase to themselves a good degree, and great boldness in the faith which is in Christ Jesus (1 Timothy 3:8–13).

4. Let the elders that rule well be counted worthy of double honour, especially they who labour in the word and doctrine. For the scripture saith, Thou shalt not muzzle the ox that treadeth out the corn. And, the labourer is worthy of his reward. Against an elder receive not an accusation, but before two or three

witnesses. Them that sin rebuke before all, that others also may fear (1 Timothy 5:17–20).

5. If any be blameless, the husband of one wife, having faithful children not accused of riot or unruly. For a bishop must be blameless, as the steward of God; not self-willed, not soon angry, not given to wine, no striker, not given to filthy lucre; but a lover of hospitality, a lover of good men, sober, just, holy, temperate; holding fast the faithful word as he hath been taught, that he may be able by sound doctrine both to exhort and to convince the gainsayers (Titus 1:6–9).

6. Is any among you afflicted? let him pray. Is any merry? let him sing psalms. Is any sick among you? let him call for the elders of the church; and let them pray over him, anointing him with oil in the name of the Lord (James 5:13–14).

7. The elders which are among you I exhort, who am also an elder, and a witness of the sufferings of Christ, and also a partaker of the glory that shall be revealed: feed the flock of God which is among you, taking the oversight thereof, not by constraint, but willingly; nor for filthy lucre, but of a ready mind; neither as being lords over God's heritage, but being examples to the flock. And when the chief Shepherd shall appear, ye shall receive a crown of glory that fadeth not away (1 Peter 5:1–4).

# 2
## PROMISES

There are two old gospel hymns that talk about "standing on the promises" and "every promise in the Book is mine." What are those promises? Is access to the promises automatic or are there conditions to be met?

The lists in this chapter offer a total of 452 promises. Some are unconditional, requiring no action by the receiver. Many of them are conditional; a certain course of action is required in order to be included in the promise. And there are some warnings—not as enjoyable reading but nevertheless important.

Whether it's salvation, finances, blessings, health, peace, forgiveness, or a good night's sleep, He has given promises to cover all these and more.

Most of the promises in this chapter are arranged in tabular form, giving the promise, the condition, and the Scripture reference. A few Scripture portions have been condensed or paraphrased slightly in the interest of abbreviation.

### 15. Twenty-three Unconditional New Testament Promises

1. For [Jesus'] yoke is easy, and [his] burden is light (Matthew 11:30).

2. With God all things are possible (Matthew 19:26).

3. All power is given to [Jesus] in heaven and in earth (Matthew 28:18).

4. God is no respecter of persons (Acts 10:34).

5. Every one of us shall give account of himself to God (Romans 14:12).

6. Where the Spirit of the Lord is, there is liberty (2 Corinthians 3:17).

7. Godly sorrow works repentance to salvation (2 Corinthians 7:10).

8. [In Christ] there is neither Greek nor Jew, circumcision nor uncircumcision, Barbarian, Scythian, bond nor free (Colossians 3:11).

9. [Jesus] abides faithful (2 Timothy 2:13).

10. The Lord knows them that are his (2 Timothy 2:19).

11. Jesus Christ [is] the same yesterday, and today, and forever (Hebrews 13:8).

12. God does not tempt any man (James 1:13).

13. Every good gift and every perfect gift . . . comes from the Father (James 1:17).

14. [Jesus] is gone into heaven, and is on the right hand of God; angels and authorities and powers being made subject unto him (1 Peter 3:22).

15. The Lord is not slack concerning his promise, . . . but is long-suffering toward us, not willing that any should perish, but that all should come to repentance (2 Peter 3:9).

16. [Jesus] comes with clouds; and every eye shall see him (Revelation 1:7).

17. Jesus is Lord of lords, and King of kings (Revelation 17:14).

18. Satan shall be bound a thousand years, and he will not be able to deceive the nations during that time (Revelation 20:1–3).

19. The devil will be cast into the lake of fire and brimstone and shall be tormented day and night forever (Revelation 20:7–10).

20. There shall not be anything that defiles, works abomination, or makes a lie in the New Jerusalem (Revelation 21:27).

21. There shall be no more curse in the New Jerusalem (Revelation 22:3).

22. There shall be no night in the New Jerusalem (Revelation 22:5).

23. The Lord God gives light in the New Jerusalem (Revelation 22:5).

## 16. *Twenty-nine New Testament Promises About the Future*

| PROMISE | CONDITION | REFERENCE |
|---|---|---|
| 1. You shall inherit the earth. | If you are meek. | Matthew 5:5 |
| 2. Great is your reward in heaven. | When men shall revile and persecute you for Jesus' sake. | Matthew 5:11–12 |
| 3. The Son of Man shall reward every man. | According to your works. | Matthew 16:27 |
| 4. The end shall come. | When the gospel of the kingdom shall be preached in all the world for a witness to all nations. | Matthew 24:14 |
| 5. God shall make him ruler over all his goods. | Be a faithful and wise servant. | Matthew 24:45–47 |
| 6. He shall not lose his reward. | Giving a cup of water to drink in my name, because you belong to Christ. | Mark 9:41 |
| 7. Jesus shall change our vile body that it may be fashioned like unto His glorious body. | Stand fast in the Lord. | Philippians 3:20–21; 4:1 |
| 8. When Christ shall appear, you shall appear with Him in glory. | If you are risen with Christ. | Colossians 3:1, 4 |

| PROMISE | CONDITION | REFERENCE |
|---|---|---|
| 9. The dead in Christ shall rise first. Then we which are alive and remain shall be caught up together with them in the clouds, to meet the Lord in the air: and so shall we ever be with the Lord. | If we believe that Jesus died and rose again. | 1 Thessalonians 4:14–17 |
| 10. There is laid up a crown of righteousness, which the Lord gave at that day. | To all them that love His appearing. | 2 Timothy 4:8 |
| 11. We may serve God acceptably. | With reverence and godly fear. | Hebrews 12:28 |
| 12. He shall receive the crown of life. | Endure temptation and love the Lord. | James 1:12 |
| 13. Elders [pastors] shall receive a crown of glory that fades not away. | Feed the flock of God among you, taking the oversight, not by constraint, but willingly; not for filthy lucre, but of a ready mind . . . being examples to the flock. | 1 Peter 5:1–4 |
| 14. When [Jesus] shall appear, we shall be like Him. | If we are sons of God. | 1 John 3:2 |
| 15. We shall receive a full reward. | Confess that Jesus Christ is come in the flesh. | 2 John 7–8 |
| 16. [Jesus] will give to eat of the tree of life which is in the midst of the paradise of God. | To him that overcomes. | Revelation 2:7 |
| 17. [Jesus] will give you a crown of life. | Be faithful unto death. | Revelation 2:10 |
| 18. He shall not be hurt of the second death. | He that overcomes. | Revelation 2:11 |

| PROMISE | CONDITION | REFERENCE |
|---|---|---|
| 19. [Jesus] will give to eat of the hidden manna and will give a white stone, and in the stone a new name written which no man knows save he that receives it. | To him that overcomes. | Revelation 2:17 |
| 20. [Jesus] will give to every one of you. | According to your works. | Revelation 2:23 |
| 21. [Jesus] will give power over the nations, and will give the morning star. | To him that overcomes and keeps [Jesus'] works to the end. | Revelation 2:26–28 |
| 22. He shall be clothed in white raiment, and [Jesus] will not blot out his name out of the book of life. | He that overcomes. | Revelation 3:5 |
| 23. [Jesus] will confess his name before the Father and before His angels. | He that overcomes. | Revelation 3:5 |
| 24. [Jesus] will make him a pillar in the temple of God and he shall go out no more: and [Jesus] will write upon him the name of God, and the name of the city of God, which is New Jerusalem. [Jesus] will write upon him [His] new name. | He that overcomes. | Revelation 3:12 |
| 25. [Jesus] will grant to sit with Him in His throne. | To him that overcomes. | Revelation 3:21 |

| PROMISE | CONDITION | REFERENCE |
|---|---|---|
| 26. They are before the throne of God, and serve Him day and night . . . They shall hunger no more; neither shall the sun light on them, nor any heat. For the Lamb which is in the midst of the throne shall feed them, and shall lead them unto living fountains of waters: and God shall wipe away all tears. | They have washed their robes and made them white in the blood of the Lamb. | Revelation 7:14–17 |
| 27. They shall live and reign with Christ a thousand years. | They which had not worshiped the beast, neither his image, neither had received his mark. | Revelation 20:4 |
| 28. He shall inherit all things. | He that overcomes. | Revelation 21:7 |
| 29. They shall enter into the holy Jerusalem. | They which are written in the Lamb's book of life. | Revelation 21:10, 27 |

## 17. *Twenty-nine New Testament Promises for Prosperity*

| PROMISE | CONDITION | REFERENCE |
|---|---|---|
| 1. They shall be comforted. | They that mourn. | Matthew 5:4 |
| 2. They shall obtain mercy. | Be merciful. | Matthew 5:7 |
| 3. Your Father shall reward you openly. | When you give alms, let not your left hand know what your right hand does. When you pray, enter into your closet, and . . . pray to your Father. | Matthew 6:3–6 |

| PROMISE | CONDITION | REFERENCE |
|---|---|---|
| 4. All these things shall be added unto you. | Seek first the kingdom of God and His righteousness. | Matthew 6:25–33 |
| 5. It shall be given you. | Ask. | Matthew 7:7 |
| 6. You shall find. | Seek. | Matthew 7:7 |
| 7. It shall be opened unto you. | Knock. | Matthew 7:7 |
| 8. You shall say to this mountain, "Remove hence to yonder place," and it shall remove. | If you have faith as a grain of mustard seed. | Matthew 17:20 |
| 9. You shall receive a hundredfold and shall inherit everlasting life. | Everyone that has forsaken houses, or brethren, or sisters, or father, or mother, or wife, or children, or lands, for Jesus' name's sake. | Matthew 19:29 |
| 10. You shall receive all things. | Ask in prayer, believing. | Matthew 21:22 |
| 11. He shall be exalted. | Humble yourself. | Matthew 23:12 |
| 12. Your reward shall be great, and you shall be the children of the Highest. | Love your enemies and do good, and lend, hoping for nothing again. | Luke 6:35 |
| 13. It shall be given unto you; good measure, pressed down, and running over. | Give. | Luke 6:38 |
| 14. [Jesus] will do it. | Ask anything in [Jesus'] name. | John 14:14 |
| 15. You shall ask what you will, and it will be done unto you. | Abide in me [Jesus] and let my words abide in you. | John 15:7 |

| PROMISE | CONDITION | REFERENCE |
|---|---|---|
| 16. You shall receive that your joy may be full. | Ask the Father in [Jesus'] name. | John 16:23–24 |
| 17. You shall live. | Through the Spirit mortify the deeds of the body. | Romans 8:13 |
| 18. All things work together for good. | Love God and be called according to His purpose. | Romans 8:28 |
| 19. No one can be against you. | When God is for you. | Romans 8:31 |
| 20. God is able to make all grace abound toward you; that you, having all sufficiency in all things, may abound in every good work. | Be a cheerful giver. | 2 Corinthians 9:7–8 |
| 21. I can do all things. | Through Christ's strength. | Philippians 4:13 |
| 22. You may know how you ought to answer every man. | Let your speech be with grace, seasoned with salt. | Colossians 4:6 |
| 23. You may walk honestly toward them that are without, and have lack of nothing. | Love one another; study to be quiet and to do your own business and to work with your own hands. | 1 Thessalonians 4:9–12 |
| 24. You may be perfect and entire, wanting nothing. | Let patience have her perfect work. | James 1:4 |
| 25. Wisdom shall be given. | Ask of God . . . in faith. | James 1:5–6 |
| 26. The prayer of faith shall save the sick, and the Lord shall raise him up. | Call for the elders of the church; and let them pray over you, anointing you with oil in the name of the Lord. Confess your faults one to another and pray for one another. | James 5:14–16 |

| PROMISE | CONDITION | REFERENCE |
|---------|-----------|-----------|
| 27. He will love life and see good days. | Refrain your tongue from evil, your lips from guile. Shun evil, do good, seek peace. | 1 Peter 3:10 |
| 28. Whatsoever we ask, we receive of [God]. | Keep His commandments and do those things that are pleasing in His sight. | 1 John 3:22 |
| 29. [God] hears us, whatever we ask, and we know that we have the petitions that we desired of Him. | Ask anything according to His will. | 1 John 5:15 |

## 18. *One Hundred Ten New Testament Promises for Spiritual Blessings*

| PROMISE | CONDITION | REFERENCE |
|---------|-----------|-----------|
| 1. Theirs is the kingdom of heaven. | Be poor in spirit. | Matthew 5:3 |
| 2. They shall be filled with righteousness. | Hunger and thirst after righteousness. | Matthew 5:6 |
| 3. They shall see God. | Be pure in heart. | Matthew 5:8 |
| 4. They shall be called the children of God. | Be peacemakers. | Matthew 5:9 |
| 5. Him will I confess before my Father which is in heaven. | Confess me [Jesus] before men. | Matthew 10:32 |
| 6. You shall find rest unto your soul. | Take my [Jesus'] yoke upon you and learn of me. | Matthew 11:29 |
| 7. You will be as my brother, and sister, and mother. | Do the will of my Father. | Matthew 12:50 |

| PROMISE | CONDITION | REFERENCE |
|---------|-----------|-----------|
| 8. You shall enter into the kingdom of heaven. | Be converted and become as little children. | Matthew 18:3 |
| 9. Be greatest in the kingdom of heaven. | Humble yourself as a little child. | Matthew 18:4 |
| 10. You shall receive Jesus. | Receive a little child in Jesus' name. | Matthew 18:5 |
| 11. Anything that they shall ask it shall be done for them of my Father which is in heaven. | If two of you shall agree on earth as touching anything. | Matthew 18:19 |
| 12. There am I in the midst of them. | Where two or three are gathered in my [Jesus'] name. | Matthew 18:20 |
| 13. He shall be saved. | He that endures unto the end. | Matthew 24:13 |
| 14. You can minister unto Jesus. | When you minister unto one of the least of His brethren. | Matthew 25:40 |
| 15. I [Jesus] am with you always, even unto the end of the world. | Go and teach all nations, baptizing them . . . teaching them to observe all things whatsoever I have commanded you. | Matthew 28:19–20 |
| 16. You shall not be judged. | Judge not. | Luke 6:37 |
| 17. You shall not be condemned. | Condemn not. | Luke 6:37 |
| 18. You shall be forgiven. | Forgive. | Luke 6:37 |
| 19. Your heavenly Father shall give the Holy Spirit. | Ask Him. | Luke 11:13 |

| PROMISE | CONDITION | REFERENCE |
|---|---|---|
| 20. The Son of Man shall confess [you] before the angels of God. | Confess me [Jesus] before men. | Luke 12:8 |
| 21. You shall have everlasting life. | Believe in the only begotten Son of God. | John 3:16 |
| 22. You shall have eternal life. | Eat my [Jesus'] flesh and drink my blood. | John 6:54 |
| 23. He shall not walk in darkness, but shall have the light of life. | Follow [Jesus]. | John 8:12 |
| 24. You shall know the truth, and the truth shall set you free. | Continue in [Jesus'] word. | John 8:31–32 |
| 25. You shall be free indeed. | If the Son makes you free. | John 8:36 |
| 26. Him will my [Jesus'] Father honour. | If any man serve me. | John 12:26 |
| 27. The works that I [Jesus] do shall he do also; and greater works than these shall he do also. | Believe on Him. | John 14:12 |
| 28. I [Jesus] will pray the Father, and He shall give you another Comforter that He may abide with you forever. | Love me [Jesus] and keep my commandments. | John 14:15–16 |
| 29. He that loves me [Jesus] shall be loved of my Father, and I will love him, and will manifest myself to him. | Know His commandments and keep them. | John 14:21 |
| 30. He brings forth much fruit. | Abide in me [Jesus], and I in him. | John 15:5 |

| PROMISE | CONDITION | REFERENCE |
|---|---|---|
| 31. You are [Jesus'] friend. | Do whatsoever Jesus commands you. | John 15:14 |
| 32. You shall receive power. | After the Holy Ghost is come upon you. | Acts 1:8 |
| 33. You shall receive the gift of the Holy Ghost. | Repent and be baptized every one of you in the name of Jesus Christ for the remission of sins. | Acts 2:38 |
| 34. Receive remission of sins. | Believe in Jesus. | Acts 10:43 |
| 35. There is therefore now no condemnation. | Walk not after the flesh, but after the Spirit. | Romans 8:1 |
| 36. He that raised up Christ from the dead shall quicken your mortal body. | The Spirit of Him who raised up Jesus from the dead dwells in you. | Romans 8:11 |
| 37. They are the sons of God. | If you are led by the Spirit of God. | Romans 8:14 |
| 38. We are joint-heirs with Christ. | If we are children of God. | Romans 8:17 |
| 39. In all these things we are more than conquerors. | Through Him that loved us. | Romans 8:37 |
| 40. Christ is the end of the law for righteousness. | To everyone that believes. | Romans 10:4 |
| 41. You shall be saved. | Confess with your mouth the Lord Jesus, and believe in your heart that God has raised Him from the dead. | Romans 10:9 |
| 42. You shall have faith. | Hear the Word of God. | Romans 10:17 |
| 43. Preaching of the cross is the power of God. | If you are saved. | 1 Corinthians 1:18 |

| PROMISE | CONDITION | REFERENCE |
|---|---|---|
| 44. Jesus is made unto us wisdom, righteousness, sanctification, and redemption. | If you are in Christ Jesus. | 1 Corinthians 1:30 |
| 45. We can know the things that are freely given to us of God. | If we have received the Spirit of God. | 1 Corinthians 2:12 |
| 46. You are one spirit with the Lord. | If you are joined unto the Lord. | 1 Corinthians 6:17 |
| 47. Your labor is not in vain. | In the Lord. | 1 Corinthians 15:58 |
| 48. He is a new creature; old things are passed away; behold, all things are become new. | If any man be in Christ. | 2 Corinthians 5:17 |
| 49. The weapons of our warfare are not carnal but mighty to the pulling down of strongholds. | Through God. | 2 Corinthians 10:4 |
| 50. We are justified. | By the faith of Jesus Christ. | Galatians 2:16 |
| 51. You have put on Christ. | If you have been baptized into Christ. | Galatians 3:27 |
| 52. You are Abraham's seed and an heir according to the promise. | If you are Christ's. | Galatians 3:29 |
| 53. You shall not fulfill the lust of the flesh. | Walk in the Spirit. | Galatians 5:16 |
| 54. You are not under the law. | If you are led of the Spirit. | Galatians 5:18 |
| 55. In due season we shall reap. | If we faint not. | Galatians 6:9 |

| PROMISE | CONDITION | REFERENCE |
|---|---|---|
| 56. You were sealed with the Holy Spirit. | After you believed [in Jesus]. | Ephesians 1:13 |
| 57. We have access by one Spirit to the Father. | Through [Jesus]. | Ephesians 2:18 |
| 58. The peace of God, which passes all understanding, shall keep your heart and mind through Christ Jesus. | In everything by prayer and supplication with thanksgiving let your requests be made known unto God. | Philippians 4:6–7 |
| 59. Jesus has reconciled you, in the body of His flesh through death, to present you holy and unblameable and unreprovable in His sight. | If you continue in the faith and are not moved away from the hope of the gospel. | Colossians 1:21–23 |
| 60. You shall both save yourself and them that hear you. | Take heed to yourself and to the doctrine; continue in them. | 1 Timothy 4:16 |
| 61. We shall live with [Jesus]. | If we are dead with Him. | 2 Timothy 2:11 |
| 62. We shall reign with [Jesus]. | If we suffer with Him. | 2 Timothy 2:12 |
| 63. He shall be a vessel unto honour, sanctified, and meet for the Master's use, and prepared unto every good work. | If a man purge himself from [iniquity]. | 2 Timothy 2:19, 21 |
| 64. The man of God may be perfect, thoroughly furnished unto all good works. | If scripture is used for doctrine, for reproof, for correction, for instruction in righteousness. | 2 Timothy 3:16–17 |
| 65. We may obtain mercy and find grace to help in time of need. | Come boldly unto the throne of grace. | Hebrews 4:16 |
| 66. [Jesus] is able to save them to the uttermost. | Come to God by [Jesus]. | Hebrews 7:25 |

| PROMISE | CONDITION | REFERENCE |
|---|---|---|
| 67. Jesus has perfected you forever. | If you are sanctified. | Hebrews 10:14 |
| 68. You will receive the promise. | Have patience after you have done the will of God. | Hebrews 10:36 |
| 69. It is possible to please God. | Believe that He is, and that He is a rewarder of them that diligently seek Him. | Hebrews 11:6 |
| 70. God deals with you as with a son. | If you endure chastening. | Hebrews 12:7 |
| 71. This man shall be blessed in his deed. | Whoso looks into the perfect law of liberty and continues therein, being not a forgetful hearer, but a doer of the work. | James 1:25 |
| 72. God gives grace. | To the humble. | James 4:6 |
| 73. God will draw nigh to you. | Draw nigh to God. | James 4:8 |
| 74. God shall lift you up. | Humble yourself in the sight of the Lord. | James 4:10 |
| 75. You are kept by the power of God. | Through faith. | 1 Peter 1:5 |
| 76. Receive the end of your faith, even the salvation of your soul. | Whom having not seen, you love, in whom, though now you see Him not, yet believing, you rejoice with joy unspeakable. | 1 Peter 1:8–9 |
| 77. Husbands, your prayers will not be hindered. | Dwell with your wife according to knowledge, giving honor . . . as unto the weaker vessel . . . being heirs together of the grace of life. | 1 Peter 3:7 |

| PROMISE | CONDITION | REFERENCE |
|---|---|---|
| 78. The eyes of the Lord are over you, and His ears are open to your prayers. | Be righteous. | 1 Peter 3:12 |
| 79. You are happy and Christ is glorified. | If you are reproached for the name of Christ. | 1 Peter 4:14 |
| 80. The spirit of glory and of God rests upon you. | If you are reproached for the name of Christ. | 1 Peter 4:14 |
| 81. God gives grace to you. | Be clothed with humility. | 1 Peter 5:5 |
| 82. God will exalt you in due time. | Humble yourself under the mighty hand of God. | 1 Peter 5:6 |
| 83. You shall be fruitful in the knowledge of our Lord Jesus Christ. | If these things be in you . . . faith, virtue, knowledge, temperance, patience, godliness, brotherly kindness, and love. | 2 Peter 1:5–8 |
| 84. You shall never fall. | Give diligence to make your calling and election sure. | 2 Peter 1:10 |
| 85. The Lord knows how to deliver you out of temptations. | Be godly. | 2 Peter 2:9 |
| 86. We have fellowship with one another, and the blood of Jesus cleanses us from all sin. | Walk in the light as He [God] is in the light. | 1 John 1:7 |
| 87. [God] is faithful and just to forgive us our sins and to cleanse us from all unrighteousness. | If we confess our sins. | 1 John 1:9 |
| 88. We do know that we know Him [Jesus]. | If we keep His commandments. | 1 John 2:3 |
| 89. In him verily is the love of God perfected. | Whoever keeps His word. | 1 John 2:5 |

| PROMISE | CONDITION | REFERENCE |
|---|---|---|
| 90. He abides in the light and there is no occasion of stumbling in him. | He that loves his brother. | 1 John 2:10 |
| 91. Ye need not that any man teach you. | If the anointing which ye have received of Him abides in you. | 1 John 2:27 |
| 92. He cannot sin. | Whosoever is born of God. | 1 John 3:9 |
| 93. We know that we have passed from death unto life. | If we love the brethren. | 1 John 3:14 |
| 94. We have confidence toward God. | If our heart does not condemn us. | 1 John 3:21 |
| 95. You dwell in Jesus, and He dwells in you. | Keep Jesus' commandments. | 1 John 3:24 |
| 96. He that knows God hears you. | If you are of God. | 1 John 4:6 |
| 97. God dwells in us, and His love is perfected in us. | If we love one another. | 1 John 4:12 |
| 98. God dwells in you, and you dwell in God. | Confess that Jesus is the Son of God. | 1 John 4:15 |
| 99. You dwell in God, and God dwells in you. | Dwell in love. | 1 John 4:16 |
| 100. You are born of God. | Believe that Jesus is the Christ. | 1 John 5:1 |
| 101. We know that we love the children of God. | When we love God and keep His commandments. | 1 John 5:2 |
| 102. You overcome the world. | Believe that Jesus is the Son of God. | 1 John 5:4–5 |

| PROMISE | CONDITION | REFERENCE |
|---|---|---|
| 103. He has eternal life. | He that has the Son. | 1 John 5:11–12 |
| 104. [God] shall give him life for them that sin not unto death. | If any man see his brother sin a sin not unto death, he shall ask [God]. | 1 John 5:16 |
| 105. He sins not, he keeps himself, and the wicked one touches him not. | Whoever is born of God. | 1 John 5:18 |
| 106. He has both the Father and the Son. | He that abides in the doctrine of Christ. | 2 John 9 |
| 107. I [Jesus] have set before you an open door, and no man can shut it. | Keep Jesus' word, and do not deny His name. | Revelation 3:8 |
| 108. [Jesus] will keep you from the hour of temptation. | Keep the word of Jesus' patience. | Revelation 3:10 |
| 109. I [Jesus] will come in to him, and will sup with him. | Those who hear Jesus' voice and open the door. | Revelation 3:20 |
| 110. Overcome the accuser of our brethren. | By the blood of the Lamb, and by the word of your testimony, love not your lives unto death. | Revelation 12:10–11 |

## 19. *Eighteen New Testament Warnings*

| WARNING | CONDITION | REFERENCE |
|---|---|---|
| 1. [Jesus] will deny us. | If we deny Him. | 2 Timothy 2:12 |
| 2. You shall suffer persecution. | Live godly in Christ. | 2 Timothy 3:12 |
| 3. There remains no more sacrifice for sins. | If we sin willfully after that we have received the knowledge of the truth. | Hebrews 10:26 |

| WARNING | CONDITION | REFERENCE |
|---|---|---|
| 4. He is guilty of breaking all the commandments. | Whosoever shall keep the whole law, and yet offend in one point. | James 2:10 |
| 5. You have not. | Because you ask not. | James 4:2 |
| 6. You ask and receive not. | Because you ask amiss, that you may consume it upon your lusts. | James 4:3 |
| 7. He is blind and cannot see afar off, and has forgotten that he was purged from his old sins. | He that lacks faith, virtue, knowledge, temperance, patience, godliness, brotherly kindness, and love. | 2 Peter 1:5–9 |
| 8. The latter end is worse with them than the beginning. | If after they have escaped the pollutions of the world through the knowledge of the Lord . . . they are again entangled and overcome. | 2 Peter 2:20 |
| 9. We deceive ourselves, and the truth is not in us. | If we say that we have no sin. | 1 John 1:8 |
| 10. We make [God] a liar, and His word is not in us. | If we say that we have not sinned. | 1 John 1:10 |
| 11. He is in darkness, and walks in darkness, and knows not where he goes, because that darkness has blinded his eyes. | He that hates his brother. | 1 John 2:11 |
| 12. The love of the Father is not in him. | If any man loves the world. | 1 John 2:15 |
| 13. He is a liar. | He that denies that Jesus is the Christ. | 1 John 2:22 |

| WARNING | CONDITION | REFERENCE |
|---------|-----------|-----------|
| 14. He has not God. | Whoever transgresses and abides not in the doctrine of Christ. | 2 John 9 |
| 15. All that dwell upon the earth shall worship [the beast]. | All whose names are not written in the book of life of the Lamb. | Revelation 13:8 |
| 16. The same shall drink of the wine of the wrath of God and . . . be tormented with fire and brimstone. | If any man worship the beast and . . . receive his mark in his forehead or in his hand. | Revelation 14:9–11 |
| 17. He was thrown into the lake of fire. | Whosoever was not found in the book of life. | Revelation 20:15 |
| 18. They shall have their part in the lake which burns with fire and brimstone: which is the second death. | The fearful, unbelieving, the abominable, murderers, whoremongers, sorcerers, idolaters, and all liars. | Revelation 21:8 |

## 20. Forty-three Unconditional Old Testament Promises

1. God's way is perfect (2 Samuel 22:31).
2. God controls the weather (Job 37:3–13).
3. You shall be judged righteously by God (Psalm 9:8).
4. The Lord will be a refuge in times of trouble (Psalm 9:9).
5. The Lord is King forever and ever (Psalm 10:16).
6. The Lord's throne is in heaven (Psalm 11:4).
7. The Lord loves righteousness (Psalm 11:7).
8. The heavens declare the glory of God (Psalm 19:1).
9. All the ends of the world shall remember and turn unto the Lord: and all the kindreds of the nations shall worship before thee (Psalm 22:27).
10. The Lord will bless His people with peace (Psalm 29:11).
11. God makes wars to cease unto the end of the earth (Psalm 46:9).
12. God is for me (Psalm 56:9).

13. God knows my foolishness, and my sins are not hidden from Him (Psalm 69:5).

14. God says, My covenant will I not break (Psalm 89:34).

15. The Lord's enemies shall perish (Psalm 92:9).

16. The Lord knows the thoughts of man (Psalm 94:11).

17. God's truth endures to all generations (Psalm 100:5).

18. The Lord is merciful (Psalm 103:8).

19. The Lord is gracious (Psalm 103:8).

20. The Lord is slow to anger (Psalm 103:8).

21. The Lord will not keep His anger forever (Psalm 103:9).

22. Precious in the sight of the Lord is the death of His saints (Psalm 116:15).

23. The earth is full of the Lord's mercy (Psalm 119:64).

24. [God's] faithfulness is unto all generations (Psalm 119:90).

25. The entrance of God's words gives understanding to the simple (Psalm 119:130).

26. God neither slumbers nor sleeps (Psalm 121:3–4).

27. Children are a heritage from the Lord (Psalm 127:3).

28. The Lord is good (Psalm 135:3).

29. God has magnified His word above all His name (Psalm 138:2).

30. You cannot flee from God's presence (Psalm 139:7–8).

31. God's understanding is infinite (Psalm 147:5).

32. Love covers all sins (Proverbs 10:12).

33. The Lord of hosts will defend Jerusalem (Isaiah 31:5).

34. The word of our God shall stand forever (Isaiah 40:8).

35. There is none that can deliver out of God's hand (Isaiah 43:13).

36. God's counsel shall stand, and He will do all His pleasure (Isaiah 46:10–11).

37. [God's] righteousness shall not be abolished (Isaiah 51:6).

38. Jesus was wounded for our transgressions (Isaiah 53:5).

39. God's word shall not return unto Him void, but it shall accomplish

that which [He] pleases and it shall prosper in the thing whereto [He] sent it (Isaiah 55:11).

40. God will bring upon you the good that He has promised you (Jeremiah 32:42).

41. The Lord your God in the midst of you is mighty (Zephaniah 3:17).

42. The Lord changes not (Malachi 3:6).

43. From the rising of the sun even unto the going down of the same, my (God's) name shall be great among the Gentiles (Malachi 1:11).

## 21. *Seven Old Testament Promises for Families*

| PROMISE | CONDITION | REFERENCE |
|---|---|---|
| 1. Blessed shall be the fruit of your body. | If you shall hearken unto the voice of the Lord. | Deuteronomy 28:2–4 |
| 2. God's righteousness is unto your children's children. | To such as keep His covenant and to those that remember His commandments to do them. | Psalm 103:17 |
| 3. Your wife shall be as a fruitful vine . . . your children like olive plants round about your table. You shall see your children's children. | The man that fears the Lord. | Psalm 128:1–6 |
| 4. The Lord relieves the fatherless and widow. | He that has the God of Jacob for his help, whose hope is in the Lord. | Psalm 146:5, 9 |
| 5. Your children shall be delivered. | If you are righteous. | Proverbs 11:21 |
| 6. You shall leave an inheritance to your children's children. | If you are a good man. | Proverbs 13:22 |
| 7. When a child is old, he will not depart from the way he should go. | Train up a child in the way he should go. | Proverbs 22:6 |

## 22. *Seven Old Testament Promises Concerning Nations*

| PROMISE | CONDITION | REFERENCE |
|---|---|---|
| 1. God will bless them. | That bless Israel. | Genesis 12:3 |
| 2. All the nations of the earth shall be blessed in Abraham. | Unconditional | Genesis 18:18 |
| 3. God will hear from heaven, and will forgive their sin, and will heal their land. | If my (God's) people, which are called by my name, humble themselves, pray, seek my face, and turn from their wicked ways. | 2 Chronicles 7:14 |
| 4. Blessed is the nation. | Whose God is the Lord. | Psalm 33:12 |
| 5. Happy is that people. | Whose God is the Lord. | Psalm 144:15 |
| 6. A nation is exalted. | By righteousness. | Proverbs 14:34 |
| 7. Blessed art thou, O land. | When thy king is the son of nobles, thy princes eat in due season, for strength, not for drunkenness. | Ecclesiastes 10:17 |

## 23. *Ninety-three Promises to the Individual From the Psalms*

| PROMISE | CONDITION | REFERENCE |
|---|---|---|
| 1. He shall be like a tree planted by the rivers of water, that brings forth his fruit in his season; his leaf also shall not wither; whatever he does shall prosper. | The man that walks not in the counsel of the ungodly, nor stands in the way of sinners, nor sits in the seat of the scornful. But his delight is in the law of the Lord and in his law does he meditate day and night. | Psalm 1:1–3 |
| 2. The Lord has set you apart and will hear you when you call to Him. | If you are godly. | Psalm 4:3 |

| PROMISE | CONDITION | REFERENCE |
|---|---|---|
| 3. He shall abide in the Lord's tabernacle. | He that walks uprightly, and works righteousness, and speaks the truth in his heart. | Psalm 15:1–2 |
| 4. I shall not be moved. Therefore my heart is glad, and my glory rejoices; my flesh also shall rest in hope. | I have set the Lord always before me. | Psalm 16:8–9 |
| 5. Your flesh shall rest in hope. | Set the Lord always before you. | Psalm 16:8–9 |
| 6. There is fulness of joy. | In God's presence. | Psalm 16:11 |
| 7. The Lord shall deliver you. | If He delights in you. | Psalm 18:19 |
| 8. The Lord shall reward you. | According to your righteousness. | Psalm 18:20 |
| 9. The Lord will show himself merciful. | With the merciful. | Psalm 18:25 |
| 10. There is great reward. | In keeping the law of the Lord. | Psalm 19:11 |
| 11. I shall not want. | The Lord is my shepherd. | Psalm 23:1 |
| 12. The Lord restores my soul: He leads me in the paths of righteousness. | The Lord is my shepherd. | Psalm 23:3 |
| 13. Though I walk through the valley of the shadow of death, I will fear no evil. | The Lord is my shepherd. | Psalm 23:4 |
| 14. Goodness and mercy shall follow me all the days of my life. | The Lord is my shepherd. | Psalm 23:6 |

| PROMISE | CONDITION | REFERENCE |
|---|---|---|
| 15. I will dwell in the house of the Lord forever. | The Lord is my shepherd. | Psalm 23:6 |
| 16. He shall receive the blessing from the Lord and righteousness from the God of his salvation. | He that has clean hands, and a pure heart; who has not lifted up his soul to vanity, nor sworn deceitfully. | Psalm 24:4–5 |
| 17. God will guide in judgment, and will teach His ways. | To the meek. | Psalm 25:9 |
| 18. All of the paths of the Lord are mercy and truth unto such. | Keep His covenant and His testimonies. | Psalm 25:10 |
| 19. His soul shall dwell at ease. | He that fears the Lord. | Psalm 25:12–13 |
| 20. The Lord shall strengthen your heart. | Wait upon the Lord. | Psalm 27:14 |
| 21. [The Lord] shall strengthen your heart. | Be of good courage. | Psalm 31:24 |
| 22. Blessed is he. | He whose transgression is forgiven, whose sin is covered. | Psalm 32:1 |
| 23. Mercy shall compass him about. | He that trusts in the Lord. | Psalm 32:10 |
| 24. Our heart shall rejoice in [the Lord]. | Because we have trusted in his holy name. | Psalm 33:21 |
| 25. The Lord delivered me from all my fears. | I sought the Lord. | Psalm 34:4 |
| 26. The angel of the Lord encamps round about them and delivers them. | Them that fear Him. | Psalm 34:7 |

| PROMISE | CONDITION | REFERENCE |
|---|---|---|
| 27. See that the Lord is good. | Taste Him. | Psalm 34:8 |
| 28. They shall not want any good thing. | Seek the Lord and fear Him. | Psalm 34:9–10 |
| 29. The Lord delivers them out of all of their troubles. | The righteous. | Psalm 34:17 |
| 30. Not one of his bones is broken. | The righteous. | Psalm 34:19–20 |
| 31. None shall be desolate. | Trust in the Lord. | Psalm 34:22 |
| 32. You shall dwell in the land, and you shall be fed. | Trust in the Lord and do good. | Psalm 37:3 |
| 33. The Lord shall give you the desires of your heart. | Delight yourself also in the Lord. | Psalm 37:4 |
| 34. The Lord shall bring it to pass. | Commit your way unto the Lord; trust also in Him. | Psalm 37:5 |
| 35. They shall inherit the earth. | Those that wait upon the Lord. | Psalm 37:9 |
| 36. They shall delight themselves in the abundance of peace. | The meek. | Psalm 37:11 |
| 37. A little is better than the riches of many wicked. | Be righteous. | Psalm 37:16 |
| 38. The Lord upholds them. | The righteous. | Psalm 37:17 |
| 39. In the days of famine they shall be satisfied. | The upright. | Psalm 37:19 |
| 40. His steps are ordered by the Lord. | A good man. | Psalm 37:23–24 |

| PROMISE | CONDITION | REFERENCE |
|---------|-----------|-----------|
| 41. None of his steps shall slide. | The law of his God is in his heart. | Psalm 37:31 |
| 42. [The Lord] is their strength in the time of trouble. | The righteous. | Psalm 37:39 |
| 43. The Lord shall deliver them from the wicked. | Because they trust in Him. | Psalm 37:40 |
| 44. God will incline unto you and hear your cry. | Wait patiently for the Lord. | Psalm 40:1 |
| 45. Blessed is he; the Lord shall deliver him in time of trouble. | He that considers the poor. | Psalm 41:1 |
| 46. The Lord will preserve him and keep him alive. | He that considers the poor. | Psalm 41:1–2 |
| 47. God has anointed you with the oil of gladness above your fellows. | Love righteousness and hate wickedness. | Psalm 45:7 |
| 48. We will not fear, though the earth be removed, and though the mountains be carried into the midst of the sea; though the waters roar and be troubled, though the mountains shake. | God is our refuge and strength. | Psalm 46:1–2 |
| 49. God will be your guide even unto death. | If He is your God. | Psalm 48:14 |
| 50. I (God) will deliver you, and you shall glorify me. | Offer unto God thanksgiving, pay your vows unto the Most High, and call upon Him in the day of your trouble. | Psalm 50:14–15 |
| 51. He glorifies God. | Whoso offers praise. | Psalm 50:23 |

| PROMISE | CONDITION | REFERENCE |
|---------|-----------|-----------|
| 52. You can offer a sacrifice to God that He will not despise. | Offer a broken spirit, a broken and contrite heart. | Psalm 51:17 |
| 53. God shall hear my voice. | Evening, morning, and noon, will I pray. | Psalm 55:17 |
| 54. The Lord will sustain you. | Cast your burden upon the Lord. | Psalm 55:22 |
| 55. I will not be afraid what man can do unto me. | In God have I put my trust. | Psalm 56:11 |
| 56. The earth shall yield her increase, and God shall bless us. | Let all the people praise Thee, O God. | Psalm 67:5–6 |
| 57. God gives strength and power. | To His people. | Psalm 68:35 |
| 58. God will fill your mouth. | Open your mouth wide. | Psalm 81:10 |
| 59. No good thing will He withhold. | From them that walk uprightly. | Psalm 84:11 |
| 60. He shall abide under the shadow of the Almighty. | He that dwells in the secret places of the Most High. | Psalm 91:1 |
| 61. God shall deliver you from the snare of the fowler and from the noisome pestilence. | He that dwells in the secret place of the Most High. | Psalm 91:1, 3 |
| 62. You shall not be afraid for the terror by night. | He that dwells in the secret place of the Most High. | Psalm 91:5 |
| 63. You shall not be afraid for the arrow that flies by day. | He that dwells in the secret place of the Most High. | Psalm 91:5 |
| 64. You shall not be afraid for the pestilence that walks in darkness. | He that dwells in the secret place of the Most High. | Psalm 91:6 |

| PROMISE | CONDITION | REFERENCE |
|---------|-----------|-----------|
| 65. You shall not be afraid for the destruction that wastes at noonday. | He that dwells in the secret place of the Most High. | Psalm 91:6 |
| 66. A thousand shall fall at your side, ten thousand at your right hand; it shall not come nigh you. | He that dwells in the secret place of the Most High. | Psalm 91:7 |
| 67. There shall no evil befall you, neither shall any plague come near your dwelling. | Because you have made the Lord your habitation. | Psalm 91:10 |
| 68. God shall give His angels charge over you, to keep you in all your ways. | Because you have made the Lord your habitation. | Psalm 91:11 |
| 69. With long life will I (God) satisfy him and show him my salvation. | Because he has set his love upon me. | Psalm 91:14, 16 |
| 70. He shall flourish like the palm tree. | The righteous. | Psalm 92:12 |
| 71. You are blessed. | If the Lord chastens you. | Psalm 94:12 |
| 72. As the heaven is high above the earth, so great is (God's) mercy toward them. | That fear him. | Psalm 103:11 |
| 73. The mercy of the Lord is from everlasting to everlasting upon them. | That fear him. | Psalm 103:17 |
| 74. [God] sent his word and healed them. | They cry unto the Lord in their trouble. | Psalm 107:19–20 |

| PROMISE | CONDITION | REFERENCE |
|---------|-----------|-----------|
| 75. Wealth and riches shall be in his house, and his righteousness endures forever. | Fear the Lord, delight greatly in His commandments. | Psalm 112:1, 3 |
| 76. He shall not be afraid of evil tidings. | His heart is fixed, trusting in the Lord. | Psalm 112:7 |
| 77. A young man shall cleanse his way. | By taking heed according to God's Word. | Psalm 119:9 |
| 78. You shall not perish in your affliction. | Make God's law your delight. | Psalm 119:92 |
| 79. I shall live. | Get understanding of the righteousness of God's testimonies. | Psalm 119:144 |
| 80. Great peace have they, and nothing shall offend them. | They which love thy law. | Psalm 119:165 |
| 81. The sun shall not smite you by day. | If the Lord is your keeper. | Psalm 121:5–6 |
| 82. The moon shall not smite you by night. | If the Lord is your keeper. | Psalm 121:5–6 |
| 83. The Lord shall preserve you from all evil. | If the Lord is your keeper. | Psalm 121:5, 7 |
| 84. They shall prosper. | Pray for the peace of Jerusalem. | Psalm 122:6 |
| 85. They shall be as Mount Zion, which cannot be removed, but abides forever. | Trust in the Lord. | Psalm 125:1 |
| 86. The rod of the wicked shall not rest on your lot. | If you are righteous. | Psalm 125:3 |
| 87. They shall reap in joy. | Who sowed in tears. | Psalm 126:5 |
| 88. God gives them sleep. | His beloved. | Psalm 127:2 |

| PROMISE | CONDITION | REFERENCE |
|---------|-----------|-----------|
| 89. It is good and pleasant for brethren to dwell together. | Dwell together in unity. | Psalm 133:1 |
| 90. The Lord is nigh unto all. | To all that call upon Him in truth. | Psalm 145:18 |
| 91. The Lord preserves all. | All them that love Him. | Psalm 145:20 |
| 92. The Lord loves you. | If you are righteous. | Psalm 146:8 |
| 93. God will beautify them with salvation. | The meek. | Psalm 149:4 |

## 24. Eighty-six Other Old Testament Promises to the Individual

| PROMISE | CONDITION | REFERENCE |
|---------|-----------|-----------|
| 1. God will bless your bread and your water and will take sickness away from you. | Serve the Lord. | Exodus 23:25 |
| 2. You will prolong your days upon the earth, which the Lord gives you. | Keep His statutes and His commandments. | Deuteronomy 4:40 |
| 3. It will be well with you and you will increase mightily. | Observe to do all His statutes and commandments. | Deuteronomy 6:3 |
| 4. The Lord will take away from you all sickness. | Keep the commandments, and the statutes, and the judgments which God commands you. | Deuteronomy 7:11, 15 |
| 5. You shall be blessed in the city and in the field. | Hearken to the voice of the Lord your God. | Deuteronomy 28:2–3 |
| 6. Your crops and your herds shall be blessed. | Hearken unto the voice of the Lord your God. | Deuteronomy 28:2, 4 |

| PROMISE | CONDITION | REFERENCE |
| --- | --- | --- |
| 7. You shall be blessed when you come in and go out. | Hearken to the voice of the Lord your God. | Deuteronomy 28:2, 6 |
| 8. The Lord shall cause your enemies to be smitten before your face. They shall come against you one way, and flee from you seven ways. | Hearken to the voice of the Lord your God. | Deuteronomy 28:2, 7 |
| 9. The Lord shall establish you a holy people unto himself. | Keep the commandments of the Lord your God, and walk in His ways. | Deuteronomy 28:9 |
| 10. The Lord shall give you rain in His season, and bless all the work of your hand. | Keep the commandments of the Lord your God, and walk in His ways. | Deuteronomy 28:9, 12 |
| 11. The Lord shall make you the head and not the tail. | Hearken to the commandments of the Lord to observe and to do them. | Deuteronomy 28:13 |
| 12. One man of you shall chase a thousand. | Cleave unto the Lord your God. | Joshua 23:8, 10 |
| 13. God will honour them. | Honour God. | 1 Samuel 2:30 |
| 14. You shall prosper. | Take heed to fulfill the statutes and judgments with which the Lord charged Moses. | 1 Chronicles 22:13 |
| 15. The Lord is with you. | Abide with Him. | 2 Chronicles 15:2 |
| 16. [God] will be found of you. | Seek Him. | 2 Chronicles 15:2 |
| 17. God made him to prosper. | Seek God. | 2 Chronicles 26:5 |
| 18. He shall be stronger and stronger. | Have clean hands. | Job 17:9 |

| PROMISE | CONDITION | REFERENCE |
|---|---|---|
| 19. They shall spend their days in prosperity and their years in pleasures. | Obey and serve [God]. | Job 36:11 |
| 20. I [God] will pour out my spirit unto you, I will make known my words unto you. | Respond to His reproof. | Proverbs 1:23 |
| 21. The Lord lays up sound wisdom for them. | Live a righteous life. | Proverbs 2:7 |
| 22. The Lord shall direct your paths. | Trust in the Lord with all your heart, and lean not unto your own understanding. In all your ways acknowledge Him. | Proverbs 3:5–6 |
| 23. Your barns shall be filled with plenty. | Honour the Lord with your substance and with the firstfruits of all your increase. | Proverbs 3:9–10 |
| 24. When you lie down, you shall not be afraid; your sleep shall be sweet. | Keep sound wisdom and discretion. | Proverbs 3:21–24 |
| 25. The Lord shall be your confidence and shall keep your foot from being taken. | Keep sound wisdom and discretion. | Proverbs 3:21, 26 |
| 26. You shall find wisdom. | Love wisdom and seek it early. | Proverbs 8:17 |
| 27. Have wisdom and understanding. | Have the fear of the Lord and the knowledge of the holy. | Proverbs 9:10 |
| 28. The years of your life shall be increased. | Have the fear of the Lord and the knowledge of the holy. | Proverbs 9:10–11 |

| PROMISE | CONDITION | REFERENCE |
|---------|-----------|-----------|
| 29. You shall be made rich and have no sorrow with your riches. | Have the blessing of the Lord. | Proverbs 10:22 |
| 30. Their desire shall be granted. | Live a righteous life. | Proverbs 10:24 |
| 31. He is delivered out of trouble. | Live a righteous life. | Proverbs 11:8 |
| 32. The just shall be delivered. | Acquire knowledge. | Proverbs 11:9 |
| 33. To him shall be a sure reward. | Sow righteousness. | Proverbs 11:18 |
| 34. He shall be satisfied. | Be generous. | Proverbs 11:25 |
| 35. He is wise. | Win souls. | Proverbs 11:30 |
| 36. He shall obtain favour of the Lord. | Do good. | Proverbs 12:2 |
| 37. His house shall stand. | Live a righteous life. | Proverbs 12:7 |
| 38. To them is joy. | Be a counselor of peace. | Proverbs 12:20 |
| 39. There shall no evil happen to them. | Live justly. | Proverbs 12:21 |
| 40. He shall be honoured. | Pay attention to reproof. | Proverbs 13:18 |
| 41. He shall be wise. | Walk with wise men. | Proverbs 13:20 |
| 42. Happy is he. | Have mercy on the poor. | Proverbs 14:21 |
| 43. You shall turn away wrath. | Give a soft answer. | Proverbs 15:1 |
| 44. In his house is much treasure. | Live a righteous life. | Proverbs 15:6 |
| 45. Your thoughts shall be established. | Commit your works unto the Lord. | Proverbs 16:3 |

| PROMISE | CONDITION | REFERENCE |
|---------|-----------|-----------|
| 46. Men depart from evil. | Fear the Lord. | Proverbs 16:6 |
| 47. The Lord makes your enemies to be at peace with you. | Please the Lord. | Proverbs 16:7 |
| 48. A man that has friends. | Show yourself friendly. | Proverbs 18:24 |
| 49. The Lord will repay you. | Have pity on the poor. | Proverbs 19:17 |
| 50. He finds life, righteousness, and honour. | He that follows after righteousness and mercy. | Proverbs 21:21 |
| 51. He keeps his soul from troubles. | Keep your tongue. | Proverbs 21:23 |
| 52. You shall have riches, honour, and life. | Humility and the fear of the Lord. | Proverbs 22:4 |
| 53. He falls seven times, and rises up again. | Live justly. | Proverbs 24:16 |
| 54. You shall heap coals of fire upon your enemy's head, and the Lord shall reward you. | If your enemy is hungry, give him bread to eat; and if he is thirsty, give him water to drink. | Proverbs 25:21–22 |
| 55. He shall have good things. | Live uprightly. | Proverbs 28:10 |
| 56. He shall have mercy. | Confess and forsake all sin. | Proverbs 28:13 |
| 57. He shall have plenty of bread. | Till your land. | Proverbs 28:19 |
| 58. He shall not lack. | Give to the poor. | Proverbs 28:27 |
| 59. He shall be safe. | Put your trust in the Lord. | Proverbs 29:25 |
| 60. God gives to a man wisdom, knowledge, and joy. | Be good in His sight. | Ecclesiastes 2:26 |

| PROMISE | CONDITION | REFERENCE |
|---|---|---|
| 61. Though your sins be as scarlet, they shall be white as snow. | Take counsel with the Lord. | Isaiah 1:18 |
| 62. You shall eat the good of the land. | Be willing and obedient. | Isaiah 1:19 |
| 63. Thou [God] will keep him in perfect peace. | Keep your mind stayed on the Lord. | Isaiah 26:3 |
| 64. Blessed are they. | Wait for the Lord. | Isaiah 30:18 |
| 65. He shall dwell on high. | He that walks righteously, speaks uprightly, despises the gain of oppression, shakes his hand from holding bribes, stops ears from hearing of blood, and shuts his eyes from seeing evil. | Isaiah 33:15–16 |
| 66. They shall renew their strength. | Wait upon the Lord. | Isaiah 40:31 |
| 67. They shall run and not be weary. | Wait upon the Lord. | Isaiah 40:31 |
| 68. They shall walk and not faint. | Wait upon the Lord. | Isaiah 40:31 |
| 69. God will help you and strengthen you. | God is your God. | Isaiah 41:10 |
| 70. When you pass through the waters, the Lord will be with you; and through the rivers, they shall not overflow you; when you walk through the fire, you shall not be burned. | You belong to God. | Isaiah 43:2 |
| 71. I have righteousness and strength. | Abide in the Lord. | Isaiah 45:24 |

| PROMISE | CONDITION | REFERENCE |
|---|---|---|
| 72. You shall go out with joy, and be led forth with peace. | Seek the Lord while he may be found. | Isaiah 55:6, 12 |
| 73. God will have mercy; He will abundantly pardon. | Seek the Lord while He may be found. Call upon Him while He is near. Forsake wickedness. Forsake unrighteous thoughts. Return unto the Lord. | Isaiah 55:7 |
| 74. God dwells with him to revive the spirit and the heart. | Have a humble and contrite heart. | Isaiah 57:15 |
| 75. You shall eat, drink, rejoice, and sing for joy. | Be God's servant. | Isaiah 65:13–14 |
| 76. They shall not labour in vain. | Be blessed of the Lord. | Isaiah 65:23 |
| 77. Before they call, I [God] will answer, and while they are yet speaking, I will hear. | Be blessed of the Lord. | Isaiah 65:23–24 |
| 78. You shall find rest for your soul. | Ask for the old paths, where is the good way, and walk therein. | Jeremiah 6:16 |
| 79. It shall be well with you. | Walk in all the ways that I (God) have commanded you. | Jeremiah 7:23 |
| 80. The Lord will show you great and mighty things which you know not. | Call unto the Lord. | Jeremiah 33:3 |
| 81. [God] will return unto you. | Return unto [God]. | Malachi 3:7 |

| PROMISE | CONDITION | REFERENCE |
|---------|-----------|-----------|
| 82. The Lord of hosts will open you the windows of heaven, and pour you out a blessing, that there shall not be room enough to receive it. | Bring all the tithes into the storehouse. | Malachi 3:10 |
| 83. I [the Lord] will rebuke the devourer for your sakes, and he shall not destroy the fruits of your ground. | Bring all the tithes into the storehouse. | Malachi 3:10–11 |
| 84. All nations shall call you blessed, for you shall be a delightsome land. | Bring all the tithes into the storehouse. | Malachi 3:10, 12 |
| 85. A book of remembrance was written before God for them. | Fear the Lord and think upon His name. | Malachi 3:16 |
| 86. Unto you shall the Sun of righteousness arise with healing in His wings. | Fear [the Lord's] name. | Malachi 4:2 |

## 25. *Eight Old Testament Warnings*

| WARNING | CONDITION | REFERENCE |
|---------|-----------|-----------|
| 1. You shall surely perish, and you shall not prolong your days upon the land. | If your heart turns away, so that you will not hear, and are drawn away. | Deuteronomy 30:17–18 |
| 2. [The Lord] will forsake you. | If you forsake Him. | 2 Chronicles 15:2 |
| 3. The Lord will not hear me. | If I regard iniquity in my heart. | Psalm 66:18 |
| 4. They labour in vain that build. | Except the Lord build the house. | Psalm 127:1 |

| WARNING | CONDITION | REFERENCE |
|---|---|---|
| 5. Contention will come. | By pride. | Proverbs 13:10 |
| 6. Evil shall not depart from his house. | Whoso rewards evil for good. | Proverbs 17:13 |
| 7. He shall fall into mischief. | He that hardens his heart. | Proverbs 28:14 |
| 8. The people perish. | Where there is no vision. | Proverbs 29:18 |

# 3
## NEW TESTAMENT PROVERBS AND FACTS

Many sayings of Jesus and the apostles nicely fit the pattern of the Old Testament book of Proverbs.

The dictionary definition of the word *proverb* and the content of the Old Testament book of Proverbs do not necessarily agree. Thus the proverbs of this chapter are categorized in the spirit of the Old Testament example, if not the definition in Webster's. If there were a New Testament book called Proverbs, it might have been a lot like this chapter!

The facts in this chapter are unusual in that most of them can be proven only by the Bible, and many can only be understood in the realm of faith.

### 26. Twenty-one New Testament Proverbs Concerning God

1. [Your Father] maketh his sun to shine on the evil and on the good, and he sendeth rain on the just and on the unjust (Matthew 5:45).

2. In the beginning was the Word, and the Word was with God, and the Word was God. The same was in the beginning with God. All things were made by him; and without him was not anything made that was made. In him was life; and the life was the light of men. And the light shineth in darkness; and the darkness comprehended it not (John 1:1–5).

3. The times of this ignorance God once winked at; but now commandeth all men every where to repent (Acts 17:30).

4. Why should it be thought a thing incredible with you, that God should raise the dead? (Acts 26:8).

5. The invisible things of [God] from the creation of the world are clearly seen, being understood by the things that are made, even his eternal power and Godhead (Romans 1:20).

6. The foolishness of God is wiser than men; and the weakness of God is stronger than men (1 Corinthians 1:25).

7. [God has] sealed us, and given the earnest of the Spirit in our hearts (2 Corinthians 1:22).

8. In [God] are hid all the treasures of wisdom and knowledge (Colossians 2:3).

9. God hath not appointed us to wrath, but to obtain salvation by our Lord Jesus Christ, who died for us, that, whether we wake or sleep, we should live together with him (1 Thessalonians 5:9–10).

10. It is a righteous thing with God to recompense tribulation to them that trouble you (2 Thessalonians 1:6).

11. Without controversy, great is the mystery of godliness: God was manifest in the flesh, justified in the Spirit, seen of angels, preached unto the Gentiles, believed on in the world, received up into glory (1 Timothy 3:16).

12. God resisteth the proud and giveth grace to the humble (1 Peter 5:5).

13. One day is with the Lord as a thousand years, and a thousand years as one day (2 Peter 3:8).

14. The Lord is not slack concerning his promise, as some men count slackness; but is longsuffering to us-ward, not willing that any should perish, but that all should come to repentance (2 Peter 3:9).

15. God is light, and in him is no darkness at all (1 John 1:5).

16. All that is in the world, the lust of the flesh, and the lust of the eyes, and the pride of life, is not of the Father, but is of the world (1 John 2:16).

17. Behold, what manner of love the Father hath bestowed upon us, that we should be called the sons of God: therefore, the world knoweth us not, because it knew him not (1 John 3:1).

18. Ye are of God, little children, and have overcome them: because greater is he that is in you, than he that is in the world (1 John 4:4).

19. Hereby know ye the Spirit of God: Every spirit that confesseth that Jesus Christ is come in the flesh is of God: and every spirit that confesseth not that Jesus Christ is come in the flesh is not of God: and this is the spirit of antichrist, whereof ye have heard that it should come; and even now already is it in the world (1 John 4:2–3).

20. Herein is love, not that we loved God, but that he loved us, and sent his Son to be the propitiation for our sins (1 John 4:10).

21. We love him, because he first loved us (1 John 4:19).

## 27. Sixty New Testament Proverbs Concerning Humankind

1. The light of the body is the eye: if therefore thine eye be single, thy whole body shall be full of light. But if thine eye be evil, thy whole body shall be full of darkness. If therefore the light that is in thee be darkness, how great is that darkness! (Matthew 6:22–23).

2. Take therefore no thought for the morrow: for the morrow shall take thought for the things of itself. Sufficient unto the day is the evil thereof (Matthew 6:34).

3. Ask, and it shall be given you; seek, and ye shall find; knock, and it shall be opened to you: for everyone that asketh receiveth; and he that seeketh findeth; and to him that knocketh it shall be opened (Matthew 7:7–8).

4. If ye, then, being evil, know how to give good gifts unto your children, how much more shall your Father which is in heaven give good things to them that ask him? (Matthew 7:11).

5. By their fruits ye shall know them (Matthew 7:20).

6. Jesus said unto him, Follow me; and let the dead bury their dead (Matthew 8:22).

7. How can one enter into a strong man's house, and spoil his goods, except he first bind the strong man? and then he will spoil his house (Matthew 12:29).

8. Those things which proceed out of the mouth come forth from the heart; and they defile the man. For out of the heart proceed evil

thoughts, murders, adulteries, fornications, thefts, false witness, blasphemies: these are the things which defile a man (Matthew 15:18–20).

9. Whatsoever thou shalt bind on earth shall be bound in heaven: and whatsoever thou shalt loose on earth shall be loosed in heaven (Matthew 16:19).

10. Wherefore [a man and his wife] are no more twain, but one flesh. What therefore God hath joined together, let not man put asunder (Matthew 19:5–6).

11. Whosoever shall put away his wife, except it be for fornication, and shall marry another, committeth adultery: and whoso marrieth her which is put away commits adultery (Matthew 19:9).

12. Watch and pray, that ye enter not into temptation: the spirit indeed is willing, but the flesh is weak (Matthew 26:41).

13. Remember Lot's wife (Luke 17:32).

14. If I have told you earthly things, and ye believe not, how shall ye believe, if I tell you of heavenly things? (John 3:12).

15. Everyone that doeth evil hateth the light, neither cometh to the light, lest his deeds should be reproved. But he that doeth truth cometh to the light, that his deeds may be made manifest, that they are wrought in God (John 3:20–21).

16. What shall we do, that we might work the works of God? This is the work of God, that ye believe on him whom he hath sent (John 6:28–29).

17. Judge not according to the appearance, but judge righteous judgment (John 7:24).

18. Whosoever committeth sin is the servant of sin (John 8:34).

19. It is not for you to know the times or the seasons, which God hath put in his own power (Acts 1:7).

20. If this counsel or this work be of men, it will come to nought: but if it be of God, ye cannot overthrow it; lest haply ye be found even to fight against God (Acts 5:38–39).

21. Blessed is the man to whom the Lord will not impute sin (Romans 4:8).

22. He that is dead is freed from sin (Romans 6:7).

23. Know ye not, that to whom ye yield yourselves servants to obey, his servants ye are to whom ye obey; whether of sin unto death, or of obedience unto righteousness? (Romans 6:16).

24. To be carnally minded is death; but to be spiritually minded is life and peace (Romans 8:6).

25. If any man have not the Spirit of Christ, he is none of his (Romans 8:9).

26. Let him that thinketh he standeth take heed lest he fall (1 Corinthians 10:12).

27. The spirits of the prophets are subject to the prophets (1 Corinthians 14:32).

28. The last enemy that shall be destroyed is death (1 Corinthians 15:26).

29. Godly sorrow worketh repentance to salvation not to be repented of: but the sorrow of the world worketh death (2 Corinthians 7:10).

30. He that glorieth, let him glory in the Lord. For not he that commendeth himself is approved, but whom the Lord commendeth (2 Corinthians 10:17–18).

31. The law was our schoolmaster to bring us unto Christ, that we might be justified by faith. But after that faith is come, we are no longer under a schoolmaster. For ye are all the children of God by faith in Christ Jesus (Galatians 3:24–26).

32. The law is good, if a man use it lawfully (1 Timothy 1:8).

33. If a man desire the office of a bishop, he desireth a good work (1 Timothy 3:1).

34. Every creature of God is good, and nothing to be refused, if it be received with thanksgiving: for it is sanctified by the word of God and prayer (1 Timothy 4:4–5).

35. If a man also strive for masteries, yet is he not crowned, except he strive lawfully (2 Timothy 2:5).

36. Those that oppose themselves . . . are taken captive by [the devil] at his will (2 Timothy 2:25–26).

37. In the last days, perilous times shall come (2 Timothy 3:1).

38. Evil men and seducers shall wax worse and worse, deceiving, and being deceived (2 Timothy 3:13).

39. The time will come when they will not endure sound doctrine; but after their own lusts shall they heap to themselves teachers, having itching ears; and they shall turn away their ears from the truth, and shall be turned unto fables (2 Timothy 4:3–4).

40. Unto the pure all things are pure: but unto them that are defiled and unbelieving is nothing pure; but even their mind and conscience is defiled (Titus 1:15).

41. For everyone that useth milk is unskillful in the word of righteousness: for he is a babe. But strong meat belongeth to them that are of full age, even those who by reason of use have their senses exercised to discern both good and evil (Hebrews 5:13–14).

42. It is impossible for those who were once enlightened, and have tasted of the heavenly gift, and were made partakers of the Holy Ghost, and have tasted the good word of God, and the powers of the world to come, if they shall fall away, to renew them again unto repentance; seeing they crucify to themselves the Son of God afresh, and put him to an open shame (Hebrews 6:4–6).

43. The law . . . can never with those sacrifices which they offered year by year continually make the comers thereunto perfect (Hebrews 10:1).

44. It is a fearful thing to fall into the hands of the living God (Hebrews 10:31).

45. Now faith is the substance of things hoped for, the evidence of things not seen (Hebrews 11:1).

46. Ye have not resisted unto blood, striving against sin (Hebrews 12:4).

47. No chastening for the present seemeth to be joyous, but grievous: nevertheless afterward it yieldeth the peaceable fruit of righteousness unto them which are exercised thereby (Hebrews 12:11).

48. A double-minded man is unstable in all his ways (James 1:8).

49. Every man is tempted, when he is drawn away of his own lust, and enticed. Then when lust hath conceived, it bringeth forth sin: and sin, when it is finished, bringeth forth death (James 1:14–15).

50. If any man among you seem to be religious, and bridleth not his tongue, but deceiveth his own heart, this man's religion is vain (James 1:26).

51. Thou believest that there is one God; thou doest well: the devils also believe and tremble (James 2:19).

52. The tongue is a little member, and boasteth great things. Behold, how great a matter a little fire kindleth! And the tongue is a fire, a world of iniquity: so is the tongue among our members, that it defileth the whole body, and setteth on fire the course of nature; and it is set on fire of hell. The tongue no man can tame; it is an unruly evil, full of deadly poison (James 3:5–6, 8).

53. Where envying and strife is, there is confusion and every evil work (James 3:16).

54. There is one lawgiver, who is able to save and to destroy: who art thou that judgest another? (James 4:12).

55. Ye know not what shall be on the morrow. . . . For that ye ought to say, If the Lord will, we shall live, and do this, or that (James 4:14–15).

56. He that saith he is in the light, and hateth his brother, is in darkness even until now (1 John 2:9).

57. He that loveth his brother abideth in the light, and there is none occasion of stumbling in him (1 John 2:10).

58. You have an unction from the Holy One, and ye know all things (1 John 2:20).

59. All unrighteousness is sin (1 John 5:17).

60. Whosoever transgresseth, and abideth not in the doctrine of Christ, hath not God. He that abideth in the doctrine of Christ, he hath both the Father and the Son (2 John 9).

## 28. *Nine New Testament Proverbs Concerning Scripture*

1. Man shall not live by bread alone, but by every word that proceedeth out of the mouth of God (Matthew 4:4).

2. Till heaven and earth pass, one jot or one tittle shall in no wise pass from the law, till all be fulfilled (Matthew 5:18).

3. He that is of God heareth God's words: ye therefore hear them not, because ye are not of God (John 8:47).

4. Faith cometh by hearing, and hearing by the word of God (Romans 10:17).

5. The natural man receiveth not the things of the Spirit of God: for they are foolishness unto him: neither can he know them, because they are spiritually discerned (1 Corinthians 2:14).

6. The holy scriptures are able to make thee wise unto salvation through faith which is in Christ Jesus (2 Timothy 3:15).

7. No prophecy of the scripture is of any private interpretation (2 Peter 1:20).

8. He that hath an ear, let him.hear what the Spirit saith unto the churches (Revelation 3:22).

9. The testimony of Jesus is the spirit of prophecy (Revelation 19:10).

## 29. *Twenty-six New Testament Proverbs Concerning Eternal Life*

1. Except your righteousness shall exceed the righteousness of the scribes and Pharisees, ye shall in no case enter into the kingdom of heaven (Matthew 5:20).

2. With what judgment ye judge, ye shall be judged (Matthew 7:2).

3. Strait is the gate, and narrow is the way which leadeth unto life, and few there be that find it (Matthew 7:14).

4. He that endureth to the end shall be saved (Matthew 10:22).

5. Fear not them which kill the body, but are not able to kill the soul: but rather fear him which is able to destroy both soul and body in hell (Matthew 10:28).

6. Out of the abundance of the heart the mouth speaketh. A good man out of the good treasure of the heart bringeth forth good things: and an evil man out of the evil treasure bringeth forth evil things. . . . Every idle word that men shall speak, they shall give account thereof in the day of judgment. For by thy words thou shalt be justified, and by thy words thou shalt be condemned (Matthew 12:34–37).

7. Whosoever hath, to him shall be given, and he shall have more abundance: but whosoever hath not, from him shall be taken away even that he hath (Matthew 13:12).

8. What is a man profited, if he shall gain the whole world, and

lose his own soul? or what shall a man give in exchange for his soul? (Matthew 16:26).

9. Many that are first shall be last; and the last shall be first (Matthew 19:30).

10. Rejoice not, that the spirits are subject unto you; but rather rejoice, because your names are written in heaven (Luke 10:20).

11. Whosoever shall seek to save his life shall lose it; and whosoever shall lose his life shall preserve it (Luke 17:33).

12. He that believeth on the Son hath everlasting life: and he that believeth not the Son shall not see life; but the wrath of God abideth on him (John 3:36).

13. We must through much tribulation enter into the kingdom of God (Acts 14:22).

14. As many as have sinned without law shall also perish without law: and as many as have sinned in the law shall be judged by the law (Romans 2:12).

15. All have sinned, and come short of the glory of God (Romans 3:23).

16. The wages of sin is death; but the gift of God is eternal life through Jesus Christ our Lord (Romans 6:23).

17. If, in this life only we have hope in Christ, we are of all men most miserable (1 Corinthians 15:19).

18. If our gospel be hid, it is hid to them that are lost (2 Corinthians 4:3).

19. We must all appear before the judgment seat of Christ; that everyone may receive the things done in his body, according to that he hath done, whether it be good or bad (2 Corinthians 5:10).

20. To live is Christ, and to die is gain (Philippians 1:21).

21. Bodily exercise profiteth little: but godliness is profitable unto all things, having promise of the life that now is, and of that which is to come (1 Timothy 4:8).

22. Some men's sins are open beforehand, going before to judgment; and some men they follow after. Likewise also the good works of some are manifest beforehand; and they that are otherwise cannot be hid (1 Timothy 5:24–25).

23. It is appointed unto men once to die, but after this the judgment (Hebrews 9:27).

24. Blessed are they which are called unto the marriage supper of the Lamb (Revelation 19:9).

25. Blessed and holy is he that hath part in the first resurrection: on such the second death hath no power, but they shall be priests of God and of Christ, and shall reign with him a thousand years (Revelation 20:6).

26. The Spirit and the bride say, Come. And let him that heareth say, Come. And let him that is athirst come. And whosoever will, let him take the water of life freely (Revelation 22:17).

## 30. *Eleven New Testament Proverbs Concerning Stewardship*

1. Where your treasure is, there will your heart be also (Matthew 6:21).

2. Give not that which is holy unto the dogs, neither cast ye your pearls before swine, lest they trample them under their feet, and turn again and rend you (Matthew 7:6).

3. Freely ye have received, freely give (Matthew 10:8).

4. Render therefore unto Caesar the things which are Caesar's; and unto God the things that are God's (Matthew 22:21).

5. Unto whomsoever much is given, of him shall be much required: and to whom men have committed much, of him they will ask the more (Luke 12:48).

6. He that is faithful in that which is least is faithful also in much: and he that is unjust in the least is unjust also in much. If therefore ye have not been faithful in unrighteous mammon, who will commit to your trust the true riches? And if ye have not been faithful in that which is another man's, who shall give you that which is your own? (Luke 16:10–12).

7. Remember the words of the Lord Jesus, how he said, It is more blessed to give than to receive (Acts 20:35).

8. If any provide not for his own, and specially for those of his own house, he hath denied the faith, and is worse than an infidel (1 Timothy 5:8).

9. Godliness with contentment is great gain. For we brought nothing into this world, and it is certain we carry nothing out (1 Timothy 6:6–7).

10. The love of money is the root of all evil (1 Timothy 6:10).

11. What doth it profit, my brethren, though a man say he hath faith, and have not works? Can faith save him? If a brother or sister be naked, and destitute of daily food, and one of you say unto them, Depart in peace, be ye warmed and filled; notwithstanding ye give them not those things which are needful to the body; what doth it profit? Even so faith, if it hath not works, is dead, being alone (James 2:14–17).

## 31. Ten New Testament Proverbs Concerning Witnessing

1. Jesus said unto them, Follow me, and I will make you fishers of men (Matthew 4:19).

2. Ye are the salt of the earth: but if the salt have lost his savor, where-with shall it be salted? It is thenceforth good for nothing, but to be cast out, and to be trodden under foot of men (Matthew 5:13).

3. Let your light so shine before men, that they may see your good works, and glorify your Father which is in heaven (Matthew 5:16).

4. The disciple is not above his master, nor the servant above his lord. It is enough for the disciple that he be as his master, and the servant as his lord (Matthew 10:24–25).

5. A prophet is not without honour, save in his own country, and in his own house (Matthew 13:57).

6. The servant is not greater than his lord; neither is he that is sent greater than he that sent him (John 13:16).

7. Greater love hath no man than this, that a man lay down his life for his friends (John 15:13).

8. Whether it be right in the sight of God to hearken unto [men] more than unto God, judge ye. For we cannot but speak the things which we have seen and heard (Acts 4:19–20).

9. [God] hath made us able ministers of the new testament; not of the letter, but of the spirit: for the letter killeth, but the spirit giveth life (2 Corinthians 3:6).

10. Marvel not, my brethren, if the world hate you (1 John 3:13).

## 32. Thirteen Special Facts About God the Father

1. Your Father knoweth what things ye have need of before ye ask him (Matthew 6:8).

2. Of that day and hour knoweth no man, no, not the angels, but my Father only (Matthew 24:36).

3. God is a Spirit (John 4:24).

4. Jesus said, My Father is greater than I (John 14:28).

5. God that made the world and all things therein, seeing that he is Lord of heaven and earth, dwelleth not in temples made with hands; neither is worshiped with men's hands, as though he needed anything, seeing he giveth to all life, and breath, and all things; and hath made of one blood all nations of men for to dwell on all the face of the earth, and hath determined the times before appointed, and the bounds of their habitation; that they should seek the Lord, if haply they might feel after him, and find him, though he be not far from every one of us: for in him we live, and move, and have our being (Acts 17:24–28).

6. God is not the author of confusion, but of peace, as in all churches of the saints (1 Corinthians 14:33).

7. There is . . . one God and Father of all, who is above all, and through all, and in you all (Ephesians 4:6).

8. God cannot lie (Titus 1:2).

9. Thou art the same, and thy years shall not fail (Hebrews 1:12).

10. Neither is there any creature that is not manifest in his sight: but all things are naked and opened unto the eyes of him with whom we have to do (Hebrews 4:13).

11. God is not unrighteous to forget your work and labour of love, which ye have showed toward his name, in that ye have ministered, and do minister to the saints (Hebrews 6:10).

12. Our God is a consuming fire (Hebrews 12:29).

13. There are seven Spirits of God (Revelation 4:5).

## 33. Fifty-four Special Facts About Jesus

1. [Jesus said], not everyone that saith unto me, Lord, Lord, shall enter into the kingdom of heaven; but he that doeth the will of my Father which is in heaven. Many will say to me in that day, Lord, Lord, have we not prophesied in thy name, and in thy name have cast out devils, and in thy name done many wonderful works? And then will I profess unto them, I never knew you: depart from me, ye that work iniquity (Matthew 7:21–23).

2. [Jesus said], I will have mercy, and not sacrifice: for I am not come to call the righteous, but sinners to repentance (Matthew 9:13).

3. The Son of man is Lord even of the sabbath day (Matthew 12:8).

4. [Jesus said], Think not that I am come to send peace on earth: I came not to send peace, but a sword. For I am come to set a man at variance against his father, and the daughter against her mother, and the daughter-in-law against her mother-in-law. And a man's foes shall be they of his own household (Matthew 10:34–36).

5. [Jesus said], He that loveth father or mother more than me is not worthy of me: and he that loveth son or daughter more than me is not worthy of me (Matthew 10:37).

6. [Jesus said], All things are delivered unto me of my Father: and no man knoweth the Son, but the Father; neither knoweth any man the Father, save the Son, and he to whomsoever the Son will reveal him (Matthew 11:27).

7. The Son of man shall send forth his angels, and they shall gather out of his kingdom all things that offend, and them which do iniquity; and shall cast them into a furnace of fire: there shall be wailing and gnashing of teeth. Then shall the righteous shine forth as the sun in the kingdom of their Father (Matthew 13:41–43).

8. [Jesus said], Heaven and earth shall pass away, but my words shall not pass away (Matthew 24:35).

9. The Word was made flesh, and dwelt among us, (and we beheld his glory, the glory as of the only begotten of the Father,) full of grace and truth (John 1:14).

10. The law was given by Moses, but grace and truth came by Jesus Christ (John 1:17).

11. [Jesus] is he which baptizeth with the Holy Ghost (John 1:33).

12. Hereafter ye shall see heaven open, and the angels of God ascending and descending upon the Son of man (John 1:51).

13. Jesus said . . . I am the bread of life: he that cometh to me shall never hunger; and he that believeth on me shall never thirst (John 6:35).

14. [Jesus said], All that the Father giveth me shall come to me; and him that cometh to me I will in no wise cast out. . . . No man can come to me, except the Father which hath sent me draw him: and I will raise him up at the last day (John 6:37, 44).

15. [Jesus said], The words that I speak unto you, they are spirit and they are life (John 6:63).

16. [Jesus said], If ye believe not that I am he, ye shall die in your sins (John 8:24).

17. Jesus said, For judgment I am come into this world, that they which see not might see; and that they which see might be made blind (John 9:39).

18. [Jesus said], I am the good shepherd, and know my sheep, and am known of mine. . . . And other sheep I have, which are not of this fold: them also I must bring, and they shall hear my voice; and there shall be one fold, and one shepherd (John 10:14, 16).

19. [Jesus said], If I then, your Lord and Master, have washed your feet; ye also ought to wash one another's feet. For I have given you an example, that ye should do as I have done to you (John 13:14–15).

20. [Jesus said], I will come again, and receive you unto myself; that where I am, there ye may be also (John 14:3).

21. [Jesus said], I am the way, the truth, and the life: no man cometh unto the Father, but by me (John 14:6).

22. [Jesus said], In the world ye shall have tribulation; but be of good cheer; I have overcome the world (John 16:33).

23. To [the apostles] he shewed himself alive after his passion by many infallible proofs, being seen of them forty days, and speaking of the things pertaining to the kingdom of God (Acts 1:3).

24. Heaven must receive [Jesus] until the times of restitution of all

things, which God hath spoken by the mouth of all his holy prophets since the world began (Acts 3:21).

25. Him hath God exalted with his right hand to be a Prince and a Saviour, for to give repentance to Israel, and forgiveness of sins (Acts 5:31).

26. Be it known unto you therefore, men and brethren, that through [Jesus] is preached unto you the forgiveness of sins: and by him all that believe are justified from all things, from which you could not be justified by the law of Moses (Acts 13:38–39).

27. The gospel of Christ . . . is the power of God unto salvation to every one that believeth (Romans 1:16).

28. Christ is the end of the law for righteousness to every one that believeth (Romans 10:4).

29. [God] hath made [Jesus], who knew no sin, to be sin for us; that we might be made the righteousness of God in him (2 Corinthians 5:21).

30. Ye know the grace of our Lord Jesus Christ, that, though he was rich, yet for your sakes he became poor, that ye through his poverty might be rich (2 Corinthians 8:9).

31. If righteousness come by the law, then Christ is dead in vain (Galatians 2:21).

32. Christ hath redeemed us from the curse of the law, being made a curse for us: for it is written, Cursed is everyone that hangeth on a tree (Galatians 3:13).

33. God also hath highly exalted [Jesus] and given him a name which is above every name: that at the name of Jesus every knee should bow, of things in heaven, and things in earth, and things under the earth; and that every tongue should confess that Jesus Christ is Lord, to the glory of God the Father (Philippians 2:9–11).

34. [Jesus] is the image of the invisible God, the firstborn of every creature: for by him were all things created (Colossians 1:15–16).

35. In [Christ] dwelleth all the fulness of the Godhead bodily (Colossians 2:9).

36. The Lord Jesus shall be revealed from heaven with his mighty angels, in flaming fire taking vengeance on them that know

not God, and that obey not the gospel of our Lord Jesus Christ (2 Thessalonians 1:7–8).

37. There is one God, and one mediator between God and men, the man Christ Jesus (1 Timothy 2:5).

38. Our Saviour Jesus Christ hath abolished death and hath brought life and immortality to light through the gospel (2 Timothy 1:10).

39. The Lord Jesus Christ shall judge the quick and the dead at his appearing (2 Timothy 4:1).

40. [Jesus] is the brightness of [God's] glory, and is the express image of his person, and upholding all things by the word of his power, when he had by himself purged our sins, sat down on the right hand of the Majesty on high (Hebrews 1:3).

41. [Jesus was] made so much better than the angels. . . . The angels of God worship him (Hebrews 1:4, 6).

42. [Jesus], the captain of [our] salvation, [was made] perfect through sufferings (Hebrews 2:10).

43. Through death, [Jesus] destroyed him that had the power of death, that is, the devil (Hebrews 2:14).

44. In all things it behoved [Jesus] to be made like unto his brethren, that he might be a merciful and faithful high priest in things pertaining to God, to make reconciliation for the sins of the people (Hebrews 2:17).

45. Though [Jesus] were a Son, yet learned he obedience by the things which he suffered; and being made perfect, he became the author of eternal salvation unto all them that obey him (Hebrews 5:8–9).

46. But [Jesus], because he continueth ever, hath an unchangeable priesthood (Hebrews 7:24).

47. How much more shall the blood of Christ, who through the eternal Spirit offered himself without spot to God, purge your conscience from dead works to serve the living God? (Hebrews 9:14).

48. [We have the] boldness to enter into the holiest by the blood of Jesus (Hebrews 10:19).

49. Yet a little while, and he that shall come will come, and will not tarry (Hebrews 10:37).

50. Wherefore Jesus also, that he might sanctify the people with his own blood, suffered without the gate. Let us go forth therefore unto him without the camp, bearing his reproach (Hebrews 13:12–13).

51. [By the Spirit, Christ] went and preached unto the spirits in prison; which sometime were disobedient, when once the long-suffering of God waited in the days of Noah, while the ark was a preparing (1 Peter 3:18–20).

52. [Jesus has] the keys of hell and of death (Revelation 1:18).

53. Jesus is holy and true, and he has the key of David. He opens, and no man can shut. He shuts, and no man opens (Revelation 3:7).

54. [Jesus is] the beginning of the creation of God (Revelation 3:14).

## 34. Seven New Testament Facts About Humankind

1. The light of the body is the eye (Matthew 6:22).

2. No man can serve two masters: for either he will hate the one, and love the other; or else he will hold to the one, and despise the other. Ye cannot serve God and mammon (Matthew 6:24).

3. In the resurrection they neither marry, nor are given in marriage (Matthew 22:30).

4. If I pray in an unknown tongue, my spirit prayeth (1 Corinthians 14:14).

5. [The Hebrews] could not enter in [to the rest of God] because of unbelief (Hebrews 3:7–19).

6. Every man is tempted, when he is drawn away of his own lust, and enticed (James 1:14).

7. If any man offend not in word, the same is a perfect man, and able to bridle the whole body (James 3:2).

## 35. Eleven New Testament Facts About Angels

1. Children have personal angels (Matthew 18:10).

2. Angels do not marry (Matthew 22:30).

3. There is joy in the presence of the angels of God over one sinner that repenteth (Luke 15:10).

4. Satan himself is transformed into an angel of light (2 Corinthians 11:14).

5. God maketh his angels spirits, and his ministers a flame of fire (Hebrews 1:7).

6. [Angels are] all ministering spirits, sent forth to minister for them who shall be heirs of salvation (Hebrews 1:14).

7. God spared not the angels that sinned, but cast them down to hell, and delivered them into chains of darkness, to be reserved unto judgment (2 Peter 2:4).

8. The angels which kept not their first estate, but left their own habitation, [God] hath reserved in everlasting chains under darkness unto the judgment of the great day (Jude 6).

9. Michael the archangel, when contending with the devil he disputed about the body of Moses, durst not bring against him a railing accusation, but said, The Lord rebuke thee (Jude 9).

10. [Jesus] sent and signified [the revelation] by his angel unto his servant John (Revelation 1:1).

11. There was war in heaven: Michael and his angels fought against the dragon; and the dragon fought and his angels, and prevailed not; neither was their place found any more in heaven (Revelation 12:7–8).

## 36. Seventeen New Testament Facts About Bible Characters

1. Herod laid hold upon John [the Baptist] and bound him in prison for Herodias' sake, his brother Philip's wife: for he had married her. For John had said unto Herod, It is not lawful for thee to have thy brother's wife (Mark 6:17–18).

2. The woman with the issue of blood whom Jesus healed, had been ill twelve years, and had spent all her living on physicians (Luke 8:43).

3. Peter fell into a trance and saw a vision (Acts 10:10–16).

4. Agabus gave two recorded prophecies, which were fulfilled: (1) There should be a great dearth throughout all the world: which came to pass in the days of Claudius Caesar (Acts 11:28); (2) He took Paul's girdle, and bound his own hands and feet, and

said, Thus saith the Holy Ghost, So shall the Jews at Jerusalem bind the man that owneth this girdle, and shall deliver him into the hands of the Gentiles (Acts 21:11).

5. At Lycaonia, the people called Barnabas "Jupiter," and Paul "Mercurius" (Acts 14:11–12).

6. Paul circumcised Timothy (Acts 16:3) even though Paul held circumcision to be unnecessary (Galatians 2).

7. Philip the evangelist had four virgin daughters who could prophesy (Acts 21:8–9).

8. Paul was in a trance and saw a vision (Acts 22:17–21).

9. [Paul could] deliver . . . unto Satan for the destruction of the flesh, that the spirit may be saved in the day of the Lord Jesus (1 Corinthians 5:5).

10. Paul (whether in the body or out of the body; he could not tell) was caught up to the third heaven, into paradise, and heard unspeakable words, which it is not lawful for a man to utter (2 Corinthians 12:2–4).

11. [Paul said], There was given to me a thorn in the flesh, the messenger of Satan to buffet me, lest I should be exalted above measure (2 Corinthians 12:7).

12. Adam was first formed, then Eve. And Adam was not deceived, but the woman being deceived was in the transgression. Notwithstanding she shall be saved in childbearing, if they continue in faith and charity and holiness with sobriety (1 Timothy 2:13–15).

13. Timothy received a gift, given him by prophecy, with the laying on of the hands of the presbytery (1 Timothy 4:14).

14. Timothy's grandmother was named Lois, and his mother's name was Eunice (2 Timothy 1:5). His mother was a Jewess, and his father was Greek (Acts 16:1).

15. Melchisedec was better than Abraham (Hebrews 7:7).

16. The devil, as a roaring lion, walketh about, seeking whom he may devour (1 Peter 5:8).

17. John heard the voices of over one hundred million angels (Revelation 5:11).

## 37. Six New Testament Facts About the Holy Spirit

1. [Jesus said], All manner of sin and blasphemy shall be forgiven unto men: but the blasphemy against the Holy Ghost shall not be forgiven unto men. Whosoever speaketh a word against the Holy Ghost, it shall not be forgiven him, neither in this world, neither in the world to come (Matthew 12:31–32).

2. The wind bloweth where it listeth, and thou hearest the sound thereof, but canst not tell whence it cometh, and whither it goeth: so is every one that is born of the Spirit (John 3:8).

3. [Jesus said], He that believeth on me, as the scripture hath said, out of his belly shall flow rivers of living water. (This spake he of the Spirit, which they that believe on him should receive) (John 7:38–39).

4. [Jesus said], I will send [the Holy Spirit] unto you. And when he is come, he will reprove the world of sin, and of righteousness, and of judgment. When the Spirit of truth is come, he will guide you into all truth: for he shall not speak of himself; but whatsoever he shall hear, that shall he speak: and he will show you things to come. He shall glorify me: for he shall receive of mine, and shall show it unto you (John 16:7–8, 13–14).

5. [Jesus] through the Holy Ghost had given commandments unto the apostles (Acts 1:2).

6. [The 120 disciples] were all filled with the Holy Ghost, and began to speak with other tongues, as the Spirit gave them utterance (Acts 2:1–4).

# 4
## SUPERNATURAL EVENTS

The Bible, the bestseller of all time, is in itself a "supernatural event." And within its pages is found a marvelous record of hundreds of unusual occurrences. Some may think of a miracle as only a positive action that God does for a person. The Bible, though, includes accounts of people who were supernaturally struck blind, deaf, or even dead. This chapter lists some of those "negative" miracles, as well as Ten Accounts of People Raised From the Dead and Fourteen Supernatural Journeys.

For more on the supernatural, see chapter 14, "Miracle Workers and Their Deeds."

### 38. Eleven Visions of God
1. Jacob dreamed of a ladder set up on the earth, and the top of it reached to heaven. . . . And, behold, the Lord stood above it (Genesis 28:12–13).
2. Moses, and Aaron, Nadab, and Abihu, and seventy of the elders of Israel . . . saw the God of Israel (Exodus 24:9–10).
3. Moses saw the back of God (Exodus 33:23).
4. Micaiah saw the Lord sitting upon his throne (2 Chronicles 18:18).
5. Isaiah saw the Lord sitting upon a throne, high and lifted up, and his train filled the temple (Isaiah 6:1).
6. Ezekiel saw the likeness of a throne, as the appearance of a sap-

phire stone: and . . . the likeness as the appearance of a man above it (Ezekiel 1:26).

7. Ezekiel again had a similar vision (Ezekiel 10:1).

8. Daniel beheld till the thrones were cast down, and the Ancient of days did sit (Daniel 7:9).

9. [Stephen] looked up stedfastly into heaven, and saw the glory of God, and Jesus standing on the right hand of God (Acts 7:55).

10. Paul wrote that he knew a man (likely himself), who was caught up to the third heaven (2 Corinthians 12:2).

11. John was in the spirit; and behold, a throne was set in heaven, and one sat on the throne (Revelation 4:2).

## 39. *People Who Were Struck Blind*

1. Many men of Sodom were struck blind by two angels who came to rescue Lot and his family before Sodom was destroyed (Genesis 19:11).

2. The Syrian army was struck blind at the word of Elisha when the army came to capture him (2 Kings 6:18).

3. Paul was struck blind on the road to Damascus (Acts 9:8).

4. Elymas the sorcerer was blinded when Paul spoke the word, because Elymas tried to turn Sergius Paulus from the faith (Acts 13:7–11).

## 40. *Two Men Who Were Struck Dumb*

1. Ezekiel was struck dumb by the Lord on occasion and then could speak only when the Lord gave him something to say (Ezekiel 3:25–27).

2. The angel Gabriel struck Zecharias dumb for about nine months until his son, John the Baptist, was born and named (Luke 1:5–20, 62–64).

## 41. *People Whom the Bible Says God Killed and Three Other Accounts of Strange Deaths*

1. God destroyed the entire world population, except Noah and seven others, when He caused the great flood (Genesis 6:7).

2. God killed all the people in Sodom and Gomorrah when He rained fire and brimstone. Only Lot and his daughters escaped (Genesis 19:24–25).

3. God slew Er for being wicked (Genesis 38:7).

4. God slew Onan for not producing offspring with his widowed sister-in-law (Genesis 38:9–10).

5. God killed all the firstborn of Egypt, and Pharaoh and his soldiers that pursued Israel into the Red Sea (Exodus 12:29; 14:16–19, 24–27).

6. Fire from the Lord devoured Nadab and Abihu when they offered strange fire (Leviticus 10:1–2).

7. Korah, his family, and all his men were swallowed up by the earth, and 250 other men were consumed by fire from the Lord because they sought the priesthood beyond the duties they already had (Numbers 16:1–35).

8. When Israel murmured about the incident in item 7, the Lord killed 14,700 more people with a plague (Numbers 16:41–50).

9. The Lord killed an unknown number of Amorites battling against Israel by casting down great hailstones from heaven (Joshua 10:8–14).

10. Jael, the wife of Heber, killed Sisera, the captain of the host of the Canaanites, by hammering a tent peg through his temples while he slept in her tent (Judges 4:18–21).

11. God killed Uzzah for touching the ark of God (2 Samuel 6:6–7).

12. The Lord sent a pestilence upon Israel, killing 70,000 people, because David numbered Israel and Judah (2 Samuel 24:1–15).

13. God killed 102 soldiers by sending fire down from heaven when they came to capture Elijah (2 Kings 1:10–12).

14. Bears tore up forty-two children when Elisha cursed them in God's name for making fun of his bald head (2 Kings 2:23–24).

15. Haman was hanged on the gallows that he had prepared for hanging Mordecai, and Mordecai was set over the house of Haman (Esther 7:10–8:2).

16. Ananias and Sapphira dropped dead after it was supernaturally

revealed that they had lied about the price received for a possession they sold (Acts 5:1–10).

## 42. Ten Biblical Accounts of People Raised From the Dead

1. Elijah raised the son of the Zarephath widow from the dead (1 Kings 17:17–22).

2. Elisha raised the son of the Shunammite woman from the dead (2 Kings 4:32–35).

3. A man was raised from the dead when his body touched Elisha's bones (2 Kings 13:20–21).

4. Many saints rose from the dead at the resurrection of Jesus (Matthew 27:50–53).

5. Jesus rose from the dead (Matthew 28:5–8; Mark 16:6; Luke 24:5–6).

6. Jesus raised the son of the widow of Nain from the dead (Luke 7:11–15).

7. Jesus raised the daughter of Jairus from the dead (Luke 8:41–42, 49–55).

8. Jesus raised Lazarus from the dead (John 11:1–44).

9. Peter raised Dorcas from the dead (Acts 9:36–41).

10. Eutychus was raised from the dead by Paul (Acts 20:9–10).

## 43. The Only Times the Sun Stood Still or Changed Direction

1. Then spake Joshua to the Lord in the day when the Lord delivered up the Amorites before the children of Israel, and he said in the sight of Israel, Sun, stand thou still upon Gibeon; and thou, Moon, in the valley of Ajalon. And the sun stood still, and the moon stayed, until the people had avenged themselves upon their enemies. Is not this written in the book of Jasher? So the sun stood still in the midst of heaven, and hasted not to go down about a whole day (Joshua 10:12–13).

2. And Hezekiah said unto Isaiah, What shall be the sign that the Lord will heal me, and that I shall go up into the house of the Lord the third day? And Isaiah said, This sign shalt thou have

of the Lord, that the Lord will do the thing that he hath spoken: shall the shadow go forward ten degrees, or go back ten degrees? And Hezekiah answered, It is a light thing for the shadow to go down ten degrees: nay, but let the shadow return backward ten degrees. And Isaiah the prophet cried unto the Lord: and he brought the shadow ten degrees backward, by which it had gone down in the dial of Ahaz (2 Kings 20:8–11).

## 44. *Creatures God Used Miraculously*

1. God provided Abraham a *ram* to be sacrificed instead of Isaac (Genesis 22:13).

2. Moses' rod became a *serpent* (Exodus 4:3).

3. God filled Egypt with *frogs* (Exodus 8:6).

4. God sent *lice* upon the Egyptians (Exodus 8:17).

5. The Lord sent *flies* upon Egypt (Exodus 8:22).

6. God sent *locusts* upon Egypt (Exodus 10:13).

7. God sent *quail* to the Israelites after they murmured (Exodus 16:13).

8. God sent *fiery serpents* among the Israelites (Numbers 21:6).

9. Balaam's *ass* spoke to him (Numbers 22:28).

10. The Philistines hitched two *cows*, separated from their calves, to the cart holding the ark of the covenant. The cows went straight to Israel (1 Samuel 6:7–12).

11. A prophet who disobeyed God's command was told, Thy carcase shall not come into the sepulchre of thy fathers. Riding on an ass, he was killed by a *lion* that did not devour him, and never touched the ass (1 Kings 13:24, 28).

12. When Elijah hid from Ahab at the brook Cherith, *ravens* brought him bread and flesh, morning and evening (1 Kings 17:6).

13. *Horses of fire*, pulling a chariot, parted Elijah and Elisha when Elijah was taken up by a whirlwind into heaven (2 Kings 2:11).

14. Elisha cursed children at Bethel, in the name of the Lord, that taunted him for his baldness. Two *she bears* appeared and tore forty-two of the children (2 Kings 2:24).

15. *Dogs* ate the flesh of Jezebel, as prophesied (2 Kings 9:36).

16. The mouths of *lions* were shut when Daniel was cast into their den because he worshiped God (Daniel 6:22).

17. The Lord prepared a *great fish* to swallow up Jonah (Jonah 1:17).

18. God prepared a *worm* to kill the vine that shaded Jonah (Jonah 4:7).

19. God provided Peter a *fish* with money in its mouth to pay tribute (Matthew 17:27).

20. Jesus rode into Jerusalem on an *ass* and its *colt*, fulfilling Zechariah's prophecy (Zechariah 9:9; Matthew 21:7).

21. The *cock* crowed after Peter denied Jesus three times, as Jesus prophesied (Matthew 26:74–75).

22. Jesus sent unclean spirits into a herd of *swine* (Mark 5:13).

23. Jesus fed four thousand with seven loaves and a few small *fish* (Mark 8:6–9).

24. Jesus gave Simon a great catch of *fish* after he had failed to catch any all night (Luke 5:5–6).

25. Jesus fed the five thousand men with two *fish* and five barley loaves (John 6:9–12).

26. Jesus, after His resurrection, caused seven of the disciples to catch more *fish* than they could draw in, though they had caught none all night (John 21:2–6).

27. Paul was bitten by a venomous *viper*, but was unharmed (Acts 28:3–6).

## 45. Fourteen Supernatural Journeys

1. Israel crossed the Red Sea on dry ground while the water stood as a wall on their right and on their left (Exodus 14:19–28).

2. Israel crossed the Jordan River on dry ground while the water stood in a heap (Joshua 3).

3. Elijah outran Ahab's chariot all the way from the top of Mount Carmel to the entrance of Jezreel (about ten miles) (1 Kings 18:41–46).

4. Elijah traveled forty days in the strength of a cake and water brought to him by an angel (1 Kings 19:5–8).

5. Elijah went up by a whirlwind into heaven (2 Kings 2:11).

6. Elijah and Elisha walked across the Jordan River on dry ground after Elijah smote the waters with his mantle (2 Kings 2:8).

7. Elisha walked across the Jordan River alone on dry ground after smiting the waters with Elijah's mantle (2 Kings 2:14).

8. A spirit took Ezekiel by a lock of his head and lifted him up between heaven and earth (Ezekiel 8:1–3).

9. The devil took Jesus up into a high mountain and showed Him all the kingdoms of the world in a moment. He then brought Jesus to Jerusalem and set Him on a pinnacle of the temple (Matthew 4; Luke 4).

10. Jesus and Peter walked on water in the midst of a storm (Matthew 14:22–32).

11. After Jesus got into the boat after walking on water, the ship was immediately at the land where they were headed (John 6:15–21).

12. Jesus was caught up to heaven as the apostles watched (Acts 1:9).

13. The Spirit of the Lord carried Philip from Gaza to Azotus (Acts 8:39–40).

14. Paul knew a man (probably himself) who was caught up to the third heaven. He didn't know whether he was there bodily or not (2 Corinthians 12:1–7).

## 46. *Supernatural Fire in the Bible*

1. And [God] placed at the east end of the garden of Eden Cherubims, and a flaming sword which turned every way (Genesis 3:24).

2. The Lord rained upon Sodom and Gomorrah brimstone and fire from the Lord of heaven (Genesis 19:24).

3. The angel of the Lord appeared unto [Moses] in a flame of fire out of a bush . . . and the bush was not consumed (Exodus 3:2).

4. The Lord sent thunder and hail, and the fire ran along upon the ground (Exodus 9:23).

5. The Lord went before them . . . by night in a pillar of fire (Exodus 13:21).

6. The Lord descended upon [Mount Sinai] in fire (Exodus 19:18).

7. There came a fire out from before the Lord, and consumed upon the altar the burnt offering and the fat (Leviticus 9:24).

8. There went out fire from the Lord, and devoured [Nadab and Abihu] (Leviticus 10:2).

9. There was upon the tabernacle as it were the appearance of fire, until morning (Numbers 9:15).

10. When the people complained . . . the fire of the Lord burnt among them and consumed them (Numbers 11:1).

11. There came out a fire from the Lord, and consumed the two hundred and fifty men that offered incense (Numbers 16:35).

12. The angel of the Lord put forth the end of the staff that was in his hand . . . and there rose up fire out of the rock, and consumed the flesh of the unleavened cakes (Judges 6:21).

13. The fire of the Lord fell, and consumed the burnt sacrifice (1 Kings 18:38).

14. There came down fire from heaven, and consumed [the captain of fifty] and his fifty (2 Kings 1:10).

15. The fire of God came down from heaven, and consumed [another captain of fifty] and his fifty (2 Kings 1:12).

16. There appeared a chariot of fire and horses of fire (2 Kings 2:11).

17. The mountain was full of horses and chariots of fire round about Elisha (2 Kings 6:17).

18. David . . . called upon the Lord; and he answered him from heaven by fire upon the altar of burnt offering (1 Chronicles 21:26).

19. When Solomon had made an end of praying, the fire came down from heaven (2 Chronicles 7:1).

20. The fire of God is fallen from heaven, and hath burned up the sheep, and the servants, and consumed them (Job 1:16).

21. While I [David] was musing the fire burned: then spake I with my tongue (Psalm 39:3).

22. Then flew one of the seraphims unto me, having a live coal in

his hand, which he had taken with the tongs from off the altar (Isaiah 6:6).

23. Behold, a whirlwind came out of the north, a great cloud, and a fire infolding itself, and a brightness was about it, and out of the midst thereof as the colour of amber, out of the midst of the fire (Ezekiel 1:4).

24. I beheld, and lo a likeness as the appearance of fire: from the appearance of his loins even downward, fire (Ezekiel 8:2).

25. Go in between the wheels, even under the cherub, and fill thine hand with coals of fire from between the cherubims, and scatter them over the city (Ezekiel 10:2).

26. [The Ancient of days'] throne was like the fiery flame, and his wheels as burning fire (Daniel 7:9).

27. [The rich man] cried . . . I am tormented in this flame (Luke 16:24).

28. There appeared unto them cloven tongues like as of fire, and it sat upon each of them (Acts 2:3).

29. His eyes were as a flame of fire (Revelation 1:14).

30. There were seven lamps of fire burning before the throne, which are the seven Spirits of God (Revelation 4:5).

31. And the angel took the censer and filled it with fire of the altar, and cast it into the earth (Revelation 8:5).

32. The first angel sounded, and there followed hail and fire mingled with blood (Revelation 8:7).

33. And thus [John] saw the horses in the vision, and them that sat on them, having breastplates of fire . . . and out of [the horses'] mouths issued fire and smoke and brimstone (Revelation 9:17).

34. [John] saw another mighty angel . . . and his feet as pillars of fire (Revelation 10:1).

35. And if any man hurt [the two witnesses], fire proceedeth out of their mouth, and devoureth their enemies (Revelation 11:5).

36. [The second beast] doeth great wonders, so that he maketh fire come down from heaven on the earth in the sight of men (Revelation 13:13).

37. And [John] saw as it were a sea of glass intermingled with fire (Revelation 15:2).

38. The fourth angel poured out his vial upon the sun; and power was given unto him to scorch men with fire (Revelation 16:8).

39. His eyes were as a flame of fire, and on his head were many crowns (Revelation 19:12).

40. The beast and the false prophet were cast alive into a lake of fire burning with brimstone (Revelation 19:20).

41. Fire came down from God out of heaven, and devoured them. And the devil that deceived them was cast into the lake of fire and brimstone. . . . And death and hell were cast into the lake of fire. . . . And whosoever was not found written in the book of life was cast into the lake of fire (Revelation 20:9–10, 14–15).

## 47. Dividing of Waters in the Bible

1. The children of Israel went through the Red Sea "upon the dry ground: and the waters were a wall unto them on their right hand, and on their left" (Exodus 14:22).

2. The waters of the Jordan were cut off before the ark of the covenant of the Lord (Joshua 4:7).

3. Elijah took his mantle, and wrapped it together, and smote the waters, and they were divided hither and thither, so that they two went over on dry ground (2 Kings 2:8).

4. When [Elisha] also had smitten the waters, they parted hither and thither (2 Kings 2:14).

5. The Lord shall utterly destroy the tongue of the Egyptian sea; and with his mighty wind shall he shake his hand over the river, and shall smite it in the seven streams, and make men go over dryshod (Isaiah 11:15).

# 5

## WORD POWER

Where would we be without words? Without them, it's nearly impossible to communicate. Some even theorize that we can't really think without words!

God reveals himself to man through His Word. This chapter is about God's Word, whether written, spoken through prophecy, or delivered by angels. This chapter also covers other aspects of word power, such as wisdom, rules for exhortation, yardsticks for measuring prophecy, names that Jesus called the scribes and Pharisees, the seven last sayings of Jesus, and benedictions.

One further note: No attempt was made to list all of the prophecies concerning Jesus' first and second coming. However, in the list of Old Testament prophecies fulfilled by Jesus, the passages found there are specifically quoted by New Testament writers as having been fulfilled by Jesus. For very special Old Testament prophecies concerning Jesus, see Psalm 22 and Isaiah 52:13–15; 53:1–12.

### 48. Twenty-five Facts About God's Word
1. Man doth not live by bread only, but by every word that proceedeth out of the mouth of the Lord (Deuteronomy 8:3).
2. The word is very nigh unto thee, in thy mouth, and in thy heart, that thou mayest do it (Deuteronomy 30:14).
3. The word of the Lord is right (Psalm 33:4).

4. By the word of the Lord were the heavens made (Psalm 33:6).

5. [Angels] hearken unto the voice of [God's] word (Psalm 103:20).

6. [God] sent his word and healed them (Psalm 107:20).

7. Wherewithal shall a young man cleanse his way? by taking heed thereto according to [God's] word (Psalm 119:9).

8. For ever, O Lord, thy word is settled in heaven (Psalm 119:89).

9. [God's] word is a lamp unto my feet and a light unto my path (Psalm 119:105).

10. [God's] word is true (Psalm 119:160).

11. Thou [God] hast magnified thy word about all thy name (Psalm 138:2).

12. [God's] word runneth very swiftly (Psalm 147:15).

13. Every word of God is pure (Proverbs 30:5).

14. [God's word] shall not return unto [Him] void, but it shall accomplish that which [God] pleases, and it shall prosper in the thing whereto [He] sent it (Isaiah 55:11).

15. Is not my word like as a fire? saith the Lord; and like a hammer that breaketh the rock in pieces? (Jeremiah 23:29).

16. The word that [God] shall speak shall come to pass (Ezekiel 12:25).

17. The Word was made flesh and dwelt among us (John 1:14).

18. The word of God is the sword of the Spirit (Ephesians 6:17).

19. The word of God is not bound (2 Timothy 2:9).

20. The word of God is quick (Hebrews 4:12).

21. The word of God is powerful (Hebrews 4:12).

22. The word of God is sharper than any twoedged sword, piercing even to the dividing asunder of soul and spirit (Hebrews 4:12).

23. The word of God is a discerner of the thoughts and intents of the heart (Hebrews 4:12).

24. The worlds were framed by the word of God (Hebrews 11:3).

25. The word of God liveth and abideth forever (1 Peter 1:23).

## 49. *Twenty-three Old Testament Prophecies Fulfilled by Jesus*

| | OLD TESTAMENT REFERENCE | NEW TESTAMENT FULFILLMENT |
|---|---|---|
| 1. | For thou wilt not leave my soul in hell; neither wilt thou suffer thine Holy One to see corruption (Psalm 16:10). | Whom God hath raised up, having loosed the pains of death: because it was not possible that he should be holden of it (Acts 2:24). |
| 2. | They part my garments among them, and cast lots upon my vesture (Psalm 22:18). | They crucified [Jesus], and parted his garments, casting lots (Matthew 27:35). |
| 3. | He keepeth all his bones: not one of them is broken (Psalm 34:20). | But when they came to Jesus, and saw that he was dead already, they brake not his legs (John 19:33). |
| 4. | Yea, mine own familiar friend, in whom I trusted, which did eat of my bread, hath lifted up his heel against me (Psalm 41:9). | And when [Jesus] had dipped the sop, he gave it to Judas Iscariot. . . . And after the sop Satan entered into him. Then said Jesus unto him, That thou doest, do quickly (John 13:26–27). |
| 5. | Thou hast ascended on high, thou hast led captivity captive: thou has received gifts for men (Psalm 68:18). | But unto every one of us is given grace according to the measure of the gift of Christ (Ephesians 4:7). |
| 6. | They that hate me without a cause are more than the hairs of mine head (Psalm 69:4). | [Jesus said], But now have they both seen and hated both me and my Father (John 15:24). |
| 7. | In my thirst they gave me vinegar to drink (Psalm 69:21). | And they filled a sponge with vinegar, and put it upon hyssop, and put it to his mouth (John 19:29). |
| 8. | I will open my mouth in a parable: I will utter dark sayings of old (Psalm 78:2). | All these things spake Jesus unto the multitude in parables; and without a parable spake he not unto them (Matthew 13:34). |

| | OLD TESTAMENT REFERENCE | NEW TESTAMENT FULFILLMENT |
|---|---|---|
| 9. | And he said, Go, and tell this people, Hear ye indeed, but understand not; and see ye indeed, but perceive not (Isaiah 6:9). | I [Jesus] speak to [the multitudes] in parables: because they seeing see not; and hearing they hear not, neither do they understand (Matthew 13:13). |
| 10. | Make the heart of this people fat, and make their ears heavy, and shut their eyes; lest they see with their eyes, and hear with their ears, and understand with their heart, and convert, and be healed (Isaiah 6:10). | The people could not believe Jesus because of Isaiah's prophecy (John 12:39–41). |
| 11. | Behold, a virgin shall conceive, and bear a son, and shall call his name Immanuel (Isaiah 7:14). | Jesus was born of the virgin Mary (Matthew 1:18–25). |
| 12. | He lightly afflicted the land of Zebulun and the land of Naphtali, and afterward did more grievously afflict her by the way of the sea, beyond Jordan, in Galilee of the nations. The people that walked in darkness have seen a great light (Isaiah 9:1–2). | And leaving Nazareth, he came and dwelt in Capernaum, which is upon the sea coast, in the borders of Zebulun and Naphtali (Matthew 4:13). |
| 13. | Behold my servant whom I uphold; mine elect, in whom my soul delighteth; I have put my spirit upon him: he shall bring forth judgment to the Gentiles. He shall not cry, nor lift up, nor cause his voice to be heard in the street. A bruised reed shall he not break, and the smoking flax shall he not quench: he shall bring forth judgment unto truth (Isaiah 42:1–3). | But when Jesus knew [the Pharisees were plotting to destroy Him], he withdrew himself from thence: and great multitudes followed him, and he healed them all; and charged them that they should not make him known (Matthew 12:15–16). |
| 14. | Who hath believed our report? and to whom is the arm of the Lord revealed? (Isaiah 53:1). | But though [Jesus] had done so many miracles before them, yet they believed not on him (John 12:37). |
| 15. | Surely he hath borne our griefs and carried our sorrows (Isaiah 53:4). | [Jesus] cast out spirits with his word, and healed all that were sick (Matthew 8:16). |

| | OLD TESTAMENT REFERENCE | NEW TESTAMENT FULFILLMENT |
|---|---|---|
| 16. | He was numbered with the transgressors (Isaiah 53:12). | And with him they crucify two thieves (Mark 15:27). |
| 17. | The Spirit of the Lord is upon me; because the Lord hath anointed me to preach good tidings unto the meek; he hath sent me to bind up the brokenhearted, to proclaim liberty to the captives, and the opening of the prison to them that are bound; to proclaim the acceptable year of the Lord (Isaiah 61:1–2). | And [Jesus] began to say unto them, This day is this scripture fulfilled in your ears (Luke 4:21). |
| 18. | I . . . called my son out of Egypt (Hosea 11:1). | Joseph took Mary and Jesus into Egypt and stayed there until the death of Herod (Matthew 2:13–15). |
| 19. | But thou Bethlehem Ephratah, though thou be little among the thousands of Judah, yet out of thee shall he come forth unto me that is to be ruler in Israel; whose goings forth have been from of old, from everlasting (Micah 5:2). | Jesus was born in Bethlehem of Judea (Matthew 2:1, 5–6). |
| 20. | Thus speaketh the Lord of hosts, saying, Behold the man whose name is The BRANCH; and he shall grow up out of his place, and he shall build the temple of the Lord (Zechariah 6:12). | Jesus dwelt in Nazareth [a play on words between the BRANCH and Nazarene] (Matthew 2:23). |
| 21. | Rejoice greatly, O daughter of Zion; shout, O daughter of Jerusalem: behold, thy King cometh unto thee: he is just, and having salvation; lowly, and riding upon an ass, and upon a colt the foal of an ass (Zechariah 9:9). | Jesus made his triumphal entry into Jerusalem riding on an ass and its colt (Matthew 21:1–11). |
| 22. | So they weighed for my price thirty pieces of silver. And the Lord said unto me, Cast it unto the potter: a goodly price that I was prised at of them. And I took the thirty pieces of silver, and cast them to the potter in the house of the Lord (Zechariah 11:12–13). | Judas . . . brought again the thirty pieces of silver to the chief priests and elders. He cast down the pieces of silver in the temple. They took counsel and bought with them the potter's field, to bury strangers in (Matthew 27:3, 5, 7). |

| | OLD TESTAMENT REFERENCE | NEW TESTAMENT FULFILLMENT |
|---|---|---|
| 23. | They shall look upon me whom they have pierced (Zechariah 12:10). | But one of the soldiers with a spear pierced his side, and forthwith came there out blood and water (John 19:34). |

## 50. Six Old Testament Prophecies Concerning Jesus' Second Coming

1. Out of Zion, the perfection of beauty, God hath shined. Our God shall come, and shall not keep silence: a fire shall devour before him, and it shall be very tempestuous round about him. He shall call to the heavens from above, and to the earth, that he may judge his people. Gather my saints together unto me (Psalm 50:2–5).

2. For unto us a child is born, unto us a son is given: and the government shall be upon his shoulder: and his name shall be called Wonderful, Counsellor, the Mighty God, the everlasting Father, the Prince of Peace. Of the increase of his government and peace there shall be no end, upon the throne of David, and upon his kingdom, to order it, and to establish it with judgment and with justice from henceforth even for ever. The zeal of the Lord of hosts will perform this (Isaiah 9:6–7).

3. For I know their works and their thoughts: it shall come, that I will gather all nations and tongues; and they shall come, and see my glory (Isaiah 66:18).

4. I saw in the night visions, and, behold, one like the Son of man came with the clouds of heaven, and came to the Ancient of days, and they brought him near before him. And there was given him dominion, and glory, and a kingdom, that all people, nations, and languages, should serve him: his dominion is an everlasting dominion, which shall not pass away, and his kingdom that which shall not be destroyed (Daniel 7:13–14).

5. And it shall come to pass in that day, that I will seek to destroy all the nations that come against Jerusalem. And I will pour upon the house of David, and upon the inhabitants of Jerusalem, the spirit of grace and of supplications: and they shall look upon me whom they have pierced, and they shall mourn for him, as one

mourneth for his only son, and shall be in bitterness for him, as one that is in bitterness for his firstborn (Zechariah 12:9–10).

6. And his feet shall stand in that day upon the mount of Olives, which is before Jerusalem on the east, and the mount of Olives shall cleave in the midst thereof toward the east and toward the west, and there shall be a very great valley; and half of the mountain shall remove toward the north, and half of it toward the south. And ye shall flee to the valley of the mountains; for the valley of the mountains shall reach unto Azal: yea, ye shall flee, like as ye fled from before the earthquake in the days of Uzziah king of Judah: and the Lord my God shall come, and all the saints with thee. And the Lord shall be king over all the earth (Zechariah 14:4–5, 9).

## 51. *Twenty Encounters With Angels*

1. The angel of the Lord appeared to Hagar after she had been sent away by Sarai. The angel told Hagar to return to, and to submit to, Sarai. He also told Hagar that her seed would be multiplied exceedingly and that she should call her child Ishmael (Genesis 16:1–12).

2. Two angels rescued Lot, his wife, and two daughters from Sodom. The angels told them to escape to the mountains and not to look back, because the angels were going to destroy Sodom. Lot convinced the angels to let him stay at Zoar (Genesis 19:1–22).

3. Abraham went up on the mountain to offer his son Isaac as a burnt sacrifice. As Abraham took the knife to slay Isaac, the angel of the Lord stopped Abraham and assured him that he had proven he feared God. The angel spoke again a little later and blessed Abraham by saying that the Lord would multiply Abraham's seed as the stars of heaven, and in his seed all the nations of the earth would be blessed (Genesis 22:1–18).

4. An angel appeared to Jacob and wrestled with him all night. Unable to prevail against Jacob, he disjointed the hollow of Jacob's thigh. The angel changed Jacob's name to Israel and blessed him (Genesis 32:24–30).

5. The angel of the Lord appeared to Moses in a burning bush. The

Lord then told Moses to free the Hebrews from the bondage of Egypt (Exodus 3–4:17).

6. The angel of the Lord stood in the way of Balaam and his donkey. The donkey saw the angel, but Balaam did not. When the donkey turned aside into the field, Balaam struck the donkey. The Lord caused the donkey to speak. Then Balaam finally saw the angel, who told Balaam that he could go to Balak, but he should only speak that which God gave him to say (Numbers 22:22–35).

7. Joshua was confronted by an angel who was the captain of the host of the Lord. The angel gave Joshua instructions on conquering Jericho (Joshua 5:13–15).

8. An angel of the Lord appeared to Gideon and commissioned him to save Israel from the Midianites. Gideon made a meal for the angel. The angel had Gideon put the food on a rock, then caused fire to come forth from the rock and consume it (Judges 6:11–23).

9. The angel of the Lord appeared to Samson's mother and told her she would have a son even though she had been barren. Later, the angel appeared again to both of Samson's parents and repeated his command that Samson was to be a Nazarite (Judges 13:1–20).

10. Elijah, depressed because Jezebel vowed to kill him, went into the wilderness, sat under a juniper tree, and begged God to let him die. An angel came and prepared food for Elijah. Elijah was so strengthened by those meals that he journeyed forty days without eating again (1 Kings 19:1–8).

11. One or two angels met the woman at Jesus' tomb and announced His resurrection (Matthew 28:5–7; Mark 16:5–7; Luke 24:4–7; John 20:11–18).

12. The angel Gabriel appeared to Zacharias and announced that Elizabeth, who was old and barren, would have a son and that he should be named John. He also told Zacharias about John's future ministry. Zacharias asked for a sign; he was struck dumb and couldn't speak again until John was born and named (Luke 1:5–22, 57–64).

13. The angel Gabriel also appeared to the Virgin Mary and told her that she would give birth to Jesus and God would be the Father. He also told her about Elizabeth (Luke 1:26–38).

14. The angel of the Lord announced the birth of Jesus to the shepherds and was then joined by a multitude of the heavenly host praising God (Luke 2:8–15).

15. As Jesus ascended into heaven, two angels appeared to the apostles and said, Ye men of Galilee, why stand ye gazing up into heaven? This same Jesus, which is taken up from you into heaven, shall so come in like manner as ye have seen him go into heaven (Acts 1:9–11).

16. The angel of the Lord brought the apostles out of prison and said, Go, stand and speak in the temple to the people all the words of this life (Acts 5:17–20).

17. The angel of the Lord told Philip to go to Gaza. There Philip met and converted the Ethiopian eunuch (Acts 8:26–39).

18. An angel appeared to Cornelius, telling him that God had heard his prayers and that he should send to Joppa for Peter. The angel said Peter would tell Cornelius what he should do (Acts 10:1–8).

19. Peter was asleep in prison while other Christians were praying for his release. The angel of the Lord woke Peter and released his chains. Peter followed the angel out of the prison and through the iron gate, which opened of its own accord (Acts 12:1–19).

20. Paul, sailing to Rome to be tried before Caesar, was in a storm for two weeks. The angel of God appeared to Paul and said, Fear not, Paul; thou must be brought before Caesar: and, lo, God hath given thee all of them that sail with thee (Acts 27:21–25).

## 52. Nineteen New Testament Prayers

1. Our Father which art in heaven, Hallowed be thy name. Thy kingdom come. Thy will be done in earth, as it is in heaven. Give us this day our daily bread. And forgive us our debts, as we forgive our debtors. And lead us not into temptation, but deliver us from evil: For thine is the kingdom, and the power, and the glory, for ever. Amen (Matthew 6:9–13).

2. I thank Thee, O Father, Lord of heaven and earth, because thou hast hid these things from the wise and prudent, and hast revealed

them unto babes. Even so, Father: for it seemed good in thy sight (Matthew 11:25–26).

3. Have mercy on me, O Lord, thou son of David; my daughter is grievously vexed with a devil. . . . Lord, help me. . . . Truth, Lord; yet the dogs eat of the crumbs which fall from their master's table (Matthew 15:22, 25, 27).

4. And there came a leper to [Jesus] beseeching him, and kneeling down to him, and saying to him, If thou wilt, thou canst make me clean (Mark 1:40).

5. God be merciful to me a sinner (Luke 18:13).

6. Father, if thou be willing, remove this cup from me: nevertheless not my will, but thine, be done (Luke 22:42).

7. Father, forgive them; for they know not what they do (Luke 23:34).

8. And he said unto Jesus, Lord, remember me when thou comest into thy kingdom (Luke 23:42).

9. Father, into thy hands I commend my spirit (Luke 23:46).

10. And Jesus lifted up his eyes, and said, Father, I thank thee that thou hast heard me. And I knew that thou hearest me always: but because of the people which stand by I said it, that they may believe that thou hast sent me (John 11:41–42).

11. Father, save me from this hour: but for this cause came I unto this hour. Father, glorify thy name (John 12:27–28).

12. Father, the hour is come; glorify thy Son, that thy Son also may glorify thee: As thou hast given him power over all flesh, that he should give eternal life to as many as thou hast given him. And this is life eternal, that they might know thee the only true God, and Jesus Christ whom thou hast sent.

    I have glorified thee on the earth: I have finished the work which thou gavest me to do. And now, O Father, glorify thou me with thine own self with the glory which I had with thee before the world was.

    I have manifested thy name unto the men which thou gavest me out of the world: thine they were, and thou gavest them me; and they have kept thy word. Now they have known that all things whatsoever thou hast given me are of thee. For I have given unto them the words which thou gav-est me; and they have received them, and have known surely that I came out from thee, and they have believed that thou didst send me.

I pray for them: I pray not for the world, but for them which thou hast given me; for they are thine. And all mine are thine, and thine are mine; and I am glorified in them. And now I am no more in the world, but these are in the world, and I come to thee.

Holy Father, keep through thine own name those whom thou hast given me, that they may be one, as we are. While I was with them in the world, I kept them in thy name: those that thou gavest me I have kept, and none of them is lost, but the son of perdition; that the scripture might be fulfilled.

And now I come to thee; and these things I speak in the world, that they might have my joy fulfilled in themselves. I have given them thy word; and the world hated them, because they are not of the world, even as I am not of the world. I pray not that thou shouldest take them out of the world, but that thou shouldest keep them from the evil. They are not of the world, even as I am not of the world. Sanctify them through thy truth: thy word is truth. As thou hast sent me into the world, even so have I sent them into the world. And for their sakes I sanctify myself, that they also might be sanctified through the truth.

Neither pray I for these alone, but for them also which shall believe on me through their word; that they all may be one; as thou, Father, art in me, and I in thee, that they also may be one in us: that the world may believe that thou hast sent me. And the glory which thou gavest me I have given them; that they may be one, even as we are one: I in them, and thou in me, that they may be made perfect in one; and that the world may know that thou hast sent me, and hast loved them, as thou hast loved me.

Father, I will that they also, whom thou hast given me, be with me where I am; that they may behold my glory, which thou hast given me: for thou lovedst me before the foundation of the world. O righteous Father, the world hath not known thee: but I have known thee, and these have known that thou hast sent me. And I have declared unto them thy name, and will declare it: that the love wherewith thou hast loved me may be in them, and I in them (John 17).

13. Thou Lord, which knowest the hearts of all men, show whether of these two thou hast chosen, that they may take part of this ministry and apostleship, from which Judas by transgression fell, that he might go to his own place (Acts 1:24).

14. Lord, thou art God, which hast made heaven, and earth, and the sea, and all that in them is: who by the mouth of thy servant David hast said, Why did the heathen rage, and the people imagine vain things? The kings of the earth stood up, and the rulers were gathered together against the Lord, and against his Christ. For of a truth against thy holy child Jesus, whom thou hast anointed, both Herod, and Pontius Pilate, with the Gentiles, and the people of Israel, were gathered together, for to do whatsoever thy hand and thy counsel determined before to be done. And now, Lord, behold their threatenings: and grant unto thy servants, that with all boldness they may speak thy word, by stretching forth thine hand to heal; and that signs and wonders may be done by the name of thy holy child Jesus (Acts 4:24–30).

15. Lord Jesus, receive my spirit (Acts 7:59).

16. Lord, lay not this sin to their charge (Acts 7:60).

17. Lord, what wilt thou have me to do? (Acts 9:6).

18. Thanks be unto God for his unspeakable gift (2 Corinthians 9:15).

19. Even so, come, Lord Jesus (Revelation 22:20).

## 53. Fifteen Facts About Wisdom

1. Happy is the man that findeth wisdom (Proverbs 3:13).

2. [Wisdom] is more precious than rubies, and all the things thou canst desire are not to be compared unto her (Proverbs 3:15).

3. Wisdom is the principal thing; therefore, get wisdom: and with all thy getting get understanding (Proverbs 4:7).

4. Those who seek [wisdom] early shall find [it] (Proverbs 8:17).

5. [Wisdom will] cause those that love [her] to inherit substance; and [she] will fill their treasures (Proverbs 8:21).

6. The fear of the Lord is the beginning of wisdom: and the knowledge of the Holy is understanding (Proverbs 9:10).

7. Wisdom that is from above is pure (James 3:17).

8. Wisdom that is from above is peaceable (James 3:17).

9. Wisdom that is from above is gentle (James 3:17).

10. Wisdom that is from above is easy to be entreated (James 3:17).

11. Wisdom that is from above is full of mercy (James 3:17).

12. Wisdom that is from above is full of good fruits (James 3:17).

13. Wisdom that is from above is without partiality (James 3:17).

14. Wisdom that is from above is without hypocrisy (James 3:17).

15. If any of you lack wisdom, let him ask of God (James 1:5).

## 54. Eighteen Rules of Exhortation

1. Our exhortation was not of deceit (1 Thessalonians 2:3).

2. Our exhortation was not of uncleanness (1 Thessalonians 2:3).

3. Our exhortation was not in guile (1 Thessalonians 2:3).

4. As you were allowed of God to be put in trust with the gospel, even so speak (1 Thessalonians 2:4).

5. Speak not as pleasing men (1 Thessalonians 2:4).

6. Speak as pleasing God (1 Thessalonians 2:4).

7. Use no flattering words (1 Thessalonians 2:5).

8. Use no cloak of covetousness (1 Thessalonians 2:5).

9. Do not seek glory from men (1 Thessalonians 2:6).

10. Be gentle, even as a nurse cherishes her children (1 Thessalonians 2:7).

11. Impart the gospel of God (1 Thessalonians 2:8).

12. Impart your own souls (1 Thessalonians 2:8).

13. Behave holily (1 Thessalonians 2:10).

14. Behave justly (1 Thessalonians 2:10).

15. Behave unblameably (1 Thessalonians 2:10).

16. Exhort as a father does his children (1 Thessalonians 2:11).

17. Charge everyone to walk worthy of God (1 Thessalonians 2:11–12).

18. Thank God without ceasing for those who receive the exhortation (1 Thessalonians 2:13).

## 55. Five Yardsticks by Which to Measure Prophecy

1. When a prophet speaketh in the name of the Lord, if the thing follow not, nor come to pass, that is the thing which the Lord hath not spoken, but the prophet hath spoken it presumptuously: thou shalt not be afraid of him (Deuteronomy 18:22).

2. He that prophesieth speaketh unto men to edification (1 Corinthians 14:3).

3. He that prophesieth speaketh unto men to . . . exhortation (1 Corinthians 14:3).

4. He that prophesieth speaketh unto men to . . . comfort (1 Corinthians 14:3).

5. If all prophesy, and there come in one that believeth not . . . thus are the secrets of his heart made manifest (1 Corinthians 14:24–25).

## 56. Seven Names That Jesus Called the Scribes and Pharisees

1. Blind guides (Matthew 23:16).

2. Fools (Matthew 23:17).

3. Whited sepulchres (Matthew 23:27).

4. Serpents (Matthew 23:33).

5. Generation of vipers (Matthew 23:33).

6. Hypocrites! (Luke 11:44).

7. Graves (hidden, unseen) (Luke 11:44).

## 57. *The Seven Last Sayings of Jesus on the Cross*

1. Then said Jesus, Father, forgive them; for they know not what they do (Luke 23:34).

2. Jesus said unto [the thief on the cross], Verily I say unto thee, Today shalt thou be with me in paradise (Luke 23:43).

3. He saith unto his mother, Woman, behold, thy son! Then saith he to the disciple, Behold, thy mother! (John 19:26–27).

4. Jesus cried with a loud voice, saying, Eloi, Eloi, lama sabachthani? which is, being interpreted, My God, my God, why hast thou forsaken me? (Mark 15:34).

5. Jesus . . . saith, I thirst (John 19:28).

6. Jesus . . . said, It is finished (John 19:30).

7. And when Jesus had cried with a loud voice, he said, Father, into thy hands I commend my spirit: and having said thus he gave up the ghost (Luke 23:46).

## 58. *Twelve Benedictions*

1. The Lord bless thee, and keep thee: the Lord make his face shine upon thee, and be gracious unto thee: the Lord lift up his countenance upon thee, and give thee peace (Numbers 6:24–26).

2. Grace to you and peace from God our Father, and the Lord Jesus Christ (Romans 1:7).

3. Now the God of peace be with you all. Amen (Romans 15:33).

4. The grace of our Lord Jesus Christ be with you all. Amen (Romans 16:24).

5. Peace be to the brethren, and love with faith, from God the Father and the Lord Jesus Christ. Grace be with all them that love our Lord Jesus Christ in sincerity. Amen (Ephesians 6:23–24).

6. Now the Lord of peace himself give you peace always by all means. The Lord be with you all (2 Thessalonians 3:16).

7. Grace, mercy, and peace, from God our Father and Jesus Christ our Lord (1 Timothy 1:2).

8. The Lord Jesus Christ be with thy spirit. Grace be with you. Amen (2 Timothy 4:22).

9. Now the God of peace, that brought again from the dead our Lord Jesus, that great shepherd of the sheep, through the blood of the everlasting covenant, make you perfect in every good work to do his will, working in you that which is well-pleasing in his sight, through Jesus Christ; to whom be glory for ever and ever. Amen (Hebrews 13:20–21).

10. Peace be with you all that are in Christ Jesus. Amen (1 Peter 5:14).

11. Grace and peace be multiplied unto you through the knowledge of God, and of Jesus our Lord (2 Peter 1:2).

12. Grace be unto you, and peace, from him which is, and which was, and which is to come; and from the seven Spirits which are before his throne; and from Jesus Christ, who is the faithful witness, and the first begotten of the dead, and the prince of the kings of the earth (Revelation 1:4–5).

# 6

## BOOKS

The Bible makes several references to books that are not contained within the Bible itself. Sometimes the reference is unusual and often it is intriguing. This chapter includes the following lists: Two Prophets Who Ate Books; The Most Important Directory in the Universe; Two Other Heavenly Books; Two Accounts of Book Burnings in the Bible, and Fourteen Non-Biblical Books Mentioned in the Bible.

### 59. *Two Prophets Who Ate Books*

1. Ezekiel wrote, And when I looked, behold, an hand was sent unto me; and, lo, a roll of a book was therein; and he spread it before me; and it was written within and without: and there was written therein lamentations, and mourning, and woe. Moreover he said unto me, Son of man, eat that thou findest; eat this roll, and go speak unto the house of Israel. So I opened my mouth, and he caused me to eat that roll. And he said unto me, Son of man, cause thy belly to eat, and fill thy bowels with this roll that I give thee. Then did I eat it; and it was in my mouth as honey for sweetness (Ezekiel 2:9–3:3).

2. John wrote, And I went unto the angel, and said unto him, Give me the little book, And he said unto me, Take it, and eat it up; and it shall make thy belly bitter, but it shall be in thy mouth sweet as honey. And I took the little book out of the angel's hand, and ate it up; and it was in my mouth sweet as honey: and as soon as I had eaten it, my belly was bitter (Revelation 10:9–10).

### 60. *The Most Important Directory in the Universe*

1. Jesus said, Rejoice not, that the spirits are subject unto you; but rather rejoice, because your names are written in heaven (Luke 10:20).

2. Jesus said, He that overcometh, the same shall be clothed in white raiment; and I will not blot out his name out of the book of life, but I will confess his name before my Father and before his angels (Revelation 3:5).

3. And whosoever was not found in the book of life was cast into the lake of fire (Revelation 20:15).

4. There shall in no wise enter into it anything that defileth . . . but they which are written in the Lamb's book of life (Revelation 21:27).

### 61. *Two Other Heavenly Books*

1. Then they that feared the Lord spake often one to another: and the Lord hearkened, and heard it, and a book of remembrance was written before him for them that feared the Lord, and that thought upon his name. And they shall be mine, saith the Lord of hosts, in that day when I make up my jewels; and I will spare them, as a man spareth his own son that serveth him (Malachi 3:16–17).

2. One of the elders saith to me [John], Weep not; behold, the Lion of the tribe of Judah, the Root of David, hath prevailed to open the book, and to loose the seven seals thereof (Revelation 5:5).

### 62. *Two Accounts of Book Burnings in the Bible*

1. When Jehudi read a book of God's judgments to king Jehoiakim, the king cut it with a penknife and cast it into the fire that was on the hearth, until all the roll was consumed in the fire that was on the hearth (Jeremiah 36:23).

2. And many that believed came, and confessed, and shewed their deeds. Many of them also which used curious arts brought their books together, and burned them before all men: and they counted the price of them, and found it fifty thousand pieces of silver (Acts 19:18–19).

## 63. *Fourteen Non-Biblical Books Mentioned in the Bible*

1. It is said in the book of the wars of the Lord, What he did in the Red sea, and in the brooks of Arnon. And at the stream of the brooks that goeth down to the dwelling of Ar, and lieth upon the border of Moab (Numbers 21:14–15).

2. And the sun stood still, and the moon stayed, until the people had avenged themselves upon their enemies. Is not this written in the book of Jasher? (Joshua 10:13).

3. Three men from each of seven of the tribes of Israel passed through the land, and described it by cities into seven parts in a book, and came again to Joshua to the host at Shiloh (Joshua 18:9).

4. Samuel told the people the manner of the kingdom [that they would have under King Saul], and wrote it in a book, and laid it up before the Lord (1 Samuel 10:25).

5. The rest of the acts of Solomon, and all that he did, and his wisdom, are they not written in the book of the acts of Solomon? (1 Kings 11:41).

6. The acts of David the king, first and last, behold, they are written in . . . the book of Nathan the prophet (1 Chronicles 29:29).

7. The acts of David the king, first and last, behold, they are written in . . . the book of Gad the seer (1 Chronicles 29:29).

8. The acts of Rehoboam, first and last, are they not written in the book of Shemaiah the prophet? (2 Chronicles 12:15).

9. The acts of Rehoboam, first and last, are they not written in the book . . . of Iddo the seer concerning genealogies? (2 Chronicles 12:15).

10. The rest of the acts of Jehoshaphat, first and last, behold, they are written in the book of Jehu the son of Hanani, who is mentioned in the book of the Kings of Israel (2 Chronicles 20:34).

11. Rehum the chancellor, and Shimshai the scribe wrote a letter to Artaxerxes the king and asked that search may be made in the book of the records of thy fathers: so shalt thou find in the book of the records, and know that this city is a rebellious city, and hurtful unto kings and provinces, and that they have moved sedition within the same of old time: for which cause was this city destroyed (Ezra 4:15).

12. In those days, while Mordecai sat in the king's gate, two of the king's chamberlains, Bigthan and Teresh, of those which kept the door, were wroth, and sought to lay hand on the king Ahasuerus. And the thing was known to Mordecai who told it unto Esther the queen; and Esther certified the king thereof in Mordecai's name. And when inquisition was made of the matter, it was found out; therefore they were both hanged on a tree: and it was written in the book of the chronicles before the king (Esther 2:21–23).

13. And the decree of Esther confirmed these matters of Purim; and it was written in the book (Esther 9:32).

14. And the king Ahasuerus laid a tribute upon the land, and upon the isles of the sea. And all the acts of his power and of his might, and the declaration of the greatness of Mordecai, whereunto the king advanced him, are they not written in the book of the chronicles of the kings of Media and Persia? (Esther 10:1–2).

# 7

## PEOPLE

The Bible, of course, is not just about God; it is also about people, many of whom were extraordinary. The people found in this chapter include inventors, kings, prophets, apostles, heroes, government employees, and polygamists. The lists here are short and contain brief interesting facts about them along with supporting Scripture references.

The chapter opens with these two lists: Two Men Who Never Died and Seven Men Who Lived More Than Nine Hundred Years. Can you name them without looking at the lists?

### 64. Two Men Who Never Died
1. Enoch lived 365 years (Genesis 5:23–24), and then he was translated by God (Hebrews 11:5).
2. Elijah was carried by a whirlwind into heaven (2 Kings 2:11).

### 65. Seven Men Who Lived More Than Nine Hundred Years
1. Adam lived 930 years (Genesis 5:5).
2. Seth lived 912 years (Genesis 5:8).
3. Enos lived 905 years (Genesis 5:11).
4. Cainan lived 910 years (Genesis 5:14).
5. Jared lived 962 years (Genesis 5:20).

6. Methuselah lived 969 years (Genesis 5:27).

7. Noah lived 950 years (Genesis 9:29).

## 66. Seven Suicides in the Bible

1. [Abimelech] called hastily unto the young man his armour-bearer, and said unto him, Draw thy sword, and slay me, that men say not of me, A woman slew him. And his young man thrust him through, and he died (Judges 9:54).

2. And Samson said, Let me die with the Philistines. And he bowed with all his might; and the house fell . . . upon all the people that were therein (Judges 16:30).

3. Saul took a sword and fell on it (1 Samuel 31:4).

4. When [Saul's] armour-bearer saw that Saul was dead, he fell likewise upon his sword, and died (1 Samuel 31:5).

5. When Ahithophel saw that his counsel was not followed, he . . . gat him home to his house, to his city, and put his house in order, and hanged himself, and died (2 Samuel 17:23).

6. It came to pass, when Zimri saw that the city was taken, that he went into the palace of the king's house, and burnt the king's house over him with fire, and died (1 Kings 16:18).

7. [Judas] cast down the pieces of silver in the temple, and departed, and went and hanged himself (Matthew 27:5).

## 67. The Three Kings Who Ruled All of Israel

1. Saul ruled forty years (Acts 13:21).

2. David ruled forty years (2 Samuel 5:4).

3. Solomon ruled forty years (1 Kings 11:42).

## 68. Nineteen Kings Who Ruled Judah

1. Rehoboam ruled seventeen years (1 Kings 14:21).

2. Abijam ruled three years (1 Kings 15:2).

3. Asa ruled forty-one years (1 Kings 15:10).

4. Jehoshaphat ruled twenty-five years (1 Kings 22:42).

5. Jehoram ruled eight years (2 Kings 8:17).

6. Ahaziah ruled part of one year (2 Kings 8:25–26). *Note:* Queen Athaliah ruled six years (2 Kings 11:3).

7. Jehoash ruled forty years (2 Kings 12:1).

8. Amaziah ruled twenty-nine years (2 Kings 14:2).

9. Uzziah (also known as Azariah) ruled fifty-two years (2 Kings 15:2).

10. Jotham ruled sixteen years (2 Kings 15:33).

11. Ahaz ruled sixteen years (2 Kings 16:2).

12. Hezekiah ruled twenty-nine years (2 Kings 18:1–2).

13. Manasseh ruled fifty-five years (2 Kings 21:1).

14. Amon ruled two years (2 Kings 21:19).

15. Josiah ruled thirty-one years (2 Kings 22:1).

16. Jehoahaz ruled three months (2 Kings 23:31).

17. Jehoiakim ruled eleven years (2 Kings 23:36).

18. Jehoiachin ruled three months (2 Kings 24:8).

19. Zedekiah ruled eleven years (2 Kings 24:18).

## 69. Nineteen Kings Who Ruled the Northern Kingdom of Israel

1. Jeroboam ruled twenty-two years (1 Kings 14:20).

2. Nadab ruled two years (1 Kings 15:25).

3. Baasha ruled twenty-four years (1 Kings 15:33).

4. Elah ruled two years (1 Kings 16:8).

5. Zimri ruled seven days (1 Kings 16:15).

6. Omri ruled twelve years (1 Kings 16:23).

7. Ahab ruled twenty-two years (1 Kings 16:29).

8. Ahaziah ruled two years (1 Kings 22:51).

9. Jehoram ruled twelve years (2 Kings 3:1).

10. Jehu ruled twenty-eight years (2 Kings 10:36).

11. Jehoahaz ruled seventeen years (2 Kings 13:1).

12. Jehoash ruled sixteen years (2 Kings 13:10).

13. Jeroboam ruled forty-one years (2 Kings 14:23).
14. Zachariah ruled six months (2 Kings 15:8).
15. Shallum ruled one month (2 Kings 15:13).
16. Menahem ruled ten years (2 Kings 15:17).
17. Pekahiah ruled two years (2 Kings 15:23).
18. Pekah ruled twenty years (2 Kings 15:27).
19. Hoshea ruled nine years (2 Kings 17:1).

## 70. *Gentile Kings of Israel*

1. Jacob and his sons settled in Egypt under a Pharaoh (Genesis 47:1–10).
2. The Pharaoh whom God delivered Israel from was a new king over Egypt which knew not Joseph (Exodus 1:8).
3. King Ahaz submitted to Tiglathpileser, king of Assyria (2 Kings 16:7).
4. Shalmaneser, king of Assyria, imprisoned Hoshea, king of the northern kingdom of Israel (2 Kings 17:3–4).
5. Sennacherib, king of Assyria, took control of Judah during Hezekiah's reign (2 Kings 18:13).
6. Esarhaddon succeeded Sennacherib (2 Kings 19:36–37).
7. Pharaoh-necchoh made Judah pay tribute after imprisoning king Jehoahaz (2 Kings 23:33–34).
8. Evil-merodach, king of Babylon, brought king Jehoiachin of Judah out of prison (2 Kings 25:27).
9. Ahasuerus (Artaxerxes) became king of Persia (Ezra 4:6–7).
10. Ahasuerus (possibly Xerxes) reigned from India to Ethiopia. Esther was his queen (Esther 1:1; 2:17).
11. Nebuchadnezzar took Jerusalem during Jehoiakim's reign (Daniel 1:1).
12. Daniel interpreted Belshazzar's vision (Daniel 5:1–28).
13. Darius conquered Babylon and assumed the rule of Israel (Daniel 5:31).
14. Darius the Mede was a son of Ahasuerus (Daniel 9:1).

15. Herod the king was king of Judea at Jesus' birth (Matthew 2:1).

16. Archelaus, son of Herod, reigned in Judea when Joseph brought Jesus and Mary to Nazareth (Matthew 2:22–23).

17. Caesar Augustus ruled the known world at the time of Jesus' birth (Luke 2:1, 7).

18. Tiberius Caesar reigned when John the Baptist began preaching (Luke 3:1–3).

19. Herod the tetrarch put John the Baptist in prison (Luke 3:19–20).

20. Herod the king imprisoned and killed some of the apostles (Acts 12:1–3).

21. There was a great dearth throughout the world in the reign of Claudius Caesar (Acts 11:28).

22. Paul referred to Nero when he declared, I appeal unto Caesar (Acts 25:11).

## 71. Four Major Prophets of the Old Testament

1. Isaiah prophesied of the Messiah (Isaiah 52:13–53:1–12).

2. Jeremiah prophesied of the Messiah (Jeremiah 23:5–6; 33:14–16).

3. Ezekiel prophesied of the Messiah (Ezekiel 34:11–16; 37:24–25).

4. Daniel prophesied of the Messiah (Daniel 2:44–45; 9:24–26).

## 72. Twelve Minor Prophets of the Old Testament

1. Hosea prophesied of the Messiah (Hosea 11:1).

2. Joel prophesied of the outpouring of the Holy Spirit (Joel 2:28–29).

3. Amos rebuked Israel for its sins (Amos).

4. Obadiah prophesied against Edom (Obadiah).

5. Jonah foreshadowed the death, burial, and resurrection of Jesus (Jonah; Matthew 12:38–40).

6. Micah prophesied of the Messiah (Micah 5:2).

7. Nahum prophesied against Nineveh (Nahum).

8. Habakkuk said, "The just shall live by his faith" (Habakkuk 2:4).

9. Zephaniah prophesied of the day of the Lord's wrath (Zephaniah).

10. Haggai prophesied of the Messiah (Haggai 2:7).

11. Zechariah prophesied of the Messiah (Zechariah 6:12–13; 9:9–10; 13:6–7).

12. Malachi prophesied of the Messiah (Malachi 3:1).

### 73. Eleven Other Prophets of the Old Testament

1. Abraham was revealed as a prophet to King Abimelech in a dream (Genesis 20:1–7).

2. Balaam prophesied of the Messiah (Numbers 24:17, 19).

3. Moses prophesied of the Messiah (Deuteronomy 18:15, 18–19).

4. Samuel was established to be a prophet of the Lord (1 Samuel 3:19–21).

5. King Saul prophesied on two occasions (1 Samuel 10:1–13; 19:18–24).

6. Nathan the prophet declared to King David that God knew about David's sins of adultery and murder (2 Samuel 12:1–23).

7. The prophet Gad presented to King David three choices of judgment upon Israel after David sinned in numbering Israel. The choices: (1) seven years of famine, (2) three months of being pursued by enemies, or (3) three days of pestilence (2 Samuel 24:10–14).

8. Ahijah prophesied that Jeroboam would be king over ten tribes, which God would take away from King Solomon (1 Kings 11:29–40).

9. Elijah the prophet (1 Kings 18:36) was translated (2 Kings 2:1–11).

10. Elisha the prophet (2 Kings 9:1) succeeded Elijah (2 Kings 2:1–15).

11. King David prophesied of the Messiah (Psalm 22:1, 6–8, 13, 16–18, 31).

## 74. Six New Testament Prophets

1. Jesus said that there was no greater prophet than John the Baptist (Matthew 11:7–15).

2. Jesus prophesied the destruction of Jerusalem and the events leading up to His second coming (Matthew 24).

3. Agabus prophesied that there would be a famine and that the Jews would deliver Paul into the hands of the Gentiles (Acts 11:27–28; 21:10–11).

4. Judas Barsabas was a prophet (Acts 15:22, 32).

5. Silas was a prophet (Acts 15:32).

6. John recorded the great prophetic work known as the Revelation (Revelation 1–22).

## 75. Eight Women Prophets

1. Miriam, Moses' sister, was a prophetess (Exodus 15:20).

2. Deborah, a judge in Israel, was a prophetess (Judges 4:4).

3. When Josiah was king of Judah, a book of the law was found during cleaning of the temple. Josiah commanded Hilkiah the high priest to inquire of the Lord for the king. Hilkiah then went to Huldah the prophetess (2 Kings 22).

4. The prophetess Anna recognized Jesus as being the Messiah when Jesus was brought to the temple to be circumcised (Luke 2:36–38).

5. The four virgin daughters of Philip the evangelist prophesied (Acts 21:8–9).

## 76. The Twelve Apostles

1. Peter, James, John, Andrew, Philip, Thomas, Bartholomew, Matthew, James (son of Alphaeus), Simon, Lebbaeus Thaddaeus (Judas), and Judas Iscariot (Matthew 10:2–4).

2. Peter, James, John, Andrew, Philip, Thomas, Bartholomew, Matthew, James (son of Alphaeus), Simon, Thaddaeus, and Judas Iscariot (Mark 3:16–19).

3. Peter, James, John, Andrew, Philip, Thomas, Bartholomew,

Matthew, James (son of Alphaeus), Simon Zelotes, Judas (brother of James), and Judas Iscariot (Luke 6:14–16).

4. Peter, James, John, Andrew, Philip, Thomas, Bartholomew, Matthew, James (son of Alphaeus), Simon Zelotes, Judas (brother of James), and Judas Iscariot (deceased) (Acts 1:13).

## 77. Eight More Apostles

1. Matthias was selected to be the apostle to replace Judas Iscariot, first by qualifications, and then by casting a prayerful lot (Acts 1:26).

2. Barnabas was an apostle and companion of Paul (Acts 14:14).

3. Paul was the apostle to the Gentiles (Romans 11:13).

4. Paul mentioned Andronicus as an apostle (Romans 16:7).

5. Paul mentioned Junia as an apostle (Romans 16:7).

6. Paul mentioned James, the brother of Jesus, as being an apostle (Galatians 1:19).

7. Paul called Silvanus a fellow apostle (1 Thessalonians 1:1; 2:6).

8. Paul called Timothy a fellow apostle (1 Thessalonians 1:1; 2:6).

## 78. Twenty-five Ways Old Testament Heroes Exercised Faith

1. Abel offered an acceptable sacrifice by faith (Hebrews 11:4).

2. Enoch was translated by faith (Hebrews 11:5).

3. Noah prepared the ark by faith (Hebrews 11:7).

4. Abraham went into a strange land by faith (Hebrews 11:8–10).

5. Sarah received strength to conceive a child in her old age by faith (Hebrews 11:11–12).

6. Abraham offered up Isaac by faith (Hebrews 11:17–19).

7. Isaac blessed Jacob and Esau prophetically by faith (Hebrews 11:20).

8. Jacob blessed the sons of Joseph prophetically by faith (Hebrews 11:21).

9. Joseph prophesied of Israel's departure from Egypt by faith (Hebrews 11:22).

10. Moses was hid as a baby by faith (Hebrews 11:23).

11. Moses forsook the riches of Egypt by faith (Hebrews 11:24–27).

12. Moses kept the passover by faith (Hebrews 11:28).

13. The Red Sea parted by faith (Hebrews 11:29).

14. The walls of Jericho fell by faith (Hebrews 11:30).

15. Rahab, the harlot, saved herself and her family by faith (Hebrews 11:31).

16. Gideon delivered Israel from the Midianites by faith (Hebrews 11:32).

17. Barak delivered Israel from the Canaanites by faith (Hebrews 11:32).

18. Samson delivered Israel from the Philistines by faith (Hebrews 11:32).

19. Jephtha delivered Israel from the Ammonites by faith (Hebrews 11:32).

20. David waxed valiant in fight by faith (Hebrews 11:32).

21. Samuel prophesied by faith (Hebrews 11:32).

22. Daniel stopped the mouths of lions by faith (Hebrews 11:33).

23. Shadrach, Meshach, and Abednego quenched the violence of fire by faith (Hebrews 11:34).

24. The son of the Zarephath widow was raised from the dead by faith (Hebrews 11:35).

25. The son of the Shunammite woman was raised from the dead by faith (Hebrews 11:35).

## 79. Important Servants in the Bible

1. Abraham and 318 of his servants defeated the captors of Sodom and Gomorrah (Genesis 14:14–15).

2. Hagar, the mother of Ishmael, was Sarah's handmaid (Genesis 16:1).

3. Abraham's eldest servant found a wife for Isaac (Genesis 24).

4. Jacob served Laban for several years (Genesis 29–31).

5. Zilpah and Bilhah, Leah's and Rachel's maids, bore children for Jacob (Genesis 30).

6. Joseph was Potiphar's servant (Genesis 39:1).

7. Pharaoh's chief butler and chief baker were instrumental in Joseph's eventual promotion to the position of prime minister (Genesis 41).

8. The Egyptians made the children of Israel serve with rigor (Exodus 1:13).

9. A maid of the daughter of Pharaoh took Moses in his basket from the river (Exodus 2:5).

10. Joshua was Moses' servant (Exodus 33:11).

11. The Hivites were cursed to be Israel's servants (Joshua 9:23).

12. Abimelech's armorbearer killed him, at his request (Judges 9:54).

13. Mephibosheth's nurse dropped him while fleeing the enemy. He was permanently crippled (2 Samuel 4:4).

14. Elisha poured water on the hands of Elijah (2 Kings 3:11).

15. Gehazi was Elisha's servant (2 Kings 4:12).

16. A young girl, captured from Israel, was the maid of Naaman's wife. She advised that he go to Elisha and be healed of leprosy (2 Kings 5:2–3).

17. Nehemiah was cupbearer for Artexerxes (Nehemiah 1:11).

18. The centurion's servant at Capernaum was healed by Jesus (Matthew 8:13).

19. Jesus spoke of an unforgiving servant (Matthew 18:23–34).

20. Jesus told of three servants who were each given money to invest for their master (Matthew 25:14–30).

21. Jesus told a parable of a vineyard owner, whose servants were killed or beaten by the husbandmen (Mark 12:1–5).

22. Peter cut off the ear of Malchus, the high priest's servant (John 18:10).

23. A servant girl at the house of Caiaphas asked Peter if he was one of the disciples (John 18:17).

24. Peter denied knowing Jesus the third time to a servant of the high priest (John 18:26).

25. Two of Cornelius' servants were sent to bring Peter from Joppa (Acts 10:7–8).

26. Onesimus, a servant of Philemon, was converted by Paul (Philemon).

## 80. *Fifteen Men in the Bible Who Had More Than One Wife*

1. Lamech, who was Cain's great-great-great grandson, was the first man recorded to have two wives (Adah, Zillah) (Genesis 4:19).

2. Abraham had three wives (Sarah, Hagar, and Keturah) (Genesis 23:19; 25:1; 16:3).

3. Esau had three wives (Judith, Bashemath, and Mahalath) (Genesis 26:34; 28:9).

4. Jacob had four wives (Leah, Rachel, Bilhah, and Zilpah) (Genesis 29:15–35; 30:4, 9).

5. Moses had two wives (Zipporah, and the Ethiopian woman) (Exodus 18:2; Numbers 12:1).

6. Gideon had many wives and seventy sons (Judges 8:30).

7. Samuel's father, Elkanah, had two wives (Hannah, Peninnah) (1 Samuel 1:1–2).

8. King Saul had at least two wives (Ahinoam, Rizpah) (1 Samuel 14:50; 2 Samuel 3:7).

9. David had at least eight wives (Michal, Abigail, Ahinoam, Bathsheba, Maacah, Haggith, Abital, and Eglah) plus Saul's wives (2 Samuel 12:8).

10. Solomon had 700 wives and 300 concubines (1 Kings 11:3).

11. King Ahab had more than one wife (1 Kings 20:7).

12. King Rehoboam had eighteen wives and sixty concubines (2 Chronicles 11:21).

13. King Abijah who ruled over Judah had fourteen wives (2 Chronicles 13:21).

14. King Joash had two wives (2 Chronicles 24:1–3).

15. King Ahasuerus had a harem. Two wives are mentioned by name: Vashti and Esther (Esther 1:10–12; 2:1–17).

## 81. Six Women in the Bible Who Had More Than One Husband

1. Tamar was married to Judah's two sons Er and Onan (Genesis 38:6–10).

2. Samson's wife was given to Samson's companion (Judges 14:20).

3. David's wife Michal was given to Phaltiel by Saul and was later reclaimed by David (2 Samuel 3:13–16).

4. Ruth was married to Mahlon first, and then to Boaz (Ruth 4:10, 13).

5. The Sadducees described to Jesus a woman who had successively married seven brothers (Mark 12:18–25).

6. The woman whom Jesus met at the well had had five husbands and was living with a sixth man to whom she was not married (John 4:6–19).

## 82. Widows in the Bible

1. The wives of the men of the city of Shechem, who were killed by Simeon and Levi (Genesis 34:25).

2. Tamar, the wife of Er (Genesis 38:6–7).

3. Naomi and her daughters-in-law, Orpah and Ruth, were all widows (Ruth 1:3, 5).

4. The wife of Phinehas, Eli's son (1 Samuel 4:19).

5. Abigail, who became David's wife (1 Samuel 25:37, 39).

6. Bathsheba, whose husband was murdered (2 Samuel 11:26).

7. A woman of Tekoah pretended to be a widow before David (2 Samuel 14:2–5).

8. When David returned to Jerusalem, his ten concubines were placed in widowhood (2 Samuel 20:3).

9. Hiram's mother (1 Kings 7:13–14).

10. Solomon, who had seven hundred wives, probably left many widows (1 Kings 11:3).

11. Zeruah, the mother of Jeroboam (1 Kings 11:26).

12. Jezebel, the wife of Ahab (1 Kings 16:31; 22:40).

13. The widow of Zarephath, whom Elijah stayed with (1 Kings 17:9).

14. A certain woman of the wives of the sons of the prophets (2 Kings 4:1).

15. The Sadducees told Jesus of a woman who was widowed seven times (Mark 12:22).

16. The poor widow who gave two mites to the temple treasury (Mark 12:42).

17. Anna the prophetess (Luke 2:36–37).

18. Many widows were in Israel in the days of Elias (Luke 4:25).

19. The widow at Nain whose son Jesus raised (Luke 7:12–15).

20. The widow in Jesus' parable who prevailed upon a judge to help her (Luke 18:2–5).

21. Sapphira was a widow for about three hours (Acts 5:5–10).

22. The Grecian widows of the church were neglected in the daily ministration (Acts 6:1).

23. Many widows received coats and garments from Dorcas (Acts 9:39).

24. There were widows in the Corinthian church (1 Corinthians 7:8).

25. There were widows under Timothy's jurisdiction (1 Timothy 5:3).

## 83. *Ten Remarkable Acts of Heroism in the Bible*

1. Simeon and Levi killed all of the men of a whole city with their swords to avenge the defiling of their sister, Dinah. First they convinced the men of the city to be circumcised, and then, while the men were still recovering, they slaughtered them (Genesis 34).

2. Shamgar, the son of Anath, delivered Israel by slaying 600 Philistines with an ox goad (Judges 3:31).

3. Samson, tied up with two new cords, broke the cords after the

Spirit of the Lord came upon him, and slew a thousand Philistines with the jawbone of an ass (Judges 15:9–17).

4. Jonathan and his armorbearer slew twenty Philistines, and thus began a great victory for Israel (1 Samuel 14:1–14).

5. David slew the giant, Goliath, with a sling and one stone (1 Samuel 17:38–54).

6. The chief captain in King David's army killed 800 men with his spear in one battle (2 Samuel 23:8).

7. Shadrach, Meshach, and Abednego defied the king's order to worship the king's golden image and were therefore thrown into the fiery furnace. God saved them even in the midst of the fire (Daniel 3).

8. Peter preached the gospel openly and boldly on the day of Pentecost under the anointing of the Holy Ghost, in spite of the fact that he had denied knowing Jesus less than two months before (Acts 2:1–41).

9. Stephen defended the gospel before the Sanhedrin, though it cost him his life. While he was dying, he forgave those who stoned him (Acts 6:9–15; 7:1–60).

10. Paul continued to preach the gospel even though he received thirty-nine lashes on five occasions, was beaten with rods on three other occasions, was stoned once, and was shipwrecked three times. And that is not to mention the number of times he was imprisoned or otherwise persecuted (2 Corinthians 11:23–28).

## 84. Government Employees Mentioned in the Bible

1. Joseph was *governor* over the land (of Egypt) (Genesis 42:6).

2. And David reigned over all Israel; and David executed judgment and justice unto all his people. And Joab the son of Zeruiah was *over the host*; [and Jehoshaphat the son of Ahilud was *recorder*;] and Zadok the son of Ahitub, and Ahimelech the son of Abiathar, were the priests; and Seraiah was the *scribe*; and Benaiah the son of Jehoiada was over the Cherethites and the Pelethites; and David's sons were *chief rulers* (2 Samuel 8:15–18).

3. Later, Adoram was *over the tribute* . . . Sheva was *scribe* . . .

and Ira . . . the Jairite was a *chief ruler* about David (2 Samuel 20:24–26).

4. King Solomon was king over all Israel. And these were the *princes* which he had: Azariah the son of Zadok the priest, Elihoreph and Ahiah, the sons of Shisha, *scribes;* Jehoshaphat the son of Ahilud, the *recorder.* And Benaiah the son of Jehoiada was *over the host:* and Zadok and Abiathar were the priests: and Azariah the son of Nathan was over the *officers:* and Zabud the son of Nathan was *principal officer* and the king's friend: and Ahishar was *over the household:* and Adoniram the son of Abda was *over the tribute.* And Solomon had twelve *officers over all Israel,* which provided victuals for the king and his household: each man his month in a year made provision. And these are their names: The son of Hur, in mount Ephraim: The son of Dekar, in Makaz, and in Shaalbim, and Bethshemesh, and Elonbethhanan: The son of Hesed, in Aruboth; to him pertained Sochoh, and all the land of Hepher: The son of Abinadab, in all the region of Dor; which had Taphath the daughter of Solomon to wife: Baana the son of Ahilud; to him pertained Taanach and Megiddo, and all Bethshean, which is by Zartanah beneath Jezreel, from Bethshean to Abelmeholah, even unto the place that is beyond Jokneam: The son of Geber, in Ramothgilead; to him pertained the towns of Jair the son of Manasseh, which are in Gilead; to him also pertained the region of Argob, which is in Bashan, threescore great cities with walls and brasen bars: Ahinadab the son of Iddo had Mahanaim: Ahimaaz was in Naphtali; he also took Basmath the daughter of Solomon to wife: Baanah the son of Hushai was in Asher and in Aloth: Jehoshaphat the son of Paruah, in Issachar: Shimei the son of Elah, in Benjamin: Geber the son of Uri was in the country of Gilead, in the country of Sihon king of the Amorites, and of Og king of Bashan; and he was the only *officer* which was in the land (1 Kings 4:1–19).

5. Ahab called Obadiah, which was the *governor of his house* (1 Kings 18:3).

6. The King of Israel said, Take Micaiah, and carry him back unto Amon the *governor of the city* (1 Kings 22:26).

7. Under King Hezekiah, Eliakim the son of Hilkiah . . . was *over*

*the household*, and Shebna (was) the *scribe*, and Joah the son of Asaph (was) the *recorder* (2 Kings 18:18).

8. In the eighteenth year of King Josiah . . . the king sent Shaphan . . . the *scribe* to the house of the Lord (2 Kings 22:3).

9. And Satan stood up against Israel, and provoked David to number Israel. And David said to Joab and to the *rulers* of the people, Go, number Israel from Beersheba even to Dan; and bring the number of them to me, that I may know it (1 Chronicles 21:1–2).

10. Rehum the *chancellor* and Shimshai the *scribe* wrote a letter against Jerusalem to Artaxerxes the king (Ezra 4:8).

11. Nebuchadnezzar the king sent to gather together the *princes*, the *governors*, and the *captains*, the *judges*, the *treasurers*, the *counsellors*, the *sheriffs*, and all the *rulers* of the provinces, to come to the dedication of the image which Nebuchadnezzar the king had set up (Daniel 3:2).

12. It pleased Darius to set over the kingdom an hundred and twenty *princes*, which should be over the whole kingdom; and over these three *presidents*; of whom Daniel was first (Daniel 6:1–2).

13. And as Jesus passed forth from thence, he saw a man, named Matthew, sitting at the *receipt of custom:* and he saith unto him, Follow me. And he arose, and followed him (Matthew 9:9).

14. Jesus said, When thou goest with thine adversary to the *magistrate*, as thou art in the way, give diligence that thou mayest be delivered from him; lest he hale thee to *the judge*, and the *judge* deliver thee to the *officer*, and the *officer* cast thee into prison (Luke 12:58).

15. There was a man named Zacchaeus, which was the chief among the *publicans*, and he was rich (Luke 19:2).

16. The angel of the Lord spoke unto Philip, saying, Arise, and go toward the south unto the way that goeth down from Jerusalem unto Gaza, which is desert. And he arose and went: and, behold a man of Ethiopia, an eunuch of great authority under Candace queen of the Ethiopians, who had *charge of* all her *treasure* (Acts 8:26–27).

17. There was a certain man in Caesarea called Cornelius, a *centurion* of the band called the Italian band (Acts 10:1).

18. And Herod was highly displeased with them of Tyre and Sidon:

but they came with one accord to him, and, having made Blastus the king's *chamberlain* their friend, desired peace; because their country was nourished by the king's country (Acts 12:20).

19. Paul and Barnabas went to Paphos on the island of Cyprus where the *deputy* of the country, Sergius Paulus, a prudent man . . . called for Barnabas and [Paul], and desired to hear the word of God (Acts 13:4–7).

20. After Paul and Silas saw the *jailor* converted, and his household, and when it was day, the *magistrates* sent the *sergeants*, saying, Let those men go. And the *keeper of the prison* told this saying to Paul, The magistrates have sent to let you go: now therefore depart, and go in peace (Acts 16:35–36).

21. When Gallio was the *deputy* of Achaia, the Jews made insurrection with one accord against Paul, and brought him to the judgment seat. . . . [But Gallio reacted by saying,] I will be no judge of such matters. And he drove them from the judgment seat (Acts 18:12–16).

22. Demetrius the silversmith caused a riot in Ephesus that was directed against Paul and his companions Gaius and Aristarchus. And when the *townclerk* had appeased the people, he said . . . If Demetrius, and the craftsmen which are with him, have a matter against any man, the law is open, and there are *deputies:* let them implead one another. But if ye enquire any thing concerning other matters, it shall be determined in a lawful assembly (Acts 19:23–39).

## 85. Sixteen Traitors Mentioned in the Bible

1. When *Delilah* saw that [Samson] had told her all his heart, she . . . sent for the Lords of the Philistines. . . . Then the lords of the Philistines came up unto her, and brought money. . . . And she made [Samson] sleep upon her knees; and she called for a man, and she caused him to shave . . . his head; and she began to afflict him, and his strength went from him. . . . [Then] the Philistines took him, and put out his eyes . . . and bound him with fetters of brass; and he did grind in the prison house (Judges 16:18–19, 21).

2. *Absalom* sent spies throughout all the tribes of Israel, saying, As soon as ye hear the sound of the trumpet, then ye shall say, Absalom reigneth in Hebron. . . . And the conspiracy was strong; for

the people increased continually with Absalom. And there came a messenger to David, saying, The hearts of the men of Israel are after Absalom. And David said unto all his servants. . . . Let us flee. . . . And the king went forth, and all the people after him, and tarried in a place that was far off (2 Samuel 15:10, 12–14, 17).

3. And one told David, saying, *Ahithophel* is among the conspirators with Absalom (2 Samuel 15:31).

4. *Baasha* the son of Ahijah . . . conspired against . . . Nadab . . . (and) in the third year of Asa king of Judah did Baasha slay him, and reigned in his stead (1 Kings 15:27–28).

5. Elah the son of Baasha (reigned) over Israel in Tirzah, two years. And his servant *Zimri*, captain of half his chariots, conspired against him, as he was in Tirzah drinking himself drunk in the house of Arza steward of his house in Tirzah. And Zimri went in and smote him, and killed him . . . and reigned in his stead (1 Kings 16:8–10).

6. It came to pass . . . that *[Hazael]* took a thick cloth, and dipped it in water, and spread it on [the face of Benhadad the king of Syria] so that he died; and Hazael reigned in his stead (2 Kings 8:15).

7. *Jehu* the son of Jehoshaphat the son of Nimshi conspired against Joram. . . . And it came to pass when Joram saw Jehu, that he said, Is it peace, Jehu? And he answered, What peace, so long as the whoredoms of thy mother Jezebel and her witchcrafts are so many? And Joram turned his hands, and fled, and said to Ahaziah, There is treachery, O Ahaziah. And Jehu drew a bow with his full strength, and smote Jehoram between his arms and the arrow went out at his heart, and he sunk down in his chariot. . . . But when Ahaziah the king of Judah saw this, he fled by the way of the garden house. And Jehu followed after him, and said, Smite him also in the chariot. And they did so . . . (2 Kings 9:14, 22–24, 27).

8. The servants of Joash made a conspiracy, and slew Joash in the house of Millo, which goeth down to Silla. For *Jozachar* the son of Shimeath, and *Jehozabad* the son of Shomer, his servants smote him and he died (2 Kings 12:20–21).

9. *Shallum* the son of Jabesh conspired against [Zachariah king of Israel], and smote him before the people, and slew him and reigned in his stead (2 Kings 15:10).

10. *Menahem* the son of Gadi went up from Tirzah, and came to

Samaria, and smote Shallum the son of Jabesh in Samaria, and slew him, and reigned in his stead (2 Kings 15:14).

11. *Pekah* the son of Remaliah, a captain of [Pekahiah king of Israel], conspired against [Pekahiah] and smote him in Samaria . . . and he killed him, and reigned in his room (2 Kings 15:25).

12. *Hoshea* the son of Elah made a conspiracy against Pekah the son of Remaliah, and smote him, and slew him, and reigned in his stead (2 Kings 15:30).

13. *Zabad* and *Jehozabad* conspired against [Joash] for the blood of the sons of Jehoiada the priest, and slew him on his bed, and he died (2 Chronicles 24:25).

14. Jesus said, Rise up, let us go; lo, he that betrayeth me is at hand. And immediately, while he yet spake, cometh Judas, one of the twelve, and with him a great multitude with swords and staves, from the chief priests and the scribes and the elders. And he that betrayed him had given them a token, saying, Whomsoever I shall kiss, that same is he; take him, and lead him away safely. And as soon as he was come, he goeth straightway to him, and saith, Master, master, and kissed him. And they laid their hands on him, and took him (Mark 14:42–46).

## 86. Nine of the Earliest Recorded Inventors

1. Abel invented shepherding (Genesis 4:2).

2. Cain invented farming (Genesis 4:2).

3. Cain invented the city (Genesis 4:17).

4. Jabal invented tents (Genesis 4:20).

5. Jubal invented the harp and organ (Genesis 4:21).

6. Tubalcain invented metalworking with brass and iron (Genesis 4:22).

7. Noah invented the ark and zoology (Genesis 6:14).

8. Noah invented wine (Genesis 9:20–21).

9. Nimrod invented hunting (Genesis 10:8–9).

## 87. *People in the Bible Who Wept*

1. [Hagar] sat over against him, and lift up her voice, and wept (Genesis 21:16).

2. Abraham came to mourn for Sarah, and to weep for her (Genesis 23:2).

3. Esau lifted up his voice, and wept (Genesis 27:38).

4. Jacob kissed Rachel, and lifted up his voice, and wept (Genesis 29:11).

5. Joseph . . . entered into his chamber, and wept there (Genesis 43:30).

6. Benjamin wept upon [Joseph's] neck (Genesis 45:14).

7. The babe [Moses] wept (Exodus 2:6).

8. Moses heard the people weep throughout their families (Numbers 11:10).

9. The children of Israel . . . lifted up their voice, and wept (Judges 2:4).

10. Samson's wife wept before him (Judges 14:16).

11. They lifted up their voice, and wept again: and Orpah kissed [Naomi]; but Ruth clave unto her (Ruth 1:14).

12. Then said Elkanah her husband to her, Hannah, weepest thou? (1 Samuel 1:8).

13. All the people [of Gibeah] lifted up their voices, and wept (1 Samuel 11:4).

14. [David and Jonathan] kissed one another, and wept one with another (1 Samuel 20:41).

15. Saul lifted up his voice, and wept (1 Samuel 24:16).

16. David and the people that were with him lifted up their voice and wept (1 Samuel 30:4).

17. [Michal's] husband went with her along weeping behind her (2 Samuel 3:16).

18. [David's] sons came, and lifted up their voice and wept: and the king also and all his servants wept very sore (2 Samuel 13:36).

19. The man of God [Elisha] wept (2 Kings 8:11).

20. Joash the king of Israel came down unto [Elisha], and wept over his face (2 Kings 13:14).

21. Hezekiah wept sore (2 Kings 20:3).

22. God spoke of Josiah, that he didst rend thy clothes and weep before me (2 Chronicles 34:27).

23. Many of the priests and Levites and chief of the fathers, who were ancient men . . . wept with a loud voice (Ezra 3:12).

24. Ezra had prayed . . . weeping and casting himself down (Ezra 10:1).

25. [Nehemiah] sat down and wept, and mourned certain days (Nehemiah 1:4).

26. All the people wept when they heard the words of the law (Nehemiah 8:9).

27. There was great mourning among the Jews, and fasting, and weeping [because of Ahasuerus' command to kill the Jews] (Esther 4:3).

28. Esther . . . fell down at [the king's] feet, and besought him with tears to put away the mischief of Haman (Esther 8:3).

29. [Eliphaz, Bildad, and Zophar] lifted up their voice, and wept (Job 2:12).

30. Job said, Mine eye poureth out tears unto God (Job 16:20).

31. Isaiah said, I will weep bitterly (Isaiah 22:4).

32. Rachel weeping for her children refused to be comforted (Jeremiah 31:15).

33. Ishmael the son of Nethaniah went forth from Mizpah to meet them, weeping all along as he went (Jeremiah 41:6).

34. Jeremiah cried, Mine eyes do fail with tears (Lamentations 2:11).

35. Behold, there sat women weeping for Tammuz (Ezekiel 8:14).

36. [Peter] went out, and wept bitterly (Matthew 26:75).

37. [Jesus] cometh to the house of the ruler of the synagogue, and seeth the tumult, and [the mourners] that wept (Mark 5:38).

38. The father of the child cried out, and said with tears, Lord, I believe; help thou mine unbelief (Mark 9:24).

39. [Mary Magdalene] went and told them that had been with [Jesus], as they mourned and wept (Mark 16:10).

40. When the Lord saw [the widow of Nain], he had compassion on her, and said unto her, Weep not (Luke 7:13).

41. [A woman who was a sinner] stood at [Jesus'] feet behind him weeping, and began to wash his feet with tears (Luke 7:38).

42. Jesus turning unto them said, Daughters of Jerusalem, weep not for me (Luke 23:28).

43. Jesus saw [Mary] weeping, and the Jews also weeping (John 11:33).

44. Jesus wept (John 11:35).

45. Mary stood without at the sepulchre weeping (John 20:11).

46. All the widows [at Joppa] stood by [Peter] weeping (Acts 9:39).

47. Paul said, I have been with you at all seasons, serving the Lord with all humility of mind, and with many tears (Acts 20:18–19).

48. [The elders at Ephesus] all wept sore, and fell on Paul's neck, and kissed him (Acts 20:37).

49. Paul answered, What mean ye [Paul's companions and the believers at Caesarea] to weep and to break mine heart? (Acts 21:13).

50. Paul wrote to Timothy that he was greatly desiring to see thee, being mindful of thy tears (2 Timothy 1:4).

51. Melchisedec . . . offered up prayers and supplications with strong crying and tears (Hebrews 5:6–7).

52. [John] wept much, because no man was found worthy to open and to read the book (Revelation 5:4).

53. [Those watching Babylon burn] cast dust on their heads, and cried, weeping and wailing (Revelation 18:19).

## 88. The Seven Deacons

1. Stephen was full of faith and power and did great wonders and miracles among the people (Acts 6:5, 8).

2. Philip went down to Samaria and preached Christ to them (Acts 6:5; 8:5).

3. Prochorus was of honest report, and full of the Holy Ghost and wisdom (Acts 6:3, 5).

4. Nicanor was of honest report, and full of the Holy Ghost and wisdom (Acts 6:3, 5).

5. Timon was of honest report, and full of the Holy Ghost and wisdom (Acts 6:3, 5).

6. Parmenas was of honest report, and full of the Holy Ghost and wisdom (Acts 6:3, 5).

7. Nicolas was a proselyte of Antioch (Acts 6:5).

## 89. *The Eighteen Judges of Israel*

1. Othniel judged Israel and led Israel to victory against Chushan-rishathaim the king of Mesopotamia (Judges 3:10).

2. Ehud killed Eglon the king of Moab and led Israel to victory against Moab (Judges 3:15–30).

3. Shamgar slew 600 Philistines with an ox goad and delivered Israel (Judges 3:31).

4. Deborah judged Israel and helped lead Israel to victory against Canaan (Judges 4).

5. Barak helped Deborah lead Israel to victory against Canaan (Judges 4).

6. Gideon led Israel to victory against the Midianites (Judges 6–8).

7. Abimelech killed sixty-nine of his brothers so that he could rule (Judges 8:30–9:5).

8. Tola the son of Dodo judged Israel twenty-three years (Judges 10:1–2).

9. Jair judged Israel twenty-two years (Judges 10:3).

10. Jephthah delivered Israel from the Ammonites and judged Israel six years (Judges 11 and 12:1–7).

11. Ibzan judged Israel for seven years (Judges 12:8–9).

12. Elon judged Israel for ten years (Judges 12:11).

13. Abdon judged Israel for eight years (Judges 12:14).

14. Samson fought the Philistines and judged Israel for twenty years (Judges 13–16).

15. Eli the high priest judged Israel for forty years (1 Samuel 4:18).

16. Samuel judged Israel all of the days of his life (1 Samuel 7:15–17).

17. Joel, the firstborn son of Samuel, judged Israel in Beersheba (1 Samuel 8:1–2).

18. Abiah, the second son of Samuel, also judged Israel in Beersheba (1 Samuel 8:1–2).

## 90. The Two Most Acclaimed Heroes in the Bible

1. Moses led Israel out of Egypt (Exodus).

2. Jesus died to save us from our sins (Hebrews 7:22–27).

## 91. Nine Infamous Villains in the Bible

1. Cain committed the first murder by killing his brother, Abel (Genesis 4:8).

2. Laban made many attempts to swindle Jacob, but Jacob ultimately prospered (Genesis 29–31).

3. Saul broke many oaths of love toward David and attempted to kill him several times (1 Samuel 19–27).

4. Absolom led a revolt against his father David (2 Samuel 15).

5. Ahab, king of Israel, did evil in the sight of the Lord above all that were before him (1 Kings 16:30).

6. Haman plotted to have the entire Hebrew nation legally killed (Esther).

7. Herod ordered the killing of all the babies in Bethlehem two years and under, in an attempt to kill Jesus; he also authorized John the Baptist's beheading (Matthew 2:16; 14:10).

8. Judas betrayed Jesus into the hands of the Jewish leaders (Matthew 26:14–15).

9. Pilate allowed Jesus to be crucified, though he acknowledged His innocence (John 18–19).

## 92. *The Best King in the Bible*

King David was a man after God's own heart (1 Samuel 13:14).

## 93. *The Wisest and Richest King in the Bible*

King Solomon was wiser than all men, for God gave Solomon wisdom. God also gave Solomon riches until he exceeded all the kings of the earth in riches and in wisdom (1 Kings 10:23).

## 94. *The Worst King in the Bible*

King Ahab married Jezebel and introduced the worship of Baal into Israel (1 Kings 16:29–31).

## 95. *The Six Hairiest Men in the Bible*

1. Esau was a very hairy man (Genesis 27:11–22).
2. Samson was a Nazarite from the time he was born and never shaved or had a haircut until Delilah had his head shaved (Judges 16:17).
3. Absalom had his hair cut once a year, and the amount of hair cut off weighed two hundred shekels (2 Samuel 14:26).
4. Elijah was a hairy man (2 Kings 1:8).
5. King Nebuchadnezzar's hair grew like eagles' feathers (Daniel 4:33).
6. John the Baptist was probably a Nazarite (Luke 1:15).

## 96. *The Bald Men in the Bible*

1. Samson had his head shaved by a man that Delilah called to do the job (Judges 16:19).
2. The only naturally bald man mentioned in the Bible is Elisha (2 Kings 2:23).
3. Ezra plucked off his own hair and beard (Ezra 9:3).
4. Job shaved his head (Job 1:20).
5. Paul purified himself along with four other men who were under a vow. They shaved their heads, and Paul possibly also shaved his own head (Acts 21:23–26).

## 97. *The Ten Most-Mentioned Men in the New Testament*

1. Jesus is by far the most-mentioned man in the New Testament.

2. Paul, the writer of a large share of the books of the New Testament, is the next most mentioned.

3. Peter was the chief apostle and is mentioned almost as many times as Paul.

4. John the Baptist is mentioned eight-six times.

5. Surprisingly, Pontius Pilate, who is mentioned fifty-six times, claims more attention than such people as Matthew, Mark, and Luke, who are not mentioned enough to make this list.

6. John the apostle is mentioned thirty-five times.

7. Here's another villain: Herod the tetrarch is mentioned thirty times.

8. Timothy's association with Paul accounts for his name being mentioned twenty-eight times.

9. Judas Iscariot is mentioned twenty-three times.

10. Philip the deacon, also known as the evangelist, is mentioned sixteen times.

## 98. *The Ten Most-Mentioned Men in the Old Testament*

1. King David has a clear majority with almost half again as many references as the runner-up.

2. Moses is credited with writing the first five books of the Bible and is mentioned twice as often as the third place winner.

3. Moses' brother Aaron was Israel's first high priest and was often the spokesman for Moses.

4. Jacob, as a person, is mentioned quite often. If all of the references to his new name, Israel, were taken into account, he would be the most mentioned; however, most uses of the name Israel concern the tribes or children of Israel.

5. Saul was the first king of Israel, but didn't get as much coverage as his successor, King David. Saul has to settle for fifth place.

6. Abraham was God's friend, because he believed God. That

earned him a place among the ten most famous men in the Old Testament.

7. King Solomon, the third king of Israel, was the richest and wisest king mentioned in the Bible.

8. Joseph was a dreamer and an interpreter of dreams. God used Joseph to get the tribe of Israel into Egypt. Then it took over four hundred years to get Israel out of Egypt.

9. Joshua fought the battle of Jericho. He took over Moses' position.

10. Jeremiah wept much about Israel and is one of the major prophets of the Old Testament.

    Note: The first man, Adam, is mentioned only thirty times.

## 99. The Ten Most-Mentioned Women in the Bible

1. Sarah, the wife of Abraham, had a child when she was ninety years old. She is mentioned fifty-six times in the Bible.

2. Rachel was one of Jacob's wives. Jacob loved her the most and worked fourteen years for her father so that he could marry her. Rachel is mentioned forty-seven times in the Bible.

3. Leah was Jacob's first wife. Jacob was tricked into marrying Leah, but Leah still wins the honor of being mentioned thirty-four times in the Bible.

4. Rebekah was Isaac's wife and the mother of Esau and Jacob. She is mentioned thirty-one times.

5. The women's list also includes an infamous person. Jezebel is mentioned twenty-three times.

6. The Virgin Mary, the mother of Jesus, is mentioned only nineteen times.

7. Abigail, the wife of Nabal, and later the wife of King David, is mentioned fifteen times and is tied for seventh place.

8. Also mentioned fifteen times is Miriam, the sister of Moses.

9. The last two women on this list are both mentioned fourteen times. Mary Magdalene knew Jesus personally and received deliverance and forgiveness from Him.

10. Hagar was Abraham's concubine and the mother of Ishmael.

*Note:* Eve, the mother of the human race, is mentioned only four times in the whole Bible!

## 100. *Fifteen Queens of the Bible*

1. Michal, a daughter of Saul, eventually scorned her husband, King David (1 Samuel 18:20; 2 Samuel 6:16).

2. When her husband Nabal died, Abigail became a wife of David (1 Samuel 25:39).

3. Rizpah was Saul's concubine (2 Samuel 3:7).

4. Bathsheba became David's wife after he had her husband, Uriah, murdered. She became the mother of Solomon (2 Samuel 11:15, 17, 27; 12:24).

5. When the queen of Sheba heard of the fame of Solomon concerning the name of the Lord, she came to prove him with hard questions (1 Kings 10:1).

6. Tahpenes was the wife of a pharaoh who reigned during David's and Solomon's reigns (1 Kings 11:19).

7. Jezebel married King Ahab and caused him to worship Baal (1 Kings 16:31).

8. Maacah was removed from being queen because she had made an idol in a grove (2 Chronicles 15:16).

9. Athaliah attempted to destroy all the seed royal of the house of Judah (2 Chronicles 22:10).

10. The queen Vashti refused to come at Ahasuerus' command to show the people and the princes her beauty (Esther 1:11–12).

11. Ahasuerus loved Esther above all women and made her queen instead of Vashti (Esther 2:17).

12. Belshazzar's queen (unnamed) brought Daniel's prophetic gift to her husband's attention (Daniel 5:10).

13. Herodias, wife of Herod, plotted the execution of John the Baptist (Matthew 14:3–8).

14. The eunuch who received the gospel from Philip had charge of all the treasure of Candace, queen of the Ethiopians (Acts 8:27–38).

15. Though historians indicated they were not married, but were

brother and sister, King Agrippa and Bernice acted as a royal couple (Acts 25:13).

## 101. The Antichrist

1. The antichrist will be revealed before the coming of Jesus (2 Thessalonians 2:3–9).

2. Little children, it is the last time: and as ye have heard that antichrist shall come, even now are there many antichrists; whereby we know it is the last time (1 John 2:18).

3. Many deceivers are entered into the world, who confess not that Jesus Christ is come in the flesh. This is a deceiver and an antichrist (2 John 7).

4. The number of the beast's name is 666 (Revelation 13:17–18).

## 102. Giants in the Bible

1. There were giants in the land before the great flood (Genesis 6:4).

2. Rephaim means giant; therefore it may be that the Rephaims were a race of giants. The Lord gave the land of the Rephaims to Abraham (Genesis 15:18–20).

3. Ten of the twelve spies sent to spy out the land reported that there were giants, the sons of Anak, in the land (Numbers 13:33).

4. The Emims dwelt in Ar and were tall like the Anakims, which were accounted giants (Deuteronomy 2:9–11).

5. In the land of the children of Ammon dwelt a people that the Ammonites called the Zamzummims. The Zamzummims were tall like the Anakims (Deuteronomy 2:19–21).

6. Og, king of Bashan, was a giant who had a bedstead of iron, nine cubits long and four cubits wide (Deuteronomy 3:11).

7. Arba was possibly a giant, since he was great among the Anakims (Joshua 14:15).

8. By extension, Anak himself might have been a giant. Anak was the son of Arba (Joshua 15:13).

9. Caleb drove the three sons of Anak out of Hebron. The names

of the three sons are: Sheshai, Ahiman, and Talmai. Presumably they might have been giants (Joshua 15:14).

10. The best known giant is Goliath, the one David killed with a stone and a slingshot. Goliath stood six cubits and a span in height (1 Samuel 17:4).

11. In reading the accounts given in 2 Samuel, chapter 21, and 1 Chronicles, chapter 20, it would appear that Goliath had four brothers. It would also appear that their father was a giant (2 Samuel 21:22). Assuming that the four men were Goliath's brothers, one brother's name was Saph (or Sippai), another's name was Lahmi, and the only other one named was Ishbi-benob. Although it's uncertain whether these three brothers were giants, the remaining brother had six fingers on each hand and six toes on each foot and was a man of great stature (2 Samuel 21:16–22; 1 Chronicles 20:4–8).

## 103. Thirteen Instances of Drunkenness in the Bible

1. Noah became drunk and was naked in his tent (Genesis 9:21).

2. Lot was made drunk by his daughters in order to seduce him (Genesis 19:32).

3. God's command to Aaron that the priests not drink wine implies that Nadab and Abihu had been drunk (Leviticus 10:1, 9).

4. Boaz had drunk and his heart was merry (Ruth 3:7).

5. Eli mistakenly thought Hannah was drunk (1 Samuel 1:13).

6. Nabal held a feast and became very drunk (1 Samuel 25:36).

7. David made Uriah drunk (2 Samuel 11:13).

8. Amnon was murdered by Absolom's servants while he was drunk (2 Samuel 13:28).

9. Elah was murdered while drunk (1 Kings 16:9).

10. Benhadad and thirty-two kings were drunk together (1 Kings 20:16).

11. Queen Vashti refused to display her beauty when King Ahasuerus was merry with wine (Esther 1:10).

12. Jesus was accused of being a winebibber (Luke 7:34).

13. At Pentecost, some mocked the disciples as being drunk (Acts 2:13).

## 104. Musicians of the Bible

1. Jubal was the father of all such as handle the harp and organ (Genesis 4:21).

2. Miriam took a timbrel in her hand; and all the women went out after her with timbrels and dances. And Miriam answered them, Sing ye to the Lord, for he hath triumphed gloriously; the horse and his rider hath he thrown into the sea (Exodus 15:20–21).

3. David played the harp for Saul and thus caused the evil spirit to depart from Saul (1 Samuel 16:23).

4. The women came out of all the cities of Israel, singing and dancing, to meet King Saul, with tabrets, with joy, and with instruments of music (1 Samuel 18:6).

5. King Solomon wrote 1,005 songs (1 Kings 4:32).

6. Elisha called for a minstrel, and when the minstrel played, he prophesied, Thus saith the Lord, Make this valley full of ditches (2 Kings 3:15–16).

7. Additional musicians from among the Levites were used to help bring the ark back to Jerusalem. Among those not previously listed herein are: Ethan, Zechariah, Aziel, Shemira-moth, Jehiel, Unni, Eliab, Maaseiah, Elipheleh, Mikneiah, Obededom, Azariah, Shebaniah, Jehoshaphat, Nethaneel, Amasai, and Eliezer (1 Chronicles 15:16–24).

8. Jeiel played the psaltery and the harp (1 Chronicles 16:5).

9. Asaph played the cymbals (1 Chronicles 16:5).

10. Benaiah and Jahaziel played the trumpet (1 Chronicles 16:6).

11. Heman played, or led the players of, the trumpet and cymbals (1 Chronicles 16:42).

12. Jeduthun was one of King David's chief musicians (1 Chronicles 16:42; title of Psalm 39).

13. King David had 4,000 musicians who praised the Lord with the instruments that David made (1 Chronicles 23:5).

14. The number of those that David set apart to perform music in

the house of the Lord was 288. Included in the 288, and not previously mentioned in this list, are Zaccur, Joseph, Nethaniah, Asarelah, Gedaliah, Zeri, Jeshaiah, Hashabiah, Mattithiah, Bukkiah, Mattaniah, Uzziel, Shebuel, Jerimoth, Hananiah, Hanani, Eliathah, Giddalti, Romamtiezer, Joshbekashah, Mallothi, Hothir, Mahazioth, Izri, Jesharelah, Shemei, Azareel, and Shubael (1 Chronicles 25).

15. When Solomon dedicated the temple, there were singers, cymbal players, psaltery players, and harpists along with 120 priests who played trumpets (2 Chronicles 5:11–14).

16. The priests played trumpets, and the Levites, the sons of Asaph, used cymbals to praise the Lord when the foundation was laid for the rebuilding of the temple (Ezra 3:10–11). Some of these musicians were mentioned by name in Nehemiah: Zechariah, Shemaiah, Azareel, Milalai, Gilalai, Maai, Nethaneel, Judah, and Hanani (Nehemiah 12:35–36).

17. John heard the voice of harpers harping with their harps: and they sung as it were a new song before the throne in heaven (Revelation 14:2–3).

## 105. Twenty-eight Dreamers in the Bible

1. God came to Abraham in a vision and promised him a son (Genesis 15:1).

2. Abimelech was told in a dream that he had taken Abraham's wife (Genesis 20:3).

3. Sleeping with his head on a rock, Jacob dreamed of a ladder extending from earth to heaven (Genesis 28:12).

4. Joseph (of the Old Testament) dreamed that his family bowed down to him (Genesis 37:5–8).

5. Pharaoh's butler dreamed of restoration to Pharaoh's favor (Genesis 40:9–13).

6. Pharaoh's baker dreamed of his execution (Genesis 40:16–19).

7. Pharaoh dreamed of cattle, which Joseph interpreted as symbolizing years of plenty and years of famine (Genesis 41:17–32).

8. Balaam claimed he was a man who saw the vision of the Almighty, falling into a trance, but having his eyes open (Numbers 24:4).

9. Gideon overheard a man who had dreamed that Gideon defeated Midian (Judges 7:13–14).

10. In a vision, God warned Samuel about Eli's sons (1 Samuel 3:1–15).

11. God appeared to Solomon in a dream, and granted him understanding to discern judgment (1 Kings 3:5–11).

12. Some of Solomon's deeds were recorded in the visions of Iddo the seer (2 Chronicles 9:29).

13. Isaiah's prophecy is called the vision (Isaiah 1:1).

14. Ezekiel traveled to Chaldea in one of his visions (Ezekiel 11:24).

15. Nebuchadnezzar dreamed dreams, wherewith his spirit was troubled, and his sleep brake from him (Daniel 2:1).

16. In the first year of Belshazzar king of Babylon Daniel had a dream and visions of his head upon his bed (Daniel 7:1).

17. The prophecy of Obadiah came in a vision (Obadiah 1:1).

18. Nahum's prophecy was a recorded vision (Nahum 1:1).

19. God said to Habakkuk, Write the vision, and make it plain upon tables, that he may run that readeth it (Habakkuk 2:2).

20. Jesus' stepfather, Joseph, was reassured by an angel in a dream that Mary was pregnant by the Holy Ghost (Matthew 1:20).

21. In a dream, God warned the wise men from the East not to return to Herod (Matthew 2:12).

22. After His transfiguration, Jesus told James (also Peter and John), Tell the vision to no man, until the Son of man be risen again from the dead (Matthew 17:9).

23. After his vision of an angel, Zechariah remained dumb until his son John was born and named (Luke 1:22, 63–64).

24. Ananias was told in a vision to pray for Paul, then Saul of Tarsus (Acts 9:10).

25. In a vision, Paul saw Ananias coming and praying for his sight to be restored (Acts 9:12).

26. Cornelius sent men to Peter after an angel of God spoke to him in a vision (Acts 10:3).

27. God spoke to Peter concerning unclean things in a vision (Acts 11:5).

28. John called his Revelation a vision (Revelation 9:17).

## 106. Lepers in the Bible

1. [Moses] put his hand into his bosom: and when he took it out, behold, his hand was leprous as snow (Exodus 4:6).

2. And the Lord spake unto Moses, saying, Command the children of Israel, that they put out of the camp every leper. . . . And the children of Israel did so, and put them out without the camp (Numbers 5:1–2, 4).

3. Behold, Miriam became leprous, white as snow (Numbers 12:10).

4. Naaman, captain of the host of the king of Syria . . . was a leper (2 Kings 5:1).

5. Gehazi became a leper after lying to Elisha (2 Kings 5:27).

6. There were four leprous men at the entering in of the gate of Samaria (2 Kings 7:3).

7. The Lord smote Azariah, so that he was a leper unto the day of his death (2 Kings 15:5).

8. Uzziah the king was a leper unto the day of his death (2 Chronicles 26:21).

9. There came a leper and worshiped Jesus (Matthew 8:2).

10. Go show John again those things which ye do hear and see . . . the lepers are cleansed (Matthew 11:5).

11. [Jesus was] in Bethany in the house of Simon the leper (Mark 14:3).

12. Many lepers were in Israel in the time of Eliseus the prophet (Luke 4:27).

13. As [Jesus] entered into a certain village, there met him ten men that were lepers, which stood afar off (Luke 17:12).

# 8

## SEX

No matter what advocates of the "new" morality try to claim, sex was God's idea, not theirs. Since God established the marriage relationship (including sex) in the first place, should it be surprising that God's Word covers the subject? As with other gifts He gives, God has supplied us with clear instructions for using sex as He intended it.

In this chapter, you will find thirty rules of conduct concerning sex. Other lists include biblical accounts of nudity and incest, what can happen to a practicing homosexual, and some prominent harlots in the Bible.

### 107. Thirty Rules of Conduct Concerning Sex

1. You shall not commit adultery (Exodus 20:14).
2. You shall not covet your neighbor's wife (Exodus 20:17).
3. If you get semen on you, you are unclean regardless whether it happened during sexual intercourse or while having a wet dream. Bathe for cleansing (Leviticus 15:16–18; Deuteronomy 23:10).
4. You shall not have sexual intercourse with your mother (Leviticus 18:7).
5. You shall not have sexual intercourse with your father (Leviticus 18:7).
6. You shall not have sexual intercourse with your father's wife, even if she's not your natural mother (Leviticus 18:8).

7. You shall not have sexual intercourse with your sister, even if she's only your half sister (Leviticus 18:9).

8. You shall not have sexual intercourse with your granddaughter (Leviticus 18:10).

9. You shall not have sexual intercourse with your aunt (Leviticus 18:12–13).

10. You shall not have sexual intercourse with your uncle (Leviticus 18:14).

11. You shall not have sexual intercourse with your daughter-in-law (Leviticus 18:15).

12. You shall not have sexual intercourse with your sister-in-law (Leviticus 18:16).

13. You shall not have sexual intercourse with both a woman and her daughter (Leviticus 18:17).

14. You shall not have sexual intercourse with both a woman and her granddaughter (Leviticus 18:17).

15. You shall not have sexual intercourse with two sisters while the first of the sisters is still alive (Leviticus 18:18).

16. You shall not have sexual intercourse with a woman while she is having her monthly period (Leviticus 18:19).

17. You shall not have sexual intercourse with a person of the same sex as you are (Leviticus 18:22).

18. You shall not have sexual intercourse with an animal (Leviticus 18:23).

19. You shall not prostitute your daughter to cause her to become a whore (Leviticus 19:29).

20. You shall not wear clothing pertaining to the opposite sex (Deuteronomy 22:5).

21. Do not make your neighbor drunk in order to look upon his or her nakedness (Habakkuk 2:15).

22. Do not look upon a woman to lust after her (Matthew 5:28).

23. Abstain from fornication (Acts 15:29).

24. Homosexual acts are unnatural and are results of vile affections, which can lead to reprobate minds (Romans 1:26–28).

25. Fornication is a sin against your own body (1 Corinthians 6:18).

26. To avoid fornication, let every man have his own wife, and let every woman have her own husband (1 Corinthians 7:2).

27. The husband has power over his wife's body, and the wife has power over her husband's body. The husband or the wife should not withhold sexual favors except for short periods, by mutual consent, for purposes of fasting and prayer (1 Corinthians 7:4–5).

28. Lasciviousness and concupiscence are works of the flesh and not of the Spirit (Galatians 5:19; Colossians 3:5).

29. The marriage bed is undefiled (Hebrews 13:4).

30. The lust of the eyes and the lust of the flesh are of the world and not of the Father (1 John 2:16).

   *Note:* For items 4 through 15, the taboo also forbids marriage; in those cases, marriage will not sanctify the sex act.

## 108. *Thirty Consequences of Homosexual Behavior*

1. God gives homosexuals up to uncleanness (Romans 1:24).

2. Homosexuals dishonor their own bodies between themselves (Romans 1:24).

3. Homosexuals corrupt the Word of God by changing His truth to a lie (Romans 1:25).

4. Homosexuals worship and serve the creature more than the Creator (Romans 1:25).

5. God gives homosexuals up to their vile affections (Romans 1:26–27).

6. God gives homosexuals over to a reprobate mind (Romans 1:28).

7. Homosexuals are filled with all unrighteousness (Romans 1:29).

8. Homosexuals end up being motivated to do things that are not convenient (Romans 1:28).

9. Homosexuals are filled with fornication (Romans 1:29).

10. Homosexuals are filled with wickedness (Romans 1:29).

11. Homosexuals are filled with covetousness (Romans 1:29).

12. Homosexuals are filled with maliciousness (Romans 1:29).

13. Homosexuals are filled with envy (Romans 1:29).

14. Homosexuals are filled with murder (Romans 1:29).

15. Homosexuals are filled with debate (Romans 1:29).

16. Homosexuals are filled with deceit (Romans 1:29).

17. Homosexuals are filled with malignity (Romans 1:29).

18. Homosexuals are whisperers (Romans 1:29).

19. Homosexuals are backbiters (Romans 1:30).

20. Homosexuals are haters of God (Romans 1:30).

21. Homosexuals are despiteful (Romans 1:30).

22. Homosexuals are proud (Romans 1:30).

23. Homosexuals are boasters (Romans 1:30).

24. Homosexuals are inventors of evil things (Romans 1:30).

25. Homosexuals are disobedient to parents (Romans 1:30).

26. Homosexuals are covenant breakers (Romans 1:31).

27. Homosexuals are without natural affection (Romans 1:31).

28. Homosexuals are unmerciful (Romans 1:31).

29. Homosexuals are implacable (Romans 1:31).

30. Homosexuals are without understanding (Romans 1:31).

## 109. Five Biblical Accounts of Incest

1. Lot's two daughters committed incest with their father (Genesis 19:31–36).

2. Reuben had sex with his father's concubine, Bilhah (Genesis 35:22).

3. Ammon committed incest with his sister, Tamar, by raping her (2 Samuel 13:10–14).

4. Absalom went into his father's concubines (2 Samuel 16:22).

5. A Corinthian Christian had sex with his father's wife (1 Corinthians 5:1).

## 110. *Seven Prominent Harlots in the Bible*

1. Judah's daughter-in-law tired of waiting for Judah to provide her with another husband (she had already been widowed by two of Judah's sons), so she played the harlot. Her only customer, apparently, was Judah, and he made her pregnant. She gave birth to twin boys: Pharez and Zarah (Genesis 38).

2. Rahab (Rachab in New Testament) the harlot received the two spies in Jericho and hid them (Joshua 2:1–5). She later married Salmon (King David's great-great grandfather) and is listed in the genealogy of Jesus (Matthew 1:5).

3. Jephthah's mother was a harlot. Jephthah delivered Israel from the Ammonites during the time of the Judges (Judges 11:1).

4. Samson spent half the night with a harlot in Gaza and then took the gates, gateposts, and bars to the gates of the city and carried them on his shoulders to the top of the hill before Hebron (Judges 16:1–3).

5. A Levite's concubine played the part of a harlot and went home to her father (Judges 19:1–2). This indirectly led to a situation in Gibeah where the concubine was forcibly and continuously raped until it caused her death (Judges 19:22–28). The Levite cut up the body of the concubine and sent the twelve pieces throughout the tribes of Israel. This led to a war which nearly wiped out the Benjamites and created a scarcity of wives for that tribe. This led to a slaughter of all of the inhabitants of Jabesh-gilead except for the female virgins. This provided 400 virgin wives for the Benjamites. An additional 200 virgins were required, and thus was initiated a sanctioned kidnapping of women from among the daughters of Shiloh to provide wives for the Benjamites (Judges 21).

6. Two harlots played a part in displaying the wisdom of Solomon. Each harlot had a son, but during the night one harlot accidentally killed her baby by lying on top of it during her sleep. She switched babies during the night and claimed the living baby was her own. When Solomon heard the case, he ordered the living child to be cut in half. The real mother was willing to give up the child rather than see him killed. The other harlot was willing to have the baby killed. Thus the child's real mother was discerned (1 Kings 3:16–28).

## 111. Nine Cases of Public or Semi-Public Nudity in the Bible

1. Adam and Eve were naked in the garden of Eden (Genesis 2:25).

2. Practically the whole nation of Israel had a nude orgy (Exodus 32:19–25).

3. King Saul stripped off his clothes, prophesied before Samuel, and lay down naked all day and all night (1 Samuel 19:21–24).

4. Isaiah walked barefoot and naked for three years among the Hebrews in obedience to the Lord (Isaiah 20:2–3).

5. A young man (probably Mark) was with Jesus in the garden of Gethsemane when Jesus was arrested. He was wearing only a linen cloth. When some of the arresting party grabbed for him, they tore the cloth from the young man's body, and he ran away naked (Mark 14:51–52).

6. The Gadarene demoniac ran about naked in a graveyard, until Jesus delivered him from a legion of demons (Luke 8:27).

7. The man helped by the good Samaritan was stripped of his clothes by thieves and left half dead (Luke 10:30).

8. Peter was naked in the fishing boat the last time he went fishing (John 21:7).

9. The seven sons of Sceva were stripped and wounded by a demon-possessed man when they tried to exorcise the demon (Acts 19:13–16).

# 9

## CHARACTERISTICS

When Jesus said, "By their fruits ye shall know them" (Matthew 7:20), He reflected God's concern for the visible details of our lifestyles. Therefore, His word presents many characteristics that His people should or shouldn't have.

For instance, what are the works of the flesh? List 112 includes twenty works of the flesh.

What will sinners be like in the last days? See list 114.

What are the qualifications for bishops or elders, and deacons, according to the Bible? See lists 115 and 116.

What five signs will follow believers? See list 117.

What are the qualifications for discipleship? See list 118.

### 112. *The Twenty Works of the Flesh*

1. Divisions [quarreling] (1 Corinthians 3:3).

2. Adultery (Galatians 5:19).

3. Fornication (Galatians 5:19).

4. Uncleanness (Galatians 5:19).

5. Lasciviousness (Galatians 5:19).

6. Idolatry (Galatians 5:20).

7. Witchcraft (Galatians 5:20).

8. Hatred (Galatians 5:20).

9. Variance [discord] (Galatians 5:20).

10. Emulation [jealousy] (Galatians 5:20).

11. Wrath (Galatians 5:20).

12. Strife (Galatians 5:20).

13. Sedition [dissension] (Galatians 5:20).

14. Heresy (Galatians 5:20).

15. Envying (Galatians 5:21).

16. Murder (Galatians 5:21).

17. Drunkenness (Galatians 5:21).

18. Revelling [orgies] (Galatians 5:21).

19. Inordinate affection [lust] (Colossians 3:5).

20. Evil concupiscence [evil desires] (Colossians 3:5).

### 113. Fifteen Types of People to Whom the Law Is Addressed

1. The lawless (1 Timothy 1:9).

2. The disobedient (1 Timothy 1:9).

3. The ungodly (1 Timothy 1:9).

4. Sinners (1 Timothy 1:9).

5. The unholy (1 Timothy 1:9).

6. The profane (1 Timothy 1:9).

7. Murderers of mothers (1 Timothy 1:9).

8. Murderers of fathers (1 Timothy 1:9).

9. Manslayers (1 Timothy 1:9).

10. Whoremongers (1 Timothy 1:10).

11. Homosexuals (1 Timothy 1:10).

12. Menstealers [slave traders] (1 Timothy 1:10).

13. Liars (1 Timothy 1:10).

14. Perjurers [false swearers in court of law] (1 Timothy 1:10).

15. Those guilty of any other thing that is contrary to sound doctrine (1 Timothy 1:10).

## 114. *Twenty-five Characteristics of Non-Christians in the Last Days*

1. Lovers of their own selves (2 Timothy 3:2).
2. Covetous (2 Timothy 3:2).
3. Boasters (2 Timothy 3:2).
4. Proud (2 Timothy 3:2).
5. Blasphemers (2 Timothy 3:2).
6. Disobedient to parents (2 Timothy 3:2).
7. Unthankful (2 Timothy 3:2).
8. Unholy (2 Timothy 3:2).
9. Without natural affection (2 Timothy 3:3).
10. Trucebreakers (2 Timothy 3:3).
11. False accusers (2 Timothy 3:3).
12. Without self-control (2 Timothy 3:3).
13. Fierce [brutal] (2 Timothy 3:3).
14. Despisers of those who do good (2 Timothy 3:3).
15. Traitors (2 Timothy 3:4).
16. Heady [rash] (2 Timothy 3:4).
17. Highminded (2 Timothy 3:4).
18. Lovers of pleasures more than lovers of God (2 Timothy 3:4).
19. Having a form of godliness, but denying the power thereof (2 Timothy 3:5).
20. Those who creep into houses and lead captive silly, sinful women who are led away with divers lusts (2 Timothy 3:6).
21. Learning but never able to come to the knowledge of the truth (2 Timothy 3:7).
22. Resistant to the truth (2 Timothy 3:8).
23. Corrupt minds (2 Timothy 3:8).
24. Reprobate concerning the faith (2 Timothy 3:8).
25. Without progress, their folly manifested unto all men (2 Timothy 3:9).

### 115. Qualifications for a Bishop or an Elder
1. Blameless (1 Timothy 3:2).
2. The husband of one wife (1 Timothy 3:2).
3. Vigilant (1 Timothy 3:2).
4. Sober (1 Timothy 3:2).
5. Good behavior (1 Timothy 3:2).
6. Given to hospitality (1 Timothy 3:2).
7. Apt to teach (1 Timothy 3:2).
8. Not given to wine (1 Timothy 3:3).
9. Not a striker (1 Timothy 3:3).
10. Not greedy of filthy lucre [profit] (1 Timothy 3:3).
11. Not a brawler (1 Timothy 3:3).
12. Not covetous (1 Timothy 3:3).
13. Patient (1 Timothy 3:3).
14. Ruler of his own house, his children in subjection (1 Timothy 3:4).
15. Not a novice (1 Timothy 3:6).
16. Of good reputation with outsiders (1 Timothy 3:7).
17. Not self-willed (Titus 1:7).
18. Not easily angered (Titus 1:7).
19. A lover of good (Titus 1:8).
20. Just (Titus 1:8).
21. Holy (Titus 1:8).
22. Temperate (Titus 1:8).
23. Holds fast to the faithful word he has been taught so that with sound doctrine he may be able to exhort and convince those who oppose it (Titus 1:9).

### 116. Qualifications for a Deacon
1. Honest reputation (Acts 6:3).
2. Full of the Holy Ghost (Acts 6:3).

3. Full of wisdom (Acts 6:3).

4. Worthy of respect (1 Timothy 3:8).

5. Not double-tongued (1 Timothy 3:8).

6. Not given to much wine (1 Timothy 3:8).

7. Not greedy of filthy lucre [profit] (1 Timothy 3:8).

8. Holds the mystery of the faith in a pure conscience (1 Timothy 3:9).

9. Blameless (1 Timothy 3:10).

10. The husband of one wife (1 Timothy 3:12).

11. Ruler of his own house and children (1 Timothy 3:12).

12. With a wife who is not a slanderer but respected, sober, and faithful in all things (1 Timothy 3:11).

## 117. *Five Signs That Shall Follow Believers*

1. Casting out devils in Jesus' name (Mark 16:17).

2. Speaking with new tongues (Mark 16:17).

3. Taking up serpents without harm (Mark 16:18).

4. Drinking any deadly thing without harm (Mark 16:18).

5. Laying hands on the sick and seeing them recover (Mark 16:18).

## 118. *Qualifications for Christian Discipleship*

1. You must be born again (John 3:1–8), for all have sinned, and come short of the glory of God (Romans 3:23). The wages of sin is death, but the gift of God is eternal life through Jesus Christ our Lord (Romans 6:23).

2. If we confess our sins, he is faithful and just to forgive us our sins, and to cleanse us from all unrighteousness (1 John 1:9).

3. Faith cometh by hearing, and hearing by the word of God (Romans 10:17).

4. There is no difference between the Jew and the Greek: for the same Lord over all is rich unto all that call upon him. For whosoever shall call upon the name of the Lord shall be saved (Romans 10:12–13).

5. If thou shalt confess with thy mouth the Lord Jesus, and shalt believe in thine heart that God hath raised him from the dead, thou shalt be saved. For with the heart man believeth unto righteousness: and with the mouth confession is made unto salvation (Romans 10:9–10).

6. For as many of you as have been baptized into Christ have put on Christ (Galatians 3:27).

7. Repent and be baptized every one of you for the remission of sins, and ye shall receive the gift of the Holy Ghost (Acts 2:38).

8. If ye then, being evil, know how to give good gifts unto your children; how much more shall your heavenly Father give the Holy Spirit to them that ask him? (Luke 11:13).

9. Ye shall receive power, after that the Holy Ghost is come upon you: and ye shall be witnesses unto me both in Jerusalem, and in all Judea, and in Samaria, and unto the uttermost part of the earth (Acts 1:8).

10. For we are his workmanship, created in Christ Jesus unto good works, which God hath before ordained that we should walk in them (Ephesians 2:10).

11. He that taketh not his cross, and followeth after me, is not worthy of me. He that findeth his life shall lose it: and he that loseth his life for my sake shall find it (Matthew 10:38–39).

12. Verily, verily, I say unto you, Except ye eat the flesh of the Son of man, and drink his blood, ye have no life in you (John 6:53).

13. Think not that I am come to send peace on earth: I came not to send peace, but a sword. For I am come to set a man at variance against his father, and the daughter against her mother, and the daughter-in-law against her mother-in-law. And a man's foes shall be they of his own household. He that loveth father or mother more than me is not worthy of me: and he that loveth son or daughter more than me is not worthy of me (Matthew 10:34–37).

14. If we walk in the light, as he is in the light, we have fellowship one with another, and the blood of Jesus Christ his Son cleanseth us from all sin (1 John 1:7).

15. By this shall all men know that ye are my disciples, if ye have love one to another (John 13:35).

16. If ye continue in my word, then are ye my disciples indeed; and ye shall know the truth, and the truth shall make you free (John 8:31–32).

17. Then said Jesus unto the twelve, Will ye also go away? Then Simon Peter answered him, Lord, to whom shall we go? Thou hast the words of eternal life. And we believe and are sure that thou art the Christ, the Son of the living God (John 6:67–69).

18. If ye abide in me, and my words abide in you, ye shall ask what ye will, and it shall be done unto you. Herein is my Father glorified, that ye bear much fruit; so shall ye be my disciples (John 15:7–8).

# 10

## LOVE

Poets still write, singers still sing, philosophers still discuss the concept of love. And the definitions of love stretch all the way from warm puppies to the hot flush of sexual attraction.

Divine love, what the Greeks call *agape*, is another matter. With His infinite precision, God has told us clearly what His love—real love—is, and isn't. That's what this chapter is about.

### 119. Who Is Love?

God is love (1 John 4:8, 16).

### 120. Eleven Descriptions of Love

1. Love is a commandment (John 13:34).
2. Love is shed abroad in our hearts by the Holy Ghost (Romans 5:5).
3. Love is the fulfilling of the law (Romans 13:10).
4. Love is the catalyst that gives meaning to speaking in tongues, to prophesying, to understanding, to faith, to charitable works, and to self-sacrifice (1 Corinthians 13:1–3).
5. Love is kind (1 Corinthians 13:4).
6. Love is greater than faith (1 Corinthians 13:13).
7. Love is greater than hope (1 Corinthians 13:13).
8. Love is the fruit of the Spirit (Galatians 5:22).
9. Love is the bond of perfectness (Colossians 3:14).

10. Love is of God (1 John 4:7).

11. Love is living according to God's commandments (2 John 6).

## 121. Ten Things That Cannot Separate Us From the Love of God

1. Death (Romans 8:38).

2. Life (Romans 8:38).

3. Angels (Romans 8:38).

4. Principalities (Romans 8:38).

5. Powers (Romans 8:38).

6. Things present (Romans 8:38).

7. Things to come (Romans 8:38).

8. Height (Romans 8:39).

9. Depth (Romans 8:39).

10. No creature (Romans 8:39).

## 122. Nine Things That Love Does

1. Love suffers long (1 Corinthians 13:4).

2. Love rejoices in truth (1 Corinthians 13:6).

3. Love bears all things (1 Corinthians 13:7).

4. Love believes all things (1 Corinthians 13:7).

5. Love hopes all things (1 Corinthians 13:7).

6. Love endures all things (1 Corinthians 13:7).

7. Love abides now (1 Corinthians 13:13).

8. Love covers a multitude of sins (1 Peter 4:8).

9. Perfect love casts out fear (1 John 4:18).

## 123. Three Things That Love Is Not

1. Love is not envious (1 Corinthians 13:4).

2. Love is not puffed up (1 Corinthians 13:4).

3. Love is not easily provoked (1 Corinthians 13:5).

## 124. Seven Things That Love Does Not Do

1. Love does not vaunt itself (1 Corinthians 13:4).

2. Love does not behave unseemly (1 Corinthians 13:5).

3. Love does not seek its own (1 Corinthians 13:5).

4. Love thinks no evil (1 Corinthians 13:5).

5. Love does not rejoice in iniquity (1 Corinthians 13:6).

6. Love never fails (1 Corinthians 13:8).

7. Love works no ill to his neighbor (Romans 13:10).

# 11

## GOD'S GIFTS TO MEN

Paul wrote in 1 Corinthians 14:1 that we should desire spiritual gifts. Many have missed out by saying, "But which gift should I seek?" Others have sold themselves short by limiting the number of spiritual gifts to nine, or twelve, or eighteen. Even this chapter does not claim to list them all, but perhaps there are enough here to expand our spiritual horizons.

Could it be that there are more gifts available in the Lord than we seek to obtain?

### 125. Nine Gifts of the Spirit

1. To one is given by the Spirit the word of wisdom (1 Corinthians 12:8).
2. To another . . . the word of knowledge by the same Spirit (1 Corinthians 12:8).
3. To another . . . faith by the same Spirit (1 Corinthians 12:9).
4. To another is given the gifts of healing (1 Corinthians 12:9).
5. To another . . . the working of miracles (1 Corinthians 12:10).
6. To another . . . prophecy (1 Corinthians 12:10).
7. To another is given the discerning of spirits (1 Corinthians 12:10).
8. To another . . . divers kinds of tongues (1 Corinthians 12:10).
9. To yet another is given the interpretation of tongues (1 Corinthians 12:10).

## 126. Nine Ministries God Gave to the Church

1. Exhorters have a ministry in the church (Romans 12:4, 8).

2. Those who give have a . . . ministry in the church (Romans 12:4, 8).

3. God gave apostles to the church (1 Corinthians 12:28).

4. God gave prophets (1 Corinthians 12:28).

5. God gave teachers (1 Corinthians 12:28).

6. God gave helpers (1 Corinthians 12:28).

7. God gave administrators to the church (1 Corinthians 12:28).

8. The Lord gave evangelists . . . to help perfect and edify the body of Christ (Ephesians 4:11–12).

9. The Lord gave pastors to the church for the work of the ministry and to help perfect and edify the body of Christ (Ephesians 4:11–12).

## 127. Eleven Fruits of the Spirit

1. The fruit of the Spirit is love (Galatians 5:22).

2. The fruit of the Spirit is joy (Galatians 5:22).

3. The fruit of the Spirit is peace (Galatians 5:22).

4. The fruit of the Spirit is long-suffering (Galatians 5:22).

5. The fruit of the Spirit is gentleness (Galatians 5:22).

6. The fruit of the Spirit is goodness (Galatians 5:22).

7. The fruit of the Spirit is faith (Galatians 5:22).

8. The fruit of the Spirit is meekness (Galatians 5:23).

9. The fruit of the Spirit is temperance (Galatians 5:23).

10. The fruit of the Spirit is in all righteousness (Ephesians 5:9).

11. The fruit of the Spirit is in all truth (Ephesians 5:9).

## 128. Seven Virtues

1. Give all diligence to add faith (to your other virtues) (2 Peter 1:5).

2. . . . add knowledge (2 Peter 1:5).

3. . . . add temperance (2 Peter 1:6).

4. . . . add patience (2 Peter 1:6).

5. . . . add godliness (2 Peter 1:6).

6. . . . add brotherly kindness (2 Peter 1:7).

7. Give all diligence to add charity (2 Peter 1:7).

## 129. Armor Every Christian Should Have

1. Cast off the works of darkness, and put on the *armor of light* (Romans 13:12).

2. Put on the *whole armor of God*, that you may be able to stand against the wiles of the devil and to withstand in the evil day. Start by having your loins girt about with *truth* (Ephesians 6:11–14).

3. Have on the *breastplate of righteousness* (Ephesians 6:14).

4. Have your feet shod with the *preparation of the gospel of peace* (Ephesians 6:15).

5. Above all, take the *shield of faith* to quench all of the fiery darts of the wicked (Ephesians 6:16).

6. Take the *helmet of salvation* (Ephesians 6:17).

7. Take the *sword of the Spirit* which is the Word of God (Ephesians 6:17).

# 12

## SIN

In a book of lists with a chapter titled "Sin," you might expect to find a list of several thousand sins. This chapter, however, is not of that sort.

What is sin anyway? Paul said, "Whatsoever is not of faith is sin" (Romans 14:23).

James wrote, "To him that knoweth to do good, and doeth it not, to him it is sin" (James 4:17).

John declared, "Sin is the transgression of the law" (1 John 3:4).

The list of possible sins could be very long. This chapter focuses on sin from some different points of view. Here we look at six sins that King David committed, six accounts of people whom Jesus personally forgave, and ten things that you can do about sin. For specific revelation of sin in one's life, the Holy Spirit will illuminate a person's God-given conscience (Romans 2:15).

In this section is included some information about Satan, since he is the father of lies and attempts to draw mankind into sin.

### 130. Six Sins That King David Committed

1. He took back Michal as his wife after she was married to another man (2 Samuel 3:13–16; Deuteronomy 24:1–4).

2. He coveted his neighbor's wife (2 Samuel 11:2–3).

3. He committed adultery with Bathsheba (2 Samuel 11:4–5).

4. He tried to cover up the adultery (2 Samuel 11:6–13).

5. He ordered the murder of Uriah (2 Samuel 11:14–17).

6. He numbered Israel (1 Chronicles 21:1, 17).

### 131. *Murderers in the Bible*

1. Cain rose up against Abel his brother, and slew him (Genesis 4:8).

2. Simeon and Levi . . . slew all the males of Shalem (Genesis 34:25).

3. Moses slew the Egyptian and hid him in the sand (Exodus 2:12).

4. Achan, through disobedience, was responsible for the deaths of thirty-six Israelites (Joshua 7:5, 20).

5. Abimelech murdered his seventy half brothers (Judges 9:5).

6. Certain sons of Belial raped the Levite's concubine until she died (Judges 19:22–28).

7. Saul ordered the killing of eighty-five priests and the people and animals of Nob because they aided David (1 Samuel 22:18–19).

8. Joab and Abishai his brother slew Abner (2 Samuel 3:30).

9. The sons of Rimmon, Rechab, and Baanah killed Ishbosheth on his bed (2 Samuel 4:5–6).

10. David arranged Uriah's death (2 Samuel 11:14–15).

11. The servants of Absolom [killed] Amnon as Absolom had commanded (2 Samuel 13:28–29).

12. Joab killed Absolom as he hung from a tree (2 Samuel 18:14).

13. Joab tricked Amasa, then killed him (2 Samuel 20:10).

14. Solomon had his brother Adonijah killed by Benaiah (1 Kings 2:23–25).

15. Baasha killed Nadab at Gebbethon (1 Kings 15:27).

16. Elah was killed by Zimri, captain of half his chariots (1 Kings 16:9–10).

17. Jezebel slew the prophets of the Lord (1 Kings 18:13).

18. Jezebel plotted Naboth's death (1 Kings 21:7–14).

19. Hazael smothered Benhadad as he lay sick (2 Kings 8:15).

20. Shallum killed Zachariah and took the throne of Israel (2 Kings 15:10).

21. Menahem killed Shallum and reigned for a month (2 Kings 15:14).

22. Pekah killed Pekahiah and took the throne (2 Kings 15:25).

23. Hoshea murdered Pekah and succeeded him (2 Kings 15:30).

24. Sennacherib was killed by his sons, Adramelech and Sharezer, as he worshiped Nisroch (2 Kings 19:36–37).

25. The servants of Amon conspired against him, and slew the king in his own household (2 Kings 21:23).

26. The children of Israel killed Hadoram with stones (2 Chronicles 10:18).

27. Joash commanded Zechariah to be stoned (2 Chronicles 24:20–22).

28. Herod ordered all the male children in Bethlehem to be killed, and in all the coasts thereof, two years old and under (Matthew 2:16).

29. Herodias requested John the Baptist's beheading (Matthew 14:8).

30. Judas betrayed Jesus into the hands of the Jews (Matthew 26:14–15).

31. Jesus said the devil was a murderer from the beginning (John 8:44).

32. Peter speaks of Barabbas as a murderer (Acts 3:14).

33. Stephen was stoned by furious Jews (Acts 7:57–59).

34. An Egyptian led out into the wilderness four thousand men that were murderers (Acts 21:38).

## 132. Six People Jesus Forgave During His Earthly Ministry

1. The man who was let down through the ceiling was forgiven by Jesus and also healed of palsy (Matthew 9:2).

2. Mary was forgiven of her sins when she anointed Jesus' feet (Luke 7:47–50).

3. Jesus forgave those who crucified Him (Luke 23:34).

4. The thief on the cross was told by Jesus that he would be in paradise with Jesus (Luke 23:39–43).

5. The impotent man that Jesus healed at the pool of Bethesda was probably forgiven by Jesus, since Jesus told him to sin no more (John 5:14).

6. To the woman taken in adultery, Jesus said, Neither do I condemn thee: go and sin no more (John 8:3–11).

## 133. Twenty-eight Names of Satan

1. Abaddon (Revelation 9:11).

2. Accuser of our brethren (Revelation 12:10).

3. Adversary (1 Peter 5:8).

4. Angel of the bottomless pit (Revelation 9:11).

5. Apollyon (Revelation 9:11).

6. Beelzebub (Matthew 12:24).

7. Belial (2 Corinthians 6:15).

8. The devil (Matthew 4:1).

9. Enemy (Matthew 13:39).

10. Evil spirit (1 Samuel 16:14).

11. Father of lies (John 8:44).

12. God of this world (2 Corinthians 4:4).

13. Great red dragon (Revelation 12:3, 9).

14. King of Tyrus (Ezekiel 28:12).

15. Liar (John 8:44).

16. Lucifer (Isaiah 14:12).

17. Old serpent (Revelation 12: 9).

18. Power of darkness (Colossians 1:13).

19. Prince of this world (John 12:31).

20. Prince of the devils (Matthew 12:24).

21. Prince of the power of the air (Ephesians 2:2).

22. Ruler of the darkness of this world (Ephesians 6:12).

23. Satan (1 Chronicles 21:1).

24. Serpent (Genesis 3:4).

25. Spirit that worketh in the children of disobedience (Ephesians 2:2).

26. Tempter (Matthew 12:43).

27. Unclean spirit (Matthew 12:43).

28. Wicked one (Matthew 13:19, 38).

## 134. Twenty-one Facts About Satan

1. God said to Satan, I will put enmity between thee and the woman, and between thy seed and her seed; it shall bruise thy head, and thou shalt bruise his heel (Genesis 3:15).

2. How art thou fallen from heaven, O Lucifer, son of the morning! how art thou cut down to the ground, which didst weaken the nations! For thou hast said in thine heart, I will ascend into heaven, I will exalt my throne above the stars of God: I will sit also upon the mount of the congregation, in the sides of the north: I will ascend above the heights of the clouds; I will be like the most High (Isaiah 14:12–14).

3. Thou hast been in Eden the garden of God; every precious stone was thy covering, the sardius, topaz, and the diamond, the beryl, the onyx, and the jasper, the sapphire, the emerald, and the carbuncle, and gold: the workmanship of thy tabrets and of thy pipes was prepared in thee in the day that thou wast created. Thou art the anointed cherub that covereth; and I have set thee so: thou wast upon the holy mountain of God; thou hast walked up and down in the midst of the stones of fire. Thou wast perfect in thy ways from the day that thou wast created, till iniquity was found in thee. Thine heart was lifted up because of thy beauty, thou hast corrupted thy wisdom by reason of thy brightness: I will cast thee to the ground, I will lay thee before kings, that they may behold thee (Ezekiel 28:13–15, 17).

4. When any one heareth the word of the kingdom and understandeth it not, then cometh the wicked one, and catcheth away that which was sown in his heart (Matthew 13:19).

5. [The devil] was a murderer from the beginning, and abode not in

the truth, because there is no truth in him. When he speaketh a lie, he speaketh of his own: for he is a liar, and the father of it (John 8:44).

6. The devil . . . put into the heart of Judas Iscariot, Simon's son, to betray [Jesus] (John 13:2).

7. [Jesus said], the prince of this world . . . hath nothing in me (John 14:30).

8. The prince of this world is judged (John 16:11).

9. Satan filled [Ananias'] heart to lie to the Holy Ghost, and to keep back part of the price of the land (Acts 5:3).

10. The God of peace shall bruise Satan under your feet shortly (Romans 16:20).

11. We are not ignorant of [Satan's] devices (2 Corinthians 2:11).

12. The God of this world hath blinded the minds of them which believe not, lest the light of the glorious gospel of Christ, who is the image of God, should shine unto them (2 Corinthians 4:4).

13. Satan himself is transformed into an angel of light (2 Corinthians 11:14).

14. Having spoiled principalities and powers, [Jesus] made a shew of them openly, triumphing over them in it (Colossians 2:15).

15. Resist the devil and he will flee from you (James 4:7).

16. Your adversary the devil, as a roaring lion, walketh about, seeking whom he may devour (1 Peter 5:8).

17. He that committeth sin is of the devil; for the devil sinneth from the beginning (1 John 3:8).

18. He that is begotten of God keepeth himself, and that wicked one toucheth him not (1 John 5:18).

19. Michael the archangel, when contending with the devil . . . durst not bring against him a railing accusation, but said, The Lord rebuke thee (Jude 9).

20. [Satan] accused them before our God day and night (Revelation 12:10).

21. The devil that deceived them was cast into the lake of fire and

brimstone, where the beast and the false prophet are, and shall be tormented day and night for ever and ever (Revelation 20:10).

## 135. Ten Things You Can Do About Sin

1. For if ye forgive men their trespasses, your heavenly Father will also forgive you: but if ye forgive not men their trespasses, neither will your Father forgive your trespasses (Matthew 6:14–15).

2. Repent, and be baptized every one of you in the name of Jesus Christ for the remission of sins (Acts 2:38).

3. This I say then, Walk in the Spirit, and ye shall not fulfill the lust of the flesh (Galatians 5:16).

4. For whom the Lord loveth he chasteneth, and scourgeth every son whom he receiveth. If ye endure chastening, God dealeth with you as with sons (Hebrews 12:6–7).

5. And the prayer of faith shall save the sick, and the Lord shall raise him up; and if he have committed sins, they shall be forgiven him (James 5:15).

6. Brethren, if any of you do err from the truth, and one convert him; let him know, that he which converteth the sinner from the error of his way shall save a soul from death, and shall hide a multitude of sins (James 5:19–20).

7. And above all things have fervent charity among yourselves: for charity shall cover the multitude of sins (1 Peter 4:8).

8. But if we walk in the light, as he is in the light, we have fellowship one with another, and the blood of Jesus Christ his Son cleanseth us from all sin (1 John 1:7).

9. If we confess our sins, he is faithful and just to forgive us our sins, and to cleanse us from all unrighteousness (1 John 1:9).

10. If any man see his brother sin a sin which is not unto death, he shall ask, and he shall give him life for them that sin not unto death. There is a sin unto death: I do not say that he shall pray for it (1 John 5:16).

# *13*

## LIES

The Bible contains many intriguing and sometimes appalling accounts of liars and their lies. The reasons for some lies *seem* justifiable. For example, the Gibeonites lied to save their lives. The Bible is very clear, though, concerning God's view of lying: "And all liars shall have their part in the lake which burneth with fire" (Revelation 21:8).

### 136. The Only Animal in the Bible That Lied

Now the serpent was more subtle than any beast of the field which the Lord God had made. And he said unto the woman, Yea, hath God said, Ye shall not eat of every tree of the garden? And the woman [Eve] said unto the serpent, We may eat of the fruit of the trees of the garden: but the fruit of the tree which is in the midst of the garden, God hath said, Ye shall not eat of it, neither shall ye touch it, lest ye die. And the serpent said unto the woman, Ye shall not surely die: for God doth know that in the day ye eat thereof, then your eyes shall be opened, and ye shall be as gods, knowing good and evil (Genesis 3:1–5).

### 137. The First Cover-Up

And Cain talked with Abel his brother: and it came to pass, when they were in the field, that Cain rose up against Abel his brother, and slew him. And the Lord said unto Cain, where is Abel thy brother? And he said, I know not: Am I my brother's keeper? (Genesis 4:8–9).

## 138. *Five Accounts of Lying Relatives in the Bible*

1. And Rebekah spake unto Jacob her son, saying, Behold, I heard thy father speak unto Esau thy brother, saying, Bring me venison . . . that I may eat and bless thee before the Lord before my death. Now therefore, my son [Jacob], obey my voice according to that which I command thee. . . . And Rebekah took goodly raiment of her eldest son Esau . . . and put them upon Jacob. . . . And she put the skins of . . . kids of . . . goats upon his hands and . . . his neck: and she gave the savoury meat and the bread, which she had prepared, [to] Jacob. And he came unto his father, and said, My father: and he said, Here am I; who art thou, my son? And Jacob said unto his father, I am Esau thy firstborn; I have done according as thou badest me. . . . And Isaac said . . . How is it that thou hast found it so quickly, my son? And he said, Because the Lord thy God brought it to me (Genesis 27:6–8, 15–20).

2. Laban said unto Jacob . . . What shall thy wages be? . . . And Jacob . . . said, I will serve thee seven years for Rachel. . . . And Laban said, It is better that I give her to thee, than . . . to another man. . . . And Jacob served seven years . . . and said to Laban, Give me my wife. [But Laban tricked Jacob.] He took Leah his daughter, and brought her to him; and he went in unto her. . . . And it came to pass, that in the morning, behold it was Leah; and he said to Laban, What is this that thou hast done unto me? did I not serve with thee for Rachel? wherefore then hast thou beguiled me? (Genesis 29:15, 18, 19–21, 23, 25).

3. Laban went to shear his sheep: and Rachel had stolen the images that were her father's. And Jacob stole away unawares to Laban. . . . And it was told Laban on the third day that Jacob was fled. And he . . . pursued after him. . . . Then Laban overtook Jacob . . . and said, . . . Wherefore hast thou stolen my gods? . . . And Laban . . . entered into Rachel's tent. Now Rachel had taken the images, and put them in the camel's furniture, and sat upon them. And Laban searched all the tent, but found them not. And she said unto her father, Let it not displease my lord that I cannot rise up before thee; for the custom of women is upon me (Genesis 31:19–20, 22–23, 25, 30, 33–34).

4. Joseph's brothers sold Joseph to the Ishmaelites for twenty pieces of silver: and they brought Joseph into Egypt. . . . And they [Joseph's

brothers] took Joseph's coat, and killed a kid of the goats, and dipped the coat in the blood; and they sent the coat of many colours, and they brought it to their father; and said, This have we found: know now whether it be thy son's coat or no. And he knew it, and said, It is my son's coat; an evil beast hath devoured him; Joseph is without doubt rent in pieces (Genesis 37:28, 31–33).

5. And all the people brake off the golden earrings which were in their ears, and brought them to Aaron. And he received them at their hand, and fashioned it with a graving tool, after he had made it a molten calf. . . . And Moses said unto Aaron, What did this people unto thee, that thou hast brought so great a sin upon them? And Aaron said, Let not the anger of my lord wax hot: thou knowest the people, that they are set on mischief. For they said unto me, Make us gods. . . . And I said unto them, Whosoever hath any gold, let them break it off. So they gave it me: then I cast it into the fire, and there came out this calf (Exodus 32:3–4, 21–24).

## 139. Accounts of "Good" People Who Lied

1. And Isaac dwelt in Gerar: and the men of the place asked him of his wife; and he said, She is my sister: for he feared to say, She is my wife; lest, said he, the men of the place should kill me for Rebekah; because she was fair to look upon (Genesis 26:6–7).

2. Delilah said to Samson, Tell me, I pray thee, wherein thy great strength lieth, and wherewith thou mightest be bound to afflict thee. And Samson said unto her, If they bind me with seven green withs that were never dried, then shall I be weak, and be as another man. [When this didn't prove to be true], Delilah said unto Samson, Behold, thou hast mocked me, and told me lies. . . . [He lied in a similar manner twice more before he got his head shaved.] (Judges 16:6–7, 10).

3. David said unto Jonathan, Behold, tomorrow is the new moon, and I should not fail to sit with the king at meat: but let me go, that I may hide myself in the field unto the third day at even. If thy father at all miss me, then say, David earnestly asked leave of me that he might run to Bethlehem his city: for there is a yearly sacrifice there for all the family [and this plan was carried out by Jonathan] (1 Samuel 20:5–6).

4. When David was sure that Saul meant to kill him, he fled. Then came David to Nob to Ahimelech the priest: and Ahimelech was afraid at the meeting of David, and said unto him, Why art thou alone, and no man with thee? And David said unto Ahimelech the priest, The king hath commanded me a business, and hath said unto me, Let no man know any thing of the business whereabout I send thee, and what I have commanded thee: and I have appointed my servants to such and such a place (1 Samuel 21:1–2).

5. David and his men dwelt in Ziklag in the country of the Philistines which was ruled by King Achish. And David and his men went up, and invaded the Geshurites, and the Gezrites, and the Amalekites. . . . And David smote the land, and left neither man nor woman alive . . . and returned and came to Achish. And Achish said, Whither have ye made a road to day? And David said, Against the south of Judah, and against the south of the Jerahmeelites, and against the south of the Kenites. And David saved neither man nor woman alive, to bring tidings to Gath, saying, Lest they should tell on us. . . . And Achish believed David, saying, He hath made his people Israel to abhor him; therefore he shall be my servant for ever (1 Samuel 27:8–12).

6. Now Peter sat without in the palace: and a damsel came unto him, saying, Thou also wast with Jesus of Galilee. But he denied before them all, saying, I know not what thou sayest. And when he was gone out into the porch, another maid saw him, and said unto them that were there, This fellow was also with Jesus of Nazareth. And again he denied with an oath, I do not know the man. And after a while came unto him they that stood by, and said to Peter, Surely thou also art one of them; for thy speech betrayeth thee. Then began he to curse and to swear, saying, I know not the man (Matthew 26:69–74).

## 140. The Father of Lies

Jesus said that the devil abode not in the truth, because there is no truth in him. When he speaketh a lie, he speaketh of his own: for he is a liar, and the father of it (John 8:44).

## 141. Three Lying Prophets

1. There was a prophet who prophesied against the altar at Bethel and who besought the Lord for the healing of King Jeroboam. After the king was healed, the king said unto the man of God, Come home with me, and refresh thyself, and I will give thee a reward. And the man of God said unto the king, . . . I will not go in with thee . . . for . . . the Lord [said], Eat no bread, nor drink water, nor turn again by the same way that thou camest. . . . Now there dwelt an old prophet in Bethel . . . [who] went after the man of God, and found him sitting under an oak: and he said unto him, . . . I am a prophet also as thou art; and an angel spake unto me by the word of the Lord, saying, Bring him back with thee into thine house, that he may eat bread and drink water. But he lied unto him. So he went back with him, and did eat bread in his house, and drank water. [Because of his disobedience, the man of God was slain by a lion.] (1 Kings 13:7–9, 11, 14, 18–19).

2. Pashur . . . who was . . . chief governor in the house of the Lord . . . smote Jeremiah the prophet, and put him in . . . stocks. . . . On the morrow . . . Pashur brought forth Jeremiah out of the stocks. Then said Jeremiah unto him . . . Thou, Pashur, and all that dwell in thine house shall go into captivity . . . and there thou shalt die . . . thou, and all thy friends, to whom thou hast prophesied lies (Jeremiah 20:1–3, 6).

3. Then came the word of the Lord unto Jeremiah, saying, Send to all of the captivity, saying, Thus saith the Lord concerning Shemaiah the Nehelamite; Because that Shemaiah hath prophesied unto you, and I sent him not, and he caused you to believe a lie; therefore thus saith the Lord; Behold, I will punish Shemaiah the Nehelamite, and his seed: he shall not have a man to dwell among this people; neither shall he behold the good that I will do for my people, saith the Lord; because he hath taught rebellion against the Lord (Jeremiah 29:30–32).

## 142. Lies That Helped Destroy Two Cities

1. The sons of Jacob answered Shechem and Hamor his father deceitfully, and said, Because he [Shechem] had defiled Dinah their sister: . . . we cannot . . . give our sister to one that is uncircumcised . . . but . . . if . . . every male of you [will] be circumcised;

then will we give our daughters unto you, and we will take your daughters to us, and we will dwell with you, and we will become one people. . . . And every male was circumcised. . . . And it came to pass on the third day, when they were sore, that . . . Simeon and Levi, Dinah's brethren . . . came upon the city boldly and slew all the males . . . and spoiled the city because they had defiled their sister (Genesis 34:13–16, 24–25, 27).

2. Joshua . . . sent . . . two men to spy secretly. . . . And they went, and came into an harlot's house, named Rahab. . . . And it was told the king of Jericho. . . . And the king of Jericho sent unto Rahab, saying, Bring forth the men that are come to thee. . . . And the woman took the two men, and hid them, and said thus, There came men unto me, but I wist not whence they were: and it came to pass about the time of shutting of the gate, when it was dark, that the men went out: whither the men went I wot not: pursue after them quickly; for ye shall overtake them (Joshua 2:1–5).

### 143. The Woman Who Yelled "Rape!"

Potiphar bought Joseph as a slave and made him overseer over his house. And it came to pass after these things, that his master's wife cast her eyes upon Joseph; and she said, Lie with me. But he refused. . . . And it came to pass, as she spake to Joseph day by day, that he hearkened not unto her, to lie by her, or to be with her. And it came to pass about this time that Joseph went into the house to do his business; and there was none of the men of the house there within. And she caught him by his garment, saying, Lie with me: and he left his garment in her hand, and fled, and got him out. . . . Then she called unto the men of her house, and spake unto them, saying, See, he hath brought in an Hebrew to mock us; he came in unto me to lie with me, and I cried with a loud voice . . . [then] he left his garment with me, and fled. . . . And it came to pass, when his master heard the words of his wife . . . Joseph's master . . . put him into the prison (Genesis 39:7–8, 10–12, 14–15, 19–20).

### 144. The Lie That Saved the Gibeonites

And when the inhabitants of Gibeon heard what Joshua had done unto Jericho and to Ai, they did work wilily, and went

215

and made as if they had been ambassadors, and took old sacks upon their asses, and wine bottles, old and rent, and bound up; and old shoes and clouted upon their feet, and old garments upon them; and all the bread of their provision was dry and mouldy. And they went to Joshua . . . and said unto him and to the men of Israel, we be come from a far country: now therefore make ye a league with us. . . . The men [of Israel] took of their victuals and asked not counsel at the mouth of the Lord. And Joshua made peace with them, and made a league with them, to let them live: and the princes of the congregation sware unto them. And . . . at the end of three days . . . they heard they were their neighbours . . . And the children of Israel smote them not, because the princes . . . had sworn unto them by the Lord God of Israel (Joshua 9:3–6, 14–16, 18).

### 145. Lies That Led to Leprosy

Gehazi, the servant of Elisha . . . said, Behold, my master hath spared Naaman . . . in not receiving . . . that which he brought: but . . . I will run after him, and take [something] of him. . . . And when Naaman saw him running after him, he lighted down from the chariot to meet him, and said, Is all well? And he said, All is well. My master hath sent me, saying, Behold, even now there [are coming] . . . two young . . . sons of the prophets: give them, I pray thee, a talent of silver, and two changes of garments. And Naaman said, [By all means,] take two talents. . . . And when he [Gehazi] came to the tower, he took [the goods] from their hand, and bestowed them in the house: and he let the men go. . . . But he went in, and stood before his master. And Elisha said unto him, Whence comest thou, Gehazi? And he said, Thy servant went [nowhere.] And he said unto him, . . . Is it a time to receive money? . . . The leprosy therefore of Naaman shall cleave unto thee, and unto thy seed for ever. And [Gehazi] went out from his presence, a leper as white as snow (2 Kings 5:20–27).

### 146. The Lie That God Seemed to Condone

Ahab said, Micaiah, shall we go to battle, or shall we forbear? And he answered him, Go, and prosper: for the Lord shall deliver it into the hand of the king. And the king said unto him, How many times shall I adjure thee that thou tell me nothing but that which is true in the name of the Lord? And he said, I saw all Israel scattered upon the hills, as sheep that have not a shepherd: and the Lord said, These have no master: Let them return every man to his house in peace. . . . And Micaiah continued, Hear thou therefore the word of the Lord: I saw the Lord sitting on his throne, and all the host of heaven standing by him on his right hand and on his left. And the Lord said, Who shall persuade Ahab, that he may go up and fall at Ramoth-gilead? . . . And there came forth a spirit, and stood before the Lord, and said, I will persuade him. And the Lord said to him, Wherewith? And he said, I will go forth, and I will be a lying spirit in the mouth of all his prophets. And he said, Thou shalt persuade him, and prevail also: go forth, and do so. Now therefore, behold, the Lord hath put a lying spirit in the mouth of all these thy prophets, and the Lord hath spoken evil concerning thee. . . . So the king of Israel [Ahab] and Jehoshaphat the king of Judah went up to Ramoth-gilead [anyway]. . . . And it came to pass . . . that . . . a certain man drew a bow at a venture, and smote the king of Israel . . . so the king died (1 Kings 22:15–17, 19–23, 29, 32, 34, 37).

### 147. Lies That Killed a Man

Ahab spake unto Naboth, saying, Give me thy vineyard, that I may have it for a garden of herbs, because it is near unto my house: and I will give thee for it a better vineyard than it; or, if it seem good to thee, I will give thee the worth of it in money. And Naboth said to Ahab, The Lord forbid me, that I should give the inheritance of my fathers [the vineyard] unto thee. And Ahab came into his house heavy and displeased. . . . And Jezebel his wife said unto him, Dost thou now govern the kingdom of Israel? . . . I will give thee the vineyard of Naboth. . . . And she wrote letters in Ahab's name . . . and sent them to the nobles that were in his [Naboth's] city. . . . She wrote . . . saying, Proclaim a fast, and set Naboth on high . . . and set two men . . . before him, to bear false witness against him, saying, Thou didst blaspheme God and the king. And then carry him out, and stone him, that he may die. And the men of his city . . . did as Jezebel had sent unto them. . . . When Jezebel heard that Naboth . . . was dead, . . . Jezebel said to Ahab, Arise, take possession of

the vineyard. . . . When Ahab heard that Naboth was dead . . .
Ahab took possession of the vineyard (1 Kings 21:2–4, 7–11,
15–16).

## 148. The Lie That Helped Destroy the Worshipers of Baal

And Jehu gathered all the people together, and said unto them,
Ahab served Baal a little; but Jehu shall serve him much. Now
therefore call unto me all the prophets of Baal, all his servants and
all his priests; let [no one be mssing]: for I have a great sacrifice
to do to Baal; whosoever [fails to come], he shall not live. But
Jehu did it in subtilty, to the intent that he might destroy the
worshippers of Baal. And Jehu said, Proclaim a solemn assembly for Baal, and they proclaimed it. And Jehu sent through all
Israel: and all the worshippers of Baal came . . . into the house
of Baal. . . . And when they went in to offer sacrifices . . . Jehu
appointed fourscore men without, and said, If any of the men
whom I have brought into your hands escape, he that letteth him
go, his life shall be for the life of him . . . Thus Jehu destroyed
Baal out of Israel (2 Kings 10:18–21, 24, 28).

## 149. Two People Who Falsely Reported Their Income

Ananias [and] Sapphira his wife sold a possession, and kept back
part of the price . . . and brought a certain part, and laid it at
the apostles' feet. But Peter said, Ananias, why hath Satan filled
thine heart to lie to the Holy Ghost, and to keep back part of
the price of the land? . . . And Ananias hearing these words fell
down, and gave up the ghost. . . . And the young men . . . carried
him out, and buried him. . . . About . . . three hours later . . . his
wife, not knowing what was done, came in. And Peter answered
unto her, Tell me whether ye sold the land for so much? And she
said, Yea, for so much. Then Peter said unto her, How is it that ye
have agreed together to tempt the Spirit of the Lord? . . . Then
fell she down . . . and yielded up the ghost (Acts 5:1–3, 5–9).

# 14

## MIRACLE WORKERS
## AND THEIR DEEDS

This chapter is about six men who accomplished marvelous things. But they didn't do it by themselves; they did it as God miraculously intervened in the affairs of men through them.

You will marvel at the variety (yet similarity) and magnitude of the miracles associated with Moses, Elijah, Elisha, Peter, Paul, and, of course—the greatest miracle worker of them all—Jesus Christ.

### 150. Thirty-eight Miracles Associated With Moses

1. Moses' rod turned into a serpent and then back into a rod (Exodus 4:2–4).

2. Moses' hand became leprous and then returned to normal (Exodus 4:7).

3. Aaron's rod became a serpent and swallowed up the sorcerers' serpents (Exodus 7:10–12).

4. The water in Egypt turned into blood (Exodus 7:19–25).

5. Frogs were brought forth upon the land of Egypt (Exodus 8:5–7).

6. All of the frogs were killed (Exodus 8:12–13).

7. Dust was changed into lice (Exodus 8:16–17).

8. Swarms of flies were produced everywhere in Egypt except in the land of Goshen (Exodus 8:20–24).

9. The flies in Egypt were made to depart (Exodus 8:29–31).

10. Murrain (a plague) was brought upon the Egyptian cattle but not upon Israel's cattle. The infected cattle died (Exodus 9:1–7).

11. Ashes were changed into dust. Wherever the dust landed on Egyptians or upon their beasts, it caused boils (Exodus 9:8–12).

12. A grievous hailstorm, with fire that ran along the ground, was sent upon the Egyptians (Exodus 9:22–26).

13. The thunder and hail stopped upon command (Exodus 9:33).

14. Then a plague of locusts was brought against the Egyptians (Exodus 10:12–15).

15. Upon request, the locusts were blown away (Exodus 10:16–20).

16. Thick darkness was brought upon Egypt for three days, but the Hebrews had light (Exodus 10:21–23).

17. All of the firstborn in Egypt were slain unless there was Passover blood on their doorposts and the people were inside (Exodus 12:21–30).

18. The Lord hid the Hebrews with a cloud (Exodus 14:19–20).

19. The Red Sea was parted (Exodus 14:21).

20. The sea bottom was made dry land (Exodus 14:21).

21. The wheels were taken off of the Egyptian chariots when they tried to cross over the dry sea bottom (Exodus 14:23–25).

22. The waters of the Red Sea returned and drowned the Egyptian army (Exodus 14:27–28).

23. Moses cast a tree into the bitter waters at Marah and made the water sweet (Exodus 15:23–25).

24. The Hebrews were fed with quail (Exodus 16:11–13).

25. The Hebrews were fed with manna (Exodus 16:14–15).

26. The manna wouldn't store until morning except on the Sabbath (Exodus 16:19–20, 23–24).

27. Each Hebrew gathered manna per his exact needs including twice as much on the sixth day (Exodus 16:16–22).

28. Moses struck the rock in Horeb to produce water for the Hebrews (Exodus 17:1–6).

29. Fire from the Lord consumed the burnt offering (Leviticus 9:22–24).

30. Miriam was made leprous and then healed (Numbers 12).

31. Complaining Hebrews were burned up by fire from the Lord, until Moses intervened by prayer (Numbers 11:1–2).

32. Fire came out from the Lord and consumed 250 men who offered incense (Numbers 16:16–18, 35).

33. The earth opened up and swallowed Korah and his men (Numbers 16:28–33).

34. A plague that killed 14,700 was stayed by making an offering of incense (Numbers 16:46–50).

35. Aaron's rod, placed before the Lord by Moses, budded, blossomed, and produced almonds (Numbers 17).

36. Moses struck the rock twice to bring forth water (Numbers 20:1–11).

37. Moses made a brass serpent and put it on a pole. If anyone was bitten by a fiery serpent and then looked upon the brass serpent, his life was saved (Numbers 21:5–9).

38. Moses appeared on the mount of transfiguration with Jesus (Luke 9:28–36).

## 151. Eleven Miracles Associated With Elijah

1. Elijah prayed, and it didn't rain for three and a half years (1 Kings 17:1).

2. A continuous supply of meal and oil was supplied for a widow and her son from nearly empty containers of the same (1 Kings 17:13–16).

3. A widow's son was raised from the dead (1 Kings 17:17–23).

4. When Elijah prayed, a fire came down from heaven and burned up a sacrifice, the altar, and the water that was placed in a trench around the altar (1 Kings 18:17–38).

5. When Elijah prayed at the end of a three-and-a-half-year drought, there was an abundance of rain (1 Kings 18:41–46).

6. Elijah was fed two miraculous meals that sustained him for forty days (1 Kings 19:4–8).

7. Elijah was fed by ravens (1 Kings 17:2–7).

8. Fire from heaven came down at the word of Elijah to burn up two different bands of soldiers (102 men) (2 Kings 1:10–12).

9. Elijah parted the waters of the Jordan River by hitting it with his mantle. He and Elisha walked across the Jordan River on dry ground (2 Kings 2:8).

10. Elijah was taken into heaven by a whirlwind (2 Kings 2:11).

11. Elijah appeared atop the mount of transfiguration with Jesus and Moses (Luke 9:28–36).

## 152. *Fifteen Miracles Associated With Elisha*

1. Elisha parted the waters of the Jordan River with Elijah's mantle and walked across the riverbed on dry ground (2 Kings 2:13–14).

2. Elisha healed a water source by throwing a bowl of salt into the water (2 Kings 2:19–22).

3. Forty-two children were torn up by two bears when they were cursed by Elisha because they mocked him (2 Kings 2:23–25).

4. Water was supplied for the kings of Israel, Judah, and Edom, and for their armies and cattle (2 Kings 3:14–20).

5. A widow's pot of oil was made to produce large quantities of oil (2 Kings 4:1–7).

6. A Shunammite woman was healed so that she conceived and had a son as prophesied by Elisha (2 Kings 4:14–17).

7. Elisha raised the Shunammite's son from the dead (2 Kings 4:32–37).

8. Elisha counteracted the poison pottage made of wild gourds by putting meal in the pottage (2 Kings 4:38–41).

9. One hundred men were fed with twenty loaves of barley and some ears of corn (2 Kings 4:42–44).

10. Naaman was healed of leprosy by following Elisha's instructions (2 Kings 5:1–14).

11. Elisha made an iron ax head float to the top of the water by throwing a stick in the water (2 Kings 6:4–7).

12. Elisha's servant's spiritual eyes were opened, in response to Elisha's prayer, to see an angelic army (2 Kings 6:15–17).

13. The Syrian army was struck blind by the Lord when Elisha prayed (2 Kings 6:18).

14. The men in the Syrian army were healed of their blindness after Elisha led them to Samaria and prayed for their eyes to be opened (2 Kings 6:19–20).

15. The bones of Elisha caused a man to be raised from the dead (2 Kings 13:20–21).

## 153. Forty-three Miracles That Happened During Jesus' Earthly Ministry

1. Jesus was conceived by the Holy Ghost and the Virgin Mary (Matthew 1:18–25).

2. Jesus healed a leper who worshiped Him (Matthew 8:1–4).

3. Jesus healed a centurion's servant of palsy by speaking a word only (Matthew 8:5–13).

4. Jesus healed Peter's mother-in-law of a fever by touching her hand (Matthew 8:14–15).

5. Jesus cast out devils (demons) with His word (Matthew 8:16).

6. Jesus rebuked the wind and the raging sea and caused them to be calm (Matthew 8:23–27).

7. Jesus cast a legion of demons out of two men and let the demons go into a herd of swine (Matthew 8:28–34).

8. Jesus healed a palsied man and also forgave his sins (Matthew 9:1–8).

9. A woman with an issue of blood was healed when she touched the hem of Jesus' garment (Matthew 9:20–22).

10. Jesus raised Jairus' daughter from the dead (Matthew 9:23–25).

11. Two blind men were healed when Jesus touched their eyes (Matthew 9:27–30).

12. Jesus exorcised a dumb demoniac, and then the demoniac was able to speak (Matthew 9:32–33).

13. Jesus healed a man who had a withered hand (Matthew 12:10–13).

14. A blind and dumb demoniac was exorcised by Jesus and was then able to speak and to see (Matthew 12:22).

15. Jesus fed five thousand-plus people with five loaves and two fish (Matthew 14:15–21).

16. Jesus walked on the water of a raging sea (Matthew 14:25).

17. Jesus made it possible for Peter to walk on the water (Matthew 14:28–31).

18. Jesus cast a demon out of a Canaanite woman's daughter without even going to her (Matthew 15:22–28).

19. Jesus healed the lame, blind, dumb, and the maimed (Matthew 15:30–31).

20. Jesus fed four thousand men plus women and children with seven loaves and a few fish (Matthew 15:32–39).

21. Jesus was transfigured (Matthew 17:1–9).

22. Jesus cast a demon out of a young boy (Matthew 17:14–18).

23. Jesus sent Peter to catch a fish with money in its mouth, so that Peter could pay the temple tax (Matthew 17:24–27).

24. Jesus healed two blind men at the wayside by touching their eyes (Matthew 20:30–34).

25. Jesus healed the blind and the lame in the temple (Matthew 21:14).

26. Jesus cursed a fig tree and thus caused it to wither and die very quickly (Matthew 21:17–20).

27. Jesus was resurrected (Matthew 28:5–10).

28. Jesus healed a deaf and dumb man at Decapolis (Mark 7:31–35).

29. Jesus healed a blind man at Bethsaida by spitting on his eyes (Mark 8:22–26).

30. Jesus walked right through a crowd that was trying to throw Him off a cliff (Luke 4:29–30).

31. Jesus exorcised an unclean demon from a man in a synagogue (Luke 4:33–36).

32. Jesus caused Peter to make a great catch of fish, which filled two ships (Luke 5:4–11).

33. Jesus brought to life the dead son of the widow of Nain (Luke 7:11–15).

34. Jesus healed a woman who was bent over and couldn't straighten up (Luke 13:11–13).

35. Jesus healed a man of dropsy in the house of one of the chief Pharisees (Luke 14:1–4).

36. Jesus healed ten lepers at the same time (Luke 17:11–19).

37. Jesus healed the ear of Malchus after Peter struck it off with a sword (Luke 22:50–51).

38. Jesus turned water into wine (John 2:1–11).

39. Jesus healed a nobleman's son of a fever (John 4:46–54).

40. Jesus healed an impotent man who was sick for thirty-eight years at the pool of Bethesda (John 5:2–9).

41. Jesus healed a man who was born blind (John 9:1–7).

42. Jesus raised Lazarus from the dead (John 11:41–44).

43. Jesus caused the apostles to make a miraculous catch of fish after Jesus was resurrected (John 21:3–11).

## 154. Ten Miracles Associated With Peter

1. Peter walked on water in a stormy sea (Matthew 14:28–31).

2. The man at the Beautiful Gate of the temple was healed when Peter spoke to him (Acts 3:1–8).

3. Peter discerned the secret of Ananias and Sapphira when they agreed to withhold money from the sale of their property (Acts 5:1–11).

4. There was a multitude of healings when Peter's shadow fell upon the sick (Acts 5:15–16).

5. The apostles were delivered from prison by the angel of the Lord (Acts 5:17–29).

6. The Holy Ghost was imparted by the laying on of Peter's hands at Samaria (Acts 8:14–17).

7. Aeneas was healed of palsy after he had been sick for eight years (Acts 9:33–34).

8. Dorcas was raised from the dead by Peter (Acts 9:36–41).

9. The outpouring of the Holy Ghost at the house of Cornelius occurred while Peter was preaching (Acts 10:34–48).

10. Peter was delivered from prison a second time (Acts 12:1–17).

## 155. Eleven Miracles Associated With Paul

1. Paul had a miraculous conversion on the road to Damascus (Acts 9:1–9).

2. Paul's eyes were healed (Acts 9:10–18).

3. Elymas the sorcerer was blinded for a season at Paul's word (Acts 13:8–11).

4. A crippled man at Lystra was healed by Paul (Acts 14:8–10).

5. A girl in Philippi was exorcised by Paul (Acts 16:16–18).

6. Paul and Silas were delivered from prison by a divine earthquake (Acts 16:25–33).

7. The Holy Ghost was imparted at Ephesus by the laying on of Paul's hands (Acts 19:1–7).

8. Healings and exorcisms took place via handkerchiefs and aprons that had been placed on Paul's body (Acts 19:1–12).

9. Eutychus was raised from the dead at Troas after he had fallen from a third-story window (Acts 20:9–10).

10. Paul was unaffected after being bitten by a viper (Acts 28:3–6).

11. Publius' father and others were healed through Paul's ministry (Acts 28:8–9).

# *15*

# NUMBERS

This section is not about the biblical book of Numbers. Rather, it is about the quality, quantity, and size of things and people referred to in the Bible. Are you curious about how many words there are in the Bible, the oddest verse in the Bible, or the two longest words in the Bible? Then this is the place to look for these and many more.

### 156. *The Shortest Reign in the Bible*

King Zimri ruled Israel for seven days and then committed suicide by burning down his palace around himself (1 Kings 16:15).

### 157. *The Longest Reign in the Bible*

King Manasseh started his reign when he was twelve years old, and ruled Judah for fifty-five years (2 Kings 21:1).

### 158. *The Youngest King in the Bible*

Joash (also known as Jehoash) was seven years old when he began to reign as king of Judah. He reigned for forty years (2 Chronicles 24:1).

### 159. *The Largest Assembled Army in the Bible*

Zerah the Ethiopian had a host of one million, which he brought against King Asa (2 Chronicles 14:9).

## 160. The Largest Numbers in the Bible

1. The largest general number is "thousands of millions." Rebekah's family blessed her by saying, "Be thou the mother of thousands of millions" (Genesis 24:60).

2. The largest specific number is the army of 200 million horsemen mentioned in Revelation (9:16).

## 161. The Longest Book in the Old Testament

The longest book in the Old Testament is Psalms, with 150 chapters and a total of 2,461 verses. Psalms is also the longest book in the whole Bible.

## 162. The Shortest Book in the Old Testament

The shortest book in the Old Testament is Obadiah, which is comprised of twenty-one verses with a total of only 670 words.

## 163. The Longest Book in the New Testament

The longest book in the New Testament is Luke, which has 1,151 verses.

## 164. The Shortest Book in the New Testament

The shortest book in the New Testament is 2 John, which is comprised of thirteen verses with a total of only 298 words, thus making it the shortest book in the whole Bible.

## 165. The Longest Chapter in the Bible

The longest chapter in the Bible is Psalm 119, which has 176 verses.

## 166. The Shortest Chapter in the Bible

The shortest chapter in the Bible is Psalm 117, which has only two verses with a total of thirty-three words.

## 167. The Two Shortest Verses in the Bible

1. Jesus wept (John 11:35).

2. Eber, Peleg, Reu (1 Chronicles 1:25).

### 168. The Longest Verse in the Bible

The longest verse in the Bible is Esther 8:9, which contains ninety words.

### 169. The Total Number of Verses in the Bible

The total number of verses in the Bible is 30,442 (Old Testament: 22,485; New Testament: 7,957).

### 170. The Oddest Verse in the Bible

At Parbar westward, four at the causeway, and two at Parbar (1 Chronicles 26:18).

### 171. The Total Number of Words in the Bible

In round numbers, the total number of words in the Bible is 845,000 (Old Testament: 647,000; New Testament: 198,000).

### 172. The Most-Used Words in the Bible

The most-used word in the Bible is *the*, which appears approximately 58,000 times. The most-used noun in the Bible is *Lord*, which appears 7,736 times (non-capitalized usages also counted).

### 173. The Two Longest Words in the Bible

Two names tie for the honor of being the longest words in the Bible: *Jonathelemrechokim* and *Mahershalalhashbaz*. Both names have eighteen letters in them. Jonathelemrechokim is found in the title of Psalm 56 and means "a silent dove of far off lands." Mahershalalhashbaz is found in Isaiah 8:1 and 8:3; it is the name of Isaiah's son, and means "spoil speedeth, prey hasteth."

### 174. The Shortest Prayer in the Bible

When Peter was walking on the water and became afraid, he cried out, "Lord, save me" (Matthew 14:30)—the shortest prayer in the Bible.

### 175. The Longest Prayers in the Bible

1. Since it is directed toward God, Psalm 119 may be considered the longest prayer in the Bible.

2. The longest prayer that is not a Psalm is found in Nehemiah 9:5–38. It is a prayer of praise, confession, and covenant.

3. The longest prayer in the New Testament is Jesus' high priestly prayer, found in John 17.

## 176. *The Biggest Animal in the Bible*

The biggest animal in the Bible is the whale. It is mentioned in the first chapter of the first book of the Bible (Genesis 1:21).

## 177. *The Five Smallest Things Mentioned in the Bible*

1. David said to King Saul, After whom is the king of Israel come out? . . . after a *flea* (1 Samuel 24:14).

2. King Solomon, said, Go to the *ant,* thou sluggard (Proverbs 6:6).

3. Jesus said, One jot or one *tittle* shall in no wise pass from the law (a tittle is a small part of a Hebrew letter) (Matthew 5:18).

4. Jesus said, Ye blind guides, which strain at a *gnat,* and swallow a camel (Matthew 23:24).

5. Jesus said, A grain of *mustard seed* is the smallest seed of all the seeds in the earth (Mark 4:31).

# 16

## FLORA AND FAUNA

The Bible is a book about life and all of the things that affect life. As well as speaking about God and people, the Bible has much to say about plants, trees, animals, birds, insects, and reptiles.

In many cases, Bible scholars have not been able to positively identify the flora and fauna mentioned in the Bible. Therefore, in this chapter, most names given for the various animals, birds, etc., are as they are found in the King James Version.

### 178. Plants and Trees Mentioned in the Bible

1. Noah built the ark out of *gopher wood* (Genesis 6:14).

2. Leah bought a night in bed with Jacob from Rachel with some *mandrakes* (Genesis 30:14–16).

3. Jacob used rods of green *poplar, hazel,* and *chestnut trees* to make his cattle bring forth offspring that were ringstraked ( had circular stripes), speckled, and spotted (Genesis 30:37–39).

4. Jacob told his sons to take some *almonds*, as part of a gift to Joseph, when they went to Egypt a second time for food (Genesis 43:11).

5. The *rie* in Egypt was not smitten by the hail because it was not grown up yet (Exodus 9:32).

6. The *bitter herbs* that were supposed to be eaten with the Passover are said to consist of *lettuce, watercress, endive, chicory, sorrel,* and *dandelion greens* (Exodus 12:8).

7. Manna looked like *coriander seed* (Exodus 16:31).

8. Spice from the *cassia tree* was used in the making of the holy anointing oil for anointing the tabernacle of the congregation (Exodus 30:24).

9. The Hebrews ate *cucumbers, melons, leeks, onions,* and *garlic* when they were in Egypt (Numbers 11:5).

10. The *vine of Sodom* is mentioned in an unfavorable light in Deuteronomy 32:32.

11. Rahab hid the Hebrew spies on her roof under stalks of *flax* (Joshua 2:6).

12. The *brambles* mentioned in Judges are thought to be *wild blackberry bushes* (Judges 9:14–15).

13. The sound of a going in the tops of the *mulberry trees* was the signal used to indicate that the Lord had begun to smite the host of the Philistines (2 Samuel 5:24).

14. Solomon spoke of the *cedar trees of Lebanon* and of *hyssop* (1 Kings 4:33).

15. The navy of Hiram brought *almug trees* to King Solomon (1 Kings 10:11).

16. Elijah sat under a *juniper tree* (1 Kings 19:4).

17. Bildad the Shuhite asked, Can the *rush* grow up without mire? Can the *flag* grow up without water? (Job 8:11).

18. Job spoke of *mallows* and *nettles* (Job 30:4, 7).

19. Job spoke of *thistles, wheat, cockle,* and *barley* in one sentence (Job 31:40).

20. The Lord, speaking to Job, said that behemoth eats *grass*, lies in the covert of the *reed*, and that the *willows* of the brook compass him about (Job 40:15–22).

21. The *green bay tree* is mentioned in Psalm 37:35.

22. I am the *rose of Sharon*, and the *lily of the valleys* (Song of Solomon 2:1).

23. As the *apple tree* among the trees of the wood . . . (Song of Solomon 2:3).

24. In the Song of Solomon, *pomegranate trees, camphire trees,*

spikenard plants, saffron plants, calamus plants, cinnamon trees, frankincense trees, myrrh trees, and aloe trees are all mentioned (Song of Solomon 4:13–14).

25. *Wild grapes* are mentioned in Isaiah (Isaiah 5:2).

26. Isaiah spoke of a *teil tree* (Isaiah 6:13).

27. Isaiah spoke of vessels made of *bulrushes* (Isaiah 18:2).

28. God, speaking to Isaiah, said, I will plant in the wilderness the *cedar*, the *shittah tree*, the *myrtle*, and the *oil tree* [olive]; I will set in the desert the *fir tree*, and the *pine*, and the *box tree* together (Isaiah 41:19).

29. The Lord accused Israel of not bringing Him *sweet cane* (Isaiah 43:24).

30. Likewise, the prophet Isaiah mentioned in quick order: *cedars*, *cypress trees*, *oak trees*, and *ash trees* (Isaiah 44:14).

31. The Lord spoke of feeding *wormwood* to backslidden Israel (Jeremiah 9:15).

32. The Lord mentioned *desert heath* to Jeremiah (Jeremiah 17:5–6).

33. Ezekiel was told by God to make bread of *wheat*, *barley*, *beans*, *lentiles*, *millet*, and *fitches* (Ezekiel 4:9).

34. Ezekiel said that the men of Dedan brought a present of *ebony* to Tyrus (Ezekiel 27:15).

35. Hosea said that the people made sacrifices on the tops of the mountains under *oaks*, *poplars*, and *elms* (Hosea 4:13).

36. Hosea spoke of *hemlock* springing up in the furrows of the field (Hosea 10:4).

37. The prophet Joel mentioned, in quick succession, the following trees and plants: *corn*, *grape vines*, *olive trees*, *wheat*, *barley*, *fig trees*, *palm trees*, and *apple trees* (Joel 1:10–12).

38. God prepared a *gourd vine* that grew up overnight and shaded Jonah (Jonah 4:6).

39. Jesus mentioned *tares* in a parable (Matthew 13:25).

40. Jesus spoke of the *mustard seed* in a parable about faith (Matthew 13:31).

41. Jesus said that the scribes and Pharisees paid tithes on their *mint, anise,* and *cummin* (Matthew 23:23).

42. Jesus mentioned that the scribes and Pharisees tithed *mint* and *rue* (Luke 11:42).

43. Jesus mentioned the *sycamine tree* in a lesson about faith (Luke 17:6).

44. Zacchaeus climbed up a *sycamore tree* so that he could see Jesus (Luke 19:1–4).

45. *Thyine wood* is mentioned in Revelation 18:12.

    *Note:* Though we do not know what kind of trees they were, the tree of the knowledge of good and evil (Genesis 2:17) and the tree of life (Genesis 3:22) could also be included.

## 179. Animals Mentioned in the Bible

1. *Whales* are the biggest animals listed in the Bible. The whale is mentioned in the first chapter of the Bible (Genesis 1:21).

2. Rebekah fooled Isaac by cooking a couple of young *goats.* He thought that he was eating venison (Genesis 27:1–10).

3. Jacob and his sons brought their *cattle* with them to Egypt (Genesis 46:6).

4. Joseph exchanged bread for *horses* during the seven-year famine in Egypt (Genesis 47:17).

5. *Badger* skins were used in the making of the tabernacle in the wilderness (Exodus 25:5).

6. *Bats* were classified as unclean and not to be eaten (Leviticus 11:13–19).

7. *Weasels* were also listed as being unclean (Leviticus 11:29).

8. The Lord told Moses that *mice* should not be eaten, because they are unclean (Leviticus 11:29).

9. The *hart* (*hind* being the female) was listed as a clean animal and therefore good to eat (Deuteronomy 12:15).

10. A *roebuck* or a *pygarg* could also be eaten (Deuteronomy 14:5).

11. The *wild ox* could be eaten (Deuteronomy 14:5).

12. The *chamois* was listed as one of the eatable clean animals (Deuteronomy 14:5).

13. *Hares* were listed as unclean and unfit for human consumption (Deuteronomy 14:7).

14. The *coney* was listed as an unclean animal (Deuteronomy 14:7).

15. Samson killed a young *lion* with his bare hands (Judges 14:5–6).

16. David was in charge of his father's *sheep* (1 Samuel 16:11–13).

17. David killed a *bear* and thus saved one of his *lambs* (1 Samuel 17:34–35).

18. Goliath said to David, "Am I a *dog*, that thou comest to me with staves?" (1 Samuel 17:43).

19. King David rode a *mule* (1 Kings 1:32–33).

20. Indirect reference is made in the Bible to *elephants*, since King Solomon had a throne made of ivory (1 Kings 10:18).

21. Elijah prophesied that the *dogs* would eat Jezebel by the wall of Jezreel (1 Kings 21:20–23), and this prophecy was fulfilled (2 Kings 9:30–37).

22. King Solomon's ships went to Tarshish and brought back *apes* (2 Chronicles 9:21).

23. Job had 3,000 *camels* (Job 1:3).

24. The Lord spoke to Job about *behemoth*, which eats grass like an ox (Job 40:15).

25. The *wild boar* is mentioned in Psalm 80:13.

26. Solomon said, "The little *foxes* spoil the vines: for our vines have tender grapes" (Song of Solomon 2:15).

27. *Moles* were mentioned by Isaiah (Isaiah 2:20).

28. Both *camels* and *dromedaries* (one-humped camels) were mentioned by Isaiah (Isaiah 60:6).

29. Jeremiah asked if it was possible for a *leopard* to change his spots (Jeremiah 13:23).

30. Jesus warned of *wolves* in *sheeps'* clothing (Matthew 7:15).

31. Jesus allowed a legion of demons to go into a herd of *swine* (Mark 5:1–13).

32. Jesus rode into Jerusalem on an *ass* (John 12:12–15).

## 180. *Birds of the Bible*

1. The following birds are listed as being unclean: *eagle, ossifrage, osprey, vulture, kite, raven, owl, nighthawk, cuckoo, hawk, little owl, cormorant, great owl, swan, pelican, gier eagle, stork, heron,* and *lapwing* (Leviticus 11:13–19).

2. God sent *quails* to feed the children of Israel during their exodus from Egypt (Exodus 16:13).

3. The *glede* is also listed as being an unclean fowl (Deuteronomy 14:13).

4. King Solomon imported *peacocks* (1 Kings 10:21–22).

5. The *sparrow* and the *swallow* are both mentioned in a psalm (Psalm 84:3).

6. Isaiah prophesied that the Lord would destroy Idumea and that the *cormorant, bittern, owl,* and the *raven* would live there (Isaiah 34:1–11).

7. King Hezekiah, in writing about his sickness, described his situation in part by writing, Like a *crane* or a *swallow*, so did I chatter: I did mourn as a *dove* (Isaiah 38:14).

8. Jeremiah likened his heritage unto a *speckled bird* (Jeremiah 12:9).

9. Thus saith the Lord, As the *partridge* sitteth on eggs and hatcheth them not; so he that getteth riches, and not by right, shall leave them in the midst of his days, and at his end shall be a fool (Jeremiah 17:11).

10. Jesus said, O Jerusalem, Jerusalem . . . how often would I have gathered thy children together, even as a *hen* gathereth her *chicks* under her wings, and ye would not! (Matthew 23:37).

11. Jesus accurately predicted that before the *cock* crowed, Peter would deny Him three times (Matthew 26:34).

12. Mary and Joseph made an offering of two *turtledoves* or two young *pigeons* when Jesus was circumcised (Luke 2:21–24).

### 181. Insects of the Bible

1. Two of the plagues that God brought upon Egypt were swarms of *flies* and an abundance of *lice* (Exodus 8:16–24).

2. God promised Israel that He would send *hornets* before them to drive out the Hivites and the Canaanites (Exodus 23:28).

3. The following insects are listed as being edible: *locusts*, *bald locusts*, *beetles*, and *grasshoppers* (Leviticus 11:22).

4. Moses told the children of Israel that the Amorites chased them as *bees* do (Deuteronomy 1:44).

5. Moses said that there were *scorpions* in the wilderness (Deuteronomy 8:15).

6. David compared himself to a *flea* when he was being chased by King Saul (1 Samuel 24:14).

7. Melting *snails* are mentioned in Psalm 58:8.

8. *Ants* are mentioned twice in Proverbs. King Solomon thought highly of them (Proverbs 6:6; 30:25).

9. The *horseleach* is mentioned in Proverbs 30:15.

10. Agur the son of Jakeh noted that *spiders* live in kings' palaces (Proverbs 30:28).

11. Isaiah had confidence that his enemies would wax old as a garment; the *moth* shall eat them up (Isaiah 50:9).

12. The prophet Joel spoke about *palmerworms*, *locusts*, *cankerworms*, and *caterpillars* (Joel 1:4).

13. Jesus accused the scribes and Pharisees of straining at a *gnat* and swallowing a camel (Matthew 23:23–24).

14. Herod didn't give God the glory for his fine oration; therefore, he was eaten of *worms*, and gave up the ghost (Acts 12:20–23).

### 182. Reptiles and Amphibians of the Bible

1. The term *serpent* covers a multitude of reptiles and is sometimes used in referring to Satan (Genesis 3:1).

2. God brought a plague of *frogs* upon Egypt (Exodus 8:2–15).

3. The *tortoise*, *chameleon*, and the *lizard* are listed as being unclean (Leviticus 11:29–30).

4. Moses sang of the cruel venom of *asps* (Deuteronomy 32:33).

5. The *leviathan* mentioned in Job is actually the *crocodile* (Job 41:1).

6. The wicked are likened unto the deaf *adder* (Psalm 58:4).

7. The *cockatrice* is thought to be the great yellow viper, which is poisonous (Jeremiah 8:17).

8. Paul was bitten by a *viper* but was unharmed (Acts 28:3–5).

# 17
## NAMES

This section includes all names of the men and women in the Bible, the names of all the firstborn in the Bible, and thirty-nine names given to Jesus.

Spelling variations within the King James Version are treated as separate entries. Spelling variations because of translations from the Greek in the New Testament concerning Old Testament characters may or may not be included.

In the two lists dealing with all the names of Bible characters, the meaning of each name, when known, is given. For the firstborn, the name of the firstborn's father is given, except in a few cases where the firstborn's mother is given.

Being the firstborn was very important to these Bible characters—his/her share of the father's estate was a double portion.

### 183. The Names of the Men in the Bible

Aaron—*enlightened.*
Abagtha—*happy.*
Abda—*worshiper.*
Abdeel—*servant of God.*
Abdi—*servant of Jehovah.*
Abdiel—*servant of God.*
Abdon—*cloud of judgment.*
Abednego—*servant of light.*

Abel—*meadow.*
Abia—*Jehovah is Father.*
Abiah—*Jehovah is Father.*
Abialbon—*father of strength.*
Abiasaph—*remover of reproach.*
Abiathar—*excellent father.*
Abida—*father of knowledge.*
Abidah—*father of knowledge.*

Abidan—*the father judges.*
Abiel—*father of strength.*
Abiezer—*father of help.*
Abihail—*father of might.*
Abihu—*he is my father.*
Abihud—*father of majesty.*
Abijah—*Jehovah is my Father.*
Abijam—*father of light.*
Abimael—*my Father is God.*
Abimelech—*father of the king.*
Abinadab—*father of liberality.*
Abinoam—*father of beauty.*
Abiram—*father is the exalted one.*
Abishai—*possessor of all that is desirable.*
Abishalom—*father of peace.*
Abishua—*father of safety.*
Abishur—*father of oxen.*
Abitub—*father of goodness.*
Abiud—*father of honor.*
Abner—*father of light.*
Abraham—*the father of a multitude.*
Abram—*father of height.*
Absalom—*father of peace.*
Achaicus—*belonging to Achaia.*
Achan—*trouble.*
Achar—*trouble.*
Achaz—*Jehovah sustains.*
Achbor—*a mouse.*
Achim—*Jehovah will establish.*
Achish—*serpent charmer.*
Adaiah—*Jehovah hath adorned.*
Adalia—*the honor of Ized.*
Adam—*taken out of the red earth.*
Adar—*fire God.*
Adbeel—*languishing for God.*

Addar—*height.*
Addi—*my witness.*
Ader—*a flock.*
Adiel—*ornament of God.*
Adin—*delicate.*
Adina—*ornament.*
Adino—*delicate.*
Adlai—*weary.*
Admatha—*God-given.*
Adna—*pleasure.*
Adnah—*pleasure.*
Adonibezek—*Lord of lightning.*
Adonijah—*Jehovah is Lord.*
Adonikam—*my Lord has raised me.*
Adoniram—*my Lord is high.*
Adonizedek—*Lord of justice.*
Adoram—*strength.*
Adrammelech—*Adar is king.*
Adriel—*flock of God.*
Aeneas—*praise.*
Agabus—*a locust.*
Agag—*warlike.*
Agee—*fugitive.*
Agrippa—*one who at birth causes pain.*
Agur—*gatherer.*
Ahab—*father's brother.*
Aharah—*a smiling brother.*
Aharhel—*brother of Rachel.*
Ahasai—*clearsighted.*
Ahasbai—*shining.*
Ahasuerus—*mighty man.*
Ahaz—*Jehovah sustains.*
Ahaziah—*Jehovah possesses.*
Ahban—*brother of intelligence.*
Aher—*another.*

Ahi—*Jehovah's brother.*
Ahiah—*Jehovah's brother.*
Ahiam—*a mother's brother.*
Ahian—*brotherly.*
Ahiezer—*brother of help.*
Ahihud—*brother of mystery.*
Ahijah—*a brother in Jehovah.*
Ahikam—*my brother has risen.*
Ahilud—*a brother of one born.*
Ahimaaz—*a rascal.*
Ahiman—*brother of man.*
Ahimelech—*brother of the king.*
Ahimoth—*brother of death.*
Ahinadab—*brother of liberality.*
Ahio—*his brother.*
Ahira—*brother of evil.*
Ahiram—*exalted brother.*
Ahisamach—*brother of support.*
Ahishahar—*brother of the dawn.*
Ahishar—*brother of song.*
Ahithophel—*brother of folly.*
Ahitub—*brother of benevolence.*
Ahlai—*Jehovah is staying.*
Ahoah—*a brother's need.*
Aholah—*a tent.*
Aholiab—*a tent.*
Aholibah—*a tent.*
Aholibamah—*a tent.*
Ahumai—*brother of water.*
Ahuzam—*possession.*
Ahuzzath—*holding fast.*
Aiah—*a vulture.*
Ajah—*bird of prey.*
Akan—*acute.*
Akkub—*cunning.*
Alameth—*youthful vigor.*
Alemeth—*covering.*

Alexander—*defender.*
Aliah—*sublimity.*
Alian—*sublime.*
Allon—*an oak.*
Almodad—*the agitator.*
Alphaeus—*transient.*
Alvah—*high.*
Alvan—*sublime.*
Amal—*sorrow.*
Amalek—*dweller in the vale.*
Amariah—*Jehovah has promised.*
Amasa—*burden-bearer.*
Amasai—*burdensome.*
Amashai—*carrying spoil.*
Amasiah—*Jehovah is strong.*
Amaziah—*Jehovah has strength.*
Ami—*the beginning.*
Aminadab—*the kinsman is
  generous.*
Amittai—*truthful.*
Ammiel—*kinsman of God.*
Ammihud—*my people are
  honorable.*
Amminadab—*my kinsman is
  generous.*
Amminadib—*my people are
  princely.*
Ammishaddai—*the Almighty is
  an ally.*
Ammizabad—*the kinsman has
  endowed.*
Ammon—*pertaining to the nation.*
Amnon—*tutelage.*
Amok—*deep.*
Amon—*security.*
Amos—*one with a burden.*
Amoz—*brass.*

Amplias—*enlarged.*
Amram—*inexperience.*
Amraphel—*powerful people.*
Amzi—*robust.*
Anah—*answering.*
Anaiah—*Jehovah has answered.*
Anak—*giant.*
Anan—*he covers.*
Anani—*covered with God.*
Ananiah—*Jehovah is a protector.*
Ananias—*Jehovah is gracious.*
Anath—*answer.*
Anathoth—*answered prayers.*
Andrew—*manliness.*
Andronicus—*conqueror.*
Aner—*waterfall.*
Aniam—*sighing of the people.*
Annas—*grace of Jehovah.*
Antipas—*likeness of his father.*
Antothijah—*Jehovah's answer.*
Anub—*strong.*
Apelles—*I exclude.*
Aphiah—*striving.*
Aphses—*the dispersed.*
Apollos—*youthful god of music.*
Appaim—*presence.*
Aquila—*eagle.*
Ara—*strong.*
Arad—*fugitive.*
Arah—*wayfarer.*
Aram—*exalted.*
Aran—*firmness.*
Araunah—*Jehovah is firm.*
Arba—*the croucher.*
Archelaus—*people's chief.*
Archippus—*master of the horse.*
Ard—*descent.*

Ardon—*descendant.*
Areli—*heroic.*
Aretas—*pleasing.*
Argob—*strong.*
Aridai—*the bull.*
Aridatha—*great birth.*
Arieh—*lion of Jehovah.*
Ariel—*lion of God.*
Arioch—*lion-like.*
Arisai—*meaning unknown.*
Aristarchus—*the best ruler.*
Aristobulus—*the best counselor.*
Armoni—*pertaining to the palace.*
Arnan—*agile.*
Arod—*posterity.*
Arphaxad—*one that releases.*
Artaxerxes—*possessor of an exalted kingdom.*
Artemas—*whole.*
Arza—*delight.*
Asa—*physician.*
Asahel—*God has made.*
Asahiah—*Jehovah has made.*
Asaiah—*Jehovah is a doer.*
Asaph—*he that removed reproach.*
Asareel—*God is joined.*
Asarelah—*upright toward God.*
Ashbea—*man of Baal.*
Ashbel—*man of Baal.*
Ashchenaz—*a fire that spreads.*
Asher—*happiness.*
Ashkenaz—*a fire that spreads.*
Ashpenaz—*horse's nose.*
Ashriel—*God is joined.*
Ashur—*freeman.*
Ashvath—*wrought.*
Asiel—*God has made.*

Asnah—*a dweller in the thornbush.*
Asnapper—*Asnap the great.*
Aspatha—*horse-given.*
Asriel—*God is joined.*
Asshur—*level plain.*
Asshurim—*mighty ones.*
Assir—*captive.*
Assur—*level plain.*
Asyncritus—*incomparable.*
Ater—*bound.*
Athaiah—*Jehovah is helper.*
Athaliah—*has afflicted.*
Athlai—*Jehovah is strong.*
Attai—*seasonable.*
Augustus—*sacred.*
Azaliah—*Jehovah is noble.*
Azaniah—*Jehovah is a hearer.*
Azarael—*God is a helper.*
Azareel—*God is a helper.*
Azariah—*Jehovah is a keeper.*
Azaz—*strong.*
Azaziah—*Jehovah is strong.*
Azbuk—*pardon.*
Azel—*noble.*
Azgad—*worship.*
Aziel—*God is might.*
Aziza—*strong.*
Azmaveth—*counsel.*
Azor—*helper.*
Azriel—*help of God.*
Azrikam—*my help has risen.*
Azur—*helper.*
Azzan—*sharp.*
Azzur—*helper.*

Baal—*controller.*

Baal-hanan—*the Lord is gracious.*
Baalis—*Lord of joy.*
Baana—*son of grief.*
Baanah—*son of grief.*
Baaseiah—*Jehovah is bold.*
Baasha—*boldness.*
Bakbakkar—*diligent searcher.*
Bakbuk—*a flagon.*
Bakbukiah—*wasted by Jehovah.*
Balaam—*Lord of the people.*
Balac—*waster.*
Baladan—*having power.*
Balak—*waster.*
Bani—*built.*
Barabbas—*son of return.*
Barachel—*God has blessed.*
Barak—*thunder.*
Bariah—*fugitive.*
Bar-jesus—*son of Joshua.*
Barkos—*partly-colored.*
Barnabas—*son of prophecy.*
Barsabas—*a son that suspends the water.*
Barsabbas—*a son that suspends the water.*
Bartholomew—*son of Tolmai.*
Bartimaeus—*honorable.*
Baruch—*blessed.*
Barzillai—*made of iron.*
Bavai—*wishes.*
Bazlith—*asking.*
Bazluth—*asking.*
Bealiah—*Jehovah is Lord.*
Bebai—*fatherly.*
Becher—*firstborn.*
Bechorath—*first birth.*
Bedad—*separation.*

Bedan—*son of judgment.*
Bedeiah—*servant of Jehovah.*
Beeliada—*the Lord knows.*
Beera—*a well.*
Beerah—*expounder.*
Beeri—*man of the well.*
Bela—*devouring.*
Belah—*devouring.*
Belshazzar—*the Lord's leader.*
Belteshazzar—*the Lord's leader.*
Benaiah—*Jehovah has built.*
Ben-Ammi—*son of my people.*
Ben-Hadad—*son of the God Hadah.*
Ben-Hail—*son of valiant.*
Ben-Hanan—*son of kind one.*
Beninu—*our son.*
Benjamin—*son of the right hand.*
Beno—*his son.*
Benoni—*son of my sorrow.*
Ben-Zoheth—*strong.*
Beor—*shepherd.*
Bera—*gift.*
Berachah—*blessing.*
Berachiah—*Jehovah is blessing.*
Beraiah—*Jehovah has created.*
Berechiah—*Jehovah is blessing.*
Bered—*seed.*
Beri—*expounder.*
Beriah—*in evil.*
Berodachbaladan—*bold.*
Besai—*treading down.*
Besodeiah—*familiar with Jehovah.*
Bethgader—*walled place.*
Bethlehem—*house of bread.*
Beth-rapha—*place of fear.*
Bethuel—*dweller in God.*

Bethzur—*place of rock.*
Bezai—*high.*
Bezaleel—*under God's shadow.*
Bezer—*strong.*
Bichri—*firstfruits.*
Bidkar—*sharp pain.*
Bigtha—*given by fortune.*
Bigthan—*gift of fortune.*
Bigthana—*gift of fortune.*
Bigvai—*happy.*
Bildad—*son of contention.*
Bilgah—*cheerful.*
Bilgai—*firstborn.*
Bilhan—*tender.*
Bilshan—*searcher.*
Bimhal—*son of circumcision.*
Binea—*wanderer.*
Binnui—*familyship.*
Birsha—*thick.*
Birzavith—*wounds.*
Bishlam—*peaceful.*
Biztha—*eunuch.*
Blastus—*a bud.*
Boaz—*strength.*
Bocheru—*youth.*
Booz—*Greek for Boaz.*
Bukki—*devastation sent by Jehovah.*
Bukkiah—*mouth of Jehovah.*
Bunah—*understanding.*
Bunni—*my understanding.*
Buz—*contempt.*
Buzi—*my contempt.*

Caesar—*one cut out.*
Caiaphas—*a searcher.*
Cain—*fabrication.*

Cainan—*acquisition*.
Calcol—*who nourishes*.
Caleb—*bold*.
Canaan—*lowland*.
Carcas—*severe*.
Careah—*bald head*.
Carmi—*noble*.
Carpus—*fruit*.
Carshena—*spoiler*.
Cephas—*rock*.
Chalcol—*who nourishes*.
Chedorlaomer—*sheaf band*.
Chelluh—*union*.
Chelub—*wicker basket*.
Chelubai—*binding together of the Lord*.
Chenaanah—*subduer*.
Chenani—*creator*.
Chenaniah—*Jehovah is firm*.
Cheran—*union*.
Chesed—*a devil*.
Chileab—*perfection of the father*.
Chilion—*wasting away*.
Chimham—*longing*.
Chislon—*trust*.
Chushanrishathaim—*blackness of iniquities*.
Chuza—*modest*.
Cis—*snaring*.
Claudius—*lame*.
Clement—*kind*.
Cleopas—*the whole glory*.
Cleophas—*the whole glory*.
Colhozeh—*a seer*.
Conaniah—*Jehovah has established*.
Coniah—*God-appointed*.
Cononiah—*Jehovah has established*.
Core—*hard*.
Cornelius—*the sunbeam*.
Cosam—*most abundant*.
Coz—*nimble*.
Crescens—*increase*.
Crispus—*curled*.
Cush—*black*.
Cushi—*black*.
Cyrenius—*one who governs*.
Cyrus—*an heir*.

Dalaiah—*Jehovah is the deliverer*.
Dalphon—*dropping*.
Dan—*he that judges*.
Daniel—*God is my judge*.
Dara—*bearer*.
Darda—*a pearl of wisdom*.
Darius—*he that informs himself*.
Darkon—*bearer*.
Dathan—*belonging to law*.
David—*beloved*.
Debir—*speaker*.
Dedan—*low*.
Dekar—*lance bearer*.
Delaiah—*Jehovah is the deliverer*.
Demas—*ruler of people*.
Demetrius—*belonging to Demeter*.
Deuel—*invocation of God*.
Diblaim—*double embrace*.
Dibri—*promise of the Lord*.
Didymus—*a twin*.
Diklah—*palm grove*.
Dionysius—*divinely touched*.
Diothephes—*nourished by Jupiter*.
Dishan—*leaping*.

Dishon—*leaping.*
Dodai—*beloved of Jehovah.*
Dodanim—*a leader.*
Dodavah—*Jehovah is loving.*
Dodo—*loving.*
Doeg—*timid.*
Dumah—*silence.*

Ebal—*bare.*
Ebed—*slave.*
Ebedmelech—*slave of the king.*
Eber—*a shoot.*
Ebiasaph—*the father of gathering.*
Eden—*delight.*
Eder—*a flock.*
Edom—*red earth.*
Eglon—*circle.*
Ehi—*unity.*
Ehud—*strong.*
Eker—*one transplanted.*
Eladah—*God has adorned.*
Elah—*like a tree.*
Elam—*youth.*
Elasah—*God has made.*
Eldaah—*whom God called.*
Eldad—*God has loved.*
Elead—*God is witness.*
Eleasah—*God has made.*
Eleazar—*God is helper.*
Elhanan—*mercy of God.*
Eli—*my God.*
Eliab—*God is a father.*
Eliada—*God is knowing.*
Eliadah—*God is knowing.*
Eliah—*God is Jehovah.*
Eliahba—*God hides.*
Eliakim—*God establishes.*

Eliam—*God is one of the family.*
Elias—*Greek form of Elijah.*
Eliasaph—*God has added.*
Eliashib—*God has restored.*
Eliathah—*God has come.*
Elidad—*God is a friend.*
Eliel—*God is God.*
Elienai—*my eyes are unto God.*
Eliezer—*God is my help.*
Elihoenai—*my eyes are to
    Jehovah.*
Elihoreph—*God is a reward.*
Elihu—*he is God himself.*
Elijah—*God himself.*
Elika—*God has spewed out.*
Elimelech—*God is King.*
Elioenai—*my eyes are to Jehovah.*
Eliphal—*God has judged.*
Eliphalet—*God is escape.*
Eliphaz—*God is fine gold.*
Elipheleh—*Jehovah is
    distinguished.*
Eliphelet—*God is escape.*
Eliseus—*Greek form of Elisha.*
Elisha—*God is Savior.*
Elishah—*God is Savior.*
Elishama—*God has heard.*
Elishaphat—*God is judge.*
Elishua—*God is salvation.*
Eliud—*God is my praise.*
Elizaphan—*God is protector.*
Elizur—*God is a rock.*
Elkanah—*God is jealous.*
Elmodam—*the God of measure.*
Elnaam—*God is pleasant.*
Elnathan—*God has given.*
Elon—*strong.*

Elpaal—*God is a reward.*
Elpalet—*God is escape.*
Eluzai—*God is my strength.*
Elymas—*a sorcerer.*
Elzabad—*God has endowed.*
Elzaphan—*God has protected.*
Emmor—*an ass.*
Enan—*having eyes.*
Enoch—*teacher.*
Enos—*man is his frailty.*
Enosh—*man is his frailty.*
Epaenetus—*worthy of praise.*
Epaphras—*charming.*
Epaphroditus—*handsome.*
Ephah—*darkness.*
Ephai—*fatigued.*
Epher—*mule.*
Ephlal—*judging.*
Ephod—*covering.*
Ephraim—*doubly fruitful.*
Ephron—*strong.*
Er—*on the watch.*
Eran—*watchful.*
Erastus—*beloved.*
Eri—*my watcher.*
Esaias—*Greek for Isaiah.*
Esarhaddon—*victorious.*
Esau—*hairy.*
Eshbaal—*a man of Baal.*
Eshban—*man of understanding.*
Eshcol—*cluster of grapes.*
Eshek—*strife.*
Eshtemoa—*obedience.*
Eshtemoh—*obedience.*
Eshton—*rest.*
Esli—*God at my side.*
Esrom—*enclosure.*

Etam—*wild beasts' lair.*
Ethan—*perplexity.*
Ethbaal—*with him is Baal.*
Ethnan—*gift.*
Ethni—*my gift.*
Eubulus—*well-advised.*
Eutychus—*happy.*
Evi—*desire.*
Evilmerodach—*man of the god Merodach.*
Ezar—*treasure.*
Ezbai—*beautiful.*
Ezbon—*splendor.*
Ezekias—*Greek for Hezekiah.*
Ezekiel—*God is strong.*
Ezer—*treasure.*
Ezra—*help.*
Ezri—*God is a help.*

Felix—*prosperous.*
Festus—*prosperous.*
Fortunatus—*prosperous.*

Gaal—*rejection.*
Gabbai—*ingatherer.*
Gad—*good fortune.*
Gaddi—*belonging to fortune.*
Gaddiel—*God is fortune bringer.*
Gadi—*fortunate.*
Gaham—*blackness.*
Gahar—*hiding place.*
Gaius—*I am glad.*
Galal—*rolling of one's day upon the Lord.*
Gallio—*he that sucks.*
Gamaliel—*reward of God.*
Gamul—*matured.*

Gareb—*rough.*
Gashmu—*corpulent.*
Gatam—*puny.*
Gazez—*shearer.*
Gazzam—*devourer.*
Geber—*a hero.*
Gedaliah—*Jehovah is great.*
Gedeon—*Greek for Gideon.*
Gedor—*a fortress.*
Gehazi—*valley of vision.*
Gemalli—*camel owner.*
Gemariah—*Jehovah hath fulfilled.*
Genubath—*theft.*
Gera—*enmity.*
Gershom—*a stranger there.*
Gershon—*a stranger there.*
Gesham—*firm.*
Geshem—*rain.*
Gether—*vale of trial.*
Geuel—*salvation of God.*
Gibbar—*mighty man.*
Gibea—*highlander.*
Giddalti—*I magnify God.*
Giddel—*he has magnified.*
Gideon—*great warrior.*
Gideoni—*he that bruises.*
Gilalai—*weighty.*
Gilead—*mass of testimony.*
Ginath—*protection.*
Ginnetho—*great protection.*
Ginnethon—*great protection.*
Gispa—*attentive.*
Gog—*a mountain.*
Goliath—*the exile.*
Gomer—*completion.*
Guni—*protected.*
Haahashtari—*the courier.*

Habaiah—*Jehovah has hidden.*
Habakkuk—*love's embrace.*
Habaziniah—*God's light.*
Hachaliah—*Jehovah is hidden.*
Hachmoni—*the wise.*
Hadad—*mighty.*
Hadadezer—*mighty is the help.*
Hadarezer—*mighty is the help.*
Hadlai—*frail.*
Hadoram—*Hadar is high.*
Hagab—*a locust.*
Hagaba—*a locust.*
Hagabah—*a locust.*
Haggai—*festive.*
Haggeri—*wanderer.*
Haggi—*festive.*
Haggiah—*feast of Jehovah.*
Hakkatan—*the younger.*
Hakkoz—*the nimble.*
Hakupha—*curved.*
Hallohesh—*the enchanter.*
Halohesh—*the enchanter.*
Ham—*dark, colored, swarthy.*
Haman—*well disposed.*
Hammath—*warmth.*
Hammedatha—*he that troubleth the law.*
Hammelech—*the king.*
Hammuel—*warmth of God.*
Hamor—*an ass.*
Hamuel—*warmth of God.*
Hamul—*pity.*
Hanameel—*grace of God.*
Hanamel—*grace of God.*
Hanan—*merciful.*
Hananeel—*the mercy of God.*
Hanani—*he has shown me mercy.*

Hananiah—*Jehovah is gracious.*
Haniel—*grace of God.*
Hanniel—*grace of God.*
Hanoch—*dedicated.*
Hanun—*gracious.*
Haran—*enlightened.*
Harbona—*ass driver.*
Harbonah—*ass driver.*
Hareph—*born early.*
Harhaiah—*Jehovah is protecting.*
Harhas—*splendor.*
Harhur—*distinction.*
Harim—*consecrated.*
Hariph—*autumn rain.*
Harnepher—*panting.*
Haroeh—*the seer.*
Harum—*exalted.*
Harumaph—*flat nose.*
Haruz—*industrious.*
Hasadiah—*Jehovah is kind.*
Hasenuah—*the violated.*
Hashabiah—*Jehovah is associated.*
Hashabnah—*Jehovah is a friend.*
Hashabniah—*Jehovah is a friend.*
Hashbadana—*reason.*
Hashem—*astonished.*
Hashub—*thoughtful.*
Hashubah—*esteemed.*
Hashum—*wealthy.*
Hashupha—*nakedness.*
Hasrah—*splendor.*
Hassenaah—*the thorn hedge.*
Hasshub—*thoughtful.*
Hasupha—*nakedness.*
Hatach—*a gift.*
Hathath—*bruised.*
Hatipha—*captive.*

Hatita—*exploration.*
Hattil—*decaying.*
Hattush—*contender.*
Havilah—*circle.*
Hazael—*God sees.*
Hazaiah—*Jehovah is seeing.*
Hazarmaveth—*court of death.*
Haziel—*vision of God.*
Hazo—*vision.*
Heber—*fellowship.*
Hebron—*company.*
Hegai—*venerable.*
Hege—*venerable.*
Heldai—*enduring.*
Heleb—*endurance.*
Heled—*endurance.*
Helek—*smoothness.*
Helem—*manly vigor.*
Helez—*alertness.*
Heli—*ascending.*
Helkai—*Jehovah is a portion.*
Helon—*strong.*
Hemam—*faithful.*
Heman—*faithful.*
Hemath—*warmth.*
Hemdan—*desirable.*
Hen—*grace.*
Henadad—*favor.*
Henoch—*dedicated.*
Hepher—*a well.*
Heresh—*silence.*
Hermas—*interpreter.*
Hermes—*gain.*
Hermogenes—*begotten.*
Herod—*son of the hero.*
Herodion—*conqueror of heroes.*
Hesed—*kindness.*

Heth—*terrible.*
Hezeki—*Jehovah is strength.*
Hezekiah—*Jehovah is strength.*
Hezion—*vision.*
Hezir—*returning home.*
Hezrai—*beautiful.*
Hezro—*enclosed.*
Hezron—*dart of joy.*
Hiddai—*mighty.*
Hiel—*the life of God.*
Hilkiah—*Jehovah is protection.*
Hillel—*praised greatly.*
Hinnom—*gratis.*
Hirah—*nobility.*
Hiram—*consecration.*
Hizkiah—*Jehovah is strong.*
Hizkijah—*Jehovah is strong.*
Hobab—*lover.*
Hod—*majesty.*
Hodaiah—*honorer of Jehovah.*
Hodaviah—*Jehovah is his praise.*
Hodevah—*Jehovah is honor.*
Hodiah—*splendor of Jehovah.*
Hodijah—*splendor of Jehovah.*
Hoham—*Jehovah protects the
    multitude.*
Homam—*destroyer.*
Hophni—*strong.*
Horam—*elevated.*
Hori—*free.*
Hosah—*refuge.*
Hosea—*salvation.*
Hoshaiah—*God has saved.*
Hoshama—*Jehovah has heard.*
Hoshea—*salvation.*
Hotham—*signet ring.*
Hothan—*signet ring.*

Hothir—*abundance.*
Hul—*circle.*
Hupham—*covering.*
Huppah—*a covering.*
Huppim—*coverings.*
Hur—*noble.*
Hurai—*a linen weaver.*
Huram—*ingenious.*
Huri—*linen weaver.*
Hushah—*passion.*
Hushai—*quick.*
Husham—*passion.*
Hushim—*hasting.*
Huz—*firm.*
Hymenaeus—*the god of marriage.*

Ibhar—*God chooses.*
Ibneiah—*Jehovah builds.*
Ibnijah—*Jehovah is builder.*
Ibri—*passer over.*
Ibzan—*active.*
Ichabod—*the glory is not.*
Idbash—*honey sweet.*
Iddo—*affectionate.*
Igal—*he will vindicate.*
Igdaliah—*great is Jehovah.*
Igeal—*deliverer.*
Ikkesh—*subtle.*
Ilai—*supreme.*
Imla—*fulfilling.*
Imlah—*fulfilling.*
Immer—*prominent.*
Imna—*God restrains.*
Imnah—*prosperity.*
Imrah—*stubborn.*
Imri—*eloquent.*
Iphedeiah—*redemption of the*

*Lord.*
Ir—*watcher.*
Ira—*watchful.*
Irad—*wild ass.*
Iram—*watchful.*
Iri—*Jehovah watches.*
Irijah—*God sees.*
Irnahash—*serpent.*
Iru—*watch.*
Isaac—*laughing one.*
Isaachar—*reward.*
Isaiah—*salvation is of the Lord.*
Ishbah—*appeaser.*
Ishbak—*free.*
Ishbibenob—*predictor.*
Ishbosheth—*man of shame.*
Ishi—*saving.*
Ishiah—*Jehovah forgives.*
Ishijah—*Jehovah is.*
Ishma—*elevated.*
Ishmael—*God hears.*
Ishmaiah—*Jehovah hears.*
Ishmerai—*God keeps.*
Ishod—*man of honor.*
Ishpan—*firm.*
Ishuah—*equal.*
Ishuai—*equality.*
Ishui—*equality.*
Ismachiah—*Jehovah supports.*
Ismaiah—*Jehovah hears.*
Ispah—*he will be eminent.*
Israel—*ruling with God.*
Isshiah—*Jehovah forgives.*
Isuah—*self-satisfied.*
Isui—*equality.*
Ithai—*existing.*
Ithamar—*palm tree.*

Ithiel—*God is with me.*
Ithmah—*purity.*
Ithra—*excellence.*
Ithran—*abundance.*
Ithream—*remnant.*
Ittai—*plowman.*
Izehar—*bright one.*
Izhar—*olive oil.*
Izrahiah—*Jehovah arises.*
Izri—*creative.*

Jaakan—*intelligent.*
Jaakobah—*to Jacob.*
Jaala—*doe.*
Jaalah—*elevation.*
Jaalam—*he will be hid.*
Jaanai—*Jehovah answers.*
Jaareoregim—*foresters.*
Jaasau—*Jehovah makes.*
Jaasiel—*God is maker.*
Jaazaniah—*Jehovah hearkens.*
Jaaziah—*God determines.*
Jaaziel—*God is consoling.*
Jabal—*river.*
Jabesh—*dry place.*
Jabez—*maker of sorrow.*
Jabin—*God discerns.*
Jachan—*afflicting.*
Jachin—*founding.*
Jacob—*supplanter.*
Jada—*wise.*
Jadau—*favorite.*
Jaddua—*known.*
Jadon—*he that abides.*
Jahath—*revival.*
Jahaziah—*Jehovah reveals.*
Jahaziel—*God sees.*

Jahdai—*guide*.
Jahdiel—*God gladdens*.
Jahdo—*union*.
Jahleel—*God waits*.
Jahmai—*lusty*.
Jahzeel—*God distributes*.
Jahzerah—*Jehovah protects*.
Jahziel—*God distributes*.
Jair—*Jehovah arouses*.
Jairus—*he will enlighten*.
Jakan—*intelligent*.
Jakeh—*pious*.
Jakim—*he raises up*.
Jalon—*obstinate*.
Jambres—*opposer*.
James—*supplanter*.
Jamin—*prosperity's right hand*.
Jamlech—*Jehovah rules*.
Janna—*he will answer*.
Jannes—*full of pleasure*.
Japheth—*persuader*.
Japhia—*shining*.
Japhlet—*Jehovah causes to escape*.
Jarah—*honey*.
Jareb—*avenger*.
Jared—*descending*.
Jaresiah—*the bed of the Lord*.
Jarha—*adversary*.
Jarib—*striving*.
Jaroah—*new moon*.
Jashen—*sleeping*.
Jashobeam—*the people return to God*.
Jashub—*returning*.
Jashubilehem—*bread returns*.
Jason—*healing*.
Jathniel—*God gives gifts*.

Javan—*clay*.
Jaziz—*shining*.
Jeaterai—*steadfast*.
Jeberechiah—*Jehovah blesses*.
Jecamiah—*meaning unknown*.
Jechonias—*established of the Lord*.
Jeconiah—*preparation of the Lord*.
Jedaiah—*Jehovah knows*.
Jediael—*known of God*.
Jedidiah—*beloved of Jehovah*.
Jeduthun—*choir of praise*.
Jeezer—*help*.
Jehaleleel—*he praises God*.
Jehalelel—*he praises God*.
Jehdeiah—*Jehovah's union*.
Jehezekel—*God is strong*.
Jehiah—*God lives*.
Jehiel—*God lives*.
Jehieli—*he lives by mercy*.
Jehizkiah—*Jehovah strengthens*.
Jehoadah—*Jehovah unveils*.
Jehoahaz—*Jehovah upholds*.
Jehoash—*God supplies*.
Jehohanan—*Jehovah is gracious*.
Jehoiachin—*Jehovah establishes*.
Jehoiada—*knowledge of God*.
Jehoiakim—*Jehovah sets up*.
Jehoiarib—*Jehovah contends*.
Jehonadab—*Jehovah is liberal*.
Jehonathan—*Jehovah has given*.
Jehoram—*Jehovah is exalted*.
Jehoshaphat—*Jehovah is judge*.
Jehoshua—*Jehovah saves*.
Jehoshuah—*Jehovah is salvation*.
Jehozabad—*Jehovah has endowed*.
Jehozadak—*Jehovah is just*.
Jehu—*Jehovah is He*.

Jehubbah—*hidden.*
Jehucal—*Jehovah is able.*
Jehudi—*Jew.*
Jehush—*collector.*
Jeiel—*treasure of God.*
Jekameam—*he assembles the people.*
Jekamiah—*Jehovah gathers.*
Jekuthiel—*God is mighty.*
Jemuel—*God is light.*
Jephthae—*Greek for Jephthah.*
Jephthah—*he sets free.*
Jephunneh—*it will be prepared.*
Jerah—*moon.*
Jerahmeel—*God is merciful.*
Jered—*flowing.*
Jeremai—*Jehovah is high.*
Jeremiah—*exalted of God.*
Jeremias—*Jehovah is high.*
Jeremoth—*heights.*
Jeremy—*Greek for Jeremiah.*
Jeriah—*Jehovah founded.*
Jeribai—*contentious.*
Jeriel—*God's foundation.*
Jerijah—*Jehovah has founded.*
Jerimoth—*heights.*
Jeroboam—*enlarges.*
Jeroham—*loved.*
Jerubbaal—*let Baal defend his cause.*
Jerubbesheth—*idol contender.*
Jesaiah—*Jehovah is rich.*
Jeshaiah—*Jehovah is rich.*
Jesharelah—*upright toward God.*
Jeshebeab—*father's house.*
Jesher—*uprightness.*
Jeshishai—*Jehovah is ancient.*

Jeshohaiah—*humbled by Jehovah.*
Jeshua—*Jehovah is salvation.*
Jeshuah—*Jehovah is salvation.*
Jesiah—*Jehovah is.*
Jesimiel—*God sets up.*
Jesse—*Jehovah is.*
Jesui—*Jehovah is satisfied.*
Jesus—*Jehovah is salvation.*
Jether—*abundance.*
Jetheth—*subjection.*
Jethro—*excellence.*
Jetur—*defense.*
Jeuel—*God's treasure.*
Jeush—*he will gather together.*
Jeuz—*counselor.*
Jezaniah—*Jehovah determines.*
Jezer—*formation.*
Jeziah—*Jehovah unites.*
Jeziel—*assembly of God.*
Jezliah—*Jehovah unites.*
Jezoar—*tawny.*
Jezrahiah—*the Lord arises.*
Jezreel—*God sows.*
Jibsam—*sweet.*
Jidlaph—*distiller.*
Jimna—*prosperity.*
Jimnah—*prosperity.*
Joab—*Jehovah is a good Father.*
Joah—*Jehovah is a brother.*
Joahaz—*Jehovah helps.*
Joash—*Jehovah hastens to help.*
Joatham—*the Lord is upright.*
Job—*he that weeps.*
Jobab—*howling.*
Joed—*Jehovah is witness.*
Joel—*Jehovah is God.*
Joelah—*God is snatching.*

Joezer—*Jehovah is help.*
Jogli—*exiled.*
Joha—*Jehovah lives.*
Johanan—*Jehovah is gracious.*
John—*Jehovah has been gracious.*
Joiada—*has known.*
Joiakim—*establishes.*
Joiarib—*Jehovah depends.*
Jokim—*Jehovah sets up.*
Jokshan—*fowler.*
Joktan—*little.*
Jona—*a dove.*
Jonadab—*who acts as a prince.*
Jonah—*a dove.*
Jonan—*God has been gracious.*
Jonas—*a dove.*
Jonathan—*the Lord gave.*
Jorah—*rain of autumn.*
Joram—*Jehovah is high.*
Jorim—*he that exalts the Lord.*
Jorkoam—*spreading the people.*
Josabad—*Jehovah has bestowed.*
Josaphat—*the Lord judges.*
Jose—*aid.*
Josedech—*Jehovah is righteous.*
Joseph—*may God add.*
Joses—*he that pardons.*
Joshah—*uprightness.*
Joshaphat—*Jehovah judges.*
Joshaviah—*sits upright.*
Joshbekashah—*seat of hardness.*
Joshua—*Jehovah is salvation.*
Josiah—*the fire of the Lord.*
Josias—*Greek for Josiah.*
Josibiah—*Jehovah causes to dwell.*
Josiphiah—*Jehovah will increase.*
Jotham—*Jehovah is upright.*

Jozabad—*endowed.*
Jozachar—*Jehovah remembers.*
Jozadak—*Jehovah is great.*
Jubal—*a trumpet.*
Jucal—*able.*
Juda—*praise of the Lord.*
Judah—*praise of the Lord.*
Judas—*praise of the Lord.*
Jude—*praise of the Lord.*
Julius—*curly-headed.*
Jushab-hesed—*lovingkindness is returned.*
Justus—*just.*

Kadmiel—*God is of old.*
Kallai—*swift.*
Kareah—*bald.*
Kedar—*powerful.*
Kedemah—*eastern.*
Keilah—*enclosed.*
Kelaiah—*Jehovah is light.*
Kelita—*poverty.*
Kemuel—*congregation of God.*
Kenan—*begotten.*
Kenaz—*hunting.*
Keros—*the reed of a weaver's beam.*
Kirjath-jearim—*city of forests.*
Kish—*straw.*
Kishi—*bow of Jehovah.*
Kittim—*they that bruise.*
Kohath—*assembly.*
Kolaiah—*the voice of Jehovah.*
Korah—*baldness.*
Kore—*baldness.*
Koz—*the thorn.*
Kushaiah—*bow of Jehovah.*

Laadah—*festival.*
Laadan—*festive-born.*
Laban—*glorious.*
Lael—*devoted to God.*
Lahad—*oppressed.*
Lahmi—*a warrior.*
Laish—*a lion.*
Lamech—*overthrower.*
Lapidoth—*enlightened.*
Lazarus—*God has helped.*
Lebana—*poetic designation for the moon.*
Lebanah—*poetic designation for the moon.*
Lebbaeus—*man of heart.*
Lecah—*addition.*
Lehabim—*flame.*
Lemuel—*devoted to God.*
Letushim—*oppressed.*
Leummim—*nations.*
Levi—*joined.*
Libni—*distinguished.*
Likhi—*Jehovah is doctrine.*
Linus—*nets.*
Lo-ammi—*not my people.*
Lot—*concealed.*
Lotan—*covering.*
Lucas—*light-giving.*
Lucifer—*the shining one.*
Lucius—*of the light.*
Lud—*bending.*
Ludim—*bending.*
Luke—*light-giving.*
Lysanias—*drives away sorrow.*
Lysias—*he who has the power to set free.*

Maacah—*oppression.*
Maachah—*oppression.*
Maadai—*wavering.*
Maadiah—*ornament of Jehovah.*
Maai—*Jehovah is compassionable.*
Maaseiah—*work of Jehovah.*
Maasiai—*work of Jehovah.*
Maath—*wiping away.*
Maaz—*anger.*
Maaziah—*consolation.*
Machbanai—*clothed with a cloak.*
Machi—*decrease.*
Machir—*sold.*
Machnadebai—*gift of the noble one.*
Madai—*middle.*
Madmannah—*heap.*
Magbish—*cluster of stars.*
Magdiel—*honor of God.*
Magog—*expansion.*
Magormissabib—*fear.*
Magpiash—*cluster of stars.*
Mahalah—*disease.*
Mahalaleel—*the praise of God.*
Mahali—*sick.*
Maharai—*impetuous.*
Mahath—*instrument.*
Mahazioth—*vision of significance.*
Mahershalalhashbaz—*rush on the prey.*
Mahlah—*disease.*
Mahli—*sick.*
Mahlon—*sickly.*
Mahol—*joy.*
Malachi—*messenger of Jehovah.*
Malcham—*rule.*

Malchiah—*Jehovah is King.*
Malchiel—*God is King.*
Malchijah—*Jehovah is King.*
Malchiram—*my King is exalted.*
Malchi-shua—*king of help.*
Malchus—*king.*
Maleleel—*praise of God.*
Mallothi—*Jehovah is speaking.*
Malluch—*counselor.*
Mamre—*vigor.*
Manaen—*comforter.*
Manahath—*resting place.*
Manasseh—*causing forgetfulness.*
Manasses—*causing forgetfulness.*
Manoah—*rest.*
Maoch—*poor.*
Maon—*habitation.*
Marcus—*polite.*
Mareshah—*at the head.*
Mark—*polite.*
Marsena—*worthy.*
Mash—*drawn out.*
Massa—*burden.*
Mathusala—*when he is dead, it shall be sent.*
Matri—*Jehovah is watching.*
Mattan—*gift.*
Mattaniah—*gift of Jehovah.*
Mattatha—*gift.*
Mattathah—*gift of Jehovah*
Mattathias—*gift of Jehovah.*
Mattenai—*gift of Jehovah.*
Matthan—*a gift.*
Matthat—*gift.*
Matthew—*gift of Jehovah.*
Matthias—*gift of God.*
Mattithiah—*gift of Jehovah.*

Mebunnai—*built up.*
Medad—*love.*
Medan—*judgment.*
Mehetabeel—*God blesses.*
Mehetabel—*God blesses.*
Mehida—*famous.*
Mehir—*dexterity.*
Mehujael—*God is combating.*
Mehuman—*faithful.*
Mehunim—*place of habitation.*
Melatiah—*Jehovah has set free.*
Melchi—*Jehovah is my King.*
Melchiah—*Jehovah is King.*
Melchisedec—*King of righteousness.*
Melchishua—*King of help.*
Melchizedek—*King of righteousness.*
Melea—*fullness.*
Melech—*a king.*
Melicu—*counselor.*
Melzar—*the overseer.*
Memucan—*impoverished.*
Menahem—*comforter.*
Menan—*consoling.*
Meonothai—*Jehovah's habitations.*
Mephibosheth—*destroying shame.*
Meraiah—*stubbornness.*
Meraioth—*rebellion.*
Merari—*unhappy.*
Mered—*rebellious.*
Meremoth—*strong.*
Meres—*worthy.*
Meribbaal—*contender against Baal.*
Merodachbaladan—*the son of*

death.

Mesech—*drawing out.*

Mesha—*retreat.*

Meshach—*agile.*

Meshech—*drawing out.*

Meshelemiah—*Jehovah recompenses.*

Meshezabeel—*God sets free.*

Meshillemith—*recompenses.*

Meshillemoth—*recompenses.*

Meshobab—*delivered.*

Meshullam—*associate.*

Methusael—*man of God.*

Methuselah—*when he is dead, it shall be sent.*

Meunim—*place of habitation.*

Mezahab—*offspring.*

Miamin—*fortunate.*

Mibhar—*youth.*

Mibsam—*sweet odor.*

Mibzar—*a stronghold.*

Micaiah—*who is like Jehovah.*

Micha—*who is like Jehovah.*

Michael—*who is like God.*

Michah—*who is like Jehovah.*

Michaiah—*who is like Jehovah.*

Michri—*Jehovah possesses.*

Midian—*strife.*

Mijamin—*fortunate.*

Mikloth—*sticks.*

Mikneiah—*Jehovah is jealous.*

Milalai—*eloquent.*

Miniamin—*fortunate.*

Mirma—*deceit.*

Mishael—*who is what God is.*

Misham—*swiftness.*

Mishma—*fame.*

Mishmannah—*vigor.*

Mispereth—*writing.*

Mithredath—*animating spirit of fire.*

Mizpar—*writing.*

Mizraim—*tribulations.*

Mizzah—*terror.*

Mnason—*a diligent seeker.*

Moab—*desire.*

Moadiah—*festival of Jehovah.*

Molid—*begetter.*

Mordecai—*worshiper.*

Moses—*taken out of the water.*

Moza—*a going forth.*

Muppim—*obscurities.*

Mushi—*drawn out.*

Naam—*pleasantness.*

Naaman—*pleasant.*

Naarai—*pleasantness of Jehovah.*

Naashon—*one that foretells.*

Naasson—*enchanter.*

Nabal—*foolish.*

Naboth—*prominence.*

Nachon—*stroke.*

Nachor—*snorer.*

Nadab—*of one's free will.*

Nagge—*splendor of the sun.*

Naham—*solace.*

Nahamani—*compassionate.*

Naharai—*snoring.*

Nahari—*snoring.*

Nahash—*serpent.*

Nahath—*lowness.*

Nahbi—*Jehovah's protection.*

Nahor—*snorer.*

Nahshon—*ominous.*

Nahum—*compassionate*.

Naphish—*numerous*.

Naphtali—*obtained by wrestling*.

Narcissus—*flower causing lethargy*.

Nathan—*he has given*.

Nathanael—*the gift of God*.

Nathanmelech—*the king is giver*.

Naum—*comfort*.

Neariah—*drives away*.

Nebai—*projecting*.

Nebaioth—*husbandry*.

Nebajoth—*husbandry*.

Nebat—*cultivation*.

Nebo—*height*.

Nebuchadnezzar—*defend the boundary*.

Nebuchadrezzar—*defend the boundary*.

Nebushasban—*save me*.

Nebuzaradan—*Nebo has an offspring*.

Necho—*who was beaten*.

Nedabiah—*Jehovah is willing*.

Nehemiah—*Jehovah has consoled*.

Nehum—*consolation*.

Nekoda—*herdsman*.

Nemuel—*God is spreading*.

Nepheg—*an offshoot*.

Nephish—*numerous*.

Nephthalim—*obtained by wrestling*.

Ner—*a lamp*.

Nereus—*name of a sea god*.

Nergalsharezer—*protect the king*.

Neri—*light of the Lord*.

Neriah—*lamp of Jehovah*.

Nethaneel—*God gives*.

Nethaniah—*Jehovah has given*.

Neziah—*pure*.

Nicanor—*conqueror*.

Nicodemus—*victor over the people*.

Nicolas—*conqueror of the people*.

Niger—*black*.

Nimrod—*valiant*.

Nimshi—*Jehovah reveals*.

Noadiah—*Jehovah has met*.

Noah—*rest*.

Nobah—*barking*.

Nogah—*brilliance*.

Nohah—*rest*.

Non—*fish*.

Nun—*fish*.

Nymphas—*bridegroom*.

Obad—*powerful*.

Obadiah—*worshiper of Jehovah*.

Obal—*bare*.

Obed—*worshiper*.

Obededom—*laborer of the earth*.

Obil—*one who weeps*.

Ocran—*troubler*.

Oded—*aiding*.

Og—*long-necked*.

Ohel—*a tent*.

Olympas—*heavenly*.

Oman—*that rejoices*.

Omar—*mountaineer*.

Omri—*impetuous*.

On—*sun*.

Onam—*wealthy*.

Onan—*strong*.

Onesimus—*profitable*.

Onesiphorus—*bringing advantage*.
Ophir—*fat*.
Ophrah—*hamlet*.
Oreb—*a raven*.
Oren—*fine tree*.
Osee—*salvation*.
Oshea—*God saves*.
Othni—*lion of God*.
Othniel—*lion of God*.
Ozem—*that fasts*.
Ozias—*strength from the Lord*.
Ozni—*attentive*.

Paarai—*revelation of Jehovah*.
Padon—*redemption*.
Pagiel—*God meets*.
Pahathmoab—*governor*.
Palal—*he has judged*.
Pallu—*wonderful*.
Palti—*deliverance by God*.
Paltiel—*deliverer of the Lord*.
Parmashta—*superior*.
Parmenas—*faithful*.
Parnach—*very nimble*.
Parosh—*a fugitive*.
Parshandatha—*dung of impurity*.
Paruah—*increase*.
Pasach—*limping*.
Paseah—*lame*.
Pashur—*free*.
Pathrusim—*the south land*.
Patrobas—*pursuer of his father's steps*.
Paul—*little*.
Pedahel—*God has saved*.
Pedahzur—*powerful*.

Pedaiah—*redemption*.
Pekah—*watchfulness*.
Pekahiah—*Jehovah has given sight*.
Pelaiah—*Jehovah has made illustrious*.
Pelaliah—*Jehovah judges*.
Pelatiah—*freedom-giver*.
Peleg—*division*.
Pelet—*escape*.
Peleth—*swiftness*.
Peniel—*the face of God*.
Penuel—*the face of God*.
Peresh—*separate*.
Perez—*a breach*.
Perida—*separation*.
Persis—*that which divides*.
Peter—*a rock*.
Pethahiah—*Jehovah has set free*.
Pethuel—*God delivers*.
Peulthai—*full of work*.
Phalec—*division*.
Phallu—*admirable*.
Phalti—*deliverance*.
Phaltiel—*deliverer of the Lord*.
Phanuel—*vision of God*.
Pharaoh—*the destroyer*.
Pharaohhophra—*priest of the sun*.
Pharaohnecho—*Pharaoh the lame*.
Phares—*rupture*.
Pharez—*break forth violently*.
Pharosh—*a fugitive*.
Phaseah—*lame*.
Phichol—*great*.
Philemon—*affectionate*.
Philetus—*beloved*.

Philip—*warrior.*
Philologus—*word lover.*
Phinehas—*serpent's mouth.*
Phlegon—*zealous.*
Phurah—*fruitbearer.*
Phut—*extension.*
Phuvah—*utterance.*
Phygellus—*fugitive.*
Pilate—*one armed with a dart.*
Pildash—*flame of fire.*
Pileha—*worship.*
Piltai—*Jehovah causes to escape.*
Pinon—*pearl.*
Piram—*a wild ass.*
Pispah—*expansion.*
Pithon—*gift of mouth.*
Pochereth—*binding.*
Poratha—*fruitful.*
Porcius—*meaning unknown.*
Potiphar—*who is of the sun.*
Poti-pherah—*belonging to the sun.*
Prochorus—*leading in a chorus.*
Pua—*utterance.*
Puah—*utterance.*
Publius—*common.*
Pudens—*bashful.*
Pul—*strong.*
Put—*extension.*
Putiel—*God enlightens.*

Quartus—*the fourth.*

Raamah—*trembling.*
Raamiah—*Jehovah causes trembling.*
Rabmag—*chief of the magicians.*
Rabsaris—*grand master of the eunuchs.*
Rabshakeh—*head of the cupbearers.*
Raddai—*Jehovah subdues.*
Ragau—*a friend.*
Raguel—*friend of God.*
Raham—*pity.*
Rakem—*friendship.*
Ram—*high.*
Ramiah—*exalted is Jehovah.*
Ramoth—*high places.*
Rapha—*fearful.*
Raphah—*fearful.*
Raphu—*feared.*
Reaia—*provided for.*
Reaiah—*provided for.*
Rechab—*companionship.*
Reelaiah—*trembling caused by Jehovah.*
Regem—*a friend.*
Regemmelech—*friend of the king.*
Rehabiah—*God is my extent.*
Rehob—*width.*
Rehoboam—*freer of the people.*
Rehoboth—*wide spaces.*
Rehum—*pity.*
Rei—*friendly.*
Rekem—*friendship.*
Remaliah—*Jehovah increases.*
Rephael—*God is a healer.*
Rephah—*riches.*
Rephaiah—*Jehovah heals.*
Resheph—*haste.*
Reu—*friend.*
Reuben—*behold a son.*
Reuel—*friend of God.*
Rezia—*Jehovah is pleasing.*

Rezin—*good will.*
Rezon—*noble.*
Rhesa—*will.*
Ribai—*Jehovah contends.*
Rimmon—*a pomegranate.*
Riphath—*enemies.*
Roboam—*freer of the people.*
Rohgah—*alarm.*
Romamtiezer—*highest help.*
Rosh—*prince.*
Rufus—*red.*

Sabta—*breaking through.*
Sabtah—*breaking through.*
Sabtecha—*surrender.*
Sabtechah—*surrender.*
Sacar—*merchandise.*
Sadoc—*righteous.*
Sala—*branch.*
Salah—*offshoot.*
Salathiel—*loan of God.*
Sallai—*rejected.*
Salma—*firmness.*
Salmon—*peaceable.*
Salu—*unfortunate.*
Samgarnebo—*be gracious.*
Samlah—*astonishment.*
Samson—*strong.*
Samuel—*asked of God.*
Sanballat—*the enemy.*
Saph—*preserver.*
Saraph—*burning.*
Sargon—*the constituted king.*
Sarsechim—*chief of the eunuchs.*
Saruch—*branch.*
Saul—*demanded.*
Sceva—*I dispose.*

Seba—*old man.*
Secundus—*secondary.*
Segub—*exalted.*
Seir—*rough.*
Seled—*exultation.*
Sem—*Greek for Shem.*
Semachiah—*Jehovah supports.*
Semei—*obey.*
Senaah—*thorny.*
Sennacherib—*the moon-god.*
Senuah—*the violated.*
Seorim—*fear.*
Seraiah—*the Lord is my Prince.*
Sered—*fear.*
Sergius Paulus—*small.*
Serug—*firmness.*
Seth—*appointed.*
Sethur—*hidden.*
Shaaph—*friendship.*
Shaashgaz—*servant of the
 beautiful.*
Shabbethai—*Sabbath-born.*
Shachia—*captive of the Lord.*
Shadrach—*moon-god.*
Shage—*erring.*
Shaharaim—*double dawning.*
Shallum—*recompense.*
Shallun—*recompense.*
Shalmai—*Jehovah is recompenser.*
Shalman—*peaceable.*
Shalmaneser—*peace taken away.*
Shama—*he hath heard.*
Shamed—*destroyer.*
Shamer—*preserver.*
Shamgar—*cupbearer.*
Shamhuth—*fame.*
Shamir—*oppressed.*

Shamma—*renown*.
Shammah—*loss*.
Shammai—*celebrated*.
Shammoth—*renown*.
Shammua—*famous*.
Shammuah—*famous*.
Shamsherai—*heroic*.
Shapham—*vigorous*.
Shaphan—*shy*.
Shaphat—*judge*.
Sharai—*my son*.
Sharar—*firm*.
Sharezer—*preserve the king*.
Shashai—*pale*.
Shashak—*runner*.
Shaul—*asked*.
Shavsha—*splendor*.
Sheal—*request*.
Shealtiel—*I have asked of God*.
Sheariah—*Jehovah has esteemed*.
Shearjashub—*a remnant returns*.
Sheba—*seventh*.
Shebaniah—*the Lord converts*.
Sheber—*fracture*.
Shebna—*youthfulness*.
Shebuel—*God is renowned*.
Shecaniah—*Jehovah is a neighbor*.
Shechaniah—*Jehovah is a neighbor*.
Shechem—*shoulder*.
Shedeur—*all mighty*.
Shehariah—*Jehovah is the dawn*.
Shelah—*peace*.
Shelemiah—*God is my perfection*.
Sheleph—*drawn out*.
Shelesh—*might*.
Shelomi—*Jehovah is peace*.

Shelomith—*peacefulness*.
Shelomoth—*peacefulness*.
Shelumiel—*God's peace*.
Shem—*name*.
Shema—*fame*.
Shemaah—*the fame*.
Shemaiah—*Jehovah is fame*.
Shemariah—*God is my guard*.
Shemember—*splendor*.
Shemer—*guardian*.
Shemida—*science of the heavens*.
Shemidah—*science of the heavens*.
Shemiramoth—*fame of the highest*.
Shemuel—*heard of God*.
Shenazar—*light*.
Shephatiah—*Jehovah is judge*.
Shephi—*smoothness*.
Shepho—*unconcern*.
Shephupham—*an adder*.
Shephuphan—*an adder*.
Sherebiah—*Jehovah is the originator*.
Sheresh—*root*.
Sherezer—*protect the king*.
Sheshai—*noble*.
Sheshan—*free*.
Sheshbazzar—*O Sun-god, protect the son*.
Shetarboznai—*starry splendor*.
Sheth—*compensation*.
Shethar—*star*.
Sheva—*vanity*.
Shilhi—*armed with darts*.
Shillem—*retribution*.
Shiloni—*sent one*.
Shilshah—*heroism*.

Shimea—*splendor.*
Shimeah—*splendor.*
Shimeam—*rumor.*
Shimei—*Jehovah is famous.*
Shimeon—*hearing.*
Shimhi—*Jehovah is famous.*
Shimi—*Jehovah is famous.*
Shimma—*fame.*
Shimon—*tried.*
Shimrath—*watch.*
Shimri—*Jehovah is watching.*
Shimrom—*a guard.*
Shimron—*a guard.*
Shimshai—*Jehovah is splendor.*
Shinab—*father's tooth.*
Shiphi—*Jehovah is fulness.*
Shiphtan—*judge.*
Shisha—*nobility.*
Shishak—*meaning unknown.*
Shitrai—*Jehovah is deciding.*
Shiza—*vehement love.*
Shobab—*restored.*
Shobach—*expansion.*
Shobai—*Jehovah is glorious.*
Shobal—*wandering.*
Shobek—*free.*
Shobi—*Jehovah is glorious.*
Shoham—*onyx.*
Shomer—*watchman.*
Shophach—*extension.*
Shua—*wealth.*
Shuah—*prosperity.*
Shual—*a fox.*
Shubael—*meaning unknown.*
Shuham—*depression.*
Shuni—*calm.*
Shupham—*serpent.*

Shuppim—*serpent.*
Shuthelah—*a plant.*
Sia—*congregation.*
Siaha—*congregation.*
Sibbecai—*Jehovah is intervening.*
Sibbechai—*Jehovah is intervening.*
Sichem—*shoulder.*
Sidon—*fortified.*
Sihon—*great.*
Silas—*lover of words.*
Silvanus—*lover of words.*
Simeon—*hears and obeys.*
Simon—*hearing.*
Simri—*Jehovah is watching.*
Sippai—*Jehovah is the preserver.*
Sisamai—*Jehovah is distinguished.*
Sisera—*meditation.*
So—*lifted up.*
Socho—*fortification.*
Sodi—*my secret.*
Solomon—*peace.*
Sopater—*father defender.*
Sophereth—*learning.*
Sosipater—*father defender.*
Sosthenes—*of sound strength.*
Sotai—*deviator.*
Stachys—*yoke.*
Stephanas—*crowned.*
Stephen—*wreath.*
Suah—*riches.*
Susi—*Jehovah is swift.*
Sychar—*shoulder.*
Sychem—*shoulder.*

Tabbaoth—*spots.*
Tabeal—*God is good.*
Tabeel—*God is good.*

Tabrimon—*rimmon is god.*
Tahan—*preciousness.*
Tahath—*humility.*
Tahrea—*flight.*
Talmai—*spirited.*
Talmon—*violent.*
Tamah—*laughter.*
Tanhumeth—*consolation.*
Tappuah—*apple.*
Tarah—*wild goat.*
Tarea—*adroitness.*
Tarshish—*hard.*
Tartan—*great increase.*
Tatnai—*overseer of gifts.*
Tebah—*thick.*
Tebaliah—*Jehovah has purified.*
Tehinnah—*supplication.*
Tekoa—*firm.*
Telah—*vigor.*
Telem—*lamb.*
Tema—*admiration.*
Teman—*perfect.*
Temani—*perfect.*
Temeni—*fortunate.*
Terah—*wandering.*
Teresh—*reverence.*
Tertius—*the third.*
Tertullus—*liar.*
Thaddaeus—*breast.*
Thahash—*reddish.*
Thamah—*combat.*
Thara—*turning.*
Tharshish—*hard.*
Theophilus—*lover of God.*
Theudas—*false teacher.*
Thomas—*twin.*
Tiberius—*son of Tiber.*

Tibni—*straw.*
Tidal—*renown.*
Tiglathpileser—*binds.*
Tikvah—*strength.*
Tikvath—*expectation.*
Tilgathpilneser—*hinders.*
Tilon—*scorn.*
Timaeus—*highly prized.*
Timna—*restraining.*
Timnah—*restraining.*
Timon—*deemed worthy.*
Timotheus—*honored of God.*
Timothy—*honored of God.*
Tiras—*desire of parents.*
Tirhakah—*exalted.*
Tirhanah—*kindness.*
Tiria—*foundation.*
Tirshatha—*reverence.*
Titus—*honorable.*
Toah—*humility.*
Tobadonijah—*good is my Lord Jehovah.*
Tobiah—*Jehovah is good.*
Tobijah—*Jehovah is good.*
Togarmah—*strong.*
Tohu—*humility.*
Toi—*wandering.*
Tola—*scarlet.*
Tou—*wandering.*
Trophimus—*well-educated.*
Tubal—*worldly.*
Tubalcain—*flowing forth of Cain.*
Tychicus—*fortunate.*
Tyrannus—*absolute.*

Ucal—*power.*
Uel—*will of God.*

Ulam—*solitary.*
Ulla—*burden.*
Unni—*poor.*
Ur—*light.*
Urbane—*polite.*
Uri—*light of Jehovah.*
Uriah—*Jehovah is light.*
Urias—*Jehovah is light.*
Uriel—*a light.*
Urijah—*Jehovah is light.*
Uthai—*Jehovah is help.*
Uz—*firmness.*
Uzai—*hoped for.*
Uzal—*a wanderer.*
Uzza—*strength.*
Uzzah—*strength.*
Uzzi—*the might of Jehovah.*
Uzzia—*might of Jehovah.*
Uzziah—*strength of the Lord.*
Uzziel—*God is strong.*

Vajezatha—*strong as the wind.*
Vaniah—*God is praise.*
Vashni—*God is strong.*
Vophsi—*fragrant.*

Zaavan—*causing fear.*
Zabad—*a gift.*
Zabbai—*humming.*
Zabbud—*well-remembered.*
Zabdi—*the gift of Jehovah.*
Zabdiel—*my gift is God.*
Zabud—*giver.*
Zaccai—*pure.*
Zacchaeus—*pure.*
Zacchur—*well-remembered.*
Zaccur—*well-remembered.*

Zachariah—*Jehovah is renowned.*
Zacharias—*Jehovah is renowned.*
Zacher—*fame.*
Zadok—*righteous.*
Zaham—*loathing.*
Zalaph—*purification.*
Zalmon—*shady.*
Zalmunna—*shelter is denied.*
Zanoah—*broken district.*
Zaphnathpaaneah—*giver of the nourishment of life.*
Zaphon—*dark.*
Zara—*brightness.*
Zarah—*brightness.*
Zatthu—*lovely.*
Zattu—*lovely.*
Zavan—*causing fear.*
Zaza—*projection.*
Zebadiah—*the Lord is my portion.*
Zebah—*victim.*
Zebedee—*the gift of God.*
Zebina—*one who is bought.*
Zebul—*a habitation.*
Zebulun—*dwelling.*
Zechariah—*Jehovah remembers.*
Zecher—*Jehovah remembers.*
Zedekiah—*Jehovah is righteous.*
Zeeb—*wolf.*
Zelek—*a shadow.*
Zelophehad—*the firstborn.*
Zelotes—*full of zeal.*
Zemira—*a melody.*
Zenas—*the gift of Zeus.*
Zephaniah—*God hides.*
Zephi—*watch.*
Zepho—*watch.*
Zephon—*dark.*

Zerah—*springing up of light.*
Zerahiah—*the Lord is risen.*
Zereth—*brightness.*
Zeri—*balm.*
Zeror—*a bundle.*
Zerubbabel—*an offspring of Babel.*
Zetham—*place of olives.*
Zethan—*place of olives.*
Zethar—*sacrifice.*
Zia—*terror.*
Ziba—*plantation.*
Zibeon—*wild robber.*
Zibia—*strength.*
Zichri—*renowned.*
Zidkijah—*Jehovah is might.*
Zidon—*fortress.*
Ziha—*sunniness.*
Zilthai—*shadow of the Lord.*
Zimmah—*counsel.*
Zimran—*the singer.*
Zimri—*celebrated.*
Zina—*borrowed.*
Ziph—*refining place.*

Ziphah—*lent.*
Ziphion—*serpent.*
Zippor—*a sparrow.*
Zithri—*overturn.*
Ziza—*fertility.*
Zizah—*fertility.*
Zohar—*distinction.*
Zoheth—*corpulent.*
Zophah—*watch.*
Zophai—*watcher.*
Zophar—*hairy.*
Zorobabel—*an offspring of Babel.*
Zuar—*little.*
Zuph—*honeycomb.*
Zur—*rock.*
Zuriel—*God is a rock.*
Zurishaddai—*the Almighty is a rock.*

## 184. The Names of the Women in the Bible

Abi—*God's will.*
Abia—*God is Father.*
Abiah—*God is Father.*
Abigail—*cause of joy.*
Abihail—*cause of strength.*
Abijah—*God's will.*
Abishag—*my father wanders.*
Achsa—*adorned.*
Achsah—*adorned.*
Agar—*fugitive.*
Ahinoam—*brother of pleasantries.*

Ahlai—*O would that!*
Aholibaham—*tent of the high places.*
Anah—*full of grace.*
Anna—*grace.*
Apphia—*fruitful.*
Asenath—*belongs to Neit.*
Atarah—*crown.*
Athaliah—*Jehovah has afflicted.*
Azubah—*desolation.*

Baara—*the burning one.*
Bashemath—*perfumed.*
Basmath—*perfumed.*
Bathsheba—*seventh daughter.*
Bernice—*victorious.*
Bilhah—*timid.*
Bithiah—*Jehovah's daughter.*

Candace—*queen.*
Chloe—*green herb.*
Claudia—*lame.*
Cozbi—*deceiver.*

Damaris—*a heifer.*
Deborah—*bee.*
Delilah—*delicate.*
Dinah—*justice.*
Dorcas—*a gazelle.*
Drusilla—*watered by the dew.*

Eglah—*chariot.*
Elisabeth—*a worshiper of God.*
Elisheba—*God is her oath.*
Elizabeth—*worshiper of God.*
Ephah—*darkness.*
Ephrath—*fruitland.*
Esther—*a star.*
Eunice—*conquering well.*
Euodias—*prosperous journey.*
Eve—*life.*

Gomer—*completion.*

Hadassah—*Jewish name for Esther.*
Hagar—*fugitive.*
Haggith—*dancer.*

Hammoleketh—*the queen.*
Hamutal—*kinsman of the dew.*
Hannah—*gracious.*
Hazelelponi—*deliverance of the God who regards me.*
Helah—*sick.*
Hephzibah—*my delight is in her.*
Herodias—*heroic.*
Hodesh—*new moon.*
Hodiah—*the splendor of Jehovah.*
Hoglah—*a partridge.*
Huldah—*weasel.*
Hushim—*hasten.*

Iscah—*she will look out.*

Jael—*gazelle.*
Jecholiah—*powerful.*
Jecoliah—*powerful.*
Jedidah—*Jehovah's darling.*
Jehoaddan—*her ornament is Jehovah.*
Jehoshabeath—*Jehovah is her oath.*
Jehosheba—*Jehovah is her oath.*
Jehudijah—*Jehovah's splendor.*
Jemima—*little dove.*
Jerioth—*tent curtains.*
Jerusha—*married.*
Jerushah—*married.*
Jezebel—*chaste.*
Joanna—*the Lord is gracious.*
Jochebed—*Jehovah's glory.*
Judith—*the praised one.*
Julia—*curly-headed.*
Junia—*belonging to Juno.*

Kerenhappuch—*beautifier.*
Keturah—*incense.*
Kezia—*cassia.*

Leah—*weary.*
Lois—*desirable.*
Loruhamah—*not pitied.*
Lydia—*bending.*

Maachah—*depression.*
Mahalah—*sickness.*
Mahlah—*sickness.*
Mara—*bitter.*
Martha—*mistress of the house.*
Mary—*bitterness.*
Mary Magdalene—*bitterness.*
Matred—*thrusting forward.*
Mehetabel—*benefited of God.*
Merab—*increase.*
Meshullemeth—*retribution.*
Michaiah—*who is like Jehovah?*
Michal—*who is like Jehovah?*
Milcah—*counsel.*
Miriam—*bitterness.*

Naamah—*sweetness.*
Naomi—*my joy.*
Narah—*child of the Lord.*
Nehushta—*piece of brass.*
Noadiah—*one to whom the Lord revealed himself.*
Noah—*comfort.*

Orpah—*a fawn.*
Peninnah—*coral.*
Persis—*one who takes by storm.*
Phanuel—*vision of God.*

Phebe—*pure.*
Prisca—*worthy.*
Priscilla—*worthy.*
Puah—*child-bearing.*

Rachel—*ewe.*
Rahab—*broad.*
Reba—*offspring.*
Rebecca—*captivating.*
Rebekah—*captivating.*
Reumah—*exalted.*
Rhoda—*rose.*
Rizpah—*baking stone.*
Ruth—*something worth seeing.*

Salome—*peace.*
Sapphira—*sapphire.*
Sara—*queen.*
Sarah—*queen.*
Sarai—*princess.*
Serah—*abundance.*
Shelomith—*peaceful.*
Sherah—*a female relation by blood.*
Shimeath—*fame.*
Shimrith—*keeper.*
Shiphrah—*prolific.*
Shomer—*keeper.*
Shua—*rich.*
Susanna—*a white lily.*
Syntyche—*fortunate.*

Tabitha—*gazelle.*
Tahpenes—*the head of the age.*
Tamar—*a palm tree.*
Taphath—*a drop of myrrh.*
Thamar—*palm tree.*

Timna—*restraint.*
Tirzah—*pleasantness.*
Tryphena—*dainty one.*
Tryphosa—*dainty one.*

Vashti—*beautiful woman.*
Zebudah—*a gift.*

Zeresh—*gold.*
Zeruah—*leprous.*
Zeruiah—*balsam from Jehovah.*
Zibiah—*female gazelle.*
Zillah—*protection.*
Zilpah—*meaning unknown.*
Zipporah—*little bird.*

## 185. Names of Firstborn in the Bible

Abdon—*firstborn of Jehiel.*
Abiram—*firstborn of Hiel.*
Amnon—*firstborn of David.*
Arphaxad—*firstborn of Shem.*
Asaiah—*firstborn of an unknown
    Shilonite.*

Bela—*firstborn of Benjamin.*

Cain—*firstborn of Adam.*
Cainan—*firstborn of Enos.*

Dan—*firstborn of Bilhah.*

Eber—*firstborn of Salah.*
Eliab—*firstborn of Jesse.*
Eliphaz—*firstborn of Esau.*
Enoch—*firstborn of Cain.*
Enoch—*firstborn of Jared.*
Enos—*firstborn of Seth.*
Ephraim—*the Lord said, I am a
    father to Israel, and Ephraim is
    my firstborn (Jeremiah 31:9).*
Er—*firstborn of Judah.*
Esau—*firstborn of Isaac.*

Gad—*firstborn of Zilpah.*

Gershom—*firstborn of Moses.*

Hur—*firstborn of Ephratah.*
Huz—*firstborn of Nahor.*

Irad—*firstborn of Enoch.*
Isaac—*firstborn of Sarah.*
Ishmael—*firstborn of Abram.*
Israel—*God said that Israel was
    His firstborn son (Exodus
    4:22).*
Isshiah—*firstborn of Rehabiah.*

Jared—*firstborn of Mahalaleel.*
Jehoram—*firstborn of Jehoshaphat.*
Jerahmeel—*firstborn of Hezron.*
Jeriah—*firstborn of Hebron.*
Jesus—*firstborn of Mary. First
    begotten of the Father.*
Jether—*firstborn of Gideon.*
Jezreel—*firstborn of Hosea.*
Joel—*firstborn of Samuel.*
Johanan—*firstborn of Josiah.*
John—*firstborn of Zechariah.*
Joseph—*firstborn of Rachel.*

Lamech—*firstborn of Methuselah.*

Leah—*firstborn of Laban.*

Machir—*firstborn of Manasseh.*
Mahalaleel—*firstborn of Cainan.*
Manasseh—*firstborn of Joseph.*
Mattithiah—*firstborn of Shallum.*
Mehujael—*firstborn of Irad.*
Merab—*firstborn of Saul.*
Mesha—*firstborn of Caleb.*
Methsael—*firstborn of Mehujael.*
Methuselah—*firstborn of Enoch.*
Micah—*firstborn of Uzziel.*
Miriam—*firstborn of Amram.*

Nadab—*firstborn of Aaron.*
Nahor—*firstborn of Serug.*
Nebajoth—*firstborn of Ishmael.*
Noah—*firstborn of Lamech.*

Peleg—*firstborn of Eber.*

Ram—*firstborn of Jerahmeel.*

Reu—*firstborn of Peleg.*
Reuben—*firstborn of Jacob.*

Salah—*firstborn of Arphaxad.*
Samson—*firstborn of Manoah.*
Samuel—*firstborn of Hannah.*
Serug—*firstborn of Reu.*
Shem—*firstborn of Noah.*
Shemaiah—*firstborn of Obededom.*
Sidon—*firstborn of Canaan.*

Terah—*firstborn of Nahor.*

Ulam—*firstborn of Eshek.*

Vashni—*firstborn of Samuel.*

Zechariah—*firstborn of Meshelemiah.*
Zidon—*firstborn of Canaan.*

## 186. Thirty-nine Names of Jesus

1. Alpha and Omega (Revelation 1:11).
2. Anointed (Psalm 2:2).
3. Branch (Zechariah 6:12).
4. Bright and Morning Star (Revelation 22:16).
5. Christ (Matthew 1:16).
6. Dayspring (Luke 1:78).
7. Daystar (2 Peter 1:19).
8. Door (John 10:9).
9. Everlasting Father (Isaiah 9:6).
10. Good Shepherd (John 10:14).
11. Holy One of God (Mark 1:24).

12. I Am (John 8:58).

13. Immanuel (Isaiah 7:14).

14. Jesus (Luke 2:21).

15. Jesus of Nazareth (Matthew 26:71).

16. Judge (Acts 10:42).

17. Just (Acts 3:14).

18. King of Kings (Revelation 19:16).

19. Lamb of God (John 1:29).

20. Lion of Judah (Revelation 5:5).

21. Lord (Matthew 7:21).

22. Lord God Almighty (Revelation 4:8).

23. Lord of Lords (Revelation 19:16).

24. Master (John 1:38).

25. Mighty God (Isaiah 9:6).

26. Nazarene (Matthew 2:23).

27. Potentate (1 Timothy 6:15).

28. Prince of Life (Acts 3:15).

29. Prince of Peace (Isaiah 9:6).

30. Root of David (Revelation 5:5).

31. Root of Jesse (Isaiah 11:10).

32. Son of David (Matthew 15:22).

33. Son of God (Matthew 4:3).

34. Son of Joseph (John 1:45).

35. Son of Man (Daniel 7:13).

36. Son of Mary (Mark 6:3).

37. True Vine (John 15:1).

38. Wonderful Counselor (Isaiah 9:6).

39. Word (John 1:1).

# 18

## BIBLE TREASURES

What did people use for money during Bible times? What kind of metals did they use? What kind of gemstones did they consider precious? All of these questions are answered by the lists in this chapter. It is also interesting to note that metals of all kinds were precious commodities, especially during Old Testament times.

### 187. Money Used in the Bible

1. The only actual coin mentioned in the Old Testament is the gold *dram*. And some of the chief of the fathers, when they came to the house of the Lord which is at Jerusalem, offered freely for the house of God to set it up in his place: they gave after their ability unto the treasure of the work threescore and one thousand *drams* of gold (Ezra 2:68–69).

2. Silver and gold were measured in units of weights called shekels in Old Testament times. And Abraham hearkened unto Ephron; and Abraham weighed to Ephron the silver, which he had named in the audience of the sons of Heth, four hundred *shekels* of silver, current money with the merchant (Genesis 23:16).

3. In the New Testament, several coins are mentioned. The Jews made their own silver *shekel* coins for the first time about AD 66. In the meantime, Roman and Greek coinage was used. The smallest coin in value was the *mite* that Jesus saw the widow give into the temple treasury (Luke 21:2).

4. Jesus said, Agree with thine adversary quickly, whiles thou art in the way with him; lest at any time the adversary deliver thee to the judge, and the judge deliver thee to the officer, and thou be cast into prison. Verily I say unto thee, Thou shalt by no means come out thence, till thou hast paid the uttermost *farthing* (Matthew 5:25–26).

5. For the kingdom of heaven is like unto a man that is an householder, which went out early in the morning to hire labourers into his vineyard. And when he had agreed with the labourers for a *penny* a day, he sent them into his vineyard (Matthew 20:1–2).

6. By New Testament times, there was a monetary unit known as the pound. A certain nobleman went into a far country to receive for himself a kingdom, and to return. And he called his ten servants, and delivered them ten *pounds* (Luke 19:12–13).

7. There was also a monetary unit in New Testament times known as the talent. It is mentioned in a parable which is the same as the one mentioned above in Luke. For the kingdom of heaven is as a man travelling into a far country, who called his own servants, and delivered unto them his goods. And unto one he gave five *talents*, to another two, and to another one (Matthew 25:14–15).

## 188. Eight Metals Mentioned in the Bible

1. Gold is the first metal mentioned in the Bible: . . . the whole land of Havilah, where there is *gold;* and the gold of that land is good (Genesis 2:11–12).

2. Tubalcain [was] an instructor of every artificer of *brass* and *iron* (Genesis 4:22).

3. Abram was very rich in cattle, in *silver*, and in *gold* (Genesis 13:2).

4. And Eleazar the priest said unto the men of war which went to the battle, This is the ordinance of the law which the Lord commanded Moses; only the *gold*, and the *silver*, the *brass*, the *iron*, the *tin*, and the *lead*, everything that may abide the fire, ye shall make it go through the fire, and it shall be clean (Numbers 31:21–23).

5. King David sang a psalm that included this sentence: He teacheth my hands to war; so that a bow of *steel* is broken by mine arms (2 Samuel 22:35).

6. Ezra inventoried two vessels of fine *copper*, precious as *gold* (Ezra 8:27).

## 189. *Precious Stones Mentioned in the Bible*

1. The breastplate of the high priest contained even four rows of stones: the first row shall be a *sardius*, a *topaz*, and a *carbuncle* . . . the second row shall be an *emerald*, a *sapphire*, and a *diamond*. And the third row a *ligure*, an *agate*, and an *amethyst*. And the fourth row a *beryl*, and an *onyx*, and a *jasper*: they shall be set in gold in their inclosings (Exodus 28:17–20).

2. Job said of wisdom that the gold and *crystal* cannot equal it: the exchange of it shall not be for jewels of fine gold. No mention shall be made of *coral*, or of *pearls*: for the price of wisdom is above *rubies* (Job 28:17–18).

3. The twelve foundations of the wall of the New Jerusalem were garnished with all manner of precious stones. The first foundation was *jasper*, the second, *sapphire*; the third, a *chalcedony*; the fourth, an *emerald*; the fifth, *sardonyx*; the sixth, *sardius*; the seventh, *chrysolyte*; the eighth, *beryl*; the ninth, a *topaz*; the tenth, a *chrysoprasus*; the eleventh, a *jacinth*; the twelfth, an *amethyst* (Revelation 21:19–20).

# 19
## SHIPS AND OTHER FLOATING OBJECTS

Ever since Noah built the ark, men have been going to sea in ships. The first mention of ships in the Bible is in Genesis and the last mention is in Revelation. There have been many strange tales of things that have happened at sea. This chapter highlights the normal, strange, and wonderful accounts of floating things in the Bible.

### 190. The Only Ferry Boat in the Bible

And Shimei . . . came down with the men of Judah to meet king David . . . and they went over Jordan before the king. And there went over a ferry boat to carry over the king's household (2 Samuel 19:16–18).

### 191. A Lifeboat That Was Discarded the Night Before It Was Needed

And as the shipmen were about to flee out of the ship, when they had let down the boat into the sea, under colour as though they would have cast anchors out of the foreship, Paul said to the centurion and to the soldiers, Except these abide in the ship, ye cannot be saved. Then the soldiers cut off the ropes of the boat, and let her fall off. And when it was day, [the ship ran aground,] and the hinder part was broken with the violence of the waves. . . . They which could swim . . . cast themselves . . . into the sea and [got] to land: and the rest, some on boards, and some on broken pieces of the ship. And so it came to pass, that they escaped all safe to land (Acts 27:30–32, 39, 41, 43–44).

### 192. The Only Ship Designed by God and Built by a Man

And God said unto Noah . . . Make thee an ark of gopher wood; rooms shalt thou make in the ark, and shalt pitch it within and without with pitch. And this is the fashion which thou shalt make it of: The length of the ark shall be three hundred cubits, the breadth of it fifty cubits, and the height of it thirty cubits. A window shalt thou make to the ark, and in a cubit shalt thou finish it above; and the door of the ark shalt thou set in the side thereof; with lower, second, and third stories shalt thou make it. Thus did Noah; according to all that God commanded him, so did he (Genesis 6:13–16, 22).

### 193. A Cradle Built Purposely to Float

When the mother of the baby Moses could no longer hide him from the Egyptians, she took for him an ark of bulrushes, and daubed it with slime and with pitch, and put the child therein; and she laid it in the flags by the river's brink. When the daughter of Pharaoh saw the ark among the flags, she sent her maid to fetch it. Pharaoh's daughter paid Moses' mother to nurse Moses. And when the child grew . . . she brought him unto Pharaoh's daughter, and he became her son. And she called his name Moses: and she said, Because I drew him out of the water (Exodus 2:3, 5, 9–10).

### 194. The Navy That Was Destroyed

Jehoshaphat king of Judah [joined] himself with Ahaziah king of Israel, who did very wickedly: and he joined himself with him to make ships to go to Tarshish: and they made the ships in Ezion-geber. Then Eliezer the son of Dodavah of Mareshah prophesied against Jehoshaphat, saying, Because thou hast joined thyself with Ahaziah, the Lord hath broken thy works. And the ships were broken, that they were not able to go to Tarshish (2 Chronicles 20:35–37).

### 195. The Ship That Was Saved by Throwing a Man Overboard

Then they said unto [Jonah], What shall we do unto thee, that the sea may be calm unto us? for the sea wrought, and was tempestuous. And he said unto them, Take me up, and cast me forth into the sea; so shall the sea be calm unto you: for I know that for my sake this great tempest is upon you. . . . So they took up Jonah, and cast him forth into the sea: and the sea ceased from her raging. Then the men feared the Lord exceedingly, and offered a sacrifice unto the Lord, and made vows (Jonah 1:11–12, 15–16).

## 196. The King Who Had Two Navies

1. King Solomon made a navy of ships in Eziongeber, which is beside Eloth, on the shore of the Red Sea, in the land of Edom. And Hiram sent in the navy his servants, shipmen that had knowledge of the sea, with the servants of Solomon. And they came to Ophir, and fetched from thence gold, four hundred and twenty talents, and brought it to king Solomon (1 Kings 9:26–28).

2. King Solomon had at sea a navy of Tharshish with the navy of Hiram: once in three years came the navy of Tharshish, bringing gold, and silver, ivory, and apes, and peacocks (1 Kings 10:22).

## 197. The Most Elaborate Description of Shipbuilding in the Bible

The ships of Tyrus were made of fir trees of Senir: they have taken cedars from Lebanon to make masts for thee. Of the oaks of Bashan have they made thine oars: the company of the Ashurites have made thy benches of ivory, brought out of the isles of Chittim. Fine linen with broidered work from Egypt was that which thou spreadest forth to be thy sail; blue and purple from the isles of Elishah was that which covered thee. The inhabitants of Zidon and Arvad were thy mariners: thy wise men, O Tyrus, that were in thee, were thy pilots. The ancients of Gebal and the wise men thereof were in thee thy calkers: all the ships of the sea with their mariners were in thee to occupy thy merchandise (Ezekiel 27:5–9).

## 198. A Trip on a Slow Boat to a Desert Place

And they departed into a desert place by ship privately. And the people saw them [Jesus and His disciples] departing, and many knew him, and ran afoot thither out of all cities, and outwent them, and came together unto him (Mark 6:32–33).

### 199. Two Ships That Jesus Saved From Storms

1. And straightway Jesus constrained his disciples to get into a ship, and to go before him unto the other side, while he sent the multitudes away. And when he had sent the multitudes away, he went up into a mountain apart to pray: and when the evening was come, he was there alone. But the ship was now in the midst of the sea, tossed with waves: for the wind was contrary. [Jesus then walked out to the ship on the water. And when Jesus got] into the ship, the wind ceased (Matthew 14:22–24, 32).

2. Now it came to pass on a certain day, that he [Jesus] went into a ship with his disciples: and he said unto them, Let us go over unto the other side of the lake. And they launched forth. But as they sailed, he fell asleep: and there came down a storm of wind on the lake; and they were filled with water, and were in jeopardy. And they came to him, and awoke him, saying, Master, Master, we perish. Then he arose, and rebuked the wind and the raging of the water: and they ceased, and there was a calm (Luke 8:22–24).

### 200. The Only Ship in the Bible Called by Name

After being on Melita for three months, Paul departed in a ship of Alexandria which had wintered in the isle, whose sign was Castor and Pollux (Acts 28:11).

### 201. The Signal That Shall Sound Destruction for One-Third of the Ships at Sea

And the second angel sounded [his trumpet], and as it were a great mountain burning with fire was cast into the sea . . . and the third part of the ships were destroyed (Revelation 8:8–9).

### 202. The Oddest Boat Construction Material in the Bible

Woe to the land shadowing with wings, which is beyond the rivers of Ethiopia: that sendeth ambassadors by the sea, even in vessels of bulrushes upon the waters (Isaiah 18:1–2).

### 203. The Ship That Was Used for a Pulpit

Jesus entered into one of the ships, which was Simon's, and prayed him that he would thrust out a little from the land. And he sat down, and taught the people out of the ship (Luke 5:3).

### 204. Five Facts Gleaned From a Shipwreck

1. The ship's origin: [At] Myra, a city of Lycia . . . the centurion found a ship of Alexandria sailing into Italy; and he put us [Paul and Luke] therein (Acts 27:5–6).

2. The ship's motive force: And when the ship was caught, and could not bear up into the wind, we let her drive. And running under a certain island which is called Clauda, we had much work to come by the boat: which when they had taken up, they used helps, undergirding the ship; and, fearing lest they should fall into the quicksands, struck sail, and so were driven (Acts 27:15–17).

3. The number of passengers: And we were in all in the ship two hundred threescore and sixteen souls (Acts 27:37).

4. The non-human cargo: And when they had eaten enough, they lightened the ship, and cast out the wheat into the sea (Acts 27:38).

5. The location of the shipwreck: And when they had escaped [from the shipwreck], then they knew that the island was called Melita (Acts 28:1).

### 205. Ships of War

1. Balaam the son of Beor prophesied, Ships shall come from the coast of Chittim, and shall afflict Asshur, and shall afflict Eber, and he shall perish forever (Numbers 24:24).

2. A vile person in the last days shall come in peaceably, and obtain the kingdom by flatteries. . . . The ships of Chittim shall come against him: therefore he shall be grieved. . . . And at the time of the end shall the king of the south push at him: and the king of the north shall come against him like a whirlwind, with chariots, and with horsemen, and with many ships (Daniel 11:21, 30, 40).

### 206. A Fishing Fleet

[Jesus] said unto Simon, Launch out into the deep, and let down your nets for a draught. And Simon answering said unto him, Master, we have toiled all the night, and have taken nothing: nevertheless at thy word I will let down the net. And when they had this done, they inclosed a great multitude of fishes: and their net brake. And they beckoned unto their partners, which were in the other ship, that they should come and help them. And they came, and filled both the ships, so that they began to sink. . . . James and John the sons of Zebedee . . . were partners with Simon (Luke 5:4–7, 10).

## 207. *Timber Also Floats*

Hiram sent to Solomon, saying, I have considered the things which thou sentest to me for: and I will do all thy desire concerning timber of cedar, and concerning timber of fir. My servants shall bring them down from Lebanon unto the sea: and I will convey them by sea in floats unto the place that thou shalt appoint me (1 Kings 5:8–9).

## 208. *Two Final Thoughts About Ships*

1. [In Zion,] the glorious Lord will be unto us a place of broad rivers and streams; wherein shall go no galley with oars, neither shall gallant ship pass by (Isaiah 33:21).

2. Behold also the ships, which though they be so great, and are driven of fierce winds, yet are they turned about with a very small helm, whithersoever the governor listeth (James 3:4).

# 20

## OTHER THINGS

"What else is listed in the Bible?" you might be asking.

I can't list them all, but here are some examples: Eighteen Descriptions of the Kingdom of Heaven, The Twenty-eight Seasons, Eight Things That Are Worthy to Think Upon, Four Things That Are Never Satisfied, Four Things That Are Too Wonderful, Four Things the Earth Cannot Bear, Four Creatures That Are Exceedingly Wise, Four Things That Are Comely in Moving About, Forty-three Things That God Hates, Musical Instruments Mentioned in the Bible, Tools of Bible People, and Bible Foods.

### 209. *Eighteen Descriptions of the Kingdom of Heaven*

1. The kingdom of heaven is like a field sown with good seed and bad (Matthew 13:24–30).

2. The kingdom of heaven is like a grain of mustard seed (Matthew 13:31).

3. The kingdom of heaven is like leaven hidden in meal until the whole is leavened (Matthew 13:33).

4. The kingdom of heaven is like a treasure hidden in a field (Matthew 13:44).

5. The kingdom of heaven is like a merchant, seeking goodly pearls (Matthew 13:45–46).

6. The kingdom of heaven is like a fishnet that gathers of every kind (Matthew 13:47–50).

7. Whosoever will humble himself as this little child, the same is greatest in the kingdom of heaven (Matthew 18:4).

8. The kingdom of heaven is like a king who would take account of his servants (Matthew 18:23–35).

9. A rich man shall hardly enter into the kingdom of heaven (Matthew 19:23–26).

10. The kingdom of heaven is like a householder who hired laborers for his vineyard and then paid each a day's wages even if they didn't work a full day (Matthew 20:1–16).

11. The kingdom of heaven is like a king who made a wedding feast for his son, and sent forth his servants to call them that were bidden to the wedding: and they would not come (Matthew 22:1–14).

12. The kingdom of heaven shall be likened unto ten virgins, which took their lamps, and went forth to meet the bridegroom. And five of them were wise, and five were foolish (Matthew 25:1–13).

13. The kingdom of heaven is as a man travelling into a far country, who called his own servants, and delivered unto them his goods (Matthew 25:14–30).

14. So is the kingdom of God, as if a man should cast seed into the ground; and should sleep, and rise night and day, and the seed should spring and grow up (Mark 4:26–29).

15. The kingdom of God cometh not with observation . . . the kingdom of God is within you (Luke 17:20–21).

16. The kingdom of God is not meat and drink; but is righteousness, peace, and joy in the Holy Ghost (Romans 14:17).

17. The kingdom of God is not in word but in power (1 Corinthians 4:20).

18. The kingdom of our Lord is everlasting (2 Peter 1:11).

## 210. *The Twenty-eight Seasons*

1. To everything there is a season. There is a time to be born (Ecclesiastes 3:1–2).

2. . . . a time to die (Ecclesiastes 3:2).

3. There is a time to plant (Ecclesiastes 3:2).

4. . . . a time to pluck up that which has been planted (Ecclesiastes 3:2).

5. There is a time to kill (Ecclesiastes 3:3).

6. . . . a time to heal (Ecclesiastes 3:3).

7. There is a time to break down (Ecclesiastes 3:3).

8. . . . a time to build up (Ecclesiastes 3:3).

9. There is a time to weep (Ecclesiastes 3:4).

10. . . . a time to laugh (Ecclesiastes 3:4).

11. There is a time to mourn (Ecclesiastes 3:4).

12. . . . a time to dance (Ecclesiastes 3:4).

13. There is a time to cast away stones (Ecclesiastes 3:5).

14. . . . a time to gather stones together (Ecclesiastes 3:5).

15. There is a time to embrace (Ecclesiastes 3:5).

16. . . . a time to refrain from embracing (Ecclesiastes 3:5).

17. There is a time to get (Ecclesiastes 3:6).

18. . . . a time to lose (Ecclesiastes 3:6).

19. There is a time to keep (Ecclesiastes 3:6).

20. . . . a time to cast away (Ecclesiastes 3:6).

21. There is a time to rend (Ecclesiastes 3:7).

22. . . . a time to sew (Ecclesiastes 3:7).

23. There is a time to keep silence (Ecclesiastes 3:7).

24. . . . a time to speak (Ecclesiastes 3:7).

25. There is a time to love (Ecclesiastes 3:8).

26. . . . a time to hate (Ecclesiastes 3:8).

27. There is a time of war (Ecclesiastes 3:8).

28. . . . a time of peace (Ecclesiastes 3:8).

### 211. Eight Things That Are Worthy to Think Upon

1. Whatsoever things are true (Philippians 4:8).

2. Whatsoever things are honest (Philippians 4:8).

3. Whatsoever things are just (Philippians 4:8).

4. Whatsoever things are pure (Philippians 4:8).

5. Whatsoever things are lovely (Philippians 4:8).

6. Whatsoever things are of good report (Philippians 4:8).

7. If there be any virtue (Philippians 4:8).

8. If there be any praise, think on these things (Philippians 4:8).

## 212. *Four Things That Are Never Satisfied*

1. The grave never says, It is enough (Proverbs 30:15–16).

2. The barren womb never says, It is enough (Proverbs 30:15–16).

3. The earth that is not filled with water never says, It is enough (Proverbs 30:15–16).

4. The fire never says, It is enough (Proverbs 30:15–16).

## 213. *Four Things That Are Too Wonderful*

1. The way of an eagle in the air is too wonderful for me, said Agur the son of Jakeh (Proverbs 30:1, 18–19).

2. The way of a serpent upon a rock is too wonderful (Proverbs 30:18–19).

3. The way of a ship in the midst of the sea is too wonderful (Proverbs 30:18–19).

4. The way of a man with a maid is too wonderful for me (Proverbs 30:18–19).

## 214. *Four Things the Earth Cannot Bear*

1. The earth cannot bear when a servant reigns (Proverbs 30:21–22).

2. The earth cannot bear a fool when he is filled with meat (Proverbs 30:21–22).

3. The earth cannot bear an odious woman when she is married (Proverbs 30:21, 23).

4. The earth cannot bear a handmaid that is heir to her mistress (Proverbs 30:21, 23).

### 215. *Four Little Creatures That Are Exceedingly Wise*

1. Ants prepare their food in the summer (Proverbs 30:24–25).

2. Conies make their houses in the rocks (Proverbs 30:24, 26).

3. Locusts go forth in bands although they have no leader (Proverbs 30:24, 27).

4. Spiders take hold with their hands and live in kings' palaces (Proverbs 30:24, 28).

### 216. *Four Things That Move With Stately Bearing*

1. A lion . . . mighty among beasts, who retreats for nothing (Proverbs 30:29–30 NIV).

2. A strutting rooster (Proverbs 30:31 NIV).

3. A he-goat (Proverbs 30:31 NIV).

4. A king, with his army around him (Proverbs 30:31 NIV).

### 217. *Successful and Attempted Stonings in the Bible*

1. And all the congregation brought [the man that gathered sticks upon the sabbath] without the camp, and stoned him with stones, and he died (Numbers 15:36).

2. And all Israel stoned [Achan and his family and possessions] with stones, and burned them with fire (Joshua 7:24–25).

3. The Lord cast down great stones from heaven upon them. . . . They were more which died with hailstones than they whom the children of Israel slew with the sword (Joshua 10:11).

4. And David put his hand in his bag, and took thence a stone, and slang it, and smote the Philistine in his forehead, that the stone sunk into his forehead; and he fell upon his face to the earth (1 Samuel 17:49).

5. David was greatly distressed; for the people spake of stoning him (1 Samuel 30:6).

6. [Shimei] cast stones at David, and at all the servants of king David (2 Samuel 16:5–6).

7. All Israel stoned [Adoram] with stones, that he died (1 Kings 12:18).

8. They carried [Naboth] forth out of the city, and stoned him with stones, that he died (1 Kings 21:13).

9. And they conspired against [Zechariah], and stoned him with stones at the commandment of the king in the court of the house of the Lord (2 Chronicles 24:20–22).

10. And the husbandmen took [the householder's] servants, and beat one, and killed another, and stoned another (Matthew 21:35).

11. The scribes and Pharisees intended to stone the woman caught in adultery (John 8:3–11).

12. They took up stones to cast at him: but Jesus hid himself, and went out of the temple, going through the midst of them, and so passed by (John 8:59).

13. The Jews took up stones again to stone [Jesus]. But he escaped out of their hand (John 10:31, 39).

14. They stoned Stephen, calling upon God, and saying, Lord Jesus, receive my spirit (Acts 7:59).

15. When there was an assault made both of the Gentiles, and also of the Jews with their rulers, to use [Paul and Barnabas] despitefully, and to stone them, they were aware of it and fled into Lystra and Derbe (Acts 14:5–6).

16. There came thither certain Jews from Antioch and Iconium, who persuaded the people, and, having stoned Paul, drew him out of the city, supposing him to be dead (Acts 14:19).

## 218. Forty-three Things That God Hates

1. God hates homosexual acts (Leviticus 18:22).

2. God hates sexual acts between humans and animals (Leviticus 18:23).

3. God hates idols and even the precious metals and other materials which have been used in making idols (Deuteronomy 7:25).

4. God hates blemished sacrifices (Deuteronomy 17:1).

5. God hates the worship of the sun, moon, or stars (Deuteronomy 17:3–4).

6. God hates divination (Deuteronomy 18:10).

7. God hates astrology (Deuteronomy 18:10).

8. God hates enchanters (Deuteronomy 18:10).

9. God hates witches (Deuteronomy 18:10).

10. God hates charmers (Deuteronomy 18:11).

11. God hates wizards (Deuteronomy 18:11).

12. God hates necromancers (Deuteronomy 18:11).

13. God hates the wearing of clothing of the opposite sex (Deuteronomy 22:5).

14. God hates and will not accept as an offering the hire of a whore (Deuteronomy 23:18).

15. God hates remarriage to a former wife after she has been married to another man (Deuteronomy 24:4).

16. God hates scales that are falsely calibrated to cheat the customer (Deuteronomy 25:13–16).

17. God hates the workers of iniquity (Psalm 5:5).

18. God hates the wicked (Psalm 11:5).

19. God hates those who love violence (Psalm 11:5).

20. God hates the froward (Proverbs 3:32).

21. God hates a proud look (Proverbs 6:16–17).

22. God hates a lying tongue (Proverbs 6:17).

23. God hates hands that shed innocent blood (Proverbs 6:17).

24. God hates a heart that devises wicked imaginations (Proverbs 6:18).

25. God hates feet that are swift in running to mischief (Proverbs 6:18).

26. God hates a false witness who speaks lies (Proverbs 6:19).

27. God hates anyone who sows discord among brethren (Proverbs 6:19).

28. God hates lying lips (Proverbs 12:22).

29. God hates the sacrifices of the wicked (Proverbs 15:8).

30. God hates the ways of the wicked (Proverbs 15:9).

31. God hates the thoughts of the wicked (Proverbs 15:26).

32. God hates the proud in heart (Proverbs 16:5).

33. God hates those who justify the wicked (Proverbs 17:15).

34. God hates those who condemn the just (Proverbs 17:15).

35. God hates vain sacrifices (Isaiah 1:13).

36. God hated the feasts of the new moon celebrated by the Hebrews during the days of Isaiah (Isaiah 1:14).

37. God hates robbery for burnt offering (Isaiah 61:8).

38. God hates idolatry (Jeremiah 44:2–4).

39. God hates evil plans against neighbors (Zechariah 8:17).

40. God hates false oaths (Zechariah 8:17).

41. God hated Esau (Malachi 1:1–3; Romans 9:13).

42. God hates divorce (Malachi 2:14–16).

43. God hates the deeds of the Nicolaitans (Revelation 2:6).

## 219. Important Doors and Gates in the Bible

1. God shut the door of Noah's ark (Genesis 7:16).

2. The two angels at Lot's house blinded the mob, so that they wearied themselves to find the door (Genesis 19:11).

3. At the first Passover, the Israelites were to apply lamb's blood on the side posts and the upper doorposts of their houses (Exodus 12:7).

4. Aaron and his sons were to be washed at the door of the tabernacle (Exodus 29:4).

5. The burnt offering was to be at the door of the tabernacle (Exodus 29:42).

6. God's words were to be written upon the doorposts of thine house, and upon thy gates (Deuteronomy 11:20).

7. Samson removed the doors from the gate of Gaza to a hill at Hebron (Judges 16:3).

8. Uriah slept at the door of the king's house, rather than go to his wife (2 Samuel 11:9).

9. A lord of the king of Samaria, as prophesied by Elisha, was trampled in the gate of the city (2 Kings 7:17).

10. Hezekiah removed the gold from the doors of the temple and gave it to the king of Assyria (2 Kings 18:16).

11. The sheep gate was the gate of Jerusalem rebuilt under Nehemiah's leadership (Nehemiah 3:1).

12. Mordecai sat in the king's gate (Esther 2:19).

13. God spoke to Job of the gates of death (Job 38:17).

14. David wrote of everlasting doors (Psalm 24:7).

15. God opened the doors of heaven (Psalm 78:23).

16. David wrote, The Lord loveth the gate of Zion (Psalm 87:2).

17. David asked God to open the gates of righteousness (Psalm 118:19).

18. David said the righteous enter the gate of the Lord (Psalm 118:20).

19. David desired God to keep the door of my lips (Psalm 141:3).

20. We are warned to stay away from the door of the house of the strange woman (Proverbs 5:8).

21. Wisdom crieth at the gates (Proverbs 8:3).

22. Zion's gates shall be called Praise (Isaiah 60:18).

23. Jeremiah said the gates of Zion had sunk into the ground (Lamentations 2:9).

24. Ezekiel measured the doors and gates of the house of Israel and the temple (Ezekiel 40–41).

25. The angel of the Lord rolled back the stone from the door of Jesus' tomb (Matthew 28:2).

26. Enter ye in at the strait gate: for wide is the gate, and broad is the way, that leadeth to destruction, and many there be which go in thereat: because strait is the gate, and narrow is the way, which leadeth unto life, and few there be that find it (Matthew 7:13–14).

27. Upon this rock will I [Jesus] build my church; and the gates of hell shall not prevail against it (Matthew 16:18).

28. Jesus said, I am the door: by me if any man enter in, he shall be saved (John 10:9).

29. Peter and John healed a lame man at the gate Beautiful of the temple (Acts 3:2–7).

30. An angel opened the prison doors and released the apostles (Acts 5:19).

31. The iron gate opened to them of its own accord as the angel led Peter out of prison (Acts 12:10).

32. Paul recounted how God had opened the door of faith to the Gentiles (Acts 14:27).

33. All the prison doors were opened in the earthquake in Philippi (Acts 16:26).

34. Jesus suffered without the gate (Hebrews 13:12).

35. Jesus said to the church in Philadelphia, I have set before thee an open door, and no man can shut it (Revelation 3:8).

36. Jesus said to the Laodiceans, Behold, I stand at the door and knock: if any man hear my voice, and open the door, I will come in to him (Revelation 3:20).

37. John looked, and behold, a door was opened in heaven (Revelation 4:1).

38. The New Jerusalem had twelve gates, each a pearl, with twelve angels. Each gate bore the name of a tribe of Israel, and was never shut (Revelation 21:12, 21, 25).

39. Blessed are they that do his commandments, that they may have right to the tree of life, and may enter in through the gates into the city (Revelation 22:14).

## 220. Musical Instruments Mentioned in the Bible

1. The *organ* was among the first musical instruments invented by Jubal (Genesis 4:21).

2. *Rams' horns* were blown by seven priests when they marched around Jericho (Joshua 6:4).

3. The women came out of all of the cities of Israel to meet David and King Saul with singing, dancing, *tabrets*, and other musical instruments (1 Samuel 18:5–6).

4. Asaph played the *cymbals* when King David brought the ark to Jerusalem (1 Chronicles 16:1–5).

5. Benaiah and Jahaziel the priests played *trumpets* while the ark was being brought to Jerusalem (1 Chronicles 16:6).

6. Job spoke of the *timbrel, harp,* and *organ* (Job 21:12).

7. The word *neginoth* means stringed instruments. Many of the psalms had instructions in their titles to play the psalm on neginoth or stringed instruments (Psalm 4 title).

8. The signal to worship King Nebuchadnezzar's golden image was the playing of the *cornet, flute, harp, sackbut, psaltery,* and the *dulcimer* (Daniel 3:1–7).

9. Amos complained about those who were at ease in Zion . . . who chant to the sound of the *viol* (Amos 6:1, 5).

10. *Pipers* are mentioned in Revelation 18:22.

## 221. Tools of Bible People

1. Zipporah took a *sharp stone,* and cut off the foreskin of her son (Exodus 4:25).

2. The Hebrew women used *kneading troughs* to knead their bread (Exodus 12:34).

3. If a slave preferred to remain with his master rather than be freed, "his master shall bore his ear through with an *awl*" (Exodus 21:6).

4. Moses was instructed to make *ash pans, shovels, fleshhooks,* and *firepans* to be used with the altar in the tabernacle (Exodus 27:3).

5. Aaron fashioned the golden calf with a *graving tool* (Exodus 32:4).

6. *Snuffers* were made as accessories to the lamps in the tabernacle (Exodus 37:23).

7. The Israelites went down to the Philistines, to sharpen every man his *share,* and his *coulter,* and his *ax,* and his *mattock.* Yet they had a *file* for the mattocks, and for the coulters, and for the *forks,* and for the axes, and to sharpen the *goads* (1 Samuel 13:20–21).

8. Joab fought against the city of Rabbah. The prisoners taken in this battle were forced to work with *iron harrows* (2 Samuel 12:26, 31).

9. The stones in Solomon's house were sawed with *saws,* within and without (1 Kings 7:8–9).

10. The prophets of Baal cut themselves with *knives* and *lancets* till the blood gushed out upon them (1 Kings 18:28).

11. Job said, My days are swifter than a *weaver's shuttle* (Job 7:6).

12. The Lord asked Job if he could fill leviathan's head with *fish spears* (Job 41:7).

13. One of the shepherd's main tools was his *staff* (Psalm 23:4).

14. As the *fining pot* for silver, and the *furnace* for gold; so is a man to his praise (Proverbs 27:21).

15. Solomon wrote, Though thou shouldest bray a fool in a *mortar* among wheat with *a pestle*, yet will not his foolishness depart from him (Proverbs 27:22).

16. The carpenter encouraged the goldsmith, and he that smootheth with the *hammer* him that smote the *anvil*, saying, It is ready for the sodering (Isaiah 41:7).

17. The Lord said that He would make Israel to be a new sharp *threshing instrument* having teeth (Isaiah 41:14–15).

18. The smith with the *tongs* both worketh in the coals, and fashioneth it with *hammers* (Isaiah 44:12).

19. The carpenter stretcheth out his *rule*; he marketh it out with a *line*; he fitteth it with *planes*, and he marketh it out with the *compass* (Isaiah 44:13).

20. The *balance* was used to weigh gold and silver (Isaiah 46:6).

21. *Millstones* were used to grind meal (Isaiah 47:2).

22. The *yoke* was used for carrying things (Isaiah 47:6).

23. Jeremiah "went down to the potter's house, and, behold, he wrought a work on the *wheels*" (Jeremiah 18:3).

24. God told Ezekiel to shave his head and beard with a *barber's razor* (Ezekiel 5:1).

25. Ezekiel had a vision wherein he saw an angel measure the temple with a *measuring reed* (Ezekiel 40:1–5).

26. Joel prophesied and said, Beat your *plowshares* into swords, and your *pruning hooks* into spears (Joel 3:10).

27. Joel also said, Put ye in the *sickle*, for the harvest is ripe (Joel 3:13).

28. The prophet Amos spoke of *hooks* and *fishhooks* (Amos 4:2).

29. Amos saw a vision of the Lord with a *plumbline* in His hand (Amos 7:7).

30. A *fan* was used in threshing wheat (Matthew 3:12).

31. Jesus said, It is easier for a camel to go through a *needle*'s eye, than for a rich man to enter the kingdom of God (Luke 18:25).

## 222. Bible Foods

1. Jacob traded *bread* and pottage of *lentiles* to Esau for Esau's birthright (Genesis 25:29–34).

2. Isaac liked *venison*, and Rebekah cooked him some young *goats* (Genesis 27:1–10).

3. Pharaoh had a baker who baked *bakemeats* (pastries) for him (Genesis 40:16–17).

4. The Passover meal was comprised of a cooked *lamb*, *bitter herbs*, and *unleavened bread* (Exodus 12:3–10).

5. Gideon fixed a meal for an angel. The meal included a pot of *broth* (Judges 6:19).

6. Abigail supplied David and his men with two hundred *loaves*, two bottles of *wine*, five ready-dressed *sheep*, five measures of parched *corn*, a hundred clusters of *raisins*, and two hundred cakes of *figs* (1 Samuel 25:18–20).

7. During the time that Eli was high priest, the Israelites boiled their *meat* (1 Samuel 2:12–17).

8. When King David fled from Absalom, various people brought . . . *wheat*, and *barley*, and *flour*, and parched *corn*, and *beans*, and *lentiles*, and parched *pulse*, and *honey*, and *butter*, and *sheep*, and *cheese* of kine [cow], for David, and for the people that were with him, to eat (2 Samuel 17:27–29).

9. Daniel, Hananiah, Mishael, and Azariah preferred to eat *pulse* and drink water rather than eat the king's *meat* and drink his *wine* (Daniel 1:3–16).

10. Jesus fed the multitude with *fish* and *barley bread* (John 6:9–14).

*Note:* For additional edible plants and animals, see "Flora and Fauna," chapter 16.

### 223. Trials Before the Courts and Councils

1. Moses sat to judge the people: and the people stood by Moses from the morning unto the evening. And when Moses' father-in-law saw all that he did to the people, he said, What is this thing that thou doest to the people? . . . And Moses said . . . The people come unto me to enquire of God . . . and I judge between one and another, and I do make them know the statutes of God and his laws. And Moses' father in law said . . . Thou wilt surely wear away, both thou, and this people that is with thee: for this thing is too heavy for thee; thou are not able to perform it . . . alone. Hearken now unto my voice. . . . Be thou for the people to Godward, that thou mayest bring the causes to God: and . . . provide out of all the people able men . . . and place . . . them to be rulers of thousands, and rulers of hundreds, rulers of fifties, and rulers of tens. And let them judge the people at all seasons: and it shall be, that every great matter they shall bring unto thee, but every small matter they shall judge. . . . So Moses hearkened to the voice of his father-in-law, and did all that he had said (Exodus 18:13–22, 24).

2. The son of an Israelitish woman, whose father was an Egyptian, went out among the children of Israel: and . . . [he] and a man of Israel strove together in the camp; and the Israelitish woman's son blasphemed the name of the Lord, and cursed. And they brought him unto Moses. . . . And they put him in ward, that the mind of the Lord might be shewed them. And the Lord spoke unto Moses, saying, Bring forth him that hath cursed without the camp; and let all that heard him lay their hands upon his head, and let all the congregation stone him. . . . And Moses spake to the children of Israel . . . and the children of Moses did as the Lord commanded Moses (Leviticus 24:10–14, 23).

3. These be . . . words which Moses spake unto all Israel. . . . I charged your judges . . . saying, Hear the causes between your brethren, and judge righteously between every man and his brother, and the stranger that is with him. Ye shall not respect persons in judgment; but ye shall hear the small as well as the great; ye shall not be afraid of the face of man; for the judgment is God's: and the cause that is too hard for you, bring it unto me, and I will hear it (Deuteronomy 1:1, 16–17).

4. At the mouth of two witnesses, or three witnesses, shall he that is worthy of death be put to death; but at the mouth of one witness he shall not be put to death (Deuteronomy 17:6).

5. [Jesus said,] Behold, I send you forth as sheep in the midst of wolves: be ye therefore wise as serpents, and harmless as doves. But beware of men: for they will deliver you up to the councils, and they will scourge you in their synagogues; and ye shall be brought before governors and kings for my sake, for a testimony against them and the Gentiles. But when they deliver you up, take no thought how or what ye shall speak: for it shall be given you in that same hour what ye shall speak. For it is not ye that speak, but the Spirit of your Father which speaketh in you (Matthew 10:16–20).

6. And they that had laid hold on Jesus led him away to Caiaphas the high priest, where the scribes and the elders were assembled. . . . Now the chief priests, and elders, and all the council, sought false witness against Jesus, to put him to death; but found none: yea, though many false witnesses came, yet found they none. At last came two false witnesses, and said, This fellow said, I am able to destroy the temple of God, and to build it in three days. And the high priest arose, and said unto him, Answerest thou nothing? what is it which these witness against Thee?

   But Jesus held his peace. And the high priest . . . said unto him, I adjure thee by the living God, that thou tell us whether thou be the Christ, the Son of God. Jesus saith unto him, Thou hast said: nevertheless I say unto you, Hereafter shall ye see the Son of man sitting on the right hand of power, and coming in the clouds of heaven. Then the high priest rent his clothes, saying, He hath spoken blasphemy: what further need have we of witnesses? behold, now ye have heard his blasphemy. What think ye? They answered and said, He is guilty of death (Matthew 26:57, 59–66).

7. And the whole multitude of them arose, and led him unto Pilate. And they began to accuse him, saying, We found this fellow perverting the nation, and forbidding to give tribute to Caesar, saying that he himself is Christ a King. And Pilate asked him, saying, Art thou the King of the Jews? And he answered him and said, Thou sayest it. Then said Pilate to the chief priests and to the people, I find no fault in this man. And they were the more

fierce, saying, He stirreth up the people, teaching throughout all Jewry, beginning from Galilee to this place.

When Pilate heard of Galilee, he asked whether the man were a Galilean. And as soon as he knew that he belonged unto Herod's jurisdiction, he sent him to Herod, who himself also was at Jerusalem at that time. And . . . Herod . . . questioned [Jesus] in many words; but he answered him nothing. And the chief priests and scribes stood and vehemently accused him. And Herod with his men of war set him at nought, and mocked him and arrayed him in a gorgeous robe, and sent him again to Pilate (Luke 23:1–7, 9–11).

8. Pilate therefore went forth again, and saith unto them, Behold, I bring him forth to you, that ye may know that I find no fault in him. Then came Jesus forth, wearing the crown of thorns, and the purple robe. And Pilate saith unto them, Behold the man! When the chief priests therefore and officers saw him, they cried out, saying, Crucify him, crucify him. Pilate saith unto them, Take ye him, and crucify him: for I find no fault in him. The Jews answered him, We have a law, and by our law he ought to die, because he made himself the Son of God.

When Pilate therefore heard that saying, he was the more afraid; and went again into the judgment hall, and saith unto Jesus, Whence art thou? But Jesus gave him no answer. Then saith Pilate unto him, Speakest thou not unto me? knowest thou not that I have power to crucify thee, and have power to release thee? Jesus answered, Thou couldest have no power at all against me, except it were given thee from above: therefore he that delivered me unto thee hath the greater sin.

And from thenceforth Pilate sought to release him: but the Jews cried out, saying, If thou let this man go, thou art not Caesar's friend: whosoever maketh himself a king speaketh against Caesar. When Pilate therefore heard that saying, he brought Jesus forth, and sat down in the judgment seat in a place that is called the Pavement, but in the Hebrew, Gabbatha. And it was the preparation of the passover, and about the sixth hour: and he saith unto the Jews, Behold your King! But they cried out, Away with him, away with him, crucify him. Pilate saith unto them, Shall I crucify your King? The chief priests answered, We have no king but Caesar. Then delivered he him therefore unto them to be crucified. And they took Jesus, and led him away. And he bearing his cross went forth into a place called the place of a skull, which is called in the Hebrew Golgotha: where they crucified him (John 19:4–16).

9. As Peter and John talked to the people in the temple in Solomon's porch after the healing of the lame man, the priests, and the captain of the temple, and the Sadducees, came upon them, being grieved that they taught the people, and preached through Jesus the resurrection from the dead. And they laid hands on them, and put them in hold unto the next day: for it was now eventide. . . . And it came to pass on the morrow, that their rulers, and elders, and scribes, and Annas the high priest, and Caiaphas, and John, and Alexander, and as many as were of the kindred of the high priest, were gathered together at Jerusalem.

And when they had set them in the midst, they asked, By what power, or by what name, have ye done this? Then Peter, filled with the Holy Ghost, said unto them, Ye rulers of the people, and elders of Israel, If we this day be examined of the good deed done to the impotent man, by what means he was made whole; be it known unto you all, and to all the people of Israel, that by the name of Jesus Christ of Nazareth, whom ye crucified, whom God raised from the dead, even by him doth this man stand before you whole. . . . Neither is there salvation in any other: for there is none other name under heaven given among men, whereby we must be saved.

Now when they saw the boldness of Peter and John, and perceived that they were unlearned and ignorant men, they marvelled; and they took knowledge of them, that they had been with Jesus. And beholding the man which was healed standing with them, they could say nothing against it. But when they had commanded them to go aside out of the council, they conferred among themselves, saying, What shall we do to these men? for that indeed a notable miracle hath been done by them is manifest to all them that dwell in Jerusalem; and we cannot deny it. . . . And they called them, and commanded them not to speak at all nor teach in the name of Jesus. But Peter and John answered and said unto them, Whether it be right in the sight of God to hearken unto you more than unto God, judge ye. For we cannot but speak the things which we have seen and heard. So when they had further threatened them, they let them go, finding nothing how they might punish them, because of the people: for all men glorified God for that which was done (Acts 4:1–3, 5–10, 12–16, 18–21).

10. The high priest . . . and all they that were with him, [which is the sect of the Sadducees] . . . laid their hands on the apostles and put them in the common prison. But the angel of the Lord by night opened the prison doors, and . . . said, Go, stand, and speak in the temple to the people all the words of this life. . . . [Then] the officers came and found them not in the prison. . . . Then came one and told them, saying, Behold, the men whom ye put in prison are standing in the temple, and teaching the people. Then went the captain with the officers, and brought them without violence. . . . and . . . they sat them before the council: and the high priest asked them, saying, Did not we straitly command you that ye should not teach in this name? and, behold ye have filled Jerusalem with your doctrine. . . .

Then Peter and the other apostles answered and said, We ought to obey God rather than men. The God of our fathers raised up Jesus, whom ye slew and hanged on a tree. Him hath God exalted . . . to be a Prince and a Saviour . . . to Israel. . . . And we are witnesses of these things: and so also is the Holy Ghost, whom God hath given to them that obey him. When they heard that, they were cut to the heart, and took counsel to slay them.

Then . . . Gamaliel . . . commanded to put the apostles forth a little space; and said unto them, Ye men of Israel, take heed to yourselves what ye intend to do as touching these men. . . . Refrain from these men, and let them alone: for if this counsel or this work be of men, it will come to nought: but if it be of God, ye cannot overthrow it; lest haply ye be found even to fight against God. And to him they agreed: and when they had called the apostles, and beaten them, they commanded that they should not speak in the name of Jesus, and let them go (Acts 5:17–20, 22, 25–35, 38–40).

11. There arose certain of the synagogue, disputing with Stephen. And they were not able to resist the wisdom and the spirit by which he spake. Then they [persuaded] men, which said, We have heard him speak blasphemous words against Moses, and against God. And they stirred up the people, and the elders, and

the scribes . . . and caught him and brought him to the council, and set up false witnesses, which said . . . We have heard him say, that Jesus of Nazareth shall destroy this place, and shall change the customs which Moses delivered us. . . .

Then said the high priest, Are these things so? [Then Stephen made a long speech about the patriarchs and about Moses, David, and Solomon. He ended by saying,] Ye stiffnecked and uncircumcised in heart and ears, ye do always resist the Holy Ghost: as your fathers did, so do ye. Which of the prophets have not your fathers persecuted? and they have slain them which shewed before the coming of the Just One; of whom ye have been now the betrayers and murderers: who have received the law by the disposition of angels, and have not kept it.

When they heard these things, they were cut to the heart, and they gnashed on him with their teeth. But he, being full of the Holy Ghost, looked up stedfastly into heaven . . . and said, Behold, I see the heavens opened, and the Son of man standing on the right hand of God. Then they cried out with a loud voice . . . and ran upon him with one accord, and cast him out of the city, and stoned him . . . and he kneeled down, and cried with a loud voice, Lord, lay not this sin to their charge. And when he had said this, he fell asleep. And Saul was consenting unto his death (Acts 6:9–14; 7:1, 51–58, 60).

12. A certain damsel possessed with a spirit of divination . . . which brought her masters much gain by soothsaying . . . followed Paul and us, and cried, saying, These men are the servants of the most high God, which shew unto us the way of salvation. And this she did many days. But Paul, being grieved, turned and said to the spirit, I command thee in the name of Jesus Christ to come out of her. And he came out the same hour. And when her masters saw that the hope of their gains was gone, they caught Paul and Silas, and drew them into the marketplace unto the rulers, and brought them to the magistrates, saying, These men, being Jews, do exceedingly trouble our city, and teach customs, which are not lawful for us to receive, neither to observe, being Romans.

And the multitude rose up together against them: and the magistrates rent off their clothes, and commanded to beat them. And when they had laid many stripes upon them, they cast them into prison, charging the jailor to keep them safely: who, having received such a charge, thrust them into the inner prison, and made their feet fast in the stocks (Acts 16:16–24).

13. [After Paul was mobbed in the temple and rescued by the chief Roman captain, Paul was brought before the chief priests and all their council.] And Paul, earnestly beholding the council, said, Men and brethren, I have lived in all good conscience before God until this day. And the high priest Ananias commanded them that stood by him to smite him on the mouth. Then said Paul unto him, God shall smite thee, thou whited wall: for sittest thou to judge me after the law, and commandest me to be smitten contrary to the law? And they that stood by said, Revilest thou God's high priest? Then said Paul, I wist not, brethren, that he was the high priest: for it is written, Thou shalt not speak evil of the ruler of thy people. But when Paul perceived that the one part were Sadducees, and the other Pharisees, he cried out in the council, Men and brethren, I am a Pharisee, the son of a Pharisee: of the hope and resurrection of the dead I am called in question.

   And when he had so said, there arose a dissension between the Pharisees and the Sadducees: and the multitude was divided. For the Sadducees say that there is no resurrection, neither angel, nor spirit: but the Pharisees confess both. And there arose a great cry: and the scribes that were of the Pharisees' part arose, and strove, saying, We find no evil in this man: but if a spirit or an angel hath spoken to him, let us not fight against God. And when there arose a great dissension, the chief captain, fearing lest Paul should have been pulled in pieces of them, commanded the soldiers to go down, and to take him by force from among them, and to bring him into the castle (Acts 22:30; 23:1–10).

14. [After Paul was taken from Jerusalem (to escape a conspiracy to kill him) to Caesarea, he was kept in Herod's judgment hall.] And after five days Ananias the high priest descended with the elders, and with a certain orator named Tertullus, who informed the governor against Paul . . . saying . . . Most noble Felix . . . I pray thee that thou wouldest hear us of thy clemency a few words. For we have found this man a pestilent fellow and a mover of sedition among all the Jews . . . who also hath gone about to

profane the temple. . . . And the Jews also assented, saying that these things were so.

Then Paul, after that the governor had beckoned unto him to speak, answered, Forasmuch as I know that thou hast been of many years a judge unto this nation, I do the more cheerfully answer for myself: . . . I went up to Jerusalem for to worship. And they neither found me in the temple disputing with any man, neither . . . can they prove the things whereof they now accuse me. But this I confess unto thee, that after the way which they call heresy, so worship I the God of my fathers, believing all things which are written in the law and in the prophets: and have hope toward God . . . that there shall be a resurrection of the dead, both of the just and unjust. . . .

And when Felix heard these things, having more perfect knowledge of that way, he deferred them, and said, When Lysias the chief captain shall come down, I will know the uttermost of your matter. And he commanded a centurion to keep Paul, and to let him have liberty, and that he should forbid none of his acquaintance to minister or to come to him (Acts 24:1–6, 9–15, 22–23).

15. When Festus was come into the province . . . the high priest and the chief of the Jews informed him against Paul . . . and desired . . . that he would send for him to Jerusalem, laying in wait . . . to kill him. But Festus answered, that Paul should be kept at Caesarea. . . . Let them therefore, said he, which among you are able, go down with me, and accuse this man. . . . [After] ten days, he went down unto Caesarea, and the next day sitting on the judgment seat commanded Paul to be brought.

And when he was come, the Jews . . . laid many and grievous complaints against Paul, which they could not prove. While he answered for himself, Neither against the law of the Jews, neither against the temple, nor yet against Caesar, have I offended any thing at all. But Festus . . . said, Wilt thou go up to Jerusalem, and there be judged of these things before me? Then said Paul, I stand at Caesar's judgment seat, where I ought to be judged. . . . I appeal to Caesar. Then Festus, when he had conferred with the council, answered, Hast thou appealed unto Caesar? unto Caesar shalt thou go (Acts 25:1–12).

16. And after certain days king Agrippa and Bernice came unto Caesarea to salute Festus. And when they had been there many days, Festus declared Paul's cause to the king. . . . Then Agrippa said unto Festus, I would also hear the man myself. . . . Agrippa said unto Paul, Thou art permitted to speak for thyself. [Then Paul told Agrippa the story of his life, including his persecution of the Christians and his own conversion. He ended by saying,] King Agrippa, believest thou the prophets? I know that thou believest. Then Agrippa said unto Paul, Almost thou persuadest me to be a Christian.

And Paul said, I would to God, that not only thou, but also all that hear me this day, were both almost, and altogether such as I am, except these bonds. And when he had thus spoken, the king rose up, and the governor, and Bernice, and they that sat with them: and when they were gone aside, they talked among themselves, saying, This man doeth nothing worthy of death or of bonds. Then said Agrippa unto Festus, This man might have been set at liberty, if he had not appealed unto Caesar (Acts 25:13–14, 22; 26:1, 27–32).

17. When the Son of man shall come in his glory, and all the holy angels with him, then shall he sit upon the throne of his glory: and before him shall be gathered all nations; and he shall separate them one from another, as a shepherd divideth his sheep from the goats: and he shall set the sheep on his right hand, but the goats on the left. Then shall the King say unto them on his right hand, Come, ye blessed of my Father, inherit the kingdom prepared for you from the foundation of the world: For I was an hungred, and ye gave me meat: I was thirsty, and ye gave me drink: I was a stranger, and ye took me in: naked, and ye clothed me: I was sick, and ye visited me: I was in prison, and ye came unto me. Then shall the righteous answer him, saying, Lord, when saw we thee an hungred, and fed thee? or thirsty, and gave thee drink? When saw we thee a stranger, and took thee in? or naked, and clothed thee? Or when saw we thee sick, or in prison, and came unto thee?

And the King shall answer and say unto them, Verily I say unto you, Inasmuch as ye have done it unto one of the least of these my brethren, ye have done it unto me. Then shall he say also unto them on the left hand, Depart from me, ye cursed, into everlasting fire, prepared for the devil and his angels: for I was an hungred, and ye gave me no meat: I . . . was a stranger, and ye took me not in: naked and ye clothed me not: sick, and in prison, and ye visited me not. Then shall they also answer him, saying, Lord, when saw we thee an hungred, or athirst, or a stranger, or naked, or sick, or in prison, and did not minister unto thee? Then shall he answer them, saying, Verily I say unto you, Inasmuch as ye did it not to one of the least of these, ye did it not to me. And these shall go away into everlasting punishment: but the righteous into life eternal (Matthew 25:31–46).

# 21

## FAMILY AFFAIRS

Though the Bible holds a wide variety of themes, the central theme of the Bible is the redemptive role of Jesus Christ. From the fall of Adam and Eve in the garden, God's plan of redemption through the seed of the woman (Genesis 3:15) has been the focal point. It is little wonder that from Genesis 12 onward, we see the narrowing of God's attention to the family of Abraham and his descendants. From this family Jesus Christ would be born nearly nineteen hundred years later.

Zeroing in on this family necessarily meant zeroing in on the families that came from Abraham. Thus, the Bible is very much a family book, and many of the joys and the frustrations of family life are depicted. Looking over the lists, we find that we have much in common with the families of the Bible: preparations for weddings, the rearing of large families, miraculous pregnancies, twins being born, the devastation of divorce, and death during childbirth. Few of us will have as large a family as some of these people did, however. You'd need a hotel to house them and a farm to feed them.

### 224. Five Dowries

1. Jacob served Laban for fourteen years so he could marry Rachel (Genesis 29:16–30).
2. Leah said, God hath endued me with a good dowry; now will my husband dwell with me, because I have born him six sons (Genesis 30:20).

3. When Shechem the Hivite sought to marry Dinah, her brothers responded, In this will we consent unto you: If ye will be as we be, that every male of you be circumcised; then we will give our daughters unto you (Genesis 34:1–16).

4. Boaz obtained Ruth as his wife by purchasing Naomi's property (Ruth 3–4).

5. Saul said, Thus shall ye say to David, The king desireth not any dowry, but an hundred foreskins of the Philistines, to be avenged of the king's enemies. Wherefore David arose and went, he and his men, and slew of the Philistines two hundred men; and David brought their foreskins, and they gave them in full tale to the king, that he might be the king's son in law (1 Samuel 18:25, 27).

## 225. Seven Weddings

1. God gave the bride (Eve) away in mankind's first wedding! (Genesis 2:22–24).

2. Laban made a public wedding feast before deceitfully giving his daughter Leah to Jacob in marriage (Genesis 29:22–25).

3. Samson made a seven-day feast and was given thirty attendants for his wedding. However, the festivities were cut short by Samson's fit of anger, and he never did actually marry the woman (Judges 14:10–20).

4. Jesus told a parable of a king who made a wedding feast for his son. The king invited guests and required that each wear a wedding garment provided for him (Matthew 22:1–14).

5. In another parable, Jesus told of ten virgins who waited at night to accompany the bride and bridegroom to their marriage feast (Matthew 25:1–13).

6. Jesus accepted an invitation to a wedding at Cana. There Jesus performed His first miracle—He changed water into wine for the marriage feast (John 2:1–11).

7. John described the future union of Christ and His church as a marriage. The church, Christ's bride, wore fine white linen (typifying its righteousness). People were invited to the marriage feast (Revelation 19:7–9).

### 226. Five Divorces

1. Abraham sent away Hagar, who gave birth to Ishmael, at Sarah's urging and God's approval (Genesis 21:9–14).

2. The post-exilic Jews, at Ezra's prompting, divorced their foreign wives (Ezra 10).

3. King Ahasuerus may have divorced Queen Vashti for her disobedience (Esther 1:9–22).

4. God "divorced" the Northern Kingdom for their idolatry (Jeremiah 3:8).

5. Herod and Herodias both divorced their spouses in order to marry each other (Josephus; cf. Matthew 14:3–4).

### 227. Five Men With the Most Wives

1. Solomon had 700 wives and 300 concubines (1 Kings 11:3).

2. King Rehoboam had eighteen wives and sixty concubines (2 Chronicles 11:21).

3. David likely had over seventeen wives, counting his concubines (2 Samuel 3:2–5; 5:13; 20:3).

4. King Abijah had fourteen wives (2 Chronicles 13:21).

5. Gideon had many wives and seventy sons (Judges 8:30).

### 228. Ten Miraculous Pregnancies

1. God closed all the wombs of Abimelech's household because Abimelech had taken Sarah for himself. After Sarah was restored to Abraham, Abraham prayed and the women bore children (Genesis 20:17–18).

2. Although Sarah was old, and unable to bear children before, she gave birth to Isaac when she was ninety years old, as the Lord fulfilled His promise. Abraham was 100 years old when Isaac was born (Genesis 21:1–5).

3. After Sarah's death (at which time Abraham was 137 years old), Abraham remarried and fathered more children (Genesis 25:1–6).

4. Rebekah was barren until her husband Isaac prayed for her. Then

she conceived and gave birth to twins: Jacob and Esau (Genesis 25:21–26).

5. God opened the womb of barren Rachel, and she gave birth to Joseph and Benjamin (Genesis 30:22–24; 35:18).

6. The angel of the Lord appeared to Manoah's barren wife, foretelling that she would bear a son (Samson) who would begin to deliver Israel from the Philistines (Judges 13:3, 5).

7. The Lord had shut up Hannah's womb, so that she was childless. But then, in answer to Hannah's intense prayer, she gave birth to Samuel (1 Samuel 1:1–20).

8. Although her husband was "too old," the Shunammite woman bore a son, fulfilling Elisha's word (2 Kings 4:13–17).

9. Barren Elisabeth gave birth to John (the Baptist), fulfilling Gabriel's message to her husband, Zacharias. Both Elisabeth and Zacharias were well stricken in years (Luke 1:7–9, 13, 18, 57).

10. Jesus was conceived by the Holy Spirit in the Virgin Mary (Matthew 1:18–20; Luke 1:31, 35).

## 229. Four Sets of Twins

1. The wording in Genesis 4:1–2 suggests that perhaps Cain and Abel were twins.

2. Jacob and Esau (Genesis 25:23–26).

3. Pharez and Zerah (Genesis 38:29–30).

4. The apostle Thomas was called Didymus, which means "a twin" (John 11:16).

## 230. Women Who Died in Childbirth

1. Rachel died giving birth to Benjamin (Genesis 35:16–18).

2. Phinehas' wife died right after giving birth to a son. The stress of her delivery was aggravated by her grief at much tragic news— the ark of God was captured, her husband and father-in-law had died, and Israel was defeated in battle by the Philistines (1 Samuel 4:19–22).

## 231. Youngest Sons

1. Seth was the youngest mentioned son of Adam. Seth's two older brothers were Cain and Abel (Genesis 4).

2. Ham was the youngest of Noah's three sons (Genesis 9:18–24).

3. Jacob was Esau's younger brother (Genesis 25:25–26).

4. Benjamin was youngest of twelve brothers, all of them sons of Jacob (Genesis 35:16–18; 43:29).

5. Ephraim was the youngest son of Joseph. Ephraim's older brother was Manasseh (Genesis 41:51–52).

6. Moses was three years younger than his brother Aaron (Exodus 7:7).

7. Kenaz was Caleb's younger brother (Judges 1:13).

8. Jotham was the youngest of the seventy sons of Jerubbaal (Judges 9:5).

9. David was the youngest of eight brothers (1 Samuel 17:12–14).

10. Segub was the youngest son of Hiel. Segub's older brother was Abiram (1 Kings 16:34).

11. Jehoahaz was Jehoram's youngest son (2 Chronicles 21:16–17).

12. The prodigal son was the younger of two brothers (Luke 15:11–32).

## 232. Ten Families With the Most Children

1. Rehoboam had twenty-eight sons and sixty daughters (2 Chronicles 11:21).

2. Gideon had seventy sons (Judges 8:30).

3. Ahab had seventy sons (2 Kings 10:1).

4. Ibzan had thirty sons and thirty daughters (Judges 12:8–9).

5. Abdon had forty sons and thirty nephews (Judges 12:13–14).

6. Abijah had twenty-two sons and sixteen daughters (2 Chronicles 13:21).

7. Jair had thirty sons (Judges 10:3–4).

8. Shimei had sixteen sons and six daughters (1 Chronicles 4:27).

9. David had nineteen sons and one daughter plus an unknown additional number of children by his concubines (1 Chronicles 3:1–9).

10. Heman had fourteen sons and three daughters (1 Chronicles 25:5).

*Note:* It is not known how many children Solomon had.

# 22

# DWELLINGS

From the Eskimo igloos of the North to the bamboo huts of the Asian tropics, we see a vast array of human dwellings. For some people, a house means barely having a roof over their heads. For others, it means living in a palace of extraordinary beauty and vigilant guards. The contrast in dwelling places is found wherever one goes.

Time has not changed the contrasts in dwelling places. In the Bible we find great men like Elijah and David residing temporarily in caves. We find the glory of the king's palaces in Babylon and the lowliness of tents (such as those of Noah, Abraham, Isaac, and Jacob). Lifeless gods dwelt in temples of grandeur, while powerful men of God, such as John the Baptist, and even the Son of God, had no home of their own.

In this chapter you will learn many interesting facts about Bible dwellings.

## 233. Eight Important Caves

1. After the destruction of Sodom and Gomorrah, Lot lived in a cave with his two daughters (Genesis 19:30).

2. Joshua trapped five kings of southern Canaan in the cave in which they were hiding. Later they were brought out and killed, and then entombed in the same cave (Joshua 10:16–27).

3. The Israelites fled to live in mountain caves and dens to escape the Midianite oppression (Judges 6:2).

4. In Saul's time, Israel again fled to caves and other hiding places to escape the Philistine army (1 Samuel 13:5–7).

5. David used caves as his hideouts and headquarters while Saul sought to kill him (1 Samuel 22:1–2; 23:14, 29).

6. When Jezebel cut off the prophets of the Lord . . . Obadiah took an hundred prophets, and hid them by fifty in a cave, and fed them with bread and water (1 Kings 18:4).

7. When Elijah fled from Jezebel, he came . . . unto a cave, and lodged there; and, behold, the word of the Lord came to him, and he said unto him, What doest thou here, Elijah? (1 Kings 19:9).

8. Lazarus was buried in a cave (John 11:38).

### 234. Five Buildings That Collapsed

1. [Gideon] beat down the tower of Penuel, and slew the men of the city (Judges 8:17).

2. Samson pushed on the two main pillars of a large building and caused it to fall, resulting in the deaths of thousands of Philistines and of Samson himself (Judges 16:23–30).

3. While Job's sons and daughters were feasting in their oldest brother's house, a great wind struck the house, causing it to collapse and kill them (Job 1:18–19).

4. In Jesus' parable, the foolish man's house, built on sand, collapsed when battered by rain, floods, and wind (Matthew 7:26–27).

5. Eighteen people died when the tower of Siloam fell on them (Luke 13:4).

### 235. Nine Rooftops

1. Rahab the harlot brought the two Israelite spies up to the roof of the house, and hid them with the stalks of flax, which she had laid in order upon the roof (Joshua 2:6).

2. There were upon the roof of the building that Samson pulled down about three thousand men and women, that watched while Samson made sport (Judges 16:27).

3. Samuel talked with Saul on Samuel's roof (1 Samuel 9:25–26).

4. While walking on his palace roof one evening, David saw Bathsheba bathing, and lusted after her (2 Samuel 11:2–4).

5. They spread Absalom a tent upon the top of the house; and Absalom went in unto his father's concubines in the sight of all Israel (2 Samuel 16:22).

6. Some Jews of Ezra's day built booths on their roofs to observe the Feast of Tabernacles (Nehemiah 8:14–16).

7. Jeremiah prophesied judgment on the houses of Jerusalem because the people were burning incense and offering drink offerings to idols on their roofs (Jeremiah 19:13).

8. Four men in Capernaum carried a paralytic to the house where Jesus was, seeking his healing. Being otherwise unable to get close to Jesus because of the crowd, they removed a section of the roof and lowered the man on his stretcher to Jesus (Mark 2:3–4).

9. While praying on a housetop, Peter had a vision that led to the first Gentile evangelization (Acts 10:9–16).

## 236. *Fifteen References to Important Tents*

1. Jabal was the father of such as dwell in tents (Genesis 4:20).

2. Noah lived in a tent (Genesis 9:21).

3. Abraham, Isaac, and Jacob lived in tents as they sojourned in Canaan (Hebrews 11:9).

4. Isaac took Rebekah into his mother Sarah's tent on their wedding night (Genesis 24:67).

5. When Jacob finally left Laban, each of the following people had his own tent: Jacob, Laban, Laban's brethren, Leah, Bilhah, Zilpah, and Rachel (Genesis 31:25, 33).

6. The tabernacle in the wilderness was a tent made according to God's specifications. God's presence was there in a special way (Exodus 26:1–4; 2 Samuel 7:6).

7. While the children of Israel were in the wilderness of sin, they lived in tents (Exodus 33:10).

8. Phinehas killed Zimri and Cozbi in Zimri's tent because of their immorality (Numbers 25:6–15).

9. Achan took some of the spoils from the battle of Jericho and buried them inside his tent (Joshua 7:21).

10. When Sisera fled from Israel in battle, Jael invited him into her tent to hide. Then, as he slept, Jael drove a tent peg through his temples, killing him (Judges 4:17–21).

11. A Midianite soldier dreamed that a loaf of barley bread had tumbled into the Midianite camp, striking and flattening a tent. His friend interpreted this to mean that God would give Midian over to Gideon (Judges 7:13–14).

12. After killing the giant, David stored Goliath's armor in his own tent (1 Samuel 17:54).

13. After God caused the Syrian army to flee from their camp, four Samaritan lepers, and then all the Samaritans, plundered their tents (2 Kings 7:3–16).

14. David pitched a tent in Jerusalem to house the ark of God (1 Chronicles 15:1).

15. Jonadab commanded his descendants to always live in tents (Jeremiah 35:6–10).

## 237. Sixteen Temples

1. About one thousand men and women of Shechem entered the house (temple) of the god Berith for protection from Abimelech. However, Abimelech and his men set fire to the building, killing them all (Judges 9:46–49).

2. During Samuel's earlier years, the Philistines captured the ark of the covenant and set it by their idol Dagon in his temple. Twice Dagon fell facedown before the ark (1 Samuel 5:2–4).

3. After Saul was slain, the Philistines put his armour in the house (temple) of Ashtaroth (1 Samuel 31:10).

4. Solomon built the temple of the Lord to replace the portable tabernacle-tent (1 Kings 6).

5. Ahab reared up an altar for Baal in the house (temple) of Baal, which he had built in Samaria (1 Kings 16:32).

6. When his master worshiped in the house (temple) of Rimnon, Naaman bowed down with him (2 Kings 5:18).

7. Sennacherib was assassinated by his two sons while he was worshiping in the house (temple) of Nisroch, his god (2 Kings 19:37).

8. The Philistines fastened Saul's head in the temple of Dagon (1 Chronicles 10:10).

9. Nebuchadnezzar carried some of the vessels of the house of the Lord to Babylon, and put them in his temple at Babylon (2 Chronicles 36:7).

10. After returning from exile in Babylon, the Jews rebuilt the temple, but on a smaller scale than Solomon's temple (Ezra 6:3–15).

11. While in Exile in Babylon, Ezekiel received a very detailed vision of a temple in Israel. He recorded dimensions of pillars, halls, and rooms (Ezekiel 40–42).

12. Jesus said, Destroy this temple, and in three days I will raise it up. Then said the Jews, Forty and six years was this temple in building, and wilt thou rear it up in three days? But he spake of the temple of his body (John 2:19–21).

13. There was a temple of the goddess Diana at Ephesus (Acts 19:27–28).

14. Believers are called the temple of God, both individually (1 Corinthians 6:19) and corporately (2 Corinthians 6:16).

15. In John's vision, he was told to measure the temple in Jerusalem (Revelation 11:1–2).

16. John said he saw no temple in the New Jerusalem, for the Lord God Almighty and the Lamb are the temple (Revelation 21:22).

## 238. Eleven Kings' Palaces

1. Hiram king of Tyre sent messengers to David, and cedar trees, and carpenters, and masons: and they built David an house (2 Samuel 5:11).

2. David referred to the temple that Solomon was to build as a palace for the Lord God (1 Chronicles 29:1, 19).

3. It took Solomon thirteen years to build his large, lavish palace (1 Kings 7:1–12).

4. When Zimri's coup failed, he burned Israel's royal palace over himself and died in the flames (1 Kings 16:15–18).

5. Israel's King Ahab coveted Naboth's vineyard because it was close to his palace. When Naboth refused to sell it, Queen Jezebel had him killed (1 Kings 21:1–19).

6. King Pekahiah of Israel was assassinated in his palace in a coup led by Pekah (2 Kings 15:25).

7. When ambassadors from Babylon came to King Hezekiah, the king showed them the wealth in his palace. Then Isaiah prophesied to Hezekiah that his palace would be plundered by Babylon and his sons would serve in the Babylonian palace (2 Kings 20:16–18).

8. Nehemiah served as cupbearer to the king in Persia's royal palace before going to Jerusalem to rebuild the city wall (Nehemiah 1:1; 2:1).

9. Persia's palace had beds of gold and silver and marble pillars and pavement in the garden court (Esther 1:5–6).

10. King Nebuchadnezzar went insane while walking in his palace (Daniel 4:28–33).

11. A hand appeared and wrote on the wall of the Babylonian palace during King Belshazzar's feast, foretelling the end of the Babylonian empire (Daniel 5:5).

# 23

## JUST FOR LOOKS

When was the last time you saw a true hippie—long, greasy hair, tangled moustache and beard, hip-length fringed leather coat, and patched blue jeans? It's been a while. The patched jeans have been replaced by faded ones, and the leather coat has been succeeded by Polo and Izod shirts; the tangled hair has given way to a succession of short, precise styles, even the bald head.

Westerners place great importance upon conforming to the latest styles. Conformity to the style of the day generally assumes acceptance by others, especially one's peers. Eastern cultures seldom change their styles, but conformity to style is still important.

Styles may not have been a major issue in Bible times, but any deviation from them indicated something of real importance. To shave one's head meant one thing, as did pulling out one's hair. To wear sackcloth was an indication of grief, as was the use of ashes. One did not tear his garments in public unless he was declaring something. Chains or ropes were another important "accessory" that one might be unfortunate enough to wear (not a fashion statement back then).

But to those seeking after God, there is no style or designer label that can match God's custom-designed "garments of righteousness."

### 239. Haircuts

1. Part of the ceremony for a leper who recovered involved shaving all his hair off twice, six days apart (Leviticus 14:8–9).

2. The Jews were forbidden to round the corners of their heads, referring to a certain hairstyle (Leviticus 19:27).

3. When an Israelite took a Nazarite vow, he was not to cut his hair. When this time of separation was completed, he shaved his head and burned the hair (Numbers 6:5, 13, 18).

4. The Levites shaved their whole bodies as part of the ceremony consecrating them to the Lord (Numbers 8:5–7).

5. If an Israelite took a woman from among the captives in war to be his wife, she first had to shave her head (Deuteronomy 21:10–12).

6. When Samson's head was shaved, his strength left him (Judges 16:19).

7. Absalom cut his hair once a year because it got too heavy (2 Samuel 14:25–26).

8. When Ezra heard that the Jews were intermarrying with the Canaanites and other nationalities, he was so upset that he pulled hair from his head and beard (Ezra 9:1–3).

9. In another occurrence of wrong intermarriage, Nehemiah pulled out the hair of some men of Judah as he charged them not to intermarry (Nehemiah 13:23–27).

10. After losing his children and wealth, Job shaved his head in his grief (Job 1:20).

11. The people of Jerusalem were told to cut off their hair in response to the Lord's rejection of them (Jeremiah 7:29).

12. God told Ezekiel to shave his head and beard, and then use the hair to symbolize Israel (Ezekiel 5:1–4).

13. Haircuts were prescribed for the priests. They were not to shave their heads or let their hair grow long (Ezekiel 44:20).

14. Paul shaved his head at Cenchrea, in connection with a vow (Acts 18:18).

15. Shaving one's head in relation to a vow is also seen in Acts 21:23–26.

## 240. Rings

1. When Pharaoh promoted Joseph, he put his own ring on Joseph's finger (Genesis 41:42).

2. Some Israelites gave a freewill offering for the tabernacle and its furnishings from their rings and other gold jewelry (Exodus 35:22).

3. King Ahasuerus of Persia gave his signet ring to Haman. The ring was then used to seal copies of an edict ordering the destruction of all Jews (Esther 3:10–13).

4. After Haman was hanged, Ahasuerus gave his royal signet ring to Mordecai. The ring was then used to seal copies of Mordecai's edict, which reversed Haman's decree and allowed the Jews to take vengeance on their enemies (Esther 8:2–13).

5. When Daniel was thrown into the lions' den, they laid a stone upon the mouth of the den, and the king sealed it with his signet. This signet may have been a ring (Daniel 6:17).

6. When the father welcomed back his prodigal son, he ordered that a ring be put on the son's finger (Luke 15:22).

### 241. *Perfume and Cosmetics*

1. The holy oil used for anointing Israel's priests was perfumed with aromatic spices (Exodus 30:23–33).

2. Jezebel painted her face before meeting with Jehu (2 Kings 9:30).

3. Women in King Ahasuerus' harem were purified with perfumes (Esther 2:12).

4. The adulteress of Proverbs 7 perfumed her bed with myrrh, aloes, and cinnamon (7:17).

5. Ointment and perfume rejoice the heart (Proverbs 27:9).

6. The lovers of the Song of Solomon lavishly used valuable perfumes:
   a. Solomon used myrrh, frankincense, and other spices (1:3; 3:6; 4:6).
   b. His wife used spikenard, camphire, saffron, calamus, cinnamon, frankincense, myrrh and aloes, among others (1:12; 4:10–14; 5:1, 5).

7. Jeremiah 4:30 and Ezekiel 23:40 mention fictitious women painting their eyes.

8. Daniel used no anointing oils during his three weeks of mourning (Daniel 10:3).

9. Frankincense and myrrh were given to Jesus by the wise men (Matthew 2:11).

10. A sinful woman anointed Jesus' feet with ointment (perfume) (Luke 7:37–38).

11. Mary (Lazarus' sister) anointed Jesus' feet with expensive spikenard. The odor of the ointment filled the house (John 12:3).

12. On yet another occasion, a woman came to Jesus and poured very precious ointment on his head (Matthew 26:7).

## 242. Chains, Ropes, and Threads

1. When Tamar gave birth, one of her twins put out his hand, and the midwife took and bound upon his hand a scarlet thread, saying, This came out first (Genesis 38:28).

2. Pharaoh put a gold chain about Joseph's neck (Genesis 41:42).

3. Aaron's ephod included gold chains of wreathen work (Exodus 28:14).

4. Rahab dropped a scarlet cord from her window to aid the spies to leave the city and then she used it later to show them where she lived (Joshua 2:15–19).

5. Gideon claimed for himself the gold chains that were about the necks of the Midianites' camels (Judges 8:26).

6. The Philistines bound Samson with seven fresh cords, but he broke them as soon as the Philistines came to get him (Judges 16:6–9).

7. Samson said that if he were bound with new ropes that had never been used, he would be as weak as any man, and then he broke them from his arms like a thread (Judges 16:11–12).

8. Benhadad's servants put sackcloth on their loins and ropes on their heads to beg for mercy from King Ahab (1 Kings 20:31).

9. Solomon made chains strung with pomegranates to decorate the temple (2 Chronicles 3:16).

10. Nebuchadrezzar put out Zedekiah's eyes and bound him with chains to carry him to Babylon (Jeremiah 39:7).

11. Jeremiah was bound in chains among all that were carried away captive of Jerusalem and Judah (Jeremiah 40:1).

12. Belshazzar clothed Daniel with scarlet and put a chain of gold around his neck (Daniel 5:29).

13. The Gadarene demoniac had been bound, but the chains had been torn asunder by him and the fetters broken in pieces (Mark 5:3–4).

14. When the angel woke up Peter in prison, Peter's chains fell off and he was set free (Acts 12:6–7).

15. The chief captain took Paul and commanded him to be bound with two chains; then he demanded who he was and what he had done (Acts 21:33).

16. The soldiers on Paul's ship cut the ropes holding the lifeboat so that the crew could not escape (Acts 27:30–32).

17. When Paul arrived in Rome, he was bound with a chain (Acts 28:20).

18. John saw an angel come down from heaven, having the key of the bottomless pit and a great chain in his hand. And he laid hold of that old serpent, the devil, and bound him for a thousand years (Revelation 20:1–2).

## 243. *Fourteen Colors in the Bible*

1. The middle of the fiery cloud in Ezekiel's vision was as the colour of *amber* (Ezekiel 1:4).

2. In the fourth chariot [were] *grisled* [dapple-gray] and *bay* [reddish brown] horses (Zechariah 6:3).

3. His locks are bushy, and *black* as a raven (Song of Solomon 5:11).

4. When the Israelite camp moved, various utensils in the tabernacle would be covered with *blue* cloths before being carried (Numbers 4:5–12).

5. The "man" that came to Daniel in Daniel 10 had arms and feet like in colour to polished *brass* (10:6).

6. And he [Jacob] removed . . . all the *brown* among the sheep (Genesis 30:35).

7. What be these two olive branches which through the two *golden* pipes empty the *golden* oil out of themselves? (Zechariah 4:12).

8. Then shall ye bring down my *gray* hairs with sorrow to the grave (Genesis 42:38).

9. He maketh me to lie down in *green* pastures (Psalm 23:2).

10. They put on [Jesus] a *purple* robe (John 19:2).

11. It will be fair weather: for the sky is *red* (Matthew 16:2).

12. I saw a woman sit upon a *scarlet*-colored beast (Revelation 17:3).

13. And I saw a great *white* throne (Revelation 20:11).

14. She saw . . . the images of the Chaldeans portrayed with *vermilion* (Ezekiel 23:14).

## 244. Seven Types of Fabric

1. John had his raiment of *camel's hair* (Matthew 3:4).

2. And thou shalt make curtains of *goat's hair* to be a covering upon the tabernacle (Exodus 26:7).

3. He wrapped [the body of Jesus] in a clean *linen* cloth (Matthew 27:59).

4. Lydia was a seller of *purple* [cloth dyed with natural dyes] (Acts 16:14).

5. The sun became black as *sackcloth of hair* (Revelation 6:12).

6. *Silk* was one of the items that the merchants of the earth sold to Babylon (Revelation 18:11–12).

7. Your sins . . . shall be as *wool* (Isaiah 1:18).

## 245. Sackcloth

1. Jacob put on sackcloth when he heard that Joseph had perished (Genesis 37:34).

2. Benhadad's servants wore sackcloth before Ahab (1 Kings 20:31–32).

3. Job wore sackcloth (Job 16:15).

4. Jeremiah prophesied that the people of Zion should put on sackcloth in view of the coming destroyer (Jeremiah 4:8).

5. The elders of the daughters of Zion wore sackcloth (Lamentations 2:10).

6. Daniel sought the Lord in sackcloth (Daniel 9:3).

7. Prophecy was given in order that a nation might lament in sack-cloth (Joel 1:8).

8. A pagan city wore sackcloth in repentance before the Lord (Jonah 3:8).

## 246. Uses of Ashes

1. A symbol of mourning (2 Samuel 13:19; Esther 4:1, 3).

2. A symbol of repentance (Job 42:6; Daniel 9:3; Jonah 3:6; Matthew 11:21; Luke 10:13).

3. A means of disguise (1 Kings 20:38, 41).

4. To sit in for mourning or fasting (Job 2:8; Isaiah 58:5; Jeremiah 6:26).

## 247. Twenty-one Rendings of Garments

1. Both Reuben and Jacob rent their clothes when they heard that Joseph had been killed (Genesis 37:29, 34).

2. Joseph's brothers rent their clothes upon finding the silver cup in Benjamin's sack (Genesis 44:13).

3. Joshua and Caleb rent their clothes when the people murmured against the Lord about going into the Promised Land (Numbers 14:6).

4. Jephthah rent his clothes when his hasty words came back to torment him (Judges 11:35).

5. David and all the men with him rent their clothes when they heard that King Saul was dead (2 Samuel 1:11).

6. David commanded Joab and the people with him to rend their clothes upon the death of Abner (2 Samuel 3:31).

7. Tamar rent her clothing after being raped by Amnon (2 Samuel 13:19).

8. David rent his clothes when he heard that Absalom had taken his revenge upon Amnon (2 Samuel 13:31).

9. Hushai the Archite came to meet David with rent clothes (2 Samuel 15:32).

10. Elisha rent his clothes when Elijah was taken up to heaven (2 Kings 2:12).

11. The king of Israel rent his clothes when he heard that Naaman had been sent to him to be healed of leprosy (2 Kings 5:7).

12. The unnamed king of Israel rent his clothes when he heard a woman quarreling about eating another woman's son (2 Kings 6:30).

13. Athaliah rent her clothes when Jehoiada the priest put her out of power (2 Kings 11:14).

14. King Hezekiah rent his clothes when Rabshakeh denounced the Lord before the people of Israel (2 Kings 19:1).

15. Josiah rent his clothes when the book of the law was read in his presence for the first time (2 Kings 22:11, 19).

16. Ezra rent his clothing when he heard about the mixture of marriages between God's people and the nations around them (Ezra 9:3, 5).

17. Job rent his clothes when he heard an evil report (Job 1:20).

18. Job's three friends rent their clothes when they saw Job (Job 2:12).

19. Eighty men came to the house of the Lord with rent clothes (Jeremiah 41:5).

20. The high priest rent his clothes when Jesus spoke of His being seated at the right hand of God's power (Matthew 26:65).

21. Barnabas and Paul rent their clothes when those who witnessed the miracle at Lystra began to worship them as gods (Acts 14:14).

# 24
# EAT AND DRINK

The tradition of mealtime around a table to enjoy family being together and to discuss expectations and experiences of the day has waned in our culture. With family members heading in different directions at all hours of the day, food is often gulped down while standing or driving. As a result, we have lost some of the benefit of God's original purpose for eating and drinking (beyond nourishment)—fellowship and enjoyment.

The following sixteen lists show the many aspects of the role of food and drink in the lives of those living in Bible times. Do any of these sound familiar? Family meals, banquets, meals with friends, marriage feasts, community picnics, discussions about the merits of wine (or not), times of fasting, times of famine, breads, soups, "miraculous" or unexpected meals, strange foods, poisonous foods, distasteful foods.

## 248. Twenty-seven Important Meals
1. The original sin occurred when Adam and Eve ate the fruit of the forbidden tree (Genesis 3:6).
2. When the Lord and two angels came to Abraham in human form, Abraham served a meal to them (Genesis 18:1–8).
3. After leaving Abraham, the two angels went to Sodom. Lot welcomed them into his house and made them a feast (Genesis 19:1–3).
4. Esau sold his birthright for a meal of bread and lentil soup (Genesis 25:29–34).

5. Jacob obtained his father's blessing by serving him a meal and disguising himself as his brother Esau (Genesis 27:1–29).

6. When Joseph's brothers went down to Egypt the second time, Joseph (still hiding his identity) invited them to eat with him (Genesis 43:16–34).

7. In the first Passover observance, each Jewish household killed a lamb, applied its blood to the doorposts, roasted the meat, and ate it. God commanded that the Passover meal, plus seven days of eating unleavened bread, be observed annually from then on, in remembrance of Israel's deliverance from Egypt (Exodus 12:1–20).

8. When David's daughter Tamar served some food to her half-brother Amnon (who was pretending to be sick), he raped her (2 Samuel 13:1–14).

9. Ravens brought Elijah bread and meat while he hid by the brook Cherith (1 Kings 17:3–6).

10. Later, a widow of Zarephath fed Elijah. Her supply of meal and oil was miraculously replenished during the famine (1 Kings 17:8–16).

11. When Elijah called Elisha to be a prophet, Elisha killed and boiled his yoke of oxen and gave a feast before following Elijah (1 Kings 19:19–21).

12. Queen Vashti was deposed during a seven-day banquet King Ahasuerus gave for the people of Shushan (Esther 1:5–21).

13. At the second of two banquets Queen Esther gave for the king and Haman, she revealed Haman's plot to have all the Jews killed. As a result, Haman was hanged and the Jews were saved (Esther 7).

14. The Jews feasted to celebrate their victory over Haman and their other enemies. Mordecai and Esther made this feast, called Purim, an annual event (Esther 9:17–32).

15. As Job's sons and daughters were feasting in their eldest brother's home, the house collapsed, killing them all (Job 1:18–19).

16. Daniel and his friends chose to eat vegetables rather than defile themselves with the king's rich food (Daniel 1:5–16).

17. As Belshazzar gave a great feast in his palace, the handwriting on the wall announced the end of his kingdom (Daniel 5).

18. The Pharisees criticized the disciples for plucking grain to eat on the Sabbath (Matthew 12:1–8).

19. John the Baptist was beheaded at Herodias' daughter's request after she danced at Herod's birthday supper (Mark 6:21–28).

20. Jesus miraculously fed five thousand men with five loaves and two fish (John 6:5–14). Later He fed four thousand in similar fashion (Matthew 15:32–38).

21. Martha and Mary invited Jesus to their home for a meal. Martha occupied herself with preparation for the meal, but Mary sat at Jesus' feet (Luke 10:38–42).

22. Jesus told a parable of a man who made a great banquet and invited many people. They all turned him down, so he had others brought in from the streets so that his house would be filled (Luke 14:16–24).

23. The father made a joyful feast of a fatted calf when his prodigal son returned home (Luke 15:20–25).

24. Mary anointed Jesus' feet with precious ointment while He was their supper guest (John 12:1–3). Jesus was also anointed by women at two other meals during His lifetime (Luke 7:36–50; Matthew 26:6–13).

25. Jesus' Last Supper was the Passover meal that He ate with the twelve disciples in the upper room (Matthew 26:1–30).

26. Jesus ate three meals with His disciples after His resurrection: He broke bread in Emmaus (Luke 24:30), ate fish at Jerusalem to prove that He was not a ghost (Luke 24:38–43), and ate fish and bread by the Sea of Galilee (John 21:12–14).

27. John witnessed the marriage feast of the Lamb in heaven (Revelation 19:9).

### 249. Three Forty-Day Fasts

1. Moses neither ate nor drank while he talked with God for forty days on Mount Sinai (Exodus 34:27–28).

2. The angel of the Lord fed Elijah two meals, which gave him strength for the next forty days (1 Kings 19:5–8).

3. Jesus fasted for forty days in the wilderness after His baptism (Matthew 4:1–2).

## 250. *Twenty-four Shorter Fasts*

1. The Israelites fasted for the rest of the day after the Benjamites had defeated them in two successive battles (Judges 20:26).

2. The children of Israel repented of their idolatry and fasted with Samuel at Mizpah for a day (1 Samuel 7:3–6).

3. Saul ordered a fast for his soldiers while pursuing the Philistines. His son Jonathan had not heard about it, so he ate some wild honey that day (1 Samuel 14:24–27).

4. When Saul was unsuccessfully inquiring of the Lord, he fasted all day and night (1 Samuel 28:20).

5. The inhabitants of Jabesh-gilead fasted for seven days (1 Samuel 31:11–13), and David and his men fasted the rest of the day when they heard about the deaths of Saul and his sons (2 Samuel 1:11–12).

6. The Lord struck the child that Uriah's wife bore unto David, and it was very sick. David sought God for the child, and fasted (2 Samuel 12:15–16).

7. Because her husband Ahab wanted Naboth's vineyard, Queen Jezebel proclaimed a day of fasting as part of a scheme to get it (1 Kings 21:8–10).

8. King Ahab humbled himself and fasted when Elijah accused him of Naboth's murder (1 Kings 21:27).

9. King Jehoshaphat sought the Lord and proclaimed a fast in Judah when the Moabites attacked (2 Chronicles 20:1–4).

10. Before leaving Babylonia for Jerusalem, Ezra and his troop sought the Lord and fasted (Ezra 8:21–23).

11. Nehemiah fasted when asking the Lord for favor before the king of Persia (Nehemiah 1:1–4).

12. The inhabitants of Jerusalem separated themselves from the people of the land and fasted (Nehemiah 9:1–3).

13. Mordecai and the rest of the Jews in Media-Persia fasted after

the king declared that they were all to be killed (Esther 4:1–3, 15–16).

14. The people of Judah came to Jerusalem for a fast, and Baruch read them the prophecy of Jeremiah (Jeremiah 36:9–10).

15. After Daniel had been thrown into the lions' den, King Darius spent the night fasting (Daniel 6:18).

16. Daniel fasted as he sought the Lord for the liberation of his people from Media-Persia (Daniel 9:3–4).

17. Jonah's warning of God's wrath drove the people of Nineveh to repentance, and the king declared a fast until God's wrath was turned away (Jonah 3:4–10).

18. Jesus told the disciples that they should have prayed and fasted in order to gain power over a demon that they had not been able to cast out (Matthew 17:21).

19. Saul fasted for three days in Damascus while he waited for Ananias (Acts 9:9).

20. Cornelius was fasting and praying when an angel appeared to him and told him to send for Peter (Acts 10:1–3).

21. The elders at Antioch fasted and prayed and laid hands on Paul and Barnabas before sending them out as missionaries (Acts 13:1–3).

22. Paul and Barnabas fasted and prayed as they chose elders for each new church (Acts 14:23).

23. Forty men bound themselves by oath neither to eat nor drink until they had killed Paul (Acts 23:20–21).

24. The 275 passengers on the storm-tossed ship with Paul had fasted for fourteen days (Acts 27:33).

## 251. Winepresses

1. Gideon threshed wheat by the winepress to hide it from the Midianites (Judges 6:11).

2. Gideon's army slew Zeeb the Midianite at the winepress of Zeeb (Judges 7:25).

3. Isaiah spoke of Judah as a vineyard and of God putting them into His winepress of wrath (Isaiah 5:1–2; 63:1–4).

4. Jesus told a parable about a householder who planted a vineyard, dug a winepress, and rented it out to tenants (Matthew 21:33–41).

## 252. Jesus and Wine

1. Jesus turned the water into wine at the wedding in Cana (John 2:1–10).

2. No one puts new wine into an old wineskin, otherwise the new wine will burst the wineskin and the wine will be lost as well as the wineskin. New wine must be put into a new wineskin so that both are preserved (Luke 5:37–38).

3. The Son of man came eating and drinking, and they called him gluttonous, a winebibber, and a friend of publicans and sinners (Matthew 11:19; Luke 7:34).

4. No one having drunk old wine desires new. He says, The old is better (Luke 5:39).

5. And he took the cup, and gave thanks, and gave it to them, saying, Drink ye all of it; for this is my blood of the new testament, which is shed for many for the remission of sins. But I say unto you, I will not drink henceforth of this fruit of the vine, until that day when I drink it new with you in my Father's kingdom (Matthew 26:27–29).

6. And they gave him to drink wine mingled with myrrh: but he received it not (Mark 15:23).

## 253. Nine Old Testament Admonitions About Wine

1. The Lord spoke unto Aaron, saying, Do not drink wine nor strong drink, thou, nor thy sons with thee, when ye go into the tabernacle of the congregation, lest ye die (Leviticus 10:8–9).

2. When either man or woman shall separate themselves to vow a vow of a Nazarite, to separate themselves unto the Lord: he shall separate himself from wine and strong drink, and shall drink no vinegar of wine, or vinegar of strong drink, neither shall he drink any liquor of grapes, nor eat moist grapes, or dried (Numbers 6:2–3).

3. It is not for kings, O Lemuel, it is not for kings to drink wine; nor for princes strong drink: lest they drink, and forget the law, and pervert the judgment of any of the afflicted (Proverbs 31:4–5).

4. Wine is a mocker, strong drink is raging: and whosoever is deceived thereby is not wise (Proverbs 20:1).

5. He that loveth wine and oil shall not be rich (Proverbs 21:17).

6. Who hath woe? who hath sorrow? who hath contentions? who hath babbling? who hath wounds without cause? who hath redness of eyes? They that tarry long at the wine; they that go to seek mixed wine (Proverbs 23:29–30).

7. Look not thou upon wine when it is red, when it giveth his colour in the cup, when it moveth itself aright. At the last it biteth like a serpent, and stingeth like an adder (Proverbs 23:31–32).

8. Give strong drink unto him that is ready to perish, and wine unto those that be of heavy hearts. Let him drink, and forget his poverty, and remember his misery no more (Proverbs 31:6–7).

9. Woe unto them that rise up early in the morning, that they may follow strong drink; that continue until night, till wine inflame them! (Isaiah 5:11).

## 254. *Four New Testament Admonitions About Wine*

1. It is good neither to eat flesh, nor to drink wine, nor any thing whereby thy brother stumbleth, or is offended, or is made weak (Romans 14:21).

2. Be not drunk with wine, wherein is excess; but be filled with the Spirit (Ephesians 5:18).

3. Paul wrote to Timothy, Drink no longer water, but use a little wine for thy stomach's sake and thine often infirmities (1 Timothy 5:23).

4. A bishop must be blameless . . . not given to wine (1 Timothy 3:2–3; Titus 1:7).

## 255. *Fourteen Famines*

1. There was a famine in the land: and Abram went down into Egypt to sojourn there; for the famine was grievous in the land (Genesis 12:10).

2. There was a famine in the land, beside the first famine that was

in the days of Abraham. And Isaac went unto Abimelech king of the Philistines unto Gerar (Genesis 26:1).

3. Pharaoh made Joseph the food-storage supervisor in preparation for the impending famine that eventually covered all the earth (Genesis 41).

4. God sent a dense swarm of locusts to destroy all the plants that remained in Egypt after the plague of hail had destroyed most of the crops (Exodus 10:14–15).

5. The Midianites would swoop through the land of Israel during Gideon's time, plundering and destroying all the crops and livestock they found (Judges 6:3–6).

6. Elimelech and his wife Naomi moved to Moab to escape the famine in Bethlehem (Ruth 1:1–2).

7. There was a famine in the days of David three years . . . because [Saul] slew the Gibeonites (2 Samuel 21:1).

8. Elijah prophesied a draught and Samaria suffered three years of famine until he told King Ahab that it would rain again (1 Kings 17:1; 18:2, 41–45).

9. God sent a seven-year famine upon Israel during Elisha's ministry (2 Kings 8:1–2).

10. Nebuchadnezzar king of Babylon came, he, and all his host, against Jerusalem, and pitched against it; and they built forts against it round about. And . . . the famine prevailed in the city and there was no bread for the people of the land (2 Kings 25:1–3).

11. The Chaldeans laid siege against Jerusalem, and God allowed famine and pestilence upon the people to judge them (Jeremiah 32:24, 36; 52:6).

12. The penniless prodigal son found himself in the midst of a great famine (Luke 15:14).

13. And there stood up one of them named Agabus, and signified by the Spirit that there should be great dearth throughout all the world; which came to pass in the days of Claudius Caesar (Acts 11:28).

14. The rider of the pale horse spreads famine and pestilence over the earth (Revelation 6:8).

### 256. Seven Miraculous Meals

1. God fed Israel with heaven-sent manna in the wilderness (Exodus 16:11–15).

2. Ravens brought [Elijah] bread and flesh in the morning, and bread and flesh in the evening (1 Kings 17:6).

3. The widow of Zarephath made Elijah a cake of bread and, as promised, her cruse of oil never ran dry, nor did her barrel of meal go empty (1 Kings 17:12–16).

4. An angel prepared a meal for Elijah that gave him strength for forty days and nights (1 Kings 19:5–8).

5. Elisha fed one hundred men with twenty barley biscuits. They all ate and still had leftovers (2 Kings 4:42–44).

6. Jesus fed about five thousand men (not including the women and children with them) with only five small loaves of bread and two fish. Everyone ate enough, and leftovers filled twelve baskets (Matthew 14:15–21).

7. Jesus also fed four thousand men (plus the women and children with them) with seven loaves and a few small fish. There were seven basketfuls of food left over (Matthew 15:32–38).

### 257. Three Soups

1. Jacob traded bread and pottage of lentils (meat and vegetables in a stew) for Esau's birthright (Genesis 25:29–34).

2. Gideon fixed a meal for an angel. The meal included a pot of broth (Judges 6:19).

3. Elijah fed the sons of the prophets with a pot of stew (2 Kings 4:38).

### 258. Loaves of Bread

1. Twelve loaves of bread were to be left upon the table in the tabernacle (Leviticus 24:5–7).

2. Three men confirmed Samuel's words to Saul by giving him two loaves of bread as had been prophesied (1 Samuel 10:3–4).

3. David and his men took the twelve loaves of the Bread of the

Presence from the tabernacle while Saul was chasing David to kill him (1 Samuel 21:1–6).

4. The widow of Zarephath prepared a loaf of bread for Elijah out of her last bit of flour (1 Kings 17:11–16).

5. Jesus took five loaves and fed five thousand men (Matthew 14:15–21) and later took seven loaves and fed four thousand (Matthew 15:32–38).

6. Jesus took the bread, and blessed it, and brake it, and gave it to his disciples, and said, Take, eat: this is my body (Matthew 26:26).

7. The men at Emmaus did not recognize Jesus until He took the bread, blessed it, and broke it (Luke 24:30–31).

8. The Gibeonites fooled Joshua by showing him moldy loaves of bread and telling him that the loaves had been freshly baked for their journey (Joshua 9:12).

## 259. Sweet and Sour: Flavors in the Bible

1. God commanded Israel to keep the Passover meal by eating a lamb with unleavened bread and bitter herbs (Exodus 12:8).

2. Moses was to make a special anointing oil with olive oil and cinnamon (Exodus 30:23–25).

3. Garlic, onions, and leeks were some of the pleasures of Egypt for which the Israelites longed (Numbers 11:5).

4. The psalmist said, My meditation of him shall be sweet: I will be glad in the Lord (Psalm 104:34).

5. Stolen waters are sweet, and bread eaten in secret is pleasant (Proverbs 9:17).

6. Bread of deceit is sweet to a man; but afterwards his mouth shall be filled with gravel (Proverbs 20:17).

7. My son, eat thou honey, because it is good; and the honeycomb, which is sweet to thy taste (Proverbs 24:13).

8. The full soul loatheth an honeycomb; but to the hungry soul every bitter thing is sweet (Proverbs 27:7).

9. God asks the people why they bother making sacrifices when your burnt offerings are not acceptable, nor your sacrifices sweet unto me (Jeremiah 6:20).

10. The fathers have eaten a sour grape, and the children's teeth are set on edge (Jeremiah 31:29).

11. Behold, the days come, saith the Lord, that the plowman shall overtake the reaper, and the treader of grapes him that soweth seed; and the mountains shall drop sweet wine, and all the hills shall melt (Amos 9:13).

12. Does a fountain send forth at the same place sweet water and bitter? (James 3:11).

13. Ezekiel ate a book and declared that it was as sweet as honey in his mouth (Ezekiel 2:9–3:3).

14. John also ate a book but wrote, It was in my mouth sweet as honey; and as soon as I had eaten it, my belly was bitter (Revelation 10:9–10).

## 260. Five Poisons

1. The Lord sent fiery serpents among the people, and they bit the people; and much people of Israel died (Numbers 21:6).

2. Elisha "healed" a poisonous spring of water (2 Kings 2:19–22).

3. The sons of the prophets made pottage but accidentally threw in some poisonous gourds. Elisha made it fit to eat again (2 Kings 4:41).

4. James said that the tongue is an unruly evil, full of deadly poison (James 3:8).

5. Christ promised, These things shall follow them that believe . . . if they drink any deadly thing, it shall not hurt them (Mark 16:17–18).

## 261. Instances of Cannibalism

1. A woman in Samaria boiled her son and ate him with her neighbor and then cried to the king when her neighbor would not boil her son (2 Kings 6:24–29).

2. Women boiled and ate their children during the Babylonian siege on Jerusalem (Lamentations 4:10).

## 262. Strange Foods

1. Moses took the golden calf which they had made, and burnt it in the fire, and ground it to powder, and strowed it upon the water, and made the children of Israel drink of it (Exodus 32:20).

2. God sent manna for the children of Israel to eat while they wandered in the wilderness. *Manna* means "what is it?" (Exodus 16:15).

3. Samson ate honey from the carcass of a lion (Judges 14:8–9).

4. John the Baptist ate locusts and wild honey (Matthew 3:4).

## 263. The Biggest Meals in the Bible

1. The Lord fed the entire nation of Israel for forty years on manna (Deuteronomy 8:16).

2. The people complained about the manna, so God sent them quail for an entire month (Numbers 11:19, 31).

3. Solomon's provision for one day was thirty measures of fine flour, and threescore measures of meal, ten fat oxen, and twenty oxen out of the pasture, and an hundred sheep, besides harts, and roebucks, and fallowdeer, and fatted fowl (1 Kings 4:22–23).

4. Jesus fed five thousand men with five loaves and two fish and four thousand men with seven loaves and a few fish (Matthew 14:19–21; 15:32–38).

# 25
## WATER

We sometimes hear news reports about a city's water supply that has been discovered to be contaminated or at least questionable for a time. Our oceans and lakes also can become contaminated from oil spills or algae, among other things. Life for those depending upon this water sometimes becomes chaotic and frustrating. Though we usually take it for granted, good water is absolutely essential for our survival.

In Bible times water was not taken for granted. The task of drawing water was a daily chore for each family. The following seven lists show the vital role of water in the lives of people in Bible times. We see the importance of the local wells and their prominent place in the life of the community, miracles that occurred related to water, important rivers and lakes, the use of water in baptisms, and the need for swimming lessons.

### 264. Fourteen Water Miracles

1. Moses and Aaron did so, as the Lord commanded; and he lifted up the rod, and smote the waters that were in the river . . . and all the waters that were in the river were turned to blood (Exodus 7:20).

2. While the Egyptian army pursued the children of Israel, the Lord opened a dry path across the Red Sea for the Israelites. The Egyptians followed closely behind the fleeing Hebrews but

were drowned when the walls of water collapsed and filled the walkway (Exodus 14:21–29).

3. When [the children of Israel] came to Marah, they could not drink of the waters of Marah, for they were bitter . . . and the people murmured against Moses, saying, What shall we drink? And he cried unto the Lord; and the Lord showed him a tree, which when he had cast into the waters, the waters were made sweet (Exodus 15:23–25).

4. In the desert the Israelites twice complained about having no water. Both times the Lord caused water to come out of a rock (Exodus 17:1–6; 20:1–11).

5. The waters of the Jordan rose up in a heap far upstream when the priests carrying the ark of the covenant dipped the soles of their feet into the water. The Israelites crossed the river on dry ground (Joshua 3:7–17).

6. Gideon wrung out a bowlful of water from the fleece in answer to prayer (Judges 6:38).

7. Elijah struck the waters of the Jordan with his mantle and he walked across on dry ground with Elisha. Elisha returned later with the same mantle and struck the waters. He crossed again on dry ground (2 Kings 2:8–14).

8. Elisha "healed" Jericho's water supply by throwing salt into it (2 Kings 2:19–22).

9. God gave water to the thirsty army of Israel by commanding them to dig trenches, and then He filled them during the night without making it rain (2 Kings 3:14–22).

10. Naaman, commander of the Syrian army, was healed after dipping seven times in the Jordan River (2 Kings 5:14).

11. As one was felling a beam, the axe head fell into the water: and he cried, and said, Alas, master! for it was borrowed. And [Elisha] said, Where fell it? And he showed him the place. And he cut down a stick, and cast it in thither; and the iron did swim . . . and he put out his hand and took it (2 Kings 6:5–7).

12. Jesus walked on the Sea of Galilee to meet His disciples in their ship. Peter crawled over the side to join Him, and he also walked on the water (Matthew 14:25–31).

13. Jesus spoke to the sea and calmed it (Mark 4:39).

14. Jesus turned the water into wine at the wedding feast in Cana (John 2:1–10).

## 265. *Eight Important Water Containers*

1. [Abraham's] servant ran to meet her [Rebekah], and said, Let me, I pray thee, drink a little water of thy *pitcher*. And she said, Drink, my lord: and . . . when she had done giving him drink, she said, I will draw water for thy camels also (Genesis 24:17–19).

2. The Lord spake unto Moses, saying, Thou shalt also make a *laver* of brass, and his foot also of brass, to wash withal: and thou shalt put it between the tabernacle of the congregation and the altar, and thou shalt put water therein. For Aaron and his sons shall wash their hands and their feet thereat (Exodus 30:17–19).

3. Gideon set out a fleece of wool on the threshing floor. In the morning, though the ground around it was dry, he wrung a *bowl* of water from the fleece (Judges 6:36–38).

4. David sneaked into Saul's camp and took Saul's spear and *cruse* of water (1 Samuel 26:7–11).

5. After the priests of Baal failed to call down fire upon their sacrifice, Elijah built his altar to the Lord and had four *barrels* of water poured over the sacrifice three times (2 Kings 18:31–38).

6. [Jesus'] disciples said unto him, Where wilt thou that we go and prepare that thou mayest eat the passover? And he sendeth forth two of his disciples, and saith unto them, Go ye into the city, and there shall meet you a man bearing a *pitcher* of water: follow him (Mark 14:12–13).

7. Jesus turned the water in six *waterpots of stone* into wine at Cana (John 2:6).

8. Jesus filled a *basin* with water and washed the disciples' feet (John 13:3–5).

## 266. *Twelve Important Wells*

1. The angel of the Lord spoke to Hagar at the well called Beerlahairoi between Kadesh and Bered (Genesis 16:7–14).

2. Abimelech's servants attempted to take a well called Beersheba away from Abraham. They settled their differences by making a covenant with one another (Genesis 21:22–32).

3. Abraham's servant found a wife for Isaac by the well at the city of Nahor (Genesis 24:10–67).

4. Isaac's servants dug two wells that he gave up to other herdsmen rather than fight over them. He called them Esek and Sitnah. They then dug two more wells that he kept without trouble. He called them Rehoboth and Beersheba (Genesis 26:17–33).

5. Jacob met Rachel when she came to water her sheep at a well that was covered by a stone (Genesis 29:1–12).

6. Moses met his wife Zipporah when he helped her and her sisters water their flock at a well in the land of Midian (Exodus 2:15–21).

7. It was at the well of Harod that God whittled Gideon's troops down to the courageous three hundred (Judges 7:1–7).

8. After Samson slew a thousand men with the jawbone of an ass, he was extremely thirsty. God opened the ground and water came out. Samson called the well Enhakkore (Judges 15:18–20).

9. Abner was at the well of Sirah when he was summoned to his death by Joab's vigilantes (2 Samuel 3:26–27).

10. Jonathan and Ahimaaz escaped Absalom's men by hiding in a well in Bahurim (2 Samuel 17:17–21).

11. David longed for a drink from the well at Bethlehem, so three mighty men broke through the Philistine defenses and drew water for him. He poured it out as a sacrifice to the Lord (2 Samuel 23:14–17).

12. Jesus talked with the woman of Samaria at Jacob's well (John 4:5–15).

## 267. Thirteen Important Rivers, Brooks, Lakes, and Seas

1. A great river flowed into the garden of Eden and divided into the Pison, the Gihon, the Hiddekel, and the Euphrates (Genesis 2:10–14).

2. The whole earth was covered by one huge sea during the flood (Genesis 7:17–24).

3. The Dead Sea is called the Salt Sea in Genesis 14:3.

4. The Lord made a covenant with Abram, saying, Unto thy seed have I given this land, from the river of Egypt unto the great river, the river Euphrates (Genesis 15:18).

5. The first plague that God sent upon the Egyptians turned the waters of the Nile River to blood (Exodus 7:17–25).

6. Pharaoh and his men were drowned in the Red Sea after the Israelites had crossed over it on dry ground (Exodus 15:4).

7. The Promised Land bordered on the great sea (Numbers 34:6), also called the sea of the Philistines (Exodus 23:31), the sea of Joppa (Ezra 3:7), and the sea of Cilicia (Acts 27:5). We know it today as the Mediterranean Sea.

8. The Israelites crossed the Jordan River when they entered the Promised Land (Joshua 1:1–2).

9. David fled across the brook Kidron in his escape from Absalom (2 Samuel 15:13–23).

10. Elijah lived by the brook Cherith during the years of drought (1 Kings 17:1–4).

11. Ezra proclaimed a fast at the river Ahava (Ezra 8:21).

12. Jesus taught by the lake of Gennesaret—or Galilee, as we know it today (Luke 5:1–3).

13. John saw a pure river of water of life, clear as crystal (Revelation 22:1).

## 268. Famous Swimmers

1. An iron axhead swam (2 Kings 6:5–6).

2. Peter swam to shore to meet Jesus (John 21:7–11).

3. Paul and 275 other people swam to shore or floated safely on broken pieces of their damaged ship (Acts 27:43–44).

### 269. Eleven Famous Baptisms

1. Then cometh Jesus from Galilee to Jordan unto John, to be baptized of him (Matthew 3:13).

2. Peter and the other disciples baptized about three thousand people on the day of Pentecost (Acts 2:41).

3. Simon the sorcerer and others from Samaria were baptized by Philip (Acts 8:12–13).

4. [The Ethiopian eunuch] commanded the chariot to stand still: and they went down both into the water, both Philip and the eunuch; and he baptized him (Acts 8:38).

5. Paul was baptized by Ananias in Damascus (Acts 9:18).

6. Peter baptized Cornelius and his friends (Acts 10:23–48).

7. Lydia and her household were baptized by Paul and Silas (Acts 16:14–15).

8. The Philippian jailor took Paul and Silas to his home where they baptized him and his household (Acts 16:26–33).

9. Crispus, the chief ruler of the synagogue, believed on the Lord with all his house; and many of the Corinthians hearing believed, and were baptized (Acts 18:8).

10. Paul baptized about twelve Ephesian believers who had known only John's baptism (Acts 19:1–7).

11. Moreover, brethren, I would not that ye should be ignorant, how that all our fathers were under the cloud, and all passed through the sea; and were all baptized unto Moses in the cloud and in the sea (1 Corinthians 10:1–2).

### 270. Three Drownings

1. Fifteen cubits upward did the waters prevail; and the mountains were covered. And all flesh died that moved upon the earth, both of fowl, and of cattle, and of beast, and of every creeping thing that creepeth upon the earth, and every man: all in whose nostrils was the breath of life, of all that was in the dry land, died . . . and Noah only remained alive, and they that were with him in the ark (Genesis 7:20–23).

2. The Lord is a man of war: the Lord is his name. Pharoah's chariots

and his host hath he cast into the sea: his chosen captains also are drowned in the Red sea (Exodus 15:3–4).

3. And the unclean spirits went out, and entered into the swine: and the herd ran violently down a steep place into the sea, (they were about two thousand;) and were choked in the sea (Mark 5:13).

# 26

## QUESTIONS

"Why, Daddy?" "Mommy, how do I do this?" "What is that?" *Why, how,* and *what* seem to be the only words that a two-year-old knows. Even the most patient parent is tested by this incessant bombardment. Yet by asking questions, the child learns about life and its many facets.

Thomas Macaulay wrote: "Knowledge advances by steps and not by leaps." As we mature, we may ask fewer questions, but the three-word vocabulary remains very central. If we are going to continue learning about life, we will have to continue asking questions. Questions are stepping-stones to obtaining knowledge.

God asks people questions and people ask God questions. Throughout the next seven lists, we find people wanting answers from God, and God questioning people to make them face the truth about their lives. God, of course, already knows the answer, but the person may be trying to cover the truth. In these lists you may find some questions you'd like to ask God; then again, you may find God asking you some questions.

### 271. Twenty-four Questions the Disciples Asked Jesus

1. The disciples came and said unto [Jesus], "Why speakest thou unto [the multitudes] in parables?" (Matthew 13:10).

2. Jesus said unto them, Hear, and understand: not that which goeth into the mouth defileth a man; but that which cometh out of the mouth, this defileth a man. Then came [Jesus'] disciples, and

343

said unto him, "Knowest thou that the Pharisees were offended, after they heard this saying?" (Matthew 15:10–12).

3. Jesus called his disciples unto him, and said, I have compassion on the multitude. . . . And his disciples say unto him, "Whence should we have so much bread in the wilderness, as to fill so great a multitude?" (Matthew 15:32–33).

4. Jesus' disciples asked Him, "Why then say the scribes that Elias must first come?" (Matthew 17:10).

5. Jesus rebuked the devil; and he departed out of him: and the child was cured from that very hour. Then came the disciples to Jesus apart, and said, "Why could not we cast him out?" (Matthew 17:14–19).

6. The disciples [came] unto Jesus, saying, "Who is the greatest in the kingdom of heaven?" (Matthew 18:1).

7. Peter came to Jesus, and said, "Lord, how oft shall my brother sin against me, and I forgive him? till seven times?" (Matthew 18:21).

8. Then said Jesus unto his disciples . . . It is easier for a camel to go through the eye of a needle, than for a rich man to enter into the kingdom of God. When his disciples heard it, they were exceedingly amazed, saying, "Who then can be saved?" (Matthew 19:23–25).

9. Peter asked Jesus, "Behold, we have forsaken all, and followed thee; what shall we have therefore?" (Matthew 19:27).

10. The disciples came to Jesus privately and asked, "When shall these things be? and what shall be the sign of thy coming, and of the end of the world?" (Matthew 24:3).

11. Now the first day of the feast of unleavened bread the disciples came to Jesus, saying unto him, "Where wilt thou that we prepare for thee to eat the passover?" (Matthew 26:6–9).

12. Jesus said, Verily I say unto you, that one of you shall betray me. And they were exceedingly sorrowful, and began every one of them to say unto him, "Lord, is it I?" (Matthew 26:21–22).

13. Jesus' disciples asked Him, "What might this parable [of the sower] be?" (Luke 8:9).

14. When James and John saw that the Samaritans did not receive

Jesus, they said, "Lord, wilt thou that we command fire to come down from heaven, and consume them, even as Elias did?" (Luke 9:53–54).

15. Jesus said, Be ye therefore ready also: for the Son of man cometh at an hour when ye think not. Then Peter said unto him, "Lord, speakest thou this parable unto us, or even to all?" (Luke 12:39–41).

16. Jesus said to the disciples, Two men shall be in the field; the one shall be taken, and the other left. And they answered and said unto him, "Where, Lord?" (Luke 17:36–37).

17. Many of Jesus' disciples, when they heard about eating Jesus' flesh and drinking His blood said, "This is a hard saying; who can hear it?" (John 6:60).

18. As Jesus passed by, he saw a man which was blind from his birth. And his disciples asked him, saying, "Master, who did sin, this man, or his parents, that he was born blind?" (John 9:1–2).

19. Jesus said to His disciples, Let us go into Judaea again. His disciples say unto him, "Master, the Jews of late sought to stone thee; and goest thou thither again?" (John 11:7–8).

20. Jesus began to wash His disciples' feet. When He came to Peter, Peter saith unto him, "Lord, dost thou wash my feet?" (John 13:3–6).

21. Jesus said, Whither I go, ye cannot come. . . . Simon Peter said unto him, "Lord, whither goest thou?" (John 13:33, 36).

22. Peter asked Jesus, "Lord, why cannot I follow thee now?" (John 13:37).

23. Thomas asked Jesus, "Lord, we know not whither thou goest; and how can we know the way?" (John 14:1–5).

24. Judas saith unto [Jesus], not Iscariot, "Lord, how is it that thou wilt manifest thyself unto us, and not unto the world?" (John 14:22).

## 272. Eighteen Questions the Religious Leaders Asked Jesus

1. And they asked [Jesus], saying, "Is it lawful to heal on the sabbath days?" (Matthew 12:10).

2. Then came to Jesus scribes and Pharisees, which were of Jerusalem, saying, "Why do thy disciples transgress the tradition of the elders? for they wash not their hands when they eat bread" (Matthew 15:1–2).

3. The Pharisees also came unto Jesus, tempting him, and saying unto him, "Is it lawful for a man to put away his wife for every cause?" (Matthew 19:3).

4. The Pharisees asked Jesus, "Why did Moses then command to give a writing of divorcement, and to put her away?" (Matthew 19:7).

5. When the chief priests and scribes saw the wonderful things that Jesus did, and the children crying in the temple, and saying, Hosanna to the son of David; they were sore displeased, and said unto him, "Hearest what these say?" (Matthew 21:15–16).

6. While Jesus was in the temple teaching, the chief priests and the elders came to him and asked, "By what authority doest thou these things: and who gave thee this authority?" (Matthew 21:23).

7. The Pharisees sent men to Jesus to gather evidence against Him and they asked, "What thinkest thou? Is it lawful to give tribute to Caesar, or not?" (Matthew 22:15–17).

8. The Sadducees asked Jesus, "Now there were with us seven brethren: and the first, when he had married a wife, deceased, and, having no issue, left his wife unto his brother: likewise the second also, and the third, unto the seventh. And last of all the woman died also. Therefore in the resurrection whose wife shall she be of the seven? for they all had her" (Matthew 22:23–28).

9. A lawyer asked Jesus, "Master, which is the great commandment in the law?" (Matthew 22:35–36).

10. Jesus' disciples walked through a grain field on the Sabbath and plucked some heads of grain. The Pharisees asked Jesus, "Behold, why do they on the sabbath that which is not lawful?" (Mark 2:23–24).

11. A certain lawyer stood up, and tempted [Jesus], saying, "Master, what shall I do to inherit eternal life?" (Luke 10:25).

12. Jesus told a lawyer that he must love his neighbor as himself.

But he, willing to justify himself, said unto Jesus, "And who is my neighbour?" (Luke 10:29).

13. After Jesus had chased the moneychangers out of the temple, the Jews asked Him, "What sign shewest thou unto us, seeing that thou doest these things?" (John 2:13–18).

14. Nicodemus saith unto him, "How can a man be born when he is old? can he enter the second time into his mother's womb and be born?" (John 3:3–4).

15. The scribes and Pharisees brought a woman caught in adultery to Jesus and they asked Him, "Now Moses in the law commanded us, that such should be stoned: but what sayest thou?" This they said tempting him, that they might have to accuse him (John 8:3–6).

16. Jesus said that the Father bore witness of Him. The Pharisees asked, "Where is thy Father?" (John 8:17–19).

17. The Pharisees asked Jesus, "Who art thou?" (John 8:25).

18. Jesus said, For judgment I am come into this world, that they which see not might see; and that they which see might be made blind. And some of the Pharisees which were with him heard these words, and said unto him, "Are we blind also?" (John 9:39–40).

### 273. Seven Questions That Received No Answer

1. Elijah asked the people of Israel, "How long halt ye between two opinions?" If the Lord be God, follow him: but if Baal, then follow him. And the people answered him not a word (1 Kings 18:21).

2. The King of Assyria sent his ambassador to King Hezekiah and asked him, "Who are [the gods of Samaria] among all the gods of these lands, that have delivered their land [into] my hand, that the Lord should deliver Jerusalem out of my hand?" But they held their peace, and answered him not a word (2 Kings 18:35–36).

3. The bride asked the city watchman, "Have you seen him whom my soul loves?" (Song of Solomon 3:3).

4. Pilate asked Jesus again, saying, "Answerest thou nothing?"

behold how many things they witness against thee. But Jesus answered nothing (Mark 15:4–5).

5. Jesus cried with a loud voice, saying, . . . "My God, my God, why hast thou forsaken me?" (Mark 15:34).

6. Then [Herod] questioned with him in many words; but he answered him nothing (Luke 23:9).

7. Pilate saith unto [Jesus], "What is truth?" (John 18:38).

## 274. *Twenty-five Questions People Asked God*

1. Cain asked God, "Am I my brother's keeper?" (Genesis 4:9).

2. Abram said, "Lord God, what wilt thou give me, seeing I go childless, and the steward of my house is this Eliezer of Damascus?" (Genesis 15:2).

3. God said to Abram, I am the Lord that brought thee out of Ur of the Chaldees, to give thee this land to inherit it. And he said, "Lord God, whereby shall I know that I shall inherit it?" (Genesis 15:7–8).

4. Abraham questioned God about the destruction of Sodom without separating the righteous from the wicked and asked, "Shall not the Judge of all the earth do right?" (Genesis 18:25).

5. Abimelech had taken Sarah as his wife, but God showed him that she was actually Abraham's wife. He prayed for mercy and said, "Lord, wilt thou slay also a righteous nation?" (Genesis 20:4).

6. God called Moses to go to Pharaoh and release the Israelites, but Moses said, "Who am I, that I should go unto Pharaoh, and that I should bring forth the children of Israel out of Egypt?" (Exodus 3:10–11).

7. Moses said unto God, "Behold, when I come unto the children of Israel, and shall say unto them, The God of your fathers hath sent me unto you; and they shall say to me, What is his name? what shall I say unto them?" (Exodus 3:13).

8. After Moses' first failure to convince Pharaoh to let Israel go, Moses returned unto the Lord, and said, "Lord, wherefore hast thou so evil entreated this people? why is it that thou hast sent me?" (Exodus 5:22).

9. God commanded Moses to go back to Pharaoh, but Moses balked and said, "Behold, the children of Israel have not hearkened unto me; how then shall Pharaoh hear me, who am of uncircumcised lips?" (Exodus 6:12).

10. The people murmured against Moses and Moses cried unto the Lord, saying, "What shall I do unto this people? they be almost ready to stone me" (Exodus 17:3–4).

11. Moses pleaded with God not to destroy the Israelites, praying, "Wherefore should the Egyptians speak, and say, For mischief did he bring them out, to slay them in the mountains, and to consume them from the face of the earth?" (Exodus 32:12).

12. Moses asked God, "Wherein shall it be known here that I and thy people have found grace in thy sight? is it not that thou goest with us?" (Exodus 33:16).

13. The Israelites cried to Moses for meat, and Moses said unto the Lord, "Wherefore hast thou afflicted thy servant? and wherefore have I not found favour in thy sight, that thou layest the burden of all this people upon me?" (Numbers 11:11).

14. Korah had rebelled against the authority of Moses, and God was about to destroy him. Moses and Aaron, fearing for the rest of the people, cried, "O God, the God of the spirits of all flesh, shall one man sin, and wilt thou be wroth with all the congregation?" (Numbers 16:22).

15. After Israel lost their first battle against Ai, Joshua said, "Alas, O Lord God, wherefore hast thou at all brought this people over Jordan, to deliver us into the hand of the Amorites, to destroy us?" (Joshua 7:7).

16. Now after the death of Joshua it came to pass, that the children of Israel asked the Lord, saying, "Who shall go up for us against the Canaanites first, to fight against them?" (Judges 1:1).

17. After nearly exterminating the tribe of Benjamin, the Israelites prayed, "O Lord God of Israel, why is this come to pass in Israel, that there should be today one tribe lacking in Israel?" (Judges 21:2–3).

18. The Philistines were plundering Keilah. Therefore David inquired of the Lord, saying, "Shall I go and smite these Philistines?" (1 Samuel 23:1–2).

19. After the Amalekites had taken Ziklag and had carried away the inhabitants, David inquired at the Lord, saying, "Shall I pursue after this troop? shall I overtake them?" (1 Samuel 30:3–8).

20. Solomon prayed, "Give therefore thy servant an understanding heart to judge thy people, that I may discern between good and bad: for who is able to judge this thy so great a people?" (1 Kings 3:5–9).

21. Elijah cried to the Lord, and said, "O Lord my God, hast thou also brought evil upon the widow with whom I sojourn, by slaying her son?" (1 Kings 17:20).

22. Job answered the Lord in response to a long list of hard questions, and said, "Behold, I am vile; what shall I answer thee?" (Job 40:3–4).

23. Jeremiah cried to God, "Why is my pain perpetual, and my wound incurable, which refuseth to be healed? wilt thou be altogether unto me as a liar, and as waters that fail?" (Jeremiah 15:18).

24. Ezekiel fell on his face, and cried with a loud voice, and said, "Ah Lord God! wilt thou make a full end of the remnant of Israel?" (Ezekiel 11:13).

25. The burden which Habakkuk the prophet did see: "O Lord, how long shall I cry, and thou wilt not hear! . . . Why dost thou shew me iniquity, and cause me to behold grievance?" (Habakkuk 1:1–3).

## 275. Forty-five Questions God Asked People

1. When Adam and Eve had sinned, they hid from the presence of God and the Lord God called unto Adam, and said unto him, "Where art thou?" (Genesis 3:6–9).

2. The Lord asked Adam, "Who told thee that thou wast naked? Hast thou eaten of the tree, whereof I commanded thee that thou shouldest not eat?" (Genesis 3:11).

3. And the Lord God said unto the woman, "What is this that thou hast done?" (Genesis 3:13).

4. After Cain's offering was rejected by God, Cain was very angry, and his countenance fell. And the Lord said unto Cain, "Why

art thou wroth? and why is thy countenance fallen? If thou doest well, shalt thou not be accepted?" (Genesis 4:6–7).

5. Cain rose up against Abel his brother, and slew him. And the Lord said unto Cain, "Where is Abel thy brother? What hast thou done?" (Genesis 4:8–10).

6. The Lord said unto Abraham, "Wherefore did Sarah laugh, saying, 'Shall I of a surety bear a child, which am old?' Is anything too hard for the Lord?" (Genesis 18:13).

7. The Lord said unto [Moses], "What is that in thine hand?" (Exodus 4:2).

8. Moses said unto the Lord, O my Lord, I am not eloquent. And the Lord said unto him, "Who hath made man's mouth?" (Exodus 4:10–11).

9. As Pharaoh's army approached, the people cried to Moses, and the Lord said unto Moses, "Wherefore criest thou unto me?" (Exodus 14:15).

10. The Israelites questioned God's provision of manna for the Sabbath. And the Lord said unto Moses, "How long refuse ye to keep my commandments and my laws?" (Exodus 16:27–28).

11. Moses asked the Lord how he was to get the meat that the people demanded, and the Lord said unto Moses, "Is the Lord's hand waxed short? thou shalt see whether my word shall come to pass or not" (Numbers 11:23).

12. Aaron and Miriam criticized Moses, and God said, "With him will I speak mouth to mouth . . . wherefore then were ye not afraid to speak against my servant Moses?" (Numbers 12:8).

13. Moses asked the Lord to lift the judgment of leprosy from Miriam, and the Lord said unto Moses, "If her father had but spit in her face, should she not be ashamed seven days?" (Numbers 12:13–14).

14. When the children of Israel refused to go into the Promised Land, the Lord said unto Moses, "How long will this people provoke me?" (Numbers 14:11).

15. After Moses had died, God asked Joshua, "Have not I commanded thee? Be strong and of good courage; be not afraid, neither be thou dismayed" (Joshua 1:1, 9).

16. The Lord said unto Samuel, "How long wilt thou mourn for Saul, seeing I have rejected him from reigning over Israel?" (1 Samuel 16:1).

17. The word of the Lord came unto Nathan, saying, "Go and tell my servant David, 'Thus saith the Lord, Shalt thou build me an house for me to dwell in?' " (2 Samuel 7:4–5).

18. After David had engineered the death of Uriah, God spoke to him through Nathan and said, "Wherefore hast thou despised the commandment of the Lord, to do evil in his sight?" (2 Samuel 12:9).

19. After David had sinned by numbering Israel and Judah, God offered him a choice of judgments, asking, "Shall seven years of famine come unto thee in thy land? or wilt thou flee three months before thine enemies, while they pursue thee? or that there be three days' pestilence in thy land?" (2 Samuel 24:13).

20. After Elijah ran away from Jezebel, he came to a cave, and behold, the word of the Lord came to him, and he said unto him, "What doest thou here, Elijah?" (1 Kings 19:9).

21. When Ahab had taken Naboth's vineyard, God sent Elijah, saying, Thus saith the Lord, "Hast thou killed, and also taken possession?" (1 Kings 21:19).

22. After Elijah had rebuked Ahab, God asked Elijah, "Seest thou how Ahab humbleth himself before me?" (1 Kings 21:29).

23. Isaiah heard the voice of the Lord, saying, "Whom shall I send, and who will go for us?" (Isaiah 6:8).

24. "Is there a God beside me?" (Isaiah 44:8).

25. The Lord asked Cyrus, "Shall the clay say to him that fashioneth it, What makest thou?" (Isaiah 45:1–9).

26. "Is my hand shortened at all, that it cannot redeem? or have I no power to deliver?" (Isaiah 50:2).

27. Jeremiah cried out in the temple, "Is this house, which is called by my name, become a den of robbers in your eyes? Behold, even I have seen it," saith the Lord (Jeremiah 7:11).

28. The Lord asked, "Why is this people of Jerusalem slidden back by a perpetual backsliding?" (Jeremiah 8:4–12).

29. "Am I a God at hand," saith the Lord, "and not a God afar off? Can any hide himself in secret places that I shall not see him? Do not I fill heaven and earth?" (Jeremiah 23:23–24).

30. Then came the word of the Lord unto Jeremiah, saying, "Behold, I am the Lord, the God of all flesh: is there anything too hard for me?" (Jeremiah 32:26–27).

31. Thus saith the Lord, the God of Israel, unto thee, "O Baruch . . . Seekest thou great things for thyself? seek them not" (Jeremiah 45:2, 5).

32. Ezekiel prophesied against the false prophets of Israel saying, "Have ye not seen a vain vision, and have ye not spoken a lying divination, whereas ye say, The Lord saith it; albeit I have not spoken?" (Ezekiel 13:7).

33. Several elders of Israel came to Ezekiel and God said, "Son of man, these men have set up their idols in their heart, and put the stumbling-block of their iniquity before their face: should I be inquired of at all by them?" (Ezekiel 14:1–3).

34. "Have I any pleasure at all that the wicked should die?" saith the Lord God: "and not that he should return from his ways, and live?" (Ezekiel 18:23).

35. The Lord asked Israel, "Can thine heart endure, or can thine hands be strong, in the days that I shall deal with thee?" (Ezekiel 22:14).

36. Ezekiel prophesied against Israel, Thus saith the Lord God: "Ye eat with the blood, and lift up your eyes toward your idols, and shed blood: and shall ye possess the land?" (Ezekiel 33:25).

37. God showed Ezekiel a valley of dry bones and asked him, "Son of man, can these bones live?" (Ezekiel 37:3).

38. The Lord asked Israel, "Shall a trumpet be blown in the city, and the people not be afraid? shall there be evil in a city, and the Lord hath not done it?" (Amos 3:6).

39. Jonah was angry about his gourd that had died. Then said the Lord, "Doest thou well to be angry?" (Jonah 4:9).

40. The Lord asked Jonah, "Should not I spare Nineveh, that great city, wherein are more than sixscore thousand persons that

cannot discern between their right hand and their left hand; and also much cattle?" (Jonah 4:11).

41. Thus saith the Lord of hosts: "Ask now the priests concerning the law, saying, If one bear holy flesh in the skirt of his garment, and with his skirt do touch bread, or pottage, or wine, or oil, or any meat, shall it be holy?" (Haggai 2:11–12).

42. Zechariah prophesied to the people and the priests, saying, "When ye fasted and mourned in the fifth and seventh month, even those seventy years, did ye at all fast unto me?" (Zechariah 7:4–6).

43. "A son honoureth his father, and a servant his master: if then I be a father, where is mine honour? and if I be a master where is my fear? saith the Lord of hosts unto you, O priests, that despise my name" (Malachi 1:6).

44. Malachi spoke forth the word of the Lord, asking, "If ye offer the blind sacrifice, is it not evil? and if ye offer the lame and sick, is it not evil? offer it now unto thy governor; will he be pleased with thee, or accept thy person?" (Malachi 1:8).

45. God pleaded for Israel to tithe, asking, "Will a man rob God?" (Malachi 3:8).

## 276. Thirty-four Questions God Asked Job

1. "Who is this that darkeneth counsel by words without knowledge?" (Job 38:2).

2. "Gird up now thy loins like a man; for I will demand of thee, and answer thou me. Where wast thou when I laid the foundations of the earth?" (Job 38:3–4).

3. "Who shut up the sea with doors, when it brake forth, as if it had issued out of the womb?" (Job 38:8).

4. "Hast thou commanded the morning since thy days; and caused the dayspring to know his place; that it might take hold of the ends of the earth, that the wicked might be shaken out of it?" (Job 38:12–13).

5. "Hast thou entered into the springs of the sea? or hast thou walked in the search of the depth?" (Job 38:16).

6. "Have the gates of death been opened unto thee? or hast thou seen the doors of the shadow of death?" (Job 38:17).

7. "Hast thou perceived the breadth of the earth?" (Job 38:18).

8. "Where is the way where light dwelleth? and as for darkness, where is the place thereof, that thou shouldest take it to the bound thereof, and that thou shouldest know the paths to the house thereof?" (Job 38:19–20).

9. "Hast thou entered into the treasures of the snow? or hast thou seen the treasures of the hail, which I have reserved against the time of trouble, against the day of battle and war?" (Job 38:22–23).

10. "By what way is the light parted, which scattereth the east wind upon the earth?" (Job 38:24).

11. "Who hath divided a watercourse for the overflowing of waters, or a way for the lightning of thunder; to cause it to rain on the earth, where no man is; on the wilderness, wherein there is no man; to satisfy the desolate and waste ground; and to cause the bud of the tender herb to spring forth?" (Job 38:25–27).

12. "Hath the rain a father? or who hath begotten the drops of dew?" (Job 38:28).

13. "Out of whose womb came the ice? and the hoary frost of heaven, who hath gendered it?" (Job 38:29).

14. "Canst thou bind the sweet influences of Pleiades, or loose the bands of Orion? Canst thou bring forth Mazzaroth in his season? or canst thou guide Arcturus with his sons?" (Job 38:31–32).

15. "Knowest thou the ordinances of heaven? canst thou set the dominion thereof in the earth?" (Job 38:33).

16. "Canst thou lift up thy voice to the clouds, that abundance of waters may cover thee?" (Job 38:34).

17. "Canst thou send lightnings, that they may go, and say unto thee, Here we are?" (Job 38:35).

18. "Who hath put wisdom in the inward parts? or who hath given understanding to the heart?" (Job 38:36).

19. "Who can number the clouds in wisdom? or who can stay the

bottles of heaven, when the dust groweth into hardness, and the clods cleave fast together?" (Job 38:37–38).

20. "Wilt thou hunt the prey for the lion? or fill the appetite of the young lions, when they couch in their dens, and abide in the covert to lie in wait?" (Job 38:39–40).

21. "Who provideth for the raven his food?" (Job 38:41).

22. "Knowest thou the time when the wild goats of the rock bring forth? or canst thou mark when the hinds do calve?" (Job 39:1).

23. "Who hath sent out the wild ass free? or who hath loosed the bands of the wild ass?" (Job 39:5).

24. "Canst thou bind the unicorn with his band in the furrow? or will he harrow the valleys after thee? Wilt thou trust him, because his strength is great?" (Job 39:10–11).

25. "Gavest thou the goodly wings unto the peacocks? or wings and feathers unto the ostrich?" (Job 39:13).

26. "Hast thou given the horse strength? hast thou clothed his neck with thunder? Canst thou make him afraid as a grasshopper?" (Job 39:19–20).

27. "Doth the hawk fly by thy wisdom, and stretch her wings toward the south?" (Job 39:26).

28. "Doth the eagle mount up at thy command, and make her nest on high?" (Job 39:27).

29. Moreover the Lord answered Job, and said, "Shall he that contendeth with the Almighty instruct him? he that reproveth God, let him answer it" (Job 40:1–2).

30. "Wilt thou also disannul my judgment? wilt thou condemn me, that thou mayest be righteous?" (Job 40:8).

31. "Hast thou an arm like God? or canst thou thunder with a voice like him?" (Job 40:9).

32. "Canst thou draw out leviathan with an hook? or his tongue with a cord which thou lettest down? Canst thou put an hook into his nose?" (Job 41:1–2).

33. "None is so fierce that dare stir [leviathan] up: who then is able to stand before me?" (Job 41:10).

34. "Who hath prevented me, that I should repay him? whatsoever is under the whole heaven is mine" (Job 41:11).

## 277. *Forty-five Questions Jesus Asked People*

1. When speaking about God's ability to provide, Jesus asked His disciples, "Why take ye thought for raiment . . . shall he not much more clothe you, O ye of little faith?" (Matthew 6:28–30).

2. "Why beholdest thou the mote that is in thy brother's eye, but considerest not the beam that is in thine own eye?" (Matthew 7:3).

3. "How much more shall your Father which is in heaven give good things to them that ask him?" (Matthew 7:11).

4. When the disciples were afraid the storm would sink their boat, Jesus asked, "Why are ye fearful, O ye of little faith?" (Matthew 8:26).

5. Jesus began to say unto the multitudes concerning John, "What went ye out into the wilderness to see?" (Matthew 11:7–10).

6. When Jesus spoke about removing a sheep from a pit on the Sabbath, He asked, "How much then is a man better than a sheep?" (Matthew 12:12).

7. To the Pharisees and scribes: "O generation of vipers, how can ye, being evil, speak good things?" (Matthew 12:34).

8. When confronted with feeding the multitude, Jesus asked the disciples, "How many loaves have ye?" (Matthew 15:34).

9. To a forgetful band of disciples: "Do ye not yet understand, neither remember the five loaves of the five thousand, and how many baskets ye took up?" (Matthew 16:9).

10. When speaking about discipleship, Jesus asked, "For what is a man profited, if he shall gain the whole world, and lose his own soul? or what shall a man give in exchange for his soul?" (Matthew 16:26).

11. When the disciples were unable to deliver the boy possessed by the devil, Jesus asked, "O faithless and perverse generation, how long shall I be with you? how long shall I suffer you?" (Matthew 17:17).

12. "What thinkest thou, Simon? Of whom do the kings of the earth take custom or tribute? of their children, or of strangers?" (Matthew 17:25).

13. To the person who labeled Jesus good: "Why callest thou me good?" (Matthew 19:17).

14. When the mother of James and John desired her sons to be in a prominent role, Jesus asked her, "What wilt thou?" (Matthew 20:21).

15. Jesus to the two blind men: "What will ye that I shall do unto you?" (Matthew 20:32).

16. When challenged as to the source of his authority, Jesus countered the chief priests by asking, "The baptism of John, whence was it? from heaven, or of men?" (Matthew 21:25).

17. When beginning a parable, Jesus asked, "But what think ye?" (Matthew 21:28).

18. When questioned by the Pharisees, Jesus unmasked their request by asking, "Why tempt ye me, ye hypocrites?" (Matthew 22:18).

19. Jesus took the offensive and asked the Pharisees, "What think ye of Christ? whose son is he?" (Matthew 22:42).

20. Jesus asked the scribes and Pharisees, "Ye serpents, ye generation of vipers, how can ye escape the damnation of hell?" (Matthew 23:33).

21. When His disciples questioned the woman about wasting the ointment on Jesus, He asked them, "Why trouble ye the woman?" (Matthew 26:10).

22. When the disciples fell asleep before Jesus was betrayed, He asked them, "What, could ye not watch with me one hour?" (Matthew 26:40).

23. To the scribes, who questioned Jesus' ability to forgive sins, He asked, "Why reason ye these things in your hearts?" (Mark 2:8).

24. To those who claimed that Jesus' power over demons came from Satan, He questioned, "How can Satan cast out Satan?" (Mark 3:23).

25. To the demoniac, "What is thy name?" (Mark 5:9).

26. To those who mourned the death of the ruler of the synagogue's daughter, "Why make ye this ado, and weep?" (Mark 5:39).

27. Deeply disturbed by the Pharisees tempting Him, Jesus asked, "Why doth this generation seek after a sign?" (Mark 8:12).

28. To the father whose son was demon possessed: "How long is it ago since this came unto him?" (Mark 9:21).

29. To the disciples who were discussing which of them was the greatest: "What was it that ye disputed among yourselves by the way?" (Mark 9:33).

30. To the Pharisees who were trying to find fault with Jesus' teaching: "What did Moses command you?" (Mark 10:3).

31. "My God, my God, why hast thou forsaken me?" (Mark 15:34).

32. "Why call ye me, Lord, Lord, and do not the things which I say?" (Luke 6:46).

33. "Ye hypocrites, ye can discern the face of the sky and of the earth; but how is it that ye do not discern this time?" (Luke 12:56).

34. To the inquiring of Nicodemus: "If I have told you earthly things, and ye believe not, how shall ye believe, if I tell you of heavenly things?" (John 3:12).

35. To the Jews whose trust was not rooted in God: "How can ye believe, which receive honour one of another and seek not the honour that cometh from God only?" (John 5:44).

36. When His disciples could not handle Jesus' teaching, Jesus asked them, "Doth this offend you?" (John 6:61).

37. Before a crowd of skeptical Jews He asked, "Did not Moses give you the law, and yet none of you keepeth the law? Why go ye about to kill me?" (John 7:19).

38. In challenging the Jewish belief that their heritage made them God's people: "Which of you convinceth me of sin? And if I say the truth, why do ye not believe me?" (John 8:46).

39. To His Father in heaven: "Now is my soul troubled; and what shall I say?" (John 12:27).

40. After washing the disciples' feet, "Know ye what I have done to you?" (John 13:12).

41. "Have I been so long time with you, and yet hast thou not known me, Philip?" (John 14:9).

42. To the officer who defended the high priest: "Why smitest thou me?" (John 18:23).

43. To Mary after His resurrection: "Woman, why weepest thou? whom seekest thou?" (John 20:15).

44. To a troubled, searching disciple: "Simon, son of Jonas, lovest thou me?" (John 21:17).

45. To a prostrated hater of the church: "Saul, Saul, why persecutest thou me?" (Acts 9:4).

# 27

## DECISIONS

Every day our lives are filled with decisions. Many decisions are routine—Shall I have cereal or eggs for breakfast?—and will not have a particularly profound effect on our lives. Others will have varying degrees of importance and impact upon us: Which job should I take? Whom should I marry?

There is one decision, though, that ranks far above every other decision an individual faces: Am I going to obey God or not? Even our everyday decisions reflect whether we seek to glorify God or serve our own interests.

The following three lists demonstrate the impact of decisions in the lives of people in the Bible.

### 278. Ten Decisions to Follow God

1. *Noah*
   Noah was a just man and perfect in his generations, and Noah walked with God. . . . And God said unto Noah . . . Make thee an ark of gopher wood. . . . Thus did Noah; according to all that God commanded him, so did he (Genesis 6:9, 13–14, 22).

2. *Abraham*
   Now the Lord had said unto Abram, Get thee out of thy country, and from thy kindred, and from thy father's house, unto a land that I will shew thee. . . . So Abram departed, as the Lord had spoken unto him (Genesis 12:1, 4).

3. *Moses*
   And the Lord said unto Moses in Midian, Go, return into Egypt: for all the men are dead which sought thy life. And Moses took his wife and sons, and set them upon an ass, and he returned to the land of Egypt: and Moses took the rod of God in his hand (Exodus 4:19–20).

4. *Israel*
   Joshua commanded, Choose you this day whom ye will serve; whether the gods which your fathers served that were on the other side of the flood, or the gods of the Amorites, in whose land ye dwell: but as for me and my house, we will serve the Lord. And the people answered and said, God forbid that we should forsake the Lord, to serve other gods. . . . we will serve the Lord (Joshua 24:15–16, 21).

5. *King Josiah*
   When the king had heard the words of the book of the law, he rent his clothes . . . and made a covenant before the Lord to walk after the Lord, and to keep his commandments (2 Kings 22:11; 23:3).

6. *Daniel*
   But Daniel purposed in his heart that he would not defile himself with the portion of the king's meat, nor with the wine which he drank (Daniel 1:8).

7. *Nebuchadnezzar*
   And at the end of the days I Nebuchadnezzar lifted up mine eyes unto heaven, and mine understanding returned unto me, and I blessed the most High, and I praised and honoured him that liveth for ever, whose dominion is an everlasting dominion. . . . At the same time my reason returned to me. . . . Now I Nebuchadnezzar praise and extol and honour the King of heaven (Daniel 4:34–37).

8. *The king and the people of Nineveh*
   So the people of Nineveh believed God, and proclaimed a fast, and put on sackcloth, from the greatest of them even to the least of them. For word came unto the king of Nineveh, and he arose from his throne, and he laid his robe from him, and covered him with sackcloth, and sat in ashes (Jonah 3:5–6).

9. *Peter and Andrew*

   Jesus, walking by the sea of Galilee, saw two brethren, Simon called Peter, and Andrew his brother, casting a net into the sea: for they were fishers. And he saith unto them, Follow me, and I will make you fishers of men. And they straightway left their nets, and followed him (Matthew 4:18–20).

10. *The Philippian jailor*

    The jailor fell down before Paul and Silas, and brought them out, and said, Sirs, what must I do to be saved? . . . When he had brought them into his house, he set meat before them, and rejoiced, believing in God with all his house (Acts 16:29–30, 34).

## 279. Ten Decisions to Serve the Devil

1. *Eve*

   When the woman saw that the tree was good for food, and that it was pleasant to the eyes, and a tree to be desired to make one wise, she took of the fruit thereof, and did eat, and gave also unto her husband with her and he did eat (Genesis 3:6).

2. *Lot's wife*

   But his wife looked back from behind him, and she became a pillar of salt (Genesis 19:26).

3. *Aaron and the people of Israel*

   When the people saw that Moses delayed to come down out of the mount, the people gathered themselves together unto Aaron, and said unto him, Up, make us gods, which shall go before us . . . and Aaron did so (Exodus 32:1).

4. *Solomon*

   It came to pass, when Solomon was old, that his wives turned away his heart after other gods: and his heart was not perfect with the Lord his God, as was the heart of David his father (1 Kings 11:4).

5. *Jeroboam*

   The king took counsel, and made two calves of gold, and said unto [Israel], It is too much for you to go up to Jerusalem: behold thy gods, O Israel, which brought thee up out of the land of Egypt (1 Kings 12:28).

6. *Ahab*

   And it came to pass, as if it had been a light thing for [Ahab] to walk in the sins of Jeroboam the son of Nebat, that he took to wife Jezebel the daughter of Ethbaal king of the Zidonians, and went and served Baal, and worshipped him (1 Kings 16:31).

7. *Judas Iscariot*

   Then entered Satan into Judas. . . . And he promised, and sought opportunity to betray [Jesus] unto them in the absence of the multitude (Luke 22:3, 6).

8. *Ananias*

   A certain man named Ananias, with Sapphira his wife, sold a possession, and kept back part of the price, his wife also being privy to it, and brought a certain part and laid it at the apostles' feet. But Peter said, Ananias, why hath Satan filled thine heart to lie to the Holy Ghost, and to keep back part of the price of the land? (Acts 5:1–3).

9. *Elymas*

   Elymas the sorcerer . . . withstood [Barnabas and Saul], seeking to turn away the deputy [Sergius Paulus] from the faith (Acts 13:8).

10. *Demas*

    Demas hath forsaken me, having loved this present world (2 Timothy 4:10).

## 280. Decisions and the Heart

1. O that there were such an heart in them, that they would fear me, and keep all my commandments always (Deuteronomy 5:29).

2. To prove thee, to know what was in thine heart, whether thou wouldst keep his commandments (Deuteronomy 8:2).

3. Only fear the Lord, and serve him in truth with all your heart (1 Samuel 12:24).

4. The Lord was angry with Solomon, because his heart turned away from the Lord God of Israel (1 Kings 11:9).

5. I have walked before thee in truth and with a perfect heart, and have done that which is good in thy sight (2 Kings 20:3).

6. Solomon my son, know thou the God of thy father, and serve

him with a perfect heart and with a willing mind (1 Chronicles 28:9).

7. The people rejoiced, for that they offered willingly, because with perfect heart they offered willingly to the Lord (1 Chronicles 29:9).

8. Keep thy heart with all diligence; for out of it are the issues of life (Proverbs 4:23).

9. The heart is deceitful above all things. . . . I the Lord search the heart, I try the reins, even to give every man according to his ways (Jeremiah 17:9–10).

10. Cast away from you all your transgressions, whereby ye have transgressed; and make you a new heart and a new spirit: for why will ye die? (Ezekiel 18:31).

11. But Daniel purposed in his heart that he would not defile himself (Daniel 1:8).

12. For where your treasure is, there will your heart be also (Matthew 6:21).

13. A good man out of the good treasure of the heart bringeth forth good things (Matthew 12:35).

14. For from within, out of the heart of men, proceed evil thoughts, adulteries. . . . These evil things come from within, and defile the man (Mark 7:21, 23).

15. That which fell on the good ground are they, which in an honest and good heart, having heard the word, keep it, and bring forth fruit with patience (Luke 8:15).

16. To Simon the sorcerer: Thou hast neither part nor lot in this matter: for thy heart is not right in the sight of God (Acts 8:21).

17. Ye have obeyed from the heart that form of doctrine which was delivered you (Romans 6:17).

18. Harden not your hearts. . . . Take heed, brethren, lest there be in any of you an evil heart of unbelief, in departing from the living God (Hebrews 3:8, 12).

19. I am he which searcheth the reins and hearts: and I will give unto every one of you according to your works (Revelation 2:23).

# 28
## GOD'S PERSONALITY

Devout Asians speak of God as the all-pervading "Force" in the universe. On every continent there are people who think God is the sovereign "bogeyman" in every tree, rock, and river. And in our culture, many people see God as an aloof old man who set the cosmos in motion, then retired to some deserted asteroid.

Happily, none of the above ideas is correct. In fact, *God is the most fascinating person in the universe*. And what makes God's personality most interesting is that *we* are similar to Him in many respects. We are able to reason, to create, to choose, and to feel emotion, even as God is able to do these things. We must realize, of course, that He does all these perfectly, unlike our human attempts.

Because we are created in the image of God, and because of his concern for us, we can speak to Him, listen to Him, and become more like Him in character. As you read the following lists, you may be surprised to learn what God is really like. And, hopefully, you will be motivated to study and better understand His personality.

### 281. Six Times God Expressed Contentment
1. God expresses His intense desire to find people to whom He can entrust himself: "For the eyes of the Lord run to and fro throughout the whole earth, to show himself strong in the behalf of them whose heart is perfect toward him" (2 Chronicles 16:9).
2. God expresses His happiness in extending forgiveness: "He retaineth

not his anger for ever, because he delighteth in mercy. He will turn again, he will have compassion upon us" (Micah 7:18–19).

3.  God expresses His heart of joy over an obedient people: "The Lord thy God in the midst of thee is mighty; he will save, he will rejoice over thee with joy; he will rest in his love, he will joy over thee with singing" (Zephaniah 3:17).

4.  Jesus compared His Father's compassion to that of a certain king: "One was brought unto him, which owed him ten thousand talents . . . as he had not to pay, his lord commanded him to be sold . . . . The servant . . . fell down . . . saying, Lord, have patience with me. . . . Then the lord of that servant was moved with compassion, and loosed him, and forgave him the debt" (Matthew 18:22–27).

5.  The happiness of heaven can only be a reflection of the heart of God: "There is joy in the presence of the angels of God over one sinner that repenteth" (Luke 15:7, 10).

6.  An amazing revelation of God's desire for us: "For the Father seeketh such to worship him" (John 4:23).

## 282. Six Times God Expressed Disappointment

1.  When sin ran rampant throughout mankind after the fall: "It repented the Lord that he had made man on earth, and it grieved him at his heart" (Genesis 6:5–6).

2.  A historical view of the children of Israel: "For they provoked him to anger with their high places, and moved him to jealousy with their graven images. When God heard this, he was wroth, and greatly abhorred Israel" (Psalm 78:58–59).

3.  The heart of God as He was so long-suffering with a disobedient people: "Forty years long was I grieved with this generation . . . unto whom I sware in my wrath that they should not enter my rest" (Psalm 95:10–11).

4.  "Though thou wast angry with me, thine anger is turned away, and thou comfortedst me" (Isaiah 12:1).

5.  "Because I am broken with their whorish heart" (Ezekiel 6:9).

6.  "I am jealous for Jerusalem and for Zion with a great jealousy. And I am very sore displeased with the heathen that are at ease: for I

was but a little displeased, and they helped toward the affliction" (Zechariah 1:14–15).

## 283. *Thirteen Times God Revealed New Choices*

1. God said, Let us make man in our image, after our likeness (Genesis 1:26).

2. Therefore, the Lord sent him forth from the garden of Eden (Genesis 3:23).

3. It repented the Lord that he had made man on the earth (Genesis 6:6).

4. God chose to destroy all mankind, except Noah and his family, because they were utterly corrupted (Genesis 6:12–13).

5. I will establish my covenant with you; neither shall all flesh be cut off any more by the waters of a flood (Genesis 9:11–12).

6. The Lord chose to withhold his anger and not destroy the rebellious children of Israel (Exodus 32:7–14, 30–33).

7. King Hezekiah's seeking the Lord resulted in God's changing His decision and extending Hezekiah's life fifteen years (2 Kings 20:5–6).

8. Even so the Son quickeneth whom he will (John 5:21).

9. I have power to lay it down, and I have power to take it again (John 10:18).

10. It is not for you to know the times or the seasons, which the Father hath put in his own power (Acts 1:7).

11. All these worketh that one and the self-same Spirit, dividing to every man severally as he will (1 Corinthians 12:11).

12. Of his own will begat he us with the word of truth (James 1:18).

13. The Father sent the Son to be the Saviour of the world (1 John 4:14).

## 284. *Eight Times God Revealed His Thoughts*

1. Moses by reasoning with the Lord staved off the wrath of God when Israel worshiped the golden calf (Exodus 32:7–14).

2. I will raise up a faithful priest, that shall do according to that which is in mine heart and in my mind (1 Samuel 2:35).

3. Come now, and let us reason together, saith the Lord (Isaiah 1:18).

4. Produce your cause, saith the Lord; bring forth your strong reasons, saith the King of Jacob (Isaiah 41:21).

5. For my thoughts are not your thoughts. . . . As the heavens are higher than the earth, so are . . . my thoughts than your thoughts (Isaiah 55:8–9).

6. For I know the thoughts that I think toward you, saith the Lord, thoughts of peace, and not of evil, to give you an expected end (Jeremiah 29:11).

7. Wherefore I will yet plead with you, saith the Lord, and with your children's children will I plead (Jeremiah 2:1–13).

8. For the Lord hath a controversy with his people, and he will plead with Israel. O my people, what have I done unto thee? and wherein have I wearied thee? testify against me (Micah 6:1–3).

## 285. Sixteen Times God Showed Flexibility in Dealing With Mankind

1. God regretted that man had been created. Here we find an aroused state of grief and disappointment over man's persistent rebellion (Genesis 6:3, 5–7).

2. Here we have the amazing statement from God concerning the implications of Abraham's obedience: For now I know that thou fearest God. A ram was provided in Isaac's place (Genesis 22:12).

3. Here Moses' intercessions changed the mind of God to not destroy the nation of Israel (Exodus 32:7–14).

4. God was waiting to see Israel's reaction of humility after the golden-calf incident before determining His judgment upon them (Exodus 33:5).

5. Another of God's judgments was stayed by the humility and prayer of Moses (Numbers 11:1–2).

6. God was using the forty years of wandering in the wilderness to discover Israel's true heart toward His rule (Deuteronomy 8:2).

7. God decided not to drive out some of the nations in Palestine because of Israel's sin. They would be His instrument to test and prove Israel's faithfulness (Judges 2:20–22).

8. When Saul disobeyed God's directions, God was grieved and determined a new plan of direction. God had reluctantly given Saul to be king over His people in response to their demands (1 Samuel 8:6–7; see also 1 Samuel 15:10–11, 23, 35).

9. God changed His mind and decided to add fifteen years to King Hezekiah's reign. This was in response to humble prayer (2 Kings 20:1–7).

10. God gave David three options of punishment for sin. David chose the direct hand of God, banking upon the mercy of God. God did choose to extend mercy and stayed the angel's hand from further judgment (1 Chronicles 21:11–15).

11. When King Rehoboam and his leaders humbled themselves, God changed His threatened judgment and granted them some deliverance (2 Chronicles 12:5–8).

12. God declared that He will change His purpose of judgment and blessing in accordance with man's reactions (Jeremiah 18:5–10).

13. Jeremiah proclaimed the possibility of God's changing His purpose of judgment if Israel would respond in repentance (Jeremiah 26:2–7, 12–13).

14. God might be induced to change His judgment if Israel would turn to God with sincere repentance (Joel 2:12–14).

15. God's judgment upon Nineveh was averted by one of the greatest examples of mass repentance ever recorded (Jonah 3).

16. Names can be blotted out of the Book of Life (Revelation 3:5).

# 29

## GOOD GUYS/BAD GUYS

Luke Skywalker versus Darth Vader; Superman versus sinister Lex Luthor; the Lone Ranger versus outlaws; Snow White versus the witch envious of her beauty. Whether in fiction or real life, the conflict is ever the same: good guys versus bad guys. The bad guys are almost always in the majority, while the good guys are seemingly the underdogs. At the movies, most of us cheer for the good guys to triumph and we are rarely disappointed. (These days, however, it's often hard to discern who really are the good guys.)

The next thirteen lists explore these two categories. As usual, the bad guys eclipse the good guys in number. But in the end, guess who wins?

### 286. Twenty Instances of Exile

1. God drove *Adam* and *Eve* out of the Garden of Eden (Genesis 3:24).
2. The Lord exiled *Cain* to the land of Nod (Genesis 4:13–16).
3. *Noah, Shem, Ham, Japheth,* and their wives were exiled from their homes forever by the flood (Genesis 7:23).
4. In obedience to God, *Abram* exiled himself and his family from their home in Ur (Genesis 12:1–5).
5. Abraham banished *Hagar* and *Ishmael* (Genesis 21:14).
6. *Jacob* chose exile rather than constant contention with Esau (Genesis 27:41–45).

7. *Joseph* was brought down to Egypt; and Potiphar . . . bought him (Genesis 39:1).

8. The *children of Israel* were exiles in Egypt for 430 years (Exodus 12:40).

9. Moses fled from the face of Pharaoh, and dwelt in the land of Midian (Exodus 2:15).

10. The *children of Israel* walked forty years in the wilderness (Joshua 5:6).

11. *Jephthah* fled from his brethren and dwelt in the land of Tob (Judges 11:3).

12. *David* lived in exile when he was fleeing from Saul (1 Samuel 27:1–7).

13. After he had had Amnon killed, *Absalom* fled, and went to Talmai . . . and was there three years (2 Samuel 13:37–38).

14. Solomon sought therefore to kill Jeroboam. And *Jeroboam* arose, and fled into Egypt . . . until the death of Solomon (1 Kings 11:40).

15. Assyria carried *Israel* into exile (2 Kings 17:6).

16. Nebuchadnezzar carried all in *Jerusalem* to Babylon (2 Kings 24:14–15).

17. The remnant of *Judah*, including *Jeremiah*, was exiled to Egypt (Jeremiah 43:5–7).

18. *Joseph* and *Mary* fled with *Jesus* into Egypt until Herod died (Matthew 2:13–15).

19. There was a great persecution against *the church* which was at Jerusalem; and they were all scattered abroad throughout the regions of Judaea and Samaria (Acts 8:1).

20. *John* was exiled to Patmos (Revelation 1:9).

## 287. *Prisons and Prisoners*

1. Joseph was thrown into prison, where he met Pharaoh's butler and baker (Genesis 39:20–40:3).

2. As governor of Egypt, Joseph put his brothers in prison for three

days and left Simeon there until his brothers returned with Benjamin (Genesis 42:17–24).

3. Joshua had the five Amorite kings sealed inside a cave, and then posted a guard until he could return for them (Joshua 10:16–18).

4. The Philistines put out Samson's eyes and made him grind in the prison (Judges 16:21).

5. Ahab threw the prophet Micaiah into prison because he did not like Micaiah's prophecy (1 Kings 22:26–27).

6. The king of Assyria bound King Hoshea of Israel in prison (2 Kings 17:4).

7. Jehoiachin, king of Judah, was imprisoned in Babylon (2 Kings 25:27–28).

8. King Asa threw Hanani into prison for delivering an unfavorable word from the Lord (2 Chronicles 16:10).

9. The king had Jeremiah put into prison and finally into a miry dungeon (Jeremiah 32:2; 37:16; 38:6).

10. The king of Babylon put out the eyes of Zedekiah and bound him in chains (Jeremiah 52:11).

11. Herod put John the Baptist into prison for speaking against Herod's adulterous marriage (Matthew 14:3–4).

12. Jesus was taken prisoner (John 18:12) and the convict Barabbas was released in His place (Matthew 27:26).

13. Peter and John spent a night in prison for preaching (Acts 4:3).

14. The apostles were imprisoned, but the angel of the Lord led them out at night (Acts 5:17, 19).

15. Herod put Peter into prison, but an angel released him (Acts 12:4, 6).

16. Paul was imprisoned with Silas at Philippi (Acts 16:22–24) and alone in Jerusalem (Acts 22:24–25), in Caesarea (Acts 23:33–35), and in Rome (Acts 28:16).

## 288. *Fourteen Great Escapes*

1. Lot and his two daughters escaped the destruction of Sodom after being warned by two angels (Genesis 19:15–26).

2. The ten plagues allowed the 600,000 Israelite men (plus women and children) to escape from Egypt (Exodus 12:37).

3. The two spies that went to Jericho escaped because Rahab hid them on her roof, sent their pursuers off on a wild-goose chase, and let the spies down the wall with a rope that hung from her window (Joshua 2:1–22).

4. Samson escaped the Philistines by breaking new ropes that bound him. He then found the jawbone of an ass and killed a thousand men before running away (Judges 15:11–15).

5. Samson escaped again by removing the doors from the gates of the city of Gaza and carrying them to the top of a nearby hill (Judges 16:1–3).

6. While David was fleeing from Saul, his wife let him down through a window and put an idol in his bed to fool Saul's messengers (1 Samuel 19:12–16).

7. David escaped the king of Gath by pretending to be a madman (1 Samuel 21:10–22:1).

8. Jonathan and Ahimaaz escaped from Absalom's men by hiding in a well that a woman covered to look like a pile of grain (2 Samuel 17:15–21).

9. Jonah tried to flee unto Tarshish from the presence of the Lord. It didn't work (Jonah 1:3).

10. The people of the synagogue in Nazareth were going to stone Jesus, but He passing through the midst of them went His way (Luke 4:29–30).

11. [The Jews] sought again to take [Jesus]: but He escaped out of their hand (John 10:39).

12. The apostles, and later Peter alone, were released from prison by angels (Acts 5:18–19; 12:6–10).

13. Paul escaped Jewish assassins in Damascus by leaving the city in a basket let down the side of the wall through a window (Acts 9:23–25).

14. Paul and Silas were released from prison in Philippi by an earthquake and then led out by the jailor (Acts 16:25–30).

## 289. Arsonists

1. The children of Israel burned the cities of Jericho (Joshua 6:24), Ai (Joshua 8:19), Hazor (Joshua 11:11), and all the cities of the Midianites (Numbers 31:9–10).

2. Israel stoned Achan and then burned him and all his belongings (Joshua 7:24–25).

3. Judah fought the Canaanites at Jerusalem and burned the city (Judges 1:8).

4. Abimelech and his men burned down the tower of Shechem, killing about a thousand men and women (Judges 9:49).

5. Samson tied torches to foxes' tails and let them go into the standing grain of the Philistines and burnt up both the shocks and the grain (Judges 15:4–5).

6. The men of Dan burned down the Canaanite city of Laish (Judges 18:26–27).

7. The men of Israel turned again upon the children of Benjamin, and smote them with the edge of the sword. . . . Also they set on fire all the cities that they came to (Judges 20:48).

8. The Amalekites burned David's city of Ziklag (1 Samuel 30:1).

9. Absalom burned Joab's barley field just to get his attention (2 Samuel 14:28–33).

10. Pharaoh king of Egypt had gone up, and taken Gezer, and burnt it with fire (1 Kings 9:16).

11. King Zimri committed suicide by burning down his house while he was in it (1 Kings 16:18).

12. Nebuchadnezzar burned Jerusalem (2 Kings 25:9).

13. Ephesian converts burned magic books worth fifty thousand pieces of silver (Acts 19:19).

## 290. Thieves and Robbers

1. Rachel had stolen the images that were her father's (Genesis 31:19).

2. Achan took a beautiful Babylonian garment, a bar of silver, and a bar of gold during the battle at Ai (Joshua 7:11–21).

3. The men of Shechem set liers (those that lie, as in ambush) in wait for Abimelech in the top of the mountains, and they robbed all that came along that way by them (Judges 9:25).

4. Micah stole eleven hundred shekels of silver from his mother (Judges 17:2).

5. Six hundred Danites stopped at Micah's house and stole his carved image, ephod, teraphim, and molten image (Judges 18:16–18).

6. The people of Judah were robbing the Lord of His rightful tithes (Malachi 3:8).

7. Then were there two thieves crucified with Jesus, one on the right hand, and another on the left (Matthew 27:38).

8. Judas Iscariot stole from the disciples' treasury (John 12:4–6).

9. Now Barabbas was a robber (John 18:40).

## 291. Impersonators

1. Sarai posed as Abram's sister in Egypt (Genesis 12:10–20).

2. Rebekah posed as Isaac's sister in Gerar (Genesis 26:6–11).

3. Jacob disguised himself as Esau so well that his father, Isaac, believed him (Genesis 27:1–29).

4. Leah posed as her sister Rachel when Jacob married her (Genesis 29:21–25).

5. The Gibeonites fooled Joshua by impersonating ambassadors from a distant country (Joshua 9:4–16).

6. David escaped from King Achish by pretending to be a madman (1 Samuel 21:12–22:1).

7. Saul disguised himself, and put on other raiment, and he went out to see the medium at Endor (1 Samuel 28:8).

8. Joab convinced the wise woman of Tekoah to pretend to be a

mourning widow and to ask for King David's help (2 Samuel 14:1–24).

9. Jeroboam's wife disguised herself and went to the prophet Ahijah to find out what the future held, but the Lord told him who she was (1 Kings 14:1–6).

10. A prophet disguised himself as a wounded soldier in order to get a point across to King Ahab (1 Kings 20:35–43).

11. King Ahab disguised himself when fighting the Syrians, but a fatal arrow found him anyway (1 Kings 22:30–40).

12. King Josiah also disguised himself for battle against King Necho of Egypt. He too was fatally wounded (2 Chronicles 35:20–24).

13. The chief priests and scribes sent spies, pretending to be sincere followers, to Jesus to try to trap him (Luke 20:19–20).

## 292. Four Kidnappers

1. Joseph was kidnapped and sold into slavery by his brothers (Genesis 37:17–28).

2. The men of Benjamin grabbed wives for themselves from the women of Shiloh during a festal dance (Judges 21:16–23).

3. Solomon had to judge a case in which two harlots had borne boys. One baby had died, and his mother had secretly traded the corpse for the other mother's son (1 Kings 3:16–21).

4. Prince Joash was kidnapped by his aunt Jehosheba to protect him from his murderous grandmother Athaliah (2 Kings 11:1–3).

## 293. Seven Good Kings—All From Judah

1. David was a man after God's own heart (1 Samuel 13:14; Acts 13:22).

2. Asa's heart was perfect with the Lord all his days (1 Kings 15:11, 14).

3. Jehoshaphat turned not aside from . . . doing what was right in the eyes of the Lord (1 Kings 22:42–43).

4. Uzziah (also known as Azariah) did that which was right in the eyes of the Lord (2 Kings 15:1–3).

5. Jotham did that which was right in the sight of the Lord (2 Kings 15:32–34).

6. Hezekiah did that which was right in the sight of the Lord (2 Kings 18:1–3).

7. Josiah was like no other king in turning to the Lord with all his heart, and with all his soul, and with all his might (2 Kings 22:1–2; 23:25).

## 294. Thirty Bad Kings

1. Jeroboam the son of Nebat made two golden calves and appointed priests for the high places (1 Kings 12:28; 13:33–34).

2. Rehoboam (Judah) did evil, because he prepared not his heart to seek the Lord (2 Chronicles 12:14).

3. Abijam (Judah) walked in all the sins of his father (1 Kings 15:1–3).

4. Nadab made Israel to sin (1 Kings 15:25–26).

5. Baasha walked in the way of Jeroboam (1 Kings 15:33–34).

6. Elah provoked the Lord to anger with his idols (1 Kings 16:8–14).

7. Zimri killed Elah to obtain the throne for a seven-day reign (1 Kings 16:9–20).

8. Omri did worse than all that were before him (1 Kings 16:25).

9. Ahab sold himself to work wickedness like none other before him (1 Kings 16:30; 21:25).

10. Ahaziah son of Ahab served Baal, and worshiped him (1 Kings 22:51–53).

11. Jehoram son of Ahab cleaved unto the sins of Jeroboam (2 Kings 3:1–3).

12. Jehoram (Judah) son of Jehoshaphat, walked in the way of the kings of Israel (2 Kings 8:16–18).

13. Ahaziah (Judah) son of Jehoram, did evil in the sight of the Lord (2 Kings 8:25–27).

14. Jehu took no heed to walk in the law of the Lord God of Israel (2 Kings 10:29–31).

15. Jehoahaz the son of Jehu followed the sins of Jeroboam (2 Kings 13:1–2).

16. Jehoash the son of Jehoahaz did that which was evil in the sight of the Lord (2 Kings 13:10–11).

17. Jeroboam the son of Joash did that which was evil in the sight of the Lord (2 Kings 14:23–24).

18. Zachariah did as his fathers had done (2 Kings 15:8–9).

19. Shallum slew Zachariah to gain his throne (2 Kings 15:10).

20. Menahem departed not all his days from the sins of Jeroboam (2 Kings 15:17–18).

21. Pekahiah did that which was evil in the sight of the Lord (2 Kings 15:23–24).

22. Pekah killed Pekahiah to gain the throne (2 Kings 15:27–28).

23. Ahaz (Judah) sacrificed his son to idols (2 Kings 16:2–4).

24. Hoshea did evil and was finally carried away to exile in Assyria (2 Kings 17:1–2).

25. Manasseh (Judah) built up again the high places which Hezekiah his father had destroyed (2 Kings 21:1–7).

26. Amon (Judah) forsook the Lord God of his fathers (2 Kings 21:19–22).

27. Jehoahaz (Judah) the son of Josiah did that which was evil in the sight of the Lord (2 Kings 23:31–32).

28. Jehoiakim (Judah) did according to all that his fathers had done (2 Kings 23:36–37).

29. Jehoiachin (Judah) did that which was evil in the sight of the Lord (2 Kings 24:8–9).

30. Zedekiah (Judah) did that which was evil in the sight of the Lord (2 Kings 24:18–19).

### 295. Four Good Kings Who Became Bad

1. Saul was given a new heart by God, but he chose to disobey God continually (1 Samuel 10:9; 13:13–14).

2. Solomon loved the Lord, but in his old age, he was turned to evil by his heathen wives (1 Kings 3:3; 11:4).

3. Jehoash (also known as Joash) the son of Ahaziah did that which was right in the sight of the Lord, but he later forsook the Lord (2 Kings 12:1–2; 2 Chronicles 24:20–22).

4. Amaziah did that which was right in the sight of the Lord, but he later turned away from following the Lord (2 Kings 14:1–3; 2 Chronicles 25:1–2, 27).

### 296. Four Adulterers

1. Reuben went and lay with Bilhah, his father's concubine (Genesis 35:22).

2. David lay with Uriah's wife Bathsheba (2 Samuel 11:3–4).

3. Absalom went in unto his father's concubines in the sight of all Israel (2 Samuel 16:22).

4. The scribes and Pharisees caught a woman committing adultery and brought her to Jesus (John 8:3).

### 297. Four Swindlers

1. Jacob cheated Esau out of his birthright and his blessing (Genesis 27:36).

2. Laban cheated Jacob by giving him Leah instead of Rachel. He also changed Jacob's wages ten times (Genesis 29:21–25; 31:7).

3. The Gibeonites swindled a treaty from Joshua by telling him lies (Joshua 9:4–16).

4. Ziba tried to swindle his master, Miphibosheth, by lying to David (2 Samuel 16:1–4; 19:24–30).

### 298. Traitors in the Bible

1. Absalom conspired with Ahithophel to take over the kingdom of David (2 Samuel 15:31).

2. Sheba conspired against David, and all the men of Israel except the tribe of Judah followed Sheba (2 Samuel 20:1–2).

3. Baasha conspired against King Nadab and killed him (1 Kings 15:27).

4. King Elah's servant Zimri, who was captain of half his chariots, conspired against him and killed him (1 Kings 16:8–10).

5. Hazael murdered King Benhadad and reigned in his stead (2 Kings 8:7–15).

6. Jehu conspired against King Joram and killed him and all of the house of Ahab; and Jehu reigned over Israel (2 Kings 9:14–10:36).

7. When Athaliah, the mother of Ahaziah, saw that her son was dead, she arose and destroyed all the seed royal . . . and Athaliah did reign over the land (2 Kings 11:1, 3).

8. Queen Athaliah accused Jehoiada the priest of treason for restoring the throne to Joash, the rightful ruler of Judah (2 Kings 11:14–16).

9. Jozachar and Jehozabad conspired against their master, King Joash, and slew him (2 Kings 12:20–21).

10. The people of Jerusalem conspired against King Amaziah, and he fled to Lachish; but they sent after him to Lachish, and slew him there (2 Kings 14:17–19).

11. Shallum the son of Jabesh conspired against [King Zachariah], and smote him before the people, and slew him, and reigned in his stead (2 Kings 15:10).

12. Menahem the son of Gadi went up from Tirzah, and came to Samaria, and smote Shallum the son of Jabesh in Samaria, and slew him, and reigned in his stead (2 Kings 15:14).

13. Pekah the son of Remaliah, a captain of [King Pekahiah], conspired against him, and smote him in Samaria, in the palace of the king's house (2 Kings 15:25).

14. Hoshea the son of Elah made conspiracy against Pekah the son of Remaliah, and smote him, and slew him, and reigned in his stead (2 Kings 15:30).

15. The king of Assyria found conspiracy in Hoshea: for he had sent messengers to So king of Egypt, and brought no present to the king of Assyria (2 Kings 17:4).

16. Adrammelech and Sharezer, sons of King Sennacherib of Assyria, killed him while he worshiped his god Nisroch (2 Kings 19:37).

17. The servants of Amon conspired against him, and slew the king in his own house (2 Kings 21:23).

18. Judas Iscariot was the traitor who betrayed Jesus (Luke 6:16; 22:48).

# 30

## THE SPIRIT WORLD

Many people deny that there is anything but a material world. Some acknowledge that there is a spiritual world, but that it consists of only good powers. Others say there are good powers and evil powers—some of these people would have you believe there is an evil power behind every problem and object in life. Still others claim that they not only believe in evil powers, but that they make contact with these powers and can exercise evil power any time they desire.

The rebirth of the popularity of occult practices in recent years can hardly escape our notice. An east coast university offers a degree in parapsychology—the study of occult phenomenon. Dabbling in witchcraft is not uncommon, even among young people, who call their "religion" Wicca.

The Bible is not a textbook on occult phenomenon. However, it does mention many activities of spirit beings, including angels, demons, and Satan. The following nine lists show us what to watch out for as we face this growing movement.

### 299. Names of Angels in the Bible
1. When the angel of the Lord met with Manoah and his wife, he told them that his name was a secret (Judges 13:17–18).
2. Gabriel spoke with Daniel, Zacharias, and Mary (Daniel 8:15–17; Luke 1:19, 26–27).
3. Jude 9 tells about Michael the archangel.

## 300. *Eleven Titles and Categories of Angels*

1. Angel of light (2 Corinthians 11:14).

2. Angel of the Lord (Genesis 16:7).

3. Angels of the churches (Revelation 1:20).

4. Archangel (Jude 9).

5. Cherubim (Genesis 3:24).

6. Chief prince (Daniel 10:13).

7. Devil's angels (Matthew 25:41).

8. Evil angels (Psalm 78:49).

9. Guardian angels (Matthew 18:10).

10. Seraphim (Isaiah 6:1–6).

11. Watchers (Daniel 4:13, 17, 23).

## 301. *Ten Statements by Satan and Demons*

1. In opposition to God, Satan told Eve that she would not die for eating of the tree of the knowledge of good and evil. He said that Adam and Eve would be as gods, knowing good and evil (Genesis 3:1–5).

2. A spirit told God that he would be a lying spirit in the mouths of Ahab's prophets, thus bringing about Ahab's death on the battlefield (1 Kings 22:19–22).

3. Satan told the Lord that Job would curse God if everything Job had was taken away (Job 1:9–11).

4. After Job passed the first test, Satan told God that Job would curse the Lord if his body was afflicted (Job 2:1–5).

5. Lucifer's aspirations to be like the Most High are recorded in Isaiah 14:13–14.

6. The devil spoke to Jesus in the wilderness and tempted Him by quoting Scripture out of context (Matthew 4:1–11).

7. When Jesus confronted demons who were inhabiting people, they acknowledged that Jesus was the Holy One of God (Luke 4:34) and the Son of God (Luke 4:41).

8. When Jesus confronted the Gadarene demoniac, the demons

begged not to be tormented or sent into the deep. They identi-
fied themselves as *Legion* and asked to be sent into a herd of
swine (Luke 8:26–32).

9. A demon-possessed soothsayer followed Paul and his companions,
   shouting that they were servants of God proclaiming the way of
   salvation (Acts 16:16–18).

10. When the seven sons of Sceva attempted to cast out an evil
    spirit, it answered them, Jesus I know, and Paul I know; but who
    are ye? (Acts 19:13–15).

## 302. Forty-three Past Activities of Angels

1. Cherubim guarded the tree of life in the garden of Eden (Genesis
   3:24).

2. The angel of the Lord found Hagar in the wilderness, prophesied
   to her, and sent her home (Genesis 16:7–12).

3. Two angels ate with Lot, blinded the Sodomites, and brought
   Lot and his family out of Sodom (Genesis 19:1–22).

4. The angel of God spoke to Hagar out of heaven and encouraged
   her (Genesis 21:17–18).

5. The angel of the Lord called to Abraham from heaven, stopped
   him from sacrificing Isaac, and told him that God would multiply
   his descendants (Genesis 22:11–18).

6. The angel of God spoke to Jacob in a dream and showed him
   how to get Laban's cattle (Genesis 31:11–12).

7. The angel of the Lord appeared to Moses in the burning bush
   and told him to go to Pharaoh and to bring the children of Israel
   out of Egypt (Exodus 3:1–22; 4:1–17).

8. The angel of God provided the pillar of fire and the pillar of cloud
   that went with the children of Israel as they traveled toward the
   Promised Land (Exodus 14:19–20).

9. The angel of the Lord withstood Balaam and his ass—first in
   an invisible form and then in a visible form. The angel warned
   Balaam to follow his orders (Numbers 22:21–35).

10. The captain of the Lord's host appeared unto Joshua before the
    battle of Jericho (Joshua 5:13–15).

11. The angel of the Lord rebuked the children of Israel because they didn't stay separated from the people around them (Judges 2:1–4).

12. The angel of the Lord appeared to Gideon and told him that he was to deliver Israel from the Midianites (Judges 6:11–21).

13. The angel of the Lord appeared to Samson's parents and told them of Samson's impending birth (Judges 13:2–20).

14. An angel smote Israel with a pestilence that killed seventy thousand men because David had taken a census (2 Samuel 24:15–16).

15. The angel of the Lord fed Elijah two meals (1 Kings 19:5–8).

16. The angel of the Lord gave Elijah a message for Israel's King Ahaziah, condemning his idolatry and foretelling his death (2 Kings 1:3–4).

17. The angel of the Lord went out, and smote in the camp of the Assyrians an hundred fourscore and five thousand: and when they arose early in the morning, behold, they were all dead corpses (2 Kings 19:35).

18. Isaiah saw and heard the seraphim praise and worship God (Isaiah 6:1–3).

19. A seraph touched Isaiah's lips with a live coal and declared God's forgiveness to him (Isaiah 6:5–7).

20. Nebuchadnezzar attributed the preservation of Shadrach, Meshech, and Abednego in the fiery furnace to God's angel (Daniel 3:28).

21. Daniel said, My God hath sent his angel, and hath shut the lions' mouths, that they have not hurt me (Daniel 6:22).

22. Twice Gabriel came to Daniel to give him understanding of future events (Daniel 8:15–26; 9:21–27).

23. Daniel 10:13–20 may refer to battles between good and evil angels.

24. The angel of the Lord prophesied and explained visions to Zechariah (Zechariah 1:9–21; 2:3–5; 4:1–6).

25. The angel of the Lord appeared unto Joseph in a dream, told him that the Virgin Mary's pregnancy was of the Holy Spirit, and told him not to fear taking Mary to be his wife (Matthew 1:20).

26. The angel of the Lord again appeared to Joseph in a dream and told him to flee with Mary and Jesus to Egypt (Matthew 2:13).

27. After Herod had died, an angel again appeared to Joseph in a dream and told him that it was safe to return to Israel (Matthew 2:19–20).

28. Angels ministered to Jesus after His temptation by the devil (Matthew 4:11).

29. The angel of the Lord opened Jesus' tomb and gave the news of His resurrection to Mary Magdalene and the other Mary (Matthew 28:1–7).

30. The angel Gabriel foretold the birth of John the Baptist to his father-to-be, Zacharias (Luke 1:11–19).

31. Gabriel also announced to Mary that she would have a son, but that it would be a supernatural conception (Luke 1:26–38).

32. The angel of the Lord announced the birth of Jesus to the shepherds (Luke 2:8–14).

33. An angel told Mary to name her baby Jesus (Luke 2:21).

34. The beggar Lazarus died, and was carried by the angels into Abraham's bosom (Luke 16:22).

35. An angel from heaven appeared to Jesus in the garden of Gethsemane and strengthened him (Luke 22:43).

36. An angel of the Lord effected the apostles' escape from a Jerusalem prison. He told them to go and preach in the temple (Acts 5:19–20).

37. An angel told Philip to go south to a certain road. Philip met the Ethiopian eunuch along that road (Acts 8:26).

38. An angel of God appeared to Cornelius in a vision and told him to send for the apostle Peter (Acts 10:3–6).

39. An angel woke Peter and freed him from prison in Jerusalem (Acts 12:6–10).

40. Because Herod did not give glory to God, an angel smote him (Acts 12:23).

41. As Paul was caught in a storm at sea, an angel assured him that all on board would live and that Paul would be brought before Caesar (Acts 27:23–24).

42. All the angels of God worshiped Jesus (Hebrews 1:6).

43. Angels watched over the churches (Revelation 1:20).

### 303. Eight Present Activities of Angels

1. The angel of the Lord encampeth round about them that fear him, and delivereth them (Psalm 34:7).

2. He shall give his angels charge over thee, to keep thee in all thy ways. They shall bear thee up in their hands, lest thou dash thy foot against a stone (Psalm 91:11–12).

3. It seems that children have guardian angels (Matthew 18:10).

4. There is joy in the presence of the angels of God over one sinner that repenteth (Luke 15:10).

5. Angels are ministering spirits, sent forth to minister for them who shall be heirs of salvation (Hebrews 1:14).

6. Angels desire to look into the things of salvation (1 Peter 1:12).

7. Angels watch over the churches (Revelation 1:20).

8. I Jesus have sent mine angel to testify unto you these things in the churches (Revelation 22:16).

### 304. Thirteen Future Activities of Angels

1. In the end of this world, the Son of man shall send forth his angels, and they shall gather out of his kingdom all things that offend (Matthew 13:40–41).

2. The Son of man shall come in the glory of his Father with his angels; and then he shall reward every man according to his works (Matthew 16:27).

3. The Son of man shall send his angels with a great sound of a trumpet, and they shall gather together his elect from the four winds, from one end of heaven to the other (Matthew 24:30–31).

4. Jesus said, Hereafter ye shall see heaven open, and the angels of God ascending and descending upon the Son of man (John 1:51).

5. Evil angels will be judged (2 Peter 2:4).

6. Angels will watch over the churches (Revelation 1:20).

7. John saw four angels standing on the four corners of the earth,

holding the four winds of the earth, that the wind should not blow on the earth (Revelation 7:1).

8. An angel will offer the prayers of the saints on the altar before God's throne (Revelation 8:3–5).

9. The angels will sound the seven trumpets of judgment (Revelation 8:7–10:7).

10. Michael and his angels will fight against the dragon and his angels (Revelation 12:7–10).

11. Seven angels will pour out vials of judgment upon the earth (Revelation 16:1–21).

12. An angel will cast Satan into the bottomless pit and bind him there (Revelation 20:1–3).

13. There will be an angel at each of the twelve gates of the New Jerusalem (Revelation 21:12).

## 305. Twenty-seven Past Activities of Satan and Demons

1. The serpent beguiled Eve and she ate of the forbidden fruit (Genesis 3:13).

2. Mediums were put to death in the Old Testament for dealing with familiar spirits (Leviticus 20:27).

3. God sent an evil spirit between Abimelech and the men of Shechem; and the men of Shechem dealt treacherously with Abimelech (Judges 9:23).

4. An evil spirit bothered Saul and prophesied through him (1 Samuel 16:14–23; 18:10–11).

5. A lying spirit working through false prophets convinced Ahab to go into battle (1 Kings 22:20–22).

6. Satan stood up against Israel, and provoked David to number Israel (1 Chronicles 21:1).

7. Satan took away Job's wealth, children, and health (Job 1:6–2:8).

8. Lucifer fell from heaven and weakened nations in his ambition to be like the Most High (Isaiah 14:12–14).

9. The Lord hath mingled a perverse spirit in the midst thereof:

and they have caused Egypt to err in every work thereof (Isaiah 19:14).

10. The prince of the kingdom of Persia withstood an angel and kept him from going to Daniel for twenty-one days (Daniel 10:13).

11. Satan tempted Jesus (Matthew 4:1–11).

12. They brought unto [Jesus] one possessed with a devil, blind, and dumb: and he healed him, insomuch that the blind and dumb both spake and saw (Matthew 12:22).

13. A demon often sought to kill the boy it inhabited by casting him into fire or water. It would also throw him to the ground and cause him to grind his teeth and foam at the mouth (Mark 9:17–29).

14. An unclean spirit that recognized Jesus convulsed his victim before being cast out of him by Jesus (Mark 1:23–36).

15. Legion gave his victim insanity, great strength, and an inclination to harm himself (Mark 5:1–20).

16. Satan kept a woman bound for eighteen years by a spirit of infirmity so that she could not straighten herself (Luke 13:11–16).

17. Satan entered into Judas surnamed Iscariot . . . and [Judas] went his way, and communed with the chief priests and captains, how he might betray [Jesus] unto them (Luke 22:3–4).

18. The Lord said, Simon, Simon, behold, Satan hath desired to have you, that he may sift you as wheat (Luke 22:31).

19. The devil was a murderer from the beginning, and abode not in the truth, because there is no truth in him. When he speaketh a lie, he speaketh of his own: for he is a liar, and the father of it (John 8:44).

20. Satan filled [Ananias's] heart to lie to the Holy Ghost, and to keep back part of the price of the land (Acts 5:3).

21. A certain damsel possessed with a spirit of divination . . . brought her masters much gain by soothsaying (Acts 16:16).

22. The seven sons of Sceva were overcome by an evil spirit that they were trying to cast out of a man (Acts 19:16).

23. Satan hindered Paul from going to the Thessalonians (1 Thessalonians 2:18).

24. The devil has taken people captive at his will (2 Timothy 2:26).

25. The devil had the power of death (Hebrews 2:14).

26. The devil sinneth from the beginning (1 John 3:8).

27. The devil disputed with Michael the archangel about the body of Moses (Jude 9).

## 306. Seven Present Activities of Satan and Demons

1. Demons may leave and later return to a person (Matthew 12:43–45).

2. Satan may take away the word that has been sown in people's hearts if they don't understand it (Matthew 13:19).

3. The god of this world hath blinded the minds of them which believe not, lest the light of the glorious gospel of Christ, who is the image of God, should shine unto them (2 Corinthians 4:4).

4. Satan disguises himself as an angel of light (2 Corinthians 11:14).

5. The powers of darkness fight against the saints (Ephesians 6:12).

6. The devils believe in God and tremble (James 2:19).

7. The devil accuses us before our God day and night (Revelation 12:10).

## 307. Six Future Activities of Satan and Demons

1. Lucifer shall be brought down to hell, to the sides of the pit (Isaiah 14:15).

2. In the latter times some shall depart from the faith, giving heed to seducing spirits, and doctrines of devils (1 Timothy 4:1).

3. Satan and his angels will battle Michael and his angels. Satan and his angels will be defeated and cast out of heaven to the earth (Revelation 12:7–10).

4. Spirits of devils will perform miracles to bring the nations to war (Revelation 16:13–14).

5. Satan will be cast into the bottomless pit for one thousand years (Revelation 20:1–3).

6. Satan will be released upon the earth after the thousand years, but he will finally be cast into the lake of fire (Revelation 20:7–10).

# 31
## HEATHEN PRACTICES

Most people, when first confronting the scene of fifteen or twenty devout Hare Krishna members in a local park, bowing before a picture of an Indian deity, are awestruck. To think that such a practice could take place in our American communities is shocking to most of us. It's heathen; it's something foreign; it's strange, and we don't like it. Even though we may not like it, there is little in the legal realm we can do about it.

The Bible records many pagan deities and practices that God forbade Israel to involve herself with. These pagan gods were an abomination to Him, and the practices associated with them were heinous. Worship of some of these gods went so far as human sacrifice. Recorded in the next lists are names of these gods, practicing sorcerers, and witches, and the various sacrifices made to those idols.

A pagan deity is, according to Arthur Wallis, "any person or thing that has usurped in the heart the place of preeminence that belongs to Jesus Christ." Though few around us bow with shaven head to an Eastern deity, many bow before Western values of prosperity, success, and prominence. Such "gods" may not look so strange, but the effect of worshiping them will be the same as that of worshiping idols.

### 308. Thirty-one Pagan Gods in the Bible
1. The Sepharites burned their children to Adrammelech (2 Kings 17:31).
2. The Sepharites also worshiped Anammelech (2 Kings 17:31).

3. The men of Hamath made Ashima (2 Kings 17:30).

4. Solomon worshiped Ashtoreth the goddess of the Zidonians (1 Kings 11:5), also known as the queen of heaven (Jeremiah 44:17).

5. King Ahab and Queen Jezebel served Baal (1 Kings 16:31–32).

6. After Gideon died, Israel turned to Baalberith (Judges 8:33).

7. Israel served Baalpeor, the god of Moab (Numbers 25:1–3).

8. Baalzebub was the god of Ekron (2 Kings 1:2).

9. Bel was a Babylonian god (Jeremiah 51:44).

10. Aaron made the children of Israel a molten calf to worship (Exodus 32:1–5), and King Jeroboam made golden calves (1 Kings 12:26–30).

11. Castor was a Greek god (Acts 28:11).

12. Solomon built a high place for Chemosh, the abomination of Moab (1 Kings 11:7).

13. Amos chastised Israel for serving Chiun (Amos 5:26).

14. The Philistines had a temple for Dagon (1 Samuel 5:1–5).

15. The great temple of the goddess Diana was in Ephesus (Acts 19:35).

16. The Lycaonians worshiped Jupiter (Acts 14:11–13).

17. The Roman god Mercury was also worshiped by the Lycaonians (Acts 14:11–13).

18. Solomon worshiped Milcom, the abomination of the Ammonites (1 Kings 11:5).

19. Solomon built a high place for Molech, the god of Ammon (1 Kings 11:7).

20. Isaiah said that the people served Nebo (Isaiah 46:1).

21. Israel saved the brass serpent that Moses made and worshiped it. They called it Nehushtan (2 Kings 18:4).

22. The men of Cuth worshiped Nergal (2 Kings 17:30).

23. The Avites worshiped Nibhaz (2 Kings 17:31).

24. Sennacherib, king of Assyria, was killed while worshiping Nisroch (2 Kings 19:36–37).

25. Pollux was a Greek god (Acts 28:11).

26. Israel worshiped images of Remphan (Acts 7:43).

27. Rimmon was the god of the Syrians (2 Kings 5:17–18).

28. The Babylonians worshiped Succothbenoth (2 Kings 17:30).

29. Ezekiel saw a woman weeping for the god Tammuz (Ezekiel 8:14).

30. The Avites worshiped Tartak (2 Kings 17:31).

31. Micah built a shrine for his teraphim, or household gods (Judges 17:5).

## 309. Witches and Sorcerers

1. Pharaoh called on his sorcerers and magicians to duplicate the miracles that Moses performed (Exodus 7:11–12).

2. The witch of Endor was a medium (1 Samuel 28:7–25).

3. Jezebel practiced witchcraft (2 Kings 9:22).

4. Edom, Moab, Ammon, Tyre, and Aidon all had enchanters, sorcerers, and diviners (Jeremiah 27:3–10).

5. Nebuchadnezzar's magicians, astrologers, soothsayers, and sorcerers could neither tell him his dream nor interpret it (Daniel 2:10).

6. Nahum called Nineveh the mistress of witchcrafts (Nahum 3:4).

7. Simon amazed the people of Samaria with his sorcery (Acts 8:9).

8. Elymas was a sorcerer on the island of Paphos (Acts 13:6–8).

9. Many of those who repented and believed at Ephesus had practiced curious arts (Acts 19:19).

## 310. Sacrifices Made to Idols

1. The children of Israel offered burnt offerings, and brought peace offerings to the molten calf that Aaron made (Exodus 32:6).

2. Jeroboam offered sacrifices and burned incense to the two golden calves that he had made (1 Kings 12:32–33).

3. Elijah challenged the prophets of Baal to a contest in which they offered a bullock to their god (1 Kings 18:25).

4. The king of Moab despaired in the face of battle and offered his

oldest son, the heir to the throne, as a burnt offering to his god (2 Kings 3:26–27).

5. The Sepharvites burned their children in fire to Adrammelech and Anammelech, the gods of Sepharvaim (2 Kings 17:31).

6. The children of Israel burned incense to the brazen serpent that Moses had made (2 Kings 18:4).

7. Idolatrous priests burned incense to Baal (2 Kings 23:5).

8. The Israelites offered up their children in the fire of Molech (2 Kings 23:10).

9. Ahaz burned incense and offered his children to Molech. He also sacrificed and burned incense to Asherah and the gods of Damascus (2 Chronicles 28:1–4, 23).

10. The people of Judah burned incense, sacrificed cakes, and poured out drink offerings to the queen of heaven (Ashtoreth) (Jeremiah 44:19).

11. The people of Jerusalem offered meat, fine flour, oil, honey, and even their sons and daughters to idols (Ezekiel 16:17–20).

# 32

## WORK AS UNTO THE LORD

An advertisement in major national magazines quoted Christopher Morley's maxim "There is only one success . . . to be able to spend your life in your own way." In the background, a man sits alone, fishing in a setting of idyllic beauty. The American dream has developed to the point where we are made to feel that the only satisfying thing in life is doing what *I* want, whenever *I* want. Work is often viewed as a necessary evil for sustaining the leisure that one finds satisfying. Work is seldom looked upon as a satisfying part of one's life.

The Bible lists that follow show many of the vocations of those who lived in Bible times. They may not have had computers and copying machines to speed up their work, but the vocations that most of them pursued are quite similar to the vocations that many of us have. Yet we find little discontentment among them concerning their jobs—as if they sensed God's purpose for their life while working.

Dorothy L. Sayers said, "I ask that work should be looked upon not as a necessary drudgery to be undergone for the purpose of making money, but as a way of life in which the nature of man should find its proper exercise and delight and so fulfill itself to the glory of God."

### 311. Spies
1. The Lord commanded Moses to send twelve men into Canaan to spy out the land (Numbers 13:1–16).

2. Joshua the son of Nun sent out of Shittim two men to spy secretly, saying, Go view the land, even Jericho (Joshua 2:1).

3. Spies found the entrance to the Canaanite city of Bethel before the army of Ephraim came in to destroy it (Judges 1:23–25).

4. The Danites sent five men to spy out the rest of their inheritance (Judges 18:2–28).

5. David sent spies out to see if Saul had followed him to the wilderness of Ziph. He had (1 Samuel 26:3–4).

6. Absalom sent spies throughout all the tribes of Israel, saying, As soon as ye hear the sound of the trumpet, then ye shall say, Absalom reigneth in Hebron (2 Samuel 15:10).

7. Hushai, the counselor of Absalom, was actually a spy for David (2 Samuel 15:32–37).

8. The chief priests and scribes sent spies to watch Jesus (Luke 20:20).

9. Paul wrote with concern about false brethren unawares brought in, who came in privily to spy out our liberty which we have in Christ Jesus, that they might bring us into bondage of the law (Galatians 2:4).

### 312. Godly Officials in Heathen Governments

1. Pharaoh appointed Joseph to be governor over Egypt (Genesis 41:39–41).

2. Nehemiah was Artaxerxes' cupbearer (Nehemiah 1:11–2:1).

3. Esther became queen to Ahasuerus (Esther 2:17).

4. Mordecai the Jew was next unto King Ahasuerus, and great among the Jews (Esther 10:3).

5. King Nebuchadnezzar made Daniel a great man, and gave him many gifts, and made him ruler over the whole province of Babylon, and chief of the governors over all the wise men of Babylon (Daniel 2:48).

6. Shadrach, Meshach, and Abednego were appointed administrators over the province of Babylon by King Nebuchadnezzar (Daniel 2:49).

7. A godly Roman centurion asked Jesus to heal his servant (Luke 7:2–10).

8. The Ethiopian eunuch was a man of great authority under Candace, queen of the Ethiopians, who had the charge of all her treasure, and had come to Jerusalem to worship (Acts 8:27).

9. Cornelius, a Roman centurion in Caesarea, was a devout man, and one that feared God with all his house, which gave much alms to the people, and prayed to God alway (Acts 10:1–2).

10. Sergius Paulus, the proconsul of Cyprus, became a believer (Acts 13:7–12).

11. Paul greeted the Philippian church from the saints that are of Caesar's household (Philippians 4:22).

## 313. Artists and Craftsmen

1. Jubal was the inventor of the harp and the pipe (Genesis 4:21).

2. Tubalcain was an instructor of every artificer in brass and iron (Genesis 4:22).

3. Noah built the ark of gopher wood (Genesis 6:13–22).

4. Bezaleel worked in gold, silver, brass, stone, and wood (Exodus 31:1–6).

5. Aaron made a molten calf of gold and fashioned it with a graving tool (Exodus 32:4).

6. Moses hewed two tables of stone to replace the ones he broke (Exodus 34:1, 4).

7. Aholiab was an engraver and an embroiderer (Exodus 38:23).

8. Moses made a serpent of brass (Numbers 21:9).

9. Hiram was cunning to work all works in brass (1 Kings 7:13–14).

10. Harhaiah was a goldsmith (Nehemiah 3:8).

11. Joseph was a carpenter (Matthew 13:55).

12. Jesus was a carpenter (Mark 6:3).

13. Paul, Aquila, and Priscilla were tentmakers (Acts 18:1–3).

14. Demetrius was a silversmith in Ephesus (Acts 19:24).

15. Alexander was a coppersmith (2 Timothy 4:14).

### 314. Physicians

1. Joseph commanded his servants the physicians to embalm his father: and the physicians embalmed Israel (Genesis 50:2).

2. King Asa was diseased in his feet and he sought the physicians but not the Lord (2 Chronicles 16:12–13).

3. Luke, the beloved physician, sent greetings to the saints at Colosse (Colossians 4:14).

### 315. Teachers

1. The Lord taught Moses what to say and what to do (Exodus 4:12, 15).

2. Moses taught the children of Israel ordinances and laws, and . . . the way wherein they must walk, and the work that they must do (Exodus 18:20).

3. The Lord appointed Bezaleel and Aholiab to teach those who would construct the tabernacle (Exodus 35:30–35).

4. The Lord told Aaron to teach the children of Israel all the statutes which the Lord hath spoken unto them by the hand of Moses (Leviticus 10:11).

5. The priests were to teach the children of Israel how to recognize and to deal with leprosy (Deuteronomy 24:8).

6. The king of Assyria sent one of the exiled priests back to Samaria to teach the Gentile inhabitants how they should fear God (2 Kings 17:28).

7. King Jehoshaphat sent his princes throughout Judah to teach the law of the Lord to all the people (2 Chronicles 17:7–9).

8. King Artaxerxes commissioned Ezra to teach the laws of God to Israel (Ezra 7:25).

9. Jesus taught the people (Matthew 11:1).

10. Jesus told His apostles, Go ye therefore, and teach all nations, . . . to observe all things whatsoever I have commanded you (Matthew 28:19–20).

11. Jesus said, The Comforter . . . shall teach you all things, and bring all things to your remembrance (John 14:26).

12. Paul and Barnabas continued in Antioch, teaching and preaching the word of the Lord, with many others also (Acts 15:35).

13. Apollos taught in the synagogue at Ephesus, but Aquila and Priscilla instructed him in the ways of God (Acts 18:24–26).

14. Paul disputed daily in the school of Tyrannus (Acts 19:9).

15. Paul was brought up . . . at the feet of Gamaliel, and taught according to the perfect manner of the law of the fathers (Acts 22:3).

### 316. Shepherds and Shepherdesses

1. Abel was a keeper of sheep (Genesis 4:2).

2. Abram had sheep (Genesis 12:16).

3. Rachel was a shepherdess (Genesis 29:9).

4. Laban had sheep (Genesis 29:9).

5. Jacob had sheep (Genesis 32:14).

6. Jacob's sons tended his flocks (Genesis 37:13).

7. Judah had sheep (Genesis 38:12, 13).

8. Moses' wife Zipporah and her sisters tended their father's sheep (Exodus 2:16, 17).

9. Moses became a shepherd for his father-in-law's flock (Exodus 3:1).

10. Achan kept sheep (Joshua 7:24).

11. David was a shepherd (1 Samuel 16:11–13).

12. Nabal had three thousand sheep (1 Samuel 25:2–3).

13. Job had fourteen thousand sheep (Job 42:12).

14. David said, The Lord is my shepherd (Psalm 23:1).

15. Jesus said, I am the good shepherd: the good shepherd giveth his life for the sheep (John 10:11).

16. Jesus commanded Peter to shepherd the church (John 21:15–17).

### 317. Beggars

1. Blind Bartimaeus, the son of Timaeus, sat by the highway side begging (Mark 10:46).

2. Jesus spoke about a beggar named Lazarus who died and was carried by the angels into Abraham's bosom (Luke 16:20–22).

3. Jesus healed a blind beggar by putting mud on his eyes and sending him to wash in the pool of Siloam (John 9:1–8).

4. Peter and John healed a lame beggar who had been asking for alms at the temple gate (Acts 3:2–7).

### 318. Thirteen Famous Farmers

1. The Lord God planted a garden eastward in Eden (Genesis 2:8).

2. Cain was a tiller of the ground (Genesis 4:2).

3. Noah began to be an husbandman, and he planted a vineyard (Genesis 9:20).

4. Isaac sowed in [Gerar], and received in the same year an hundredfold (Genesis 26:12).

5. Gideon raised wheat (Judges 6:11).

6. Boaz had a barley field (Ruth 1:22–2:3).

7. David commanded Ziba to till the land for Mephibosheth, Saul's grandson (2 Samuel 9:9–10).

8. Joab had a barley field (2 Samuel 14:30).

9. Elisha was plowing when Elijah threw his mantle upon him (1 Kings 19:19).

10. Naboth had a vineyard on which Ahab wanted to raise herbs (1 Kings 21:1–2).

11. King Uzziah loved husbandry (2 Chronicles 26:9–10).

12. Job was a farmer (Job 1:14).

13. Solomon planted vineyards, gardens, and orchards (Ecclesiastes 2:4–5).

### 319. One Hundred and Ninety-eight Vocations in the Bible

1. Apostle (Acts 6:1–6).

2. Apothecary (perfumer) (Nehemiah 3:8).

3. Archer (Genesis 21:20).

4. Armorbearer (1 Samuel 14:12).

5. Astrologer (Daniel 1:20).

6. Baker (Genesis 40:1).

7. Barber (Ezekiel 5:1).

8. Beggar (Acts 3:2).

9. Binder of sheaves (Psalm 129:7).

10. Bishop (or elder) (1 Timothy 3:1).

11. Brickmaker (Exodus 5:7).

12. Builder (1 Kings 5:18).

13. Butler (Genesis 40:1).

14. Calker (shipwright) (Ezekiel 27:27).

15. Camel driver (Genesis 32:13–16; 33:13).

16. Candlestick maker (Exodus 25:31).

17. Carpenter (Mark 6:3).

18. Cattleman (Genesis 46:34).

19. Centurion (Matthew 8:5).

20. Chamberlain (Acts 12:20).

21. Chancellor (Ezra 4:8).

22. Chapman (trader) (2 Chronicles 9:14).

23. Chariot driver (1 Kings 22:34).

24. Charmer (Psalm 58:5).

25. Clothes maker (Acts 9:39).

26. Confectionary (perfumer) (1 Samuel 8:13).

27. Cook (1 Samuel 8:13).

28. Coppersmith (2 Timothy 4:14).

29. Council (Sanhedrin) member (Acts 22:30).

30. Counsellor (1 Chronicles 27:33).

31. Cupbearer (Nehemiah 1:11).

32. Daysman (mediator) (Job 9:33).

33. Deacon (Acts 6:3–5; 1 Timothy 3:8).

34. Deputy (governor) (Acts 13:7).

35. Ditchdigger (Isaiah 22:11).
36. Diviner (soothsayer) (1 Samuel 6:2).
37. Doorkeeper (1 Chronicles 15:23).
38. Drawer of water (Joshua 9:21).
39. Embroiderer (Exodus 38:23).
40. Enchanter (Jeremiah 27:9).
41. Engraver (Exodus 38:23).
42. Evangelist (Acts 21:8).
43. Exchanger (banker) (Matthew 25:27).
44. Executioner (Mark 6:27).
45. Exorcist (Acts 19:13).
46. Fanner (winnower) (Jeremiah 51:2).
47. Farmer (Matthew 22:5; Genesis 9:20).
48. Feller (lumberjack) (Isaiah 14:8).
49. Fisherman (Luke 5:2).
50. Footman (1 Samuel 22:17).
51. Forest keeper (Nehemiah 2:8).
52. Fowler (Psalm 124:7).
53. Fruit gatherer (Amos 7:14).
54. Fuller (treater of cloth) (Mark 9:3).
55. Furniture maker (Exodus 31:6–9).
56. Gardener (John 20:15).
57. Garment maker (Exodus 31:6, 10).
58. Goat herder (Genesis 32:14, 16).
59. Goldsmith (Isaiah 40:19).
60. Governor (Genesis 42:6).
61. Grapegatherer (Jeremiah 6:9).
62. Guard (Genesis 40:4).
63. Harlot (Joshua 6:17).
64. Harper (Revelation 14:2).

65. Herald (Daniel 3:4).
66. Hewer of timber (2 Chronicles 2:10).
67. Hewer of wood (Joshua 9:21).
68. Horseman (2 Kings 9:17).
69. Hunter (Genesis 25:27).
70. Innkeeper (Luke 10:34–35).
71. Interpreter (Genesis 42:23).
72. Jailor (Acts 16:23).
73. Judge (2 Samuel 15:4).
74. King (Acts 25:13).
75. Lamp maker (Exodus 25:37).
76. Lawyer (Titus 3:13).
77. Lieutenant (Esther 9:3).
78. Locksmith (Nehemiah 3:3).
79. Magician (Daniel 2:2).
80. Magistrate (Acts 16:35).
81. Maid (Esther 4:4; Genesis 16:1).
82. Maidservant (Exodus 20:10).
83. Manservant (Exodus 20:10).
84. Mariner (Ezekiel 27:27).
85. Mason (2 Kings 12:12).
86. Masterbuilder (1 Corinthians 3:10).
87. Merchant (Revelation 18:11–13).
88. Messenger (1 Samuel 23:27).
89. Midwife (Genesis 35:17).
90. Miller (Matthew 24:41).
91. Miner (Job 28:1–2).
92. Minister (Jeremiah 33:21).
93. Minstrel (2 Kings 3:15).
94. Money changer (Matthew 21:12).

95. Mourner (Ecclesiastes 12:5).

96. Mover (Numbers 4:1–15).

97. Musician (Psalm 4, title).

98. Necromancer (sorcerer) (Deuteronomy 18:11).

99. Night watchman (Isaiah 21:11).

100. Nurse for children (Exodus 2:7–9).

101. Officer (Luke 12:58).

102. Orator (Acts 24:1).

103. Overseer (2 Chronicles 34:12).

104. Pastor (Ephesians 4:11).

105. Philosopher (Acts 17:18).

106. Physician (Colossians 4:14).

107. Pilot (ship) (Ezekiel 27:27).

108. Planter (Jeremiah 31:5).

109. Plowman (Amos 9:13).

110. Poet (Acts 17:28).

111. Porter (gatekeeper) (2 Kings 7:10).

112. Post (postman) (Esther 3:13).

113. Potter (Jeremiah 18:4).

114. Preacher (1 Timothy 2:7).

115. Presbyter (1 Timothy 4:14).

116. President (Daniel 6:2).

117. Priest (Hebrew) (Leviticus 1:7).

118. Priest (pagan) (1 Samuel 6:2).

119. Prince (1 Chronicles 5:6).

120. Prognosticator (Isaiah 47:13).

121. Prophet (1 Samuel 3:20).

122. Prophetess (Judges 4:4).

123. Prostitute (see Harlot) (Joshua 6:25).

124. Publican (Luke 5:27).

125. Queen (1 Kings 10:1).

126. Rabbi (John 1:38).

127. Reaper (Amos 9:13; Isaiah 17:5).

128. Recorder (2 Samuel 8:16).

129. Refiner (Malachi 3:3).

130. Robber (Job 5:5).

131. Rower (Ezekiel 27:26).

132. Runner (2 Samuel 15:1).

133. Sailor (Revelation 18:17).

134. Sawyer (2 Samuel 12:31).

135. Schoolmaster (Galatians 3:25).

136. Scientist (Daniel 1:4).

137. Scribe (2 Samuel 8:17).

138. Seamstress (Acts 9:39).

139. Seer (1 Samuel 9:9).

140. Seller (James 4:13).

141. Senator (Psalm 105:22).

142. Sergeant (Acts 16:35).

143. Servant (Genesis 24:2).

144. Sheepmaster (2 Kings 3:4).

145. Sheepshearer (Genesis 38:12).

146. Shepherd (Genesis 46:32; Amos 7:14).

147. Sheriff (Daniel 3:2).

148. Shipbuilder (1 Kings 22:48).

149. Shipmaster (Jonah 1:6).

150. Shipmen (1 Kings 9:27).

151. Silversmith (Acts 19:24; Judges 17:4).

152. Singer (1 Chronicles 9:33).

153. Slave (Revelation 18:13).

154. Slinger (armed with a sling) (2 Kings 3:25).

155. Smith (1 Samuel 13:19).

156. Snake charmer (Psalm 58:4–5).

157. Soldier (Acts 27:31).

158. Soothsayer (diviner) (Joshua 13:22).

159. Sorcerer (Exodus 7:11).

160. Sorceress (Isaiah 57:3).

161. Sower (Isaiah 55:10).

162. Spearman (Acts 23:23).

163. Spice merchant (1 Kings 10:15).

164. Spy (Joshua 2:1).

165. Stargazer (Isaiah 47:13).

166. Steward (Genesis 15:2).

167. Stonecutter (1 Kings 5:18).

168. Swineherder (Mark 5:14).

169. Swordsman (Song of Solomon 3:8).

170. Tailor (Exodus 39:22).

171. Tanner (Acts 9:43).

172. Taskmaster (Exodus 1:11).

173. Tax collector (see Publican).

174. Teacher (1 Chronicles 25:8).

175. Temple servants (Ezra 8:20).

176. Tentmaker (Acts 18:3).

177. Tetrarch (governor) (Matthew 14:1).

178. Thief (Joel 2:9).

179. Tormentor (Matthew 18:34).

180. Townclerk (Acts 19:35).

181. Treader of grapes (Amos 9:13).

182. Treasurer (Ezra 1:8).

183. Trumpeter (2 Kings 11:14).

184. Tutor (Galatians 4:2).

185. Usurer (moneylender) (Exodus 22:25).
186. Vinedresser (2 Kings 25:12).
187. Waiter (Acts 6:2).
188. Wardrobe keeper (2 Kings 22:14).
189. Watcher (Jeremiah 4:16).
190. Watchman (2 Kings 9:17).
191. Water drawer (Joshua 9:21).
192. Weapons maker (1 Samuel 8:12).
193. Weaver (Exodus 35:35).
194. Whore (Leviticus 21:7).
195. Witch (Exodus 22:18).
196. Wizard (Leviticus 20:27).
197. Woodcarver (Exodus 35:33).
198. Worker in brass (1 Kings 7:13–14).

# 33

## MONEY

"Federal Income Taxes Will Rise Thirteen Percent"—so reads a morning headline. Year after year, as government revenues fall short, more is demanded. The IRS makes sure we pay all that is required of us. In hard economic times, the burden of taxes becomes heavier, and the percentage of poor people increases. The pressure to maintain the current standard of living pushes many into illegal means of gaining money—extortion and bribery.

What is true today was also true in Bible times: taxes, government tax collectors, the poor becoming poorer, extortion, and bribery. Governments back then were known to spend money lavishly on those in power and squeeze the little people for all they could get. Maybe we don't have it as bad as we think!

You may also want to reconsider the possible benefits of *not* being rich. The first lists show poor people, and it is interesting how many of them received God's *direct care* because of their distressing situation. Had they not had such need, they might not have encountered God as they did. It's something to think about.

### 320. Poor People
1. Naomi and Ruth were poor when they came to the land of Israel from Moab (Ruth 1:21).
2. David was poor in his early days (1 Samuel 18:23).
3. A poor widow came to Elisha because a creditor wanted payment.

It seems that the only assets she had to pay him with were a pot of oil and her two sons (2 Kings 4:1–2).

4. The widow of Zarephath was very poor and might have starved to death if the Lord had not sent Elijah to her (1 Kings 17:8–16).

5. When the king of Babylon carried the people of Jerusalem away into captivity, he left only the poorest people of the land (2 Kings 24:10–14).

6. Blind Bartimaeus was a beggar before Jesus healed him (Mark 10:46).

7. Jesus commended a poor widow to His disciples for putting all she had into the temple treasury (Mark 12:41–44).

8. When Lazarus the beggar died, angels carried him to Abraham's bosom (Luke 16:20–22).

9. Jesus healed another beggar who was blind from birth (John 9:1–8).

10. Peter and John healed a beggar lame from birth as they were going to the temple to pray (Acts 3:1–8).

11. Christians in Macedonia and Achaia made a contribution for the poor among the saints in Jerusalem (Romans 15:25–27).

12. Ye know the grace of our Lord Jesus Christ, that, though he was rich, yet for your sakes he became poor, that ye through his poverty might be rich (2 Corinthians 8:9).

## 321. Taxes

1. At Joseph's advice, the Egyptians were taxed 20 percent of their produce for the seven plenteous years before the famine. This tax remained even after the famine was over (Genesis 41:34; 47:26).

2. All Israelites twenty years old or older were required to pay a half-shekel when the census was taken. The money was used for the service of the tabernacle (Exodus 30:12–16).

3. When Israel asked for a king, Samuel warned the people that he would tax them and take their children and property. Nevertheless, the people held to their request (1 Samuel 8).

4. Solomon's heavy yoke upon Israel probably included taxes (1 Kings 12:1–14).

5. The kingdoms Solomon reigned over brought presents, or tribute, to his government (1 Kings 4:21).

6. Menahem, king of Israel, taxed the rich men of his kingdom fifty shekels of silver apiece to pay Pul, king of Assyria (2 Kings 15:19–20).

7. King Hoshea of Israel paid tribute to King Shalmaneser of Assyria. When it was discovered that he had ceased payments, Shalmaneser imprisoned him (2 Kings 17:3–4).

8. King Jehoiakim of Judah taxed his subjects in order to give Pharaoh Necho the tribute he demanded (2 Kings 23:33–35).

9. Some of the Philistines brought Jehoshaphat [king of Judah] presents, and tribute silver (2 Chronicles 17:11).

10. The Jews were paying toll, tribute, and custom to Persia during Artaxerxes' reign (Ezra 4:13).

11. Later, King Artaxerxes exempted the priests, Levites, and other temple personnel from taxation (Ezra 7:24).

12. King Ahasuerus laid a tribute upon the land, and upon the isles of the sea [i.e., upon the whole empire] (Esther 10:1).

13. Jesus sent Peter fishing to pay their taxes. In the fish's mouth was a coin sufficient for the tax (Matthew 17:24–27).

14. Caesar imposed tribute on his subjects in Jerusalem in Jesus' day (Matthew 22:17–22).

15. Joseph and Mary had to go to Bethlehem to be registered before being taxed. Thus Jesus was born there (Luke 2:1–7).

### 322. Tax Collectors

1. Matthew (Levi) left his tax collecting to follow Jesus (Matthew 9:9).

2. Matthew then made a feast for Jesus, which many tax collectors (publicans) attended (Luke 5:29–32).

3. Zacchaeus, a rich chief tax collector, climbed a sycamore tree to see Jesus. When Jesus saw Zacchaeus and called him, he joyfully received Jesus into his home and was saved (Luke 19:1–10).

4. In one of Jesus' parables, a publican humbly prayed for mercy

and was justified, whereas the self-exalting Pharisee was not (Luke 18:9–14).

5. Tax collectors came to John to be baptized; he charged them not to collect more than they were supposed to (Luke 3:12–13).

## 323. Important Coins

1. The only coin mentioned in the Old Testament is the *dram* or *daric*, a gold Persian coin (Ezra 2:69; 8:27).

   Note: The coins mentioned in the New Testament were issued by three governments: Greek, Roman, and Jewish (Maccabaean). For the sake of clarity, it is necessary to refer to the names of the coins as given in the Greek text.

2. Sparrows were sold two for an *assarion* (*farthing* in KJV), a Greek coin (Matthew 10:29; cf. Luke 12:6).

3. The woman's lost coin was a *drachma*, a Greek coin worth a day's wages (Luke 15:8).

4. *Tribute money* was a half shekel per person, and the *piece of money* that Peter found in the fish's mouth, a Greek *stater*, would have paid for two people (Matthew 17:24–27).

5. The man who owned the vineyard in Jesus' parable gave each laborer a *denarius* (*penny* in KJV), a Roman coin worth about one day's wages (Matthew 20:1–2).

6. The widow's mite was a Jewish *lepton* (*mite* in KJV). It was worth half a *kodrantes* (*farthing* in KJV) and could be used in the temple because it did not picture a pagan deity (Mark 12:42).

## 324. Three Cases of Extortion

1. Jacob would not feed Esau until he could extract a promise from Esau to give up his birthright (Genesis 25:29–34).

2. Samson's wedding guests threatened his wife, saying, Entice thy husband, that he may declare unto us the riddle, lest we burn thee and thy father's house with fire (Judges 14:15).

3. The sons of Eli threatened to take the uncooked sacrificial meat by force unless those who brought it gave it to them (1 Samuel 2:12–17).

### 325. Five Bribes

1. The lords of the Philistines each offered Delilah eleven hundred pieces of silver if she would find the secret of Samson's strength and tell them (Judges 16:5).

2. When Samuel was old . . . his sons walked not in his ways, but turned aside after lucre, and took bribes, and perverted judgment (1 Samuel 8:1–3).

3. Judas Iscariot was given thirty pieces of silver to betray Jesus (Matthew 26:14–16).

4. The chief priests bribed the guards of Jesus' tomb to say that the disciples had stolen the body (Matthew 28:11–15).

5. Felix kept Paul in prison, hoping that Paul would bribe him for release (Acts 24:26).

# 34

## PEOPLE TO PEOPLE

Almost every community has a recluse; surely you remember at least one. The old man who lived by himself back in the woods—in an old dingy house—and only came to town when he was in need of food. Or the old lady who lived down the street in the foreboding, dark house and was only seen when peering out from a split in the curtains. Like Howard Hughes, these folks at some time in life decided to shut themselves off from others and try to find some semblance of happiness by themselves. Unfortunately, the recluse's life becomes one marked by eccentricity and extreme unhappiness.

Life will not be fulfilling if we try to avoid the reality of people around us. It is necessary and good that we interact with one another. It is the way of growth and maturity. Interaction with others will create difficult situations. Just as love is the fruit of interacting with others, so are anger and people who are difficult to be with. These are all a part of maturing. The following lists include some of the interpersonal relationships we will find ourselves in: times of hugs and kisses, times of people being angry with us, getting to know the in-laws, competition with one another, and the drawing of contracts in business relationships.

### 326. Thirteen Contracts

1. Abimelech swore to Abraham that the well dug by Abraham would not be bothered by his men. Abraham gave him seven ewe lambs as a witness of the deal (Genesis 21:25–32).

2. Abraham purchased a burial plot for Sarah from Ephron the Hittite. He had to pay four hundred shekels of silver for the deed (Genesis 23:10–20).

3. Jacob forced the starving Esau to swear over his birthright before Jacob would feed him any pottage (Genesis 25:29–34).

4. Jacob negotiated a work contract with Laban. He would take no wages, but only the striped, spotted, and speckled sheep from Laban's flocks. The Lord blessed Laban with many striped, spotted, and speckled lambs (Genesis 30:29–43).

5. Laban and Jacob later set up a stone pillar to witness a contract of peace between them (Genesis 31:44–53).

6. Joseph's brothers sold him to slave traders for twenty shekels of silver (Genesis 37:28).

7. The lords of the Philistines each offered Delilah eleven hundred pieces of silver if she would find out the secret of Samson's strength for them (Judges 16:4–5).

8. Micah hired a Levite to be a priest in his shrine for an annual salary of ten shekels and a suit of clothing (Judges 17:10).

9. Being Ruth's closest relative gave Boaz the right to buy Naomi's property and to marry Ruth, and he confirmed the agreement by removing and giving over his shoe (Ruth 4:1–10).

10. David pledged kindness to Jonathan and his family with an oath. He later fulfilled his oath by caring for Jonathan's son Mephibosheth (1 Samuel 20:12–17; 2 Samuel 9:6–7).

11. Solomon contracted with Hiram for the use of his servants. Hiram's men would cut cedar for the temple, and Solomon would pay their wages (1 Kings 5:2–12).

12. King Benhadad of Syria promised King Ahab the return of all the Samarian cities taken by his father in return for his safe release (1 Kings 20:34).

13. Jeremiah bought a field from Hananeel, his cousin, for seventeen shekels of silver. The payment and signing of the deed were done before witnesses (Jeremiah 32:6–12).

### 327. *Fourteen Censuses*

1. The population of the garden of Eden was one until God doubled it (Genesis 2:8, 22).

2. The post-Flood census showed only eight survivors (1 Peter 3:20).

3. The Israelites numbered seventy-five when they went into the land of Egypt (Acts 7:14).

4. Six-hundred thousand men (plus women and children) left Egypt on foot in the Exodus (Exodus 12:37).

5. God commanded Moses to number his army by recording every male twenty years old or older (Numbers 1:1–46). The results were:

   The tribe of Reuben—46,500
   The tribe of Simeon—59,300
   The tribe of Gad—45,650
   The tribe of Judah—74,600
   The tribe of Issachar—54,400
   The tribe of Zebulun—57,400
   The half tribe of Ephraim—40,500
   The half tribe of Manasseh—32,200
   The tribe of Benjamin—35,400
   The tribe of Dan—62,700
   The tribe of Asher—41,500
   The tribe of Naphtali—53,400
   Total number of Israelite fighting men—603,550

6. God also commanded that a census be taken of the Levites. Moses found 22,000 Levites more than one month old (Numbers 3:39).

7. After 24,000 had died in a plague of judgment, God again commanded Moses to number the army. Moses found 601,730 men over twenty years of age (Numbers 26:1–51).

8. The armies of Israel came against the tribe of Benjamin in judgment. A numbering of the armies showed 26,000 Benjamite soldiers and 400,000 from Israel. After the battle, only 600 Benjamite men remained (Judges 20:14–48).

9. Saul numbered the army that had gathered to fight the Ammonites, and he counted 330,000 men (1 Samuel 11:8).

10. David brought God's wrath upon Israel by numbering the kingdom. He counted 1,300,000 valiant men that drew the sword. God sent a plague that killed 70,000 of those men in one day (2 Samuel 24:1–15).

11. Under King David the Levites were numbered from the age of thirty years and upward: and their number by their polls, man by man was 38,000 (1 Chronicles 23:3).

12. And Solomon numbered all the [aliens] in the land of Israel . . . and they were found 153,600 (2 Chronicles 2:17).

13. Ezra brought 42,360 people and 7,337 of their servants back to Jerusalem from Babylon (Ezra 2:64–65).

14. And it came to pass in those days, that there went out a decree from Caesar Augustus, that all the world should be [enrolled] (Luke 2:1).

## 328. Seventeen Hugs and Kisses

1. Isaac kissed Jacob thinking that he was Esau (Genesis 27:27).

2. Jacob kissed Rachel almost as soon as he met her. These kissing cousins were later wed (Genesis 29:11).

3. Laban embraced Jacob, kissed him, and brought him into his house (Genesis 29:13).

4. When Jacob and Laban parted company, Laban kissed his sons and daughters and blessed them (Genesis 31:55).

5. Esau ran to meet [Jacob], and embraced him, and fell on his neck, and kissed him: and they wept (Genesis 33:4).

6. Joseph kissed all his brothers and wept when they were reunited (Genesis 45:15).

7. Israel kissed, embraced, and blessed Ephraim and Manasseh, Joseph's sons (Genesis 48:10, 20).

8. When Jacob died, Joseph fell upon his father's face, and wept upon him, and kissed him (Genesis 50:1).

9. Aaron met Moses in the mount of God, and kissed him (Exodus 4:27).

10. Jethro, Moses' father-in-law, came . . . unto Moses into the wilderness, . . . and Moses went out to meet his father-in-law, and did obeisance, and kissed him (Exodus 18:5, 7).

11. Naomi kissed Orpah and Ruth, her daughters-in-law, as she left them to return to her own country (Ruth 1:9).

12. Samuel took a vial of oil, and poured it upon [Saul's] head, and kissed him, and said, Is it not because the Lord hath anointed thee to be captain over his inheritance? (1 Samuel 10:1).

13. David and Jonathan kissed one another and wept when David began his flight from Saul (1 Samuel 20:41).

14. After Absalom's two years in exile, he returned to his father and King David kissed him (2 Samuel 14:33).

15. When any man came nigh to Absalom to do him obeisance, he put forth his hand, and took him, and kissed him. . . . So Absalom stole the hearts of the men of Israel (2 Samuel 15:5–6).

16. When David returned to Jerusalem from fighting Absalom, he met and kissed Barzillai, an old man who had provided supplies for David's army (2 Samuel 19:39).

17. Joab took Amasa by the beard with the right hand to kiss him. But Amasa took no heed to the sword that was in Joab's hand: so [Joab] smote him therewith . . . and he died (2 Samuel 20:9–10).

### 329. Late-Night Visitors

1. Jacob was met by a man whom he wrestled all night. He later realized that the "man" was actually God (Genesis 32:22–31).

2. The angel of death came through Egypt at midnight (Exodus 12:29–31).

3. Gideon and his three hundred men attacked the Midianite camp at night (Judges 7:19).

4. The Lord came to Samuel at night (1 Samuel 4:1–14).

5. David and Abishai visited Saul's camp at night and took Saul's spear and a jug of water (1 Samuel 26:7–12).

6. King Saul visited the witch of Endor at night (1 Samuel 28:8).

7. The shepherds in Bethlehem were visited by a host of angels while they watched their flocks at night. After the news of the

Messiah's birth had been revealed, they went to visit Joseph, Mary, and Jesus (Luke 2:8–16).

8. About the fourth watch of the night [Jesus] cometh unto them, walking upon the sea (Mark 6:48).

9. There was a man of the Pharisees named Nicodemus, a ruler of the Jews: the same came to Jesus by night (John 3:1–2).

10. Judas then, having received a band of men and officers from the chief priests and Pharisees, cometh thither with lanterns and torches and weapons. . . . Then the band and the captain and officers of the Jews took Jesus and bound him (John 18:3, 12).

11. An angel came to Peter late at night and released him from prison, and then Peter went to visit a prayer meeting at the home of John Mark's mother (Acts 12:6–17).

12. Paul was visited by an angel one night who assured him that all on board the storm-tossed boat would be safe (Acts 27:23–24).

## 330. Angry Brothers

1. Cain rose up against Abel his brother, and slew him (Genesis 4:8).

2. Esau hated Jacob because of the blessing wherewith his father blessed him: and Esau said . . . I will slay my brother Jacob (Genesis 27:41).

3. The sons of Jacob were very angry when they heard that Shechem had raped their sister Dinah (Genesis 34:7).

4. And when [Joseph's] brethren saw that their father loved him more than all his brethren, they hated him, and could not speak peaceably unto him (Genesis 37:4).

5. Moses came down the mountain and saw the golden calf that Aaron his brother had made. He angrily rebuked Aaron for causing the people to sin (Exodus 32:19–22).

6. Abimelech, the son of Gideon, killed all seventy of his brothers at once (Judges 9:1–5).

7. Jephthah was thrown out of the house by his brothers because he was an illegitimate son of their father (Judges 11:1–2).

8. Eliab, David's oldest brother, was angered by David's concern over Goliath's challenge. He said that David had come out just to see the fighting (1 Samuel 17:28–30).

9. Absalom hated [his brother] Ammon, because he had forced his sister Tamar (2 Samuel 13:22).

10. The prodigal son's older brother was angry and would not go in to the prodigal's welcome-home party (Luke 15:28).

### 331. Eight Important Mothers-in-law

1. Sarah was Rebekah's mother-in-law (Genesis 21:3; 24:67).

2. Rebekah was Leah and Rachel's mother-in-law (Genesis 27:46; 29:21–28).

3. Moses' mother Jochebed was Zipporah's mother-in-law (Exodus 2:21; Numbers 26:59).

4. Naomi was Ruth and Orpah's mother-in-law (Ruth 1:14).

5. King Saul's wife Ahinoam was David's mother-in-law (1 Samuel 14:50; 18:27).

6. Queen Jezebel was the mother-in-law of King Jehoram (1 Kings 21:4–5; 2 Kings 8:16–18).

7. Queen Athaliah was the mother-in-law of Ahaziah's wife Zibiah (2 Chronicles 22:10–12; 24:1).

8. Peter's mother-in-law was healed of a fever by Jesus (Matthew 8:14–15).

### 332. Six Important Contests

1. Rachel and Leah competed for Jacob's love. They sought to have children to earn his favor (Genesis 30:1).

2. Moses and Aaron and the magicians of Egypt competed in doing miracles. They all turned their rods into snakes, but Aaron's snake ate up the other snakes (Exodus 7:10–12).

3. Korah questioned Moses' authority so Moses had Aaron and Korah take censers of incense before the Lord to see whom God would accept. Korah lost by default. A fiery crevice opened and swallowed Korah and his men before the contest could be completed (Numbers 16:16–35).

4. God commanded each tribe to bring a rod and set it before him in the tabernacle overnight. Aaron's rod blossomed and thus proved that Aaron was God's chosen high priest (Numbers 17:1–13).

5. Elijah challenged the priests of Baal to a contest to prove who the true God really was. Jehovah sent fire down from heaven to consume Elijah's sacrifice, including the altar (1 Kings 18:25–39).

6. The soldiers cast lots for Jesus' garments (Matthew 27:35).

# 35

# THE ANIMAL WORLD

"Look over there—it's a deer!" Such exclamations remind us of the wonder of the zoological kingdom. Other phrases, like "Beware of the dog," remind us that though the animal world is wondrous, we still need to be careful. The stories of tourists being attacked by bears in Yellowstone National Park, or of a local farmer being gored by his prize bull, keep us wary.

The Bible recounts the creation of animals, and is saturated with stories about or including animals. Many of the accounts include the enchantment that the animal world provides; others include the danger that exists. Both elements are found in these lists. The lists also hold interest for those avid fishermen seeking new techniques for larger catches. There is even a section for those interested in the study of worms.

### 333. Five Animals That Attacked People
1. Two she bears attacked a group of children (2 Kings 2:24).
2. God sent hornets before Israel to drive away the Amorites (Joshua 24:12).
3. A young lion attacked Samson (Judges 14:5).
4. Jonah was swallowed by a whale (Matthew 12:40).
5. Paul was bitten by a viper on the island of Melita (Acts 28:3).

## 334. Monsters

1. Behold now behemoth which I made with thee; he eateth grass as an ox (Job 40:15).

2. In the habitation of dragons, where each lay, shall be grass with reeds and rushes (Isaiah 35:7).

3. The Lord with his sore and great and strong sword shall punish leviathan the piercing serpent (Isaiah 27:1).

4. Even the sea monsters . . . give suck to their young ones (Lamentations 4:3).

5. The Lord hath as it were the strength of an unicorn (Numbers 23:22).

## 335. Three Catches of Fish

1. Jesus told Peter to take the first fish that he caught and open its mouth. He would find a coin there to pay tribute for both Jesus and himself (Matthew 17:24–27).

2. When Jesus commanded Peter to launch out into the deep and drop his nets, Peter reminded Him of the poor fishing the previous night. Nevertheless, Peter obeyed and caught enough fish to fill two boats (Luke 5:1–7).

3. Peter was again fishing unsuccessfully when Jesus yelled out from the shore, telling him to cast his net on the other side of the boat. Peter did that and caught 153 large fish (John 21:2–11).

## 336. Worms

1. Some of them left [the manna] until the morning, and it bred worms, and stank (Exodus 16:20).

2. That which the palmerworm hath left hath the locust eaten; and that which the locust hath left hath the cankerworm eaten; and that which the cankerworm hath left hath the caterpillar eaten (Joel 1:4).

3. Job said, My flesh is clothed with worms and clods of dust (Job 7:5).

4. The Lord God prepared a gourd, and made it to come up over

Jonah. . . . But God prepared a worm when the morning rose the next day, and it smote the gourd that it withered (Jonah 4:6–7).

5. The nations shall see and be confounded. . . . They shall lick the dust like a serpent, they shall move out of their holes like worms of the earth (Micah 7:16–17).

6. Jesus said that hell is a place where the worm dieth not (Mark 9:43–44).

7. The angel of the Lord smote [Herod], because he gave not God the glory and he was eaten of worms, and gave up the ghost (Acts 12:23).

## 337. Snakes

1. And the Lord God said unto the serpent, Because thou hast done this [beguiled Eve to eat the forbidden fruit] . . . upon thy belly shalt thou go (Genesis 3:14–15).

2. In blessing his sons, Jacob said, Dan shall be a serpent by the way, an adder in the path, that biteth the horse heels, so that his rider shall fall backward (Genesis 49:17).

3. Moses' rod became a serpent when he cast it on the ground (Exodus 4:2–4).

4. The people spake against God, and against Moses. . . . And the Lord sent fiery serpents among the people, and they bit the people; and much of Israel died (Numbers 21:5–6).

5. The day of the Lord is darkness, and not light. As if a man did flee from a lion, and a bear met him; or went into the house, and leaned his hand on the wall, and a serpent bit him (Amos 5:18–19).

6. [Jesus said to His disciples,] Behold, I give unto you power to tread on serpents and scorpions, and over all the power of the enemy: and nothing shall by any means hurt you (Luke 10:19).

7. When Paul had gathered a bundle of sticks, and laid them on the fire, there came a viper out of the heat, and fastened on his hand (Acts 28:3).

## 338. Important Donkeys

1. An ass carried the wood upon which Abraham was planning to sacrifice Isaac (Genesis 22:1–3).

2. Jacob gave Esau twenty she asses and ten foals to appease him (Genesis 32:13–18).

3. Moses took his wife and his sons, and set them upon an ass, and returned to the land of Egypt (Exodus 4:20).

4. Balaam's ass verbally rebuked him for harsh treatment (Numbers 22:21–33).

5. Saul was looking for his father's lost asses when he met Samuel (1 Samuel 9:1–6).

6. Abigail rode an ass to plead with David for her husband's life (1 Samuel 25:20).

7. Absalom rode upon a mule, and the mule went under the thick boughs of a great oak, and his head caught hold of the oak (2 Samuel 18:9).

8. The Shunammite sent her servant on an ass to Elisha to tell him that her son had died (2 Kings 4:18–32).

9. Jesus rode into Jerusalem on an ass (Matthew 21:1–9).

# 36

## TRANSPORTATION

The Bible lists that follow explore some of the transportation methods used in ancient days. The standard cart and chariots would be no match for today's freeway traffic, but they certainly were economical. There are at least three methods of transportation in the lists that may be well worth our exploring as an alternative to the "gas hog" we may be driving. Check out the economy rating on the following modes of travel: the chariot of fire that transported Elijah to heaven, the chariots that Zechariah saw being driven by angels, and the speedy trip that Philip made after baptizing the Ethiopian eunuch. If you could only get somebody to duplicate these, you'd be a millionaire!

### 339. Important Carts and Chariots

1. Pharaoh said unto Joseph, See, I have set thee over all the land of Egypt. . . . And he made him to ride in the second chariot which he had (Genesis 41:41, 43).

2. Joseph sent wagons to Canaan to carry back his father and his brothers' families (Genesis 45:17–21).

3. The Egyptians pursued after [the Israelites with] all the horses and chariots of Pharaoh (Exodus 14:9).

4. The Levites were given six covered wagons in which to haul the tabernacle and its furnishings (Numbers 7:1–9).

5. The Philistines sent the ark of the covenant back to the Israelites on a cart pulled by a cow (1 Samuel 6:7–14).

6. Solomon . . . had a thousand and four hundred chariots (1 Kings 10:26).

7. King Rehoboam's tax gatherer was stoned, so Rehoboam sped away to the safety of Jerusalem in his chariot (1 Kings 12:18).

8. King Ahab rode into battle in a chariot, but was fatally hit by an Assyrian arrow (1 Kings 22:34–38).

9. There appeared a chariot of fire, and horses of fire . . . and Elijah went up by a whirlwind into heaven (2 Kings 2:11).

10. Naaman came with his horses and with his chariot, and stood at the door of the house of Elisha waiting to be healed of his leprosy (2 Kings 5:9).

11. The Lord sent many horses and chariots of fire to guard the Israelites against the invading Syrians (2 Kings 6:14–17).

12. Jehu rode in a chariot and chased the chariots of King Ahaziah and King Joram and killed them both (2 Kings 9:16–28).

13. While wiping out idolatry in the land, King Josiah burned the chariots of the sun (2 Kings 23:11).

14. King Josiah was wounded while fighting the Egyptians, so his servants took him from his own chariot and put him in the second chariot that he had; and they brought him to Jerusalem, and he died (2 Chronicles 35:23–24).

15. Zechariah saw four chariots driven by angels (Zechariah 6:1–8).

16. The Ethiopian eunuch was riding back to Ethiopia in a chariot when Philip came upon him (Acts 8:27–28).

### 340. The Longest Journeys in the Bible

1. Abraham moved his entire household from Haran to Canaan (Genesis 12:1–5).

2. Israel wandered through the wilderness for forty years after they had left Egypt to go to the Promised Land (Deuteronomy 29:5).

3. Jesus' longest journey, made when He was a baby, was from Bethlehem to Egypt (Matthew 2:14).

4. Jesus' longest journey during His ministry was from Capernaum to Jerusalem (Matthew 17:24; 20:17).

5. The Ethiopian eunuch rode by chariot from Ethiopia to Jerusalem and back (Acts 8:27).

## 341. The Fastest Travelers in the Bible

1. Elijah raced Ahab's chariot on foot between Mount Carmel and Samaria and won (1 Kings 18:44–46).

2. The Spirit caught Philip away from the eunuch and took him to Azotus (Acts 8:39–40).

# 37

## FORCES OF NATURE

Through the advances of meteorology, we are able to watch the development of weather patterns 24/7 on the Weather Channel. It's fascinating to be able to see satellite pictures of cloud cover and radar images of lines of thunderstorms or cold fronts. Somehow we get the sense that we actually understand what is happening in nature. We can easily forget that though we may now *understand* more about what is happening in nature, we still have no *say* about what happens. We still find ourselves extremely vulnerable to the powers of the wind, rain, snow, and floods.

The following lists show that the people in the Bible were also vulnerable to nature's forces. In these lists, we see not only the powerful weather patterns that the writers observed but also the ways in which God was active in using these patterns for His purposes. Recorded are many instances when God intervened via strong winds, hail, floods, lightning, thunder, and rain. He used these methods to speak to people then, and we shouldn't be surprised if He uses them to speak to us today.

### 342. Thunder and Lightning
1. Thunder and lightning accompanied the veil of clouds that hung around Mount Sinai when God gave Moses the law (Exodus 19:16).
2. The Philistines drew near to do battle against Israel: but the Lord

thundered with a great thunder on that day upon the Philistines, and discomfited them (1 Samuel 7:10).

3. Samuel called unto the Lord; and the Lord sent thunder and rain that day: and all the people greatly feared the Lord and Samuel (1 Samuel 12:18).

4. John saw thunder and lightning before the Lord poured out His wrath upon the earth (Revelation 11:19).

### 343. *Three Tornadoes (Whirlwinds)*

1. Elijah went up by a whirlwind into heaven (2 Kings 2:11).

2. The Lord answered Job out of the whirlwind (Job 38:1).

3. Ezekiel looked, and behold, a whirlwind came out of the north, a great cloud, and a fire infolding itself (Ezekiel 1:4).

### 344. *Three Important Rainstorms*

1. The rain was upon the earth forty days and forty nights while Noah was in the ark (Genesis 7:12).

2. Samuel called unto the Lord; and the Lord sent thunder and rain that day (1 Samuel 12:18).

3. After three and a half years of devastating drought in Israel, Elijah prayed for rain and it came again (1 Kings 18:45).

### 345. *Weather Miracles*

1. The Lord sent fire and hail upon the Egyptians, but He spared the land of Goshen, where the Israelites lived (Exodus 9:22–33).

2. The Lord turned a mighty strong wind, which took away the locusts, and cast them into the Red Sea (Exodus 10:19).

3. As the Amorites fled before Israel, the Lord cast down great stones from heaven upon them unto Azekah, and they died (Joshua 10:11).

4. Samuel called unto the Lord; and the Lord sent thunder and rain that day (1 Samuel 12:18).

5. Elijah prayed earnestly that it might not rain: and it rained not on the earth by the space of three years and six months. And he prayed again, and the heaven gave rain (James 5:17–18).

6. Jonah's ship was hit by a mighty tempest that died down as soon as he was thrown overboard (Jonah 1:3–16).

7. The disciples were out on the Sea of Galilee in a storm when Jesus came to them walking on the water. When He got into the boat, the wind stopped (Matthew 14:24, 33).

8. Jesus rebuked the wind, and said unto the sea, Peace, be still. And the wind ceased, and there was a great calm (Mark 4:39).

### 346. Earthquakes

1. As the Israelites waited before Mount Sinai, the Lord descended and the whole mountain quaked (Exodus 19:18).

2. Jonathan came against a Philistine garrison, and an earthquake accompanied his attack (1 Samuel 14:14–15).

3. The Lord passed by Elijah and an earthquake followed (1 Kings 19:11–12).

4. Jesus, when he had cried again with a loud voice, yielded up the ghost. And . . . the earth did quake (Matthew 27:50–51).

5. There was a great earthquake: for the angel of the Lord descended from heaven, and came and rolled back the stone from the door (Matthew 28:2).

6. Paul and Silas were in prison in Philippi when suddenly there was a great earthquake, so that the foundations of the prison were shaken (Acts 16:26).

7. Jesus declared that earthquakes in diverse places would come before the end of the world (Matthew 24:7).

# 38

## VIOLENCE

Leo Tolstoy wrote concerning mankind, "A good portion of the evils that afflict mankind is due to the erroneous belief that life can be made secure by violence." Ever since the day Cain slew Abel, violence as a means to gain something has been a way of life. Today we live in a generation when nothing seems to shock us. On the news, we can see robberies in progess, the bloodshed of warfare from some part of the world, and riots and looting in foreign cities. We are being conditioned to violence.

The human race has not changed much over the last two thousand years. The following lists show some of the acts of violence that took place during Bible times. Remember Frenchman Emile Coue's glowing statement from the late nineteenth century: "Every day in every way, I am getting better and better." It became a symbol of where mankind thought they were heading. I wonder what he would say today.

### 347. Five Riots

1. The people of Nazareth rose up, and thrust Jesus out of the city, and led him unto the brow of the hill whereon their city was built, that they might cast him down headlong (Luke 4:29).

2. Pilate bowed to the wishes of the crowd and allowed Jesus to be crucified because the mob had become uncontrollable (Matthew 27:23–24).

3. The unbelieving Thessalonian Jews took unto them certain lewd

fellows of the baser sort, and gathered a company, and set all the city in an uproar, and assaulted the house of Jason, and sought to bring [Paul and Silas] out to the people (Acts 17:5).

4. The Ephesians were full of wrath, and cried out, saying, Great is Diana of the Ephesians. And the whole city was filled with confusion . . . they rushed with one accord into the theatre (Acts 19:28–29).

5. All Jerusalem was moved, and the people ran together: and they took Paul, and drew him out of the temple. . . . He was borne of the soldiers for the violence of the people (Acts 21:30–35).

## 348. Three Ambushes

1. Joshua drew the army of Ai out of the city while another group ambushed and destroyed the city (Joshua 8:12–22).

2. The armies of Israel drew the Benjamites out of the city of Gibeah by retreating before them. But more Israelites were lurking behind the city and they ambushed Gibeah (Judges 20:29–43).

3. More than forty men were waiting in ambush for Paul, but the Roman soldiers moved him secretly out of Jerusalem at night (Acts 23:21–23).

## 349. Defensive Weapons

1. Goliath had an *helmet of brass* upon his head, and he was armed with a *coat of mail*; and the weight of the coat was five thousand shekels of brass. And he had *greaves of brass* upon his legs, and a *target of brass* between his shoulders (1 Samuel 17:4–6).

2. Uzziah prepared for them throughout all the host *shields*, and spears, and *helmets*, and *habergeons*, and bows, and slings to cast stones. And he made in Jerusalem *engines*, invented by cunning men to be on the towers and upon the bulwarks, to shoot arrows and great stones withal (2 Chronicles 26:14–15).

3. Order ye the *buckler* and *shield*, and draw near to battle. Harness the horses; and get up, ye horsemen, and stand forth with your *helmets*; furbish the spears, and put on the *brigandines* (Jeremiah 46:3–4).

## 350. Offensive Weapons

1. David took his *staff* in his hand, and chose him five smooth *stones* out of the brook, and put them in a shepherd's bag which he had, even in a scrip; and his *sling* was in his hand (1 Samuel 17:40).

2. And Saul cast the *javelin;* for he said, I will smite David even to the wall with it (1 Samuel 18:11).

3. David's men were armed with *bows*, and could use both the right hand and the left in hurling *stones* and shooting *arrows* out of a *bow* (1 Chronicles 12:2).

4. Hezekiah strengthened himself . . . and made *darts* and shields in abundance (2 Chronicles 32:5).

5. A man that beareth false witness against his neighbour is a *maul*, and a *sword*, and a sharp *arrow* (Proverbs 25:18).

6. Ezekiel was commanded to make a model of Jerusalem and set *battering rams* against it round about (Ezekiel 4:1–2).

7. One of the soldiers with a *spear* pierced his side (John 19:34).

## 351. Murder Weapons and Devices

1. Ehud killed King Eglon of Moab with a two-edged *dagger* (Judges 3:16–21).

2. Joab took three *darts* in his hand, and thrust them through the heart of Absalom (2 Samuel 18:14).

3. Hazel took a *thick cloth*, and dipped it in water, and spread it on [Ben-hadad's] face, so that he died (2 Kings 8:15).

4. Adrammelech and Sharezer killed their father, Sennacherib, with a *sword* (2 Kings 19:37).

5. King Rehoboam sent Hadoram that was over the tribute; and the children of Israel stoned him with *stones* that he died (2 Chronicles 10:18).

## 352. Unusual Weapons

1. Shamgar . . . slew of the Philistines six hundred men with an *ox goad* (Judges 3:31).

2. Jael, Heber's wife, took a *nail of the tent*, and took a hammer in

her hand, and went softly unto [Sisera], and smote the nail into his temple, and fastened it into the ground (Judges 4:17–21).

3. Samson found a new *jawbone of an ass*, and put forth his hand, and took it, and slew a thousand men therewith (Judges 15:15).

4. The staff of Goliath's spear was like a *weaver's beam;* and his spear's head weighed six hundred shekels of iron (1 Samuel 17:7).

# 39

## DEATH AND FUNERALS

Shakespeare devoted much thought in writing his plays to the theme of death. In the play *King Henry VI*, he wrote: "Why, what is pomp, rule, reign, but earth and dust? And live we how we can, yet die we must." His characters often face the issue of death, and many of them die tragically. In contrast, our Western society provides little in the way of preparation for death. It is an issue that most of us would rather not think or talk about. Shakespeare is correct, though—"yet die we must."

The following Bible lists show deaths and funerals of the people of that time. Some of the deaths recorded followed lives filled with corruption and wrongdoing. Some followed lives lived for the glory of God. In either case the sadness of the loss of a loved one was always there, but in the case of a righteous life there was always the great anticipation of the resurrection from the dead. Paul's words are always timely: "For me to live is Christ, and to die is gain." He saw death as a mere stepping into eternal life with Christ.

How we view death will profoundly affect how we live. Death in the Bible is never seen as the end of life but rather as an entrance into eternity. Catherine Booth declared on her deathbed: "The waters are rising but I am not sinking."

### 353. Nineteen Graves and Graveyards

1. Deborah, Rebekah's nurse, died, and she was buried beneath Bethel under an oak: and the name of it was called Allonbachuth (Genesis 35:8).

2. Rachel died, and was buried in the way to Ephrath, which is Bethlehem. And Jacob set a pillar upon her grave (Genesis 35:19–20).

3. Abraham, Sarah, Isaac, Rebekah, Jacob, and Leah were all buried in the cave of the field of Machpelah before Mamre (Genesis 49:30–31; 50:13).

4. The Lord buried Moses in a valley in the land of Moab, over against Bethpeor: but no man knoweth of his sepulchre unto this day (Deuteronomy 34:6).

5. A heap of stones was raised over the bodies of Achan and his family after they were stoned in the valley of Achor (Joshua 7:25–26).

6. The Israelites took the body of the king of Ai and cast it at the entering of the gate of the city, and [raised] thereon a great heap of stones (Joshua 8:29).

7. Israel buried Joshua in the border of his inheritance in Timnath-serah (Joshua 24:30).

8. The bones of Joseph, which the children of Israel brought up out of Egypt, buried they in Shechem (Joshua 24:32).

9. Gideon the son of Joash died in a good old age, and was buried in the sepulchre of Joash his father (Judges 8:32).

10. Samson was buried between Zorah and Eshtaol in the burying place of Manoah his father (Judges 16:31).

11. The men of Jabesh-gilead took the body of Saul and the bodies of his sons from the wall of Bethshan, and came to Jabesh, and burnt them there. And they took their bones, and buried them under a tree at Jabesh (1 Samuel 31:12–13).

12. Samuel died; and all the Israelites were gathered together, and lamented him, and buried him in his house at Ramah (1 Samuel 25:1).

13. Joab took Absalom, and cast him into a great pit in the wood, and laid a very great heap of stones upon him (2 Samuel 18:17).

14. King Jehoram was killed by Jehu, and his body was cast into Naboth's field (2 Kings 9:25).

15. Ahaziah's servants buried him in his sepulchre with his fathers in the city of David (2 Kings 9:28).

16. Manasseh slept with his fathers, and was buried in the garden of his own house, in the garden of Uzza (2 Kings 21:18).

17. Amon was buried in his sepulchre in the garden of Uzza (2 Kings 21:26).

18. Uzziah slept with his fathers, and they buried him with his fathers in the field of the burial which belonged to the kings; for they said, He is a leper (2 Chronicles 26:23).

19. And the chief priests took the silver pieces. . . . And they took counsel, and bought with them the potter's field, to bury strangers (Matthew 27:6–7).

## 354. Executions

1. The Roman soldiers crucified Jesus along with two common criminals at the demand of the Jews (Matthew 27:33–50).

2. Pharaoh hanged the chief baker (Genesis 40:22).

3. The Levites executed three thousand men for worshiping the golden calf (Exodus 32:26–28).

4. Joshua hung the king of Ai (Joshua 8:28–29).

5. Joshua executed Adonizedek, king of Jerusalem; Hoham, king of Hebron; Piram, king of Jarmuth; Japhia, king of Lachish; and Debir, king of Eglon (Joshua 10:1–26).

6. Samuel hewed Agag [the king of the Amalekites] in pieces before the Lord in Gilgal (1 Samuel 15:33).

7. King Saul ordered Doeg to execute eighty-five priests of the Lord (1 Samuel 22:17–18).

8. David executed a young Amalekite for claiming that he had killed King Saul (2 Samuel 1:6–15).

9. David ordered his men to kill Rechab and Baanah because they had murdered Ishbosheth, Saul's son (2 Samuel 4:9–12).

10. The Gibeonites hung seven of Saul's grandsons in retribution for one of Saul's bloody actions against them (2 Samuel 21:1–9).

11. At King Solomon's command, Benaiah executed Adonijah, Joab, and Shimei (1 Kings 2:25, 34, 46).

12. King Ahasuerus hung his chamberlains, Bigthan and Teresh (Esther 2:21, 23).

13. King Ahasuerus also hung Haman on Haman's own gallows (Esther 7:5–10).

14. Haman's ten sons were hung at Esther's request (Esther 9:13–14).

15. King Jehoiakim executed the prophet Uriah for giving unfavorable prophecies (Jeremiah 26:20–23).

### 355. Unusual Funeral Processions

1. The longest funeral procession was for Joseph. The Israelites carried his body for over forty years through the wilderness from Egypt to Canaan (Joshua 24:32).

2. The shortest funeral procession never made it to the cemetery. The young man of Nain was raised from his funeral bier by Jesus as the procession left the city (Luke 7:11–16).

### 356. Laws of Purification After Death

1. He that toucheth the dead body of any man shall be unclean seven days. He shall purify himself with [the ashes of a red heifer] on the third day, then the seventh day he shall . . . be clean (Numbers 19:11–12).

2. This is the law, when a man dieth in a tent: all that come into the tent, and all that is in the tent, shall be unclean seven days. . . . And a clean person shall take hyssop and dip it in the water, and sprinkle it upon the tent, and upon all the vessels, and upon the persons that were there (Numbers 19:14–18).

### 357. People Killed by Animals

1. The Lord sent fiery serpents among the people, and they bit the people; and much people of Israel died (Numbers 21:6).

2. A disobedient prophet was killed by a lion along the path on which he was traveling (1 Kings 13:20–32).

3. Another lion killed a man who would not strike a young prophet with a sword as he had been commanded by the Lord to do (1 Kings 20:35–36).

4. A group of children made fun of Elisha, and there came forth two she bears out of the wood, and tear forty and two children (2 Kings 2:24).

5. At the beginning of their dwelling there . . . they [foreigners who had moved into Samaria] feared not the Lord: therefore the Lord sent lions among them, which slew some of them (2 Kings 17:24–25).

6. The king commanded, and they brought those men which had accused Daniel, and they cast them into the den of lions, them, their children, and their wives; and the lions had the mastery of them (Daniel 6:24).

## 358. *The Ten Largest Mass Deaths*

1. Abijah and his people slew them with a great slaughter: so there fell down slain of Israel five hundred thousand chosen men (2 Chronicles 13:17).

2. The angel of the Lord went out, and smote in the camp of the Assyrians an hundred fourscore and five thousand (2 Kings 19:35).

3. Gideon and his men killed one hundred twenty thousand Midianites (Judges 8:10).

4. King Pekah killed twenty thousand men of Judah in one day because they had forsaken the Lord (2 Chronicles 28:6).

5. The children of Israel slew of the Syrians an hundred thousand footmen in one day (1 Kings 20:29).

6. The other Jews that were in the king's provinces gathered themselves together . . . and slew of their foes seventy and five thousand (Esther 9:15–16).

7. The Lord sent a pestilence upon Israel from the morning even to the time appointed: and there died of the people from Dan to Beersheba seventy thousand men (2 Samuel 24:15).

8. The Lord smote the men of Bethshemesh, because they had looked into the ark of the Lord, even he smote of the people fifty thousand and three score and ten men (1 Samuel 6:19).

9. David slew of the Syrians seven thousand men which fought in chariots, and forty thousand footmen (1 Chronicles 19:18).

10. The Philistines fought . . . and there was a very great slaughter; for there fell of Israel thirty thousand footmen (1 Samuel 4:10).

# 40

## INTERESTING PEOPLE

For some time a popular television theme was that of discovering people who did unique things. The offshoot was a number of programs that went anywhere to locate something that would catch the viewer's attention. The popularity of *The Guinness Book of World Records* indicates that we enjoy hearing about people who do unique things. And producers of reality TV shows go out of their way to find unique people we will not forget any time soon.

Compiled below are seven Bible lists of interesting people—those who are known for a particular reason. Something about their lives stands out as different from the ordinary. Some received their names from heavenly sources.

### 359. Five Insomniacs
1. Jacob said to Laban, This twenty years have I been with thee . . . in the day the drought consumed me, and the frost by night; and my sleep departed from my eyes (Genesis 31:38, 40).

2. On the night after Haman built a gallows for the purpose of hanging Mordecai, King Ahasuerus could not sleep (Esther 6:1).

3. The wicked sleep not, except they have done mischief; and their sleep is taken away, unless they cause some to fall (Proverbs 4:16).

4. Nebuchadnezzar dreamed dreams, wherewith his spirit was troubled, and his sleep brake from him (Daniel 2:1).

5. While Daniel was in the lions' den, King Darius stayed up all night (Daniel 6:18).

## 360. Twenty-three References to Runners

1. Abraham ran to meet the Lord in the plains of Mamre (Genesis 18:1–2).

2. Abraham's servant ran to meet Rebekah (Genesis 24:17).

3. Laban ran to meet Abraham's servant at the well (Genesis 24:29).

4. Jacob told Rachel that he was her father's [relative] . . . and she ran and told her father (Genesis 29:12).

5. When Jacob returned to his country, Esau ran to meet him, and embraced him, and fell on his neck, and kissed him: and they wept (Genesis 33:4).

6. Aaron ran into the midst of the congregation with incense to stay a plague (Numbers 16:46–48).

7. Samson's mother ran to her husband Manoah to tell him that an angel had appeared to her a second time (Judges 13:10).

8. When the Lord called the child Samuel, he ran to Eli thinking that Eli had called him (1 Samuel 3:4–5).

9. A Benjamite man ran from the battlefield to tell Eli that the ark of the Lord had been captured by the Philistines (1 Samuel 4:12–18).

10. David ran toward the Philistine camp to meet Goliath and slew him (1 Samuel 17:48–49).

11. Joab sent Cushi to run to David with the news of Absalom's death. Ahimaaz later volunteered and, in spite of his late start, beat Cushi to David with the news (2 Samuel 18:19–23).

12. Adonijah the son of Gaggith exalted himself, saying, I will be king: and he prepared him chariots and horsemen, and fifty men to run before him (1 Kings 1:5).

13. Elijah girded up his loins, and ran before Ahab to the entrance of Jezreel (1 Kings 18:46).

14. Elisha ran after Elijah to accept the appointment as his successor (1 Kings 19:19–21).

15. Gehazi ran from Elisha to meet the Shunammite woman (2 Kings 4:25–26).

16. An angel told another angel to run to Zechariah and to deliver him the message that Jerusalem would again be inhabited (Zechariah 2:3–4).

17. One of the onlookers at Jesus' crucifixion ran and found a sponge to use for giving Jesus a drink (Matthew 27:46–48).

18. Mary Magdalene and the other Mary ran from the empty tomb to tell the disciples about it (Matthew 28:8).

19. When the Gadarene demoniac saw Jesus afar off, he ran and worshiped him (Mark 5:6).

20. People ran to hear Jesus teach and to see Him perform miracles (Mark 6:33–35).

21. Zacchaeus ran before the throng around Jesus and climbed up into a sycamore tree to see Him (Luke 19:4).

22. John outran Peter to see the empty tomb (John 20:4).

23. Philip ran to the Ethiopian eunuch's chariot (Acts 8:30).

### 361. Blind People

1. When the men of Sodom attacked Lot's house, the two angels smote the men that were at the door of the house with blindness (Genesis 19:11).

2. When Isaac was old . . . his eyes were dim, so that he could not see (Genesis 27:1).

3. The eyes of Israel were dim for age, so that he could not see (Genesis 48:10).

4. The Philistines took [Samson], and put out his eyes, and brought him down to Gaza (Judges 16:21).

5. Eli was ninety and eight years old; and his eyes were dim, that he could not see (1 Samuel 4:15).

6. Ahijah could not see; for his eyes were set by reason of his age (1 Kings 14:4).

7. Elisha prayed unto the Lord, and said, Smite [the Syrian army],

I pray thee, with blindness. And he smote them with blindness (2 Kings 6:18).

8. Nebuchadnezzar put out Zedekiah's eyes, and bound him with chains to carry him to Babylon (Jeremiah 39:7).

9. Two blind men followed Jesus, crying, and saying, Thou son of David, have mercy on us. . . . Then touched he their eyes, saying, According to your faith be it unto you. And their eyes were opened (Matthew 9:27–30).

10. Two blind men sat by the road and cried out to Jesus to have mercy on them. He restored their sight instantly (Matthew 20:30–34).

11. Jesus touched one blind man and the man said, I see men as trees, walking. Jesus touched him again and he saw clearly (Mark 8:22–25).

12. Jesus healed a blind beggar named Bartimaeus near Jericho (Mark 10:46–52).

13. Jesus put mud on the eyes of one blind man and told him to go and wash in the pool of Siloam. He washed his eyes and saw again (John 9:1–7).

14. Saul was blind for three days after the Lord stopped him on the way to Damascus and spoke to him out of a great light (Acts 9:9).

15. Elymas the sorcerer stood against Paul and Barnabas as they told Sergius Paulus the gospel. Paul pronounced God's judgment upon Elymas, and he immediately became blind (Acts 13:7–12).

## 362. Eighteen Sleepers

1. And the Lord caused a deep sleep to fall upon Adam, and he slept: and he took one of his ribs (Genesis 2:21).

2. God spoke to Abram while he was in a deep sleep (Genesis 15:12–16).

3. Jacob slept at Bethel and dreamed about angels (Genesis 28:11–15).

4. Pharaoh dreamed of cows and corn while he slept (Genesis 41:1–7).

5. Jael, Heber's wife, took a nail of the tent, and took a hammer in

her hand, and went softly unto [Sisera], and smote the nail into his temple . . . for he was fast asleep and weary (Judges 4:21).

6. Samson slept while the Philistines cut off his hair (Judges 16:19).

7. David and Abishai sneaked into Saul's camp while he was asleep (1 Samuel 26:7).

8. Uriah slept at David's door while he was on leave from the battlefront (2 Samuel 11:9).

9. Elijah sarcastically suggested that Baal was asleep when Jezebel's priests could not get him to respond (1 Kings 18:27).

10. While Nebuchadnezzar slept, he had a troubling dream, which he could not remember in the morning (Daniel 2:1–9).

11. Jonah slept in the bottom of the ship while it rolled in the storm (Jonah 1:5).

12. Joseph was sleeping when an angel of the Lord came to him in a dream (Matthew 2:13).

13. While the disciples sailed, Jesus fell asleep. A storm came and they anxiously woke Him up (Luke 8:23–24).

14. Jesus told the mourners that Jairus' daughter was not dead but only sleeping (Luke 8:52).

15. While Jesus prayed in Gethsemane, His disciples slept (Luke 22:45).

16. Peter was sleeping between two soldiers in prison when an angel came to release him (Acts 12:6–7).

17. The Philippian jailor was awakened from a deep sleep by the earthquake that hit his prison (Acts 16:27).

18. Eutychus fell asleep and fell to the ground through a third-story window while Paul preached. Paul stopped the service long enough to raise him from the dead (Acts 20:9–12).

## 363. Laughers

1. Abraham fell upon his face, and laughed, and said in his heart, Shall a child be born unto him that is an hundred years old? and shall Sarah, that is ninety years old, bear? (Genesis 17:17).

2. When Sarah heard that she would have a son, she laughed (Genesis 18:10–12).

3. Hezekiah sent decrees that made an urgent plea for repentance from city to city through the country of Ephraim and Manasseh even unto Zebulun: but they laughed them to scorn (2 Chronicles 30:10).

4. When Sanballat the Horonite, and Tobiah the servant, the Ammonite, and Geshem the Arabian, heard [that Nehemiah and his group were going to rebuild Jerusalem], they laughed (Nehemiah 2:19).

5. When Jesus came into the ruler's house, and saw the minstrels and the people making a noise, he said unto them, Give place: for the maid is not dead, but sleepeth. And they laughed him to scorn (Matthew 9:23–24).

## 364. Dancers

1. Miriam the prophetess, the sister of Aaron, took a timbrel in her hand; and all the women went out after her with timbrels and with dances (Exodus 15:20).

2. The children of Israel danced before the calf that Aaron made (Exodus 32:19).

3. After Jephthah's victory over the Ammonites, his daughter came out to meet him with timbrels and with dances (Judges 11:34).

4. The men of Benjamin took wives from among the dancers at Shiloh (Judges 21:20, 23).

5. After David had returned from killing Goliath, the women of Israel came out dancing with tabrets to meet Saul (1 Samuel 18:6–7).

6. When David finally caught up with the Amalekites, they were spread abroad upon all the earth, eating and drinking, and dancing, because of all the great spoil that they had taken out of all the land of the Philistines (1 Samuel 30:16–18).

7. When the ark of the Lord was brought into Jerusalem, David danced before the Lord with all his might (2 Samuel 6:14).

8. The daughter of Herodias so enchanted Herod with a dance at his birthday party that he promised her anything she wanted. She asked for the head of John the Baptist (Matthew 14:6–8).

9. When the prodigal son came back, his father held a feast with music and dancing (Luke 15:25).

## 365. *People Named by God, Jesus, or Angels*

1. God called His human creation Adam (Genesis 5:2).

2. The angel of the Lord said to [Hagar], Behold, thou art with child and shalt bear a son, and shalt call his name Ishmael (Genesis 16:11).

3. The Lord said, Neither shall thy name be any more Abram, but thy name shall be Abraham (Genesis 17:5).

4. God told Abraham, Thou shalt not call her name Sarai, but Sarah shall her name be (Genesis 17:15).

5. God said, Sarah thy wife shall bear thee a son indeed; and thou shalt call his name Isaac (Genesis 17:19).

6. The Lord declared, Thy name shall be called no more Jacob, but Israel (Genesis 32:28).

7. The Lord told David, Behold, a son shall be born to thee, who shall be a man of rest; and I will give him a rest from all his enemies round about: for his name shall be Solomon (1 Chronicles 22:9).

8. The Lord commanded Isaiah to call his son Mahershalalhashbaz (Isaiah 8:3).

9. Jeremiah said to Pashur, The Lord hath not called thy name Pashur, but Magormissabib (Jeremiah 20:3).

10. When Hosea had a son, the Lord said, Call his name Jezreel; for yet a little while, and I will avenge the blood of Jezreel upon the house of Jehu (Hosea 1:4).

11. Hosea's wife bore a daughter. And God said unto him, Call her name Loruhamah: for I will no more have mercy upon the house of Israel (Hosea 1:6).

12. After Hosea's second son was born, God said, Call his name Loammi: for ye are not my people, and I will not be your God (Hosea 1:9).

13. [The angel told Joseph,] Thou shalt call his name Jesus: for he shall save his people from their sins (Matthew 1:21).

14. The angel said unto him, Fear not, Zacharias: for thy prayer is

heard; and thy wife Elisabeth shall bear thee a son, and thou shalt call his name John (Luke 1:13).

15. Jesus said, Thou art Simon the son of Jona: thou shalt be called Cephas (John 1:42).

# 41

## ODDS AND ENDS

It would be difficult to compile 375 lists without gathering some that don't fit under any specific heading. Though not related to each other, the following lists should be of interest to you.

Did you realize that there are some extremely important bones mentioned in the Bible? There are also at least twenty-nine important stones recorded for us. Did you know that some battles were won supernaturally? Do you know how many times God's name is mentioned in the Bible? Here's one you probably haven't considered: Did you know that the New Testament alone includes at least thirty-one descriptions of non-Christians?

### 366. Important Bones

1. And of the rib, which the Lord God had taken from man, made he a woman (Genesis 2:21–22).

2. The bones of Joseph, which the children of Israel brought up out of Egypt, buried they in Shechem (Joshua 24:32).

3. Samson found a new jawbone of an ass, and put forth his hand, and took it, and slew a thousand men therewith (Judges 15:15).

4. The men of Jabesh-gilead rescued the bones of Saul and his sons from Bethshan and buried them under a tree at Jabesh (1 Samuel 31:11–13).

5. And it came to pass, as they were burying a man, that behold, they spied a band of [Moabites]; and they cast the man into

the sepulchre of Elisha: and when the man was let down, and touched the bones of Elisha, he revived, and stood up on his feet (2 Kings 13:20–21).

6. King Josiah desecrated the heathen altar at Bethel by burning human bones on it (2 Kings 23:16).

7. Ezekiel saw a valley of dry bones in a vision (Ezekiel 37:1–14).

8. But when the soldiers came to Jesus, and saw that he was dead already, they broke not his legs. . . . For these things were done, that the scripture should be fulfilled, A bone of him shall not be broken (John 19:33, 36).

## 367. The Number of Times God, Jesus, and Satan Are Mentioned

1. The name God (capitalized) appears in the Bible 4,395 times.

2. The name Jesus appears in the Bible 979 times.

3. The name Satan appears in the Bible 56 times.

## 368. Thirty Important Stones

1. Jacob used a stone for a pillow at Bethel and dreamed about the Lord. In the morning, he took the stone and set it up as a pillar of remembrance before the Lord (Genesis 28:11–22).

2. When Jacob saw Rachel . . . Jacob went near and rolled the stone from the well's mouth, and watered the flock of Laban (Genesis 29:10–11).

3. Jacob and Laban made a heap of stones as a witness to their covenant not to bother one another (Genesis 31:44–52).

4. God appeared unto Jacob again, when he came out of Padanaram, and blessed him. . . . And Jacob set up a pillar in the place where he talked with him, even a pillar of stone (Genesis 35:9, 14).

5. The Lord told Moses, Thou shalt smite the rock, and there shall come water out of it, that the people may drink (Exodus 17:6).

6. While Amalek fought Israel, Moses sat on a stone while Aaron and Hur held his hands up to God (Exodus 17:8–12).

7. The Lord said unto Moses, Come up to me into the mount, and

be there: and I will give thee tables of stone, and a law, and commandments which I have written (Exodus 24:12).

8. Aaron's ephod held two onyx stones engraved with the names of the children of Israel (Exodus 28:9–12).

9. The Lord said unto Moses, Hew thee two tables of stone like unto the first: and I will write upon these tables the words that were in the first tables (Exodus 34:1).

10. Joshua had twelve stones taken from the dry pathway across the Jordan to be set in a heap in Canaan as a memorial. He also had twelve stones piled up where the priests had stood in the river (Joshua 4:4–8).

11. As Joshua pursued the Amorites, the Lord cast down great stones from heaven upon them (Joshua 10:11).

12. The five Amorite kings fled from Joshua and hid in a cave. He rolled large stones over the entrance to hold them in (Joshua 10:16–18).

13. After the children of Israel had covenanted to serve the Lord, Joshua set up a stone as a witness to all that had been promised (Joshua 24:27).

14. A certain woman cast a piece of a millstone on Abimelech's head, and broke his skull (Judges 9:53).

15. After the Israelites had defeated the Philistines, Samuel raised a stone pillar and called the name of it Ebenezer, saying, Hitherto hath the Lord helped us (1 Samuel 7:12).

16. David put his hand in his bag, took a stone, slung it, and smote Goliath in the forehead (1 Samuel 17:49).

17. King [Solomon] commanded, and they brought great stones, costly stones, and hewed stones, to lay the foundation of the house of the Lord (1 Kings 5:17).

18. After the priests of Baal had failed, Elijah took twelve stones, built an altar, and laid a bullock on top. The fire of the Lord fell and consumed even the stones (1 Kings 18:31–38).

19. Nebuchadnezzar dreamed about a great image and then a stone was cut out without hands, which smote the image upon his feet that were of iron and clay, and brake them to pieces (Daniel 2:34–35).

20. Daniel was thrown into the lions' den, and it was sealed with a stone and the king's own signet (Daniel 6:17).

21. Jesus said, Thou art Peter, and upon this rock I will build my church; and the gates of hell shall not prevail against it (Matthew 16:18).

22. Jesus saith unto them, Did you never read in the scriptures, The stone which the builders rejected, the same is become the head of the corner? (Matthew 21:42).

23. After laying Jesus in the tomb, Joseph of Arimathaea rolled a great stone to the door of the sepulchre (Matthew 27:59–60).

24. Jesus prophesied about the temple, saying, There shall not be left one stone upon another that shall not be thrown down (Mark 13:1–2).

25. The devil tempted Jesus, saying, If thou be the son of God, command this stone that it be made bread (Luke 4:3).

26. Jesus told the Pharisees that if the people did not hail Him king, the stones would cry out (Luke 19:40).

27. Before He called Lazarus from the grave, Jesus ordered that the stone be removed from the entrance of the tomb (John 11:38–40).

28. The children of Israel drank of that spiritual rock that followed them: and that Rock was Christ (1 Corinthians 10:4).

29. The Spirit saith unto the churches; To him that overcometh will I give . . . a white stone (Revelation 2:17).

30. An angel took up a stone like a great millstone and threw it into the sea, in John's vision (Revelation 18:21).

### 369. Lamps and Candles

1. Abraham set up a sacrifice to God to confirm the covenant, and God took a burning lamp through the midst of the sacrifice as a sign of His promise (Genesis 15:17).

2. The Lord commanded Moses to make a seven-branched candlestick to be placed within the tabernacle (Exodus 25:31–37).

3. Gideon's men blew the trumpets, and broke the pitchers, and held the lamps in their left hands . . . and they cried, The sword of the Lord, and of Gideon (Judges 7:16–21).

4. David sang, For thou art my lamp, O Lord: and the Lord will lighten my darkness (2 Samuel 22:29).

5. Thy word is a lamp unto my feet, and a light unto my path (Psalm 119:105).

6. Jesus said, Ye are the light of the world. A city that is set on a hill cannot be hid (Matthew 5:14).

7. Then shall the kingdom of heaven be likened unto ten virgins, which took their lamps, and went forth to meet the bridegroom (Matthew 25:1).

8. What woman having ten pieces of silver, if she lose one piece, doth not light a candle, and sweep the house, and seek diligently till she find it? (Luke 15:8).

9. The Philippian jailor called for a light to see if his prisoners were still in the jail (Acts 16:29).

10. John saw Jesus walking among seven golden candlesticks in his vision on Patmos (Revelation 1:12).

11. John described the New Jerusalem, saying, There shall be no night there; and they need no candle, neither light of the sun; for the Lord God giveth them light (Revelation 22:5).

## 370. *Ten Battles Won Supernaturally*

1. The Lord destroyed the Egyptian army in the Red Sea (Exodus 14:13–31).

2. And it came to pass, when Moses held up his hand, that Israel prevailed: and when he let down his hand, Amalek prevailed (Exodus 17:11).

3. When Joshua fought the kings of the Amorites, the Lord caused the sun to stand still, and He threw large hailstones down from the sky to kill the fleeing Amorites (Joshua 10:6–13).

4. The Philistines drew near to battle against Israel: but the Lord thundered with a great thunder on that day upon the Philistines, and discomfited them; and they were smitten before Israel (1 Samuel 7:10).

5. Jonathan and his armor-bearer attacked the Philistines, and the

Lord sent an earthquake that routed the enemy before them (1 Samuel 14:11–15).

6. Israel won a battle against the Syrians when the Lord struck the Syrians blind at Elisha's word (2 Kings 6:18–23).

7. The Lord had made the host of the Syrians to hear a noise of chariots, and a noise of horses, even the noise of a great host. . . . Wherefore they arose and fled in the twilight (2 Kings 7:6–7).

8. The Lord saved Jerusalem from the Syrians when the angel of the Lord went out, and smote in the camp of the Assyrians an hundred fourscore and five thousand (2 Kings 19:35).

9. As the men of Judah shouted, it came to pass, that God smote Jeroboam and all Israel before Abijah and Judah. And the children of Israel fled before Judah (2 Chronicles 13:15–16).

10. Jehoshaphat and Judah began to sing and to praise, [and] the Lord set ambushments against the children of Ammon, Moab, and mount Seir, which were come against Judah; and they were smitten (2 Chronicles 20:22).

## 371. Thirty-one New Testament Descriptions of Sinful Humanity

1. Alienated from God (Ephesians 4:18).

2. Blind (John 12:40; 2 Corinthians 4:4; 1 John 2:11).

3. Carnally minded (Romans 8:6, 13).

4. Corrupt (Matthew 7:17–18; 1 Timothy 6:5).

5. Darkened (Matthew 6:23; John 3:19; Romans 1:21; Ephesians 4:18; 1 John 1:6–7).

6. Dead in sin (John 5:24; Romans 8:6; Colossians 2:13; 1 Timothy 5:6; 1 John 3:14).

7. Deceived (Titus 3:3).

8. Defiled, or filthy (Titus 1:15; 2 Peter 2:20; Revelation 22:11).

9. Destitute of truth (Romans 1:18, 25; 1 Timothy 6:5).

10. Disobedient (Matthew 7:23; Ephesians 2:3; Titus 3:3).

11. An enemy of God (James 4:4).

12. Evil (Matthew 6:22; 12:33–34; John 3:20).

13. Foolish (Matthew 7:26; Ephesians 5:15; Titus 3:3).

14. Going astray (1 Peter 2:25).

15. Hateful (Titus 3:3).

16. Hypocritical (Matthew 6:2, 5, 16; 23:13, 28).

17. Impenitent (Romans 2:5; Hebrews 3:8).

18. Malicious and envious (Titus 3:3).

19. Pleasure- or world-loving (2 Thessalonians 2:12; 1 Timothy 5:6; 2 Timothy 3:4; Titus 3:3; 1 John 2:15).

20. Proud (Romans 1:30; 1 Timothy 6:4; 2 Timothy 3:4; James 4:6; 1 Peter 5:5).

21. Refusing belief (John 3:35; Titus 1:15).

22. Rejecting truth (2 Timothy 4:4).

23. Resisting God (Acts 7:51).

24. Guided by Satan (John 8:44; Ephesians 2:3).

25. Lovers of self (2 Timothy 3:2).

26. Self-satisfied (Revelation 3:17).

27. A slave of sin (John 8:34; Romans 6:16–17, 20; Titus 3:3).

28. Subordinating God (Romans 1:25).

29. Unconscious of bondage (John 8:33; Romans 7:7).

30. Unrighteous (1 Corinthians 6:9; Revelation 22:11).

31. Vain in their imaginations (Romans 1:21).

### 372. Thirty-eight Parables of Jesus

1. Ye are the salt of the earth: but if the salt have lost his savour, wherewith shall it be salted? it is thenceforth good for nothing, but to be cast out, and to be trodden under foot of men (Matthew 5:13).

2. Ye are the light of the world. A city that is set on an hill cannot be hid. Neither do men light a candle, and put it under a bushel, but on a candlestick; and it giveth light unto all that are in the house. Let your light so shine before men, that they may see your good works, and glorify your Father which is in heaven (Matthew 5:14–16).

3. Whosoever heareth these sayings of mine, and doeth them I will liken him unto a wise man, which built his house upon a rock: and the rain descended, and the floods came, and the winds blew, and beat upon that house; and it fell not: for it was founded upon a rock. And every one that heareth these sayings of mine, and doeth them not, shall be likened unto a foolish man, which built his house upon the sand: and the rain descended, and the floods came, and the winds blew, and beat upon that house; and it fell: and great was the fall of it (Matthew 7:24–27).

4. No man putteth a piece of new cloth unto an old garment, for that which is put in to fill it up taketh from the garment, and the rent is made worse (Matthew 9:16).

5. Neither do men put new wine into old bottles: else the bottles break, and the wine runneth out, and the bottles perish: but they put new wine into new bottles, and both are preserved (Matthew 9:17).

6. Behold, a sower went forth to sow . . . some seeds fell by the way side, and the fowls came and devoured them up: some fell upon stony places, where they had not much earth: and forthwith they sprung up, because they had no deepness of earth: and when the sun was up, they were scorched; and because they had no root, they withered away. And some fell among thorns . . . and choked them: but other fell into good ground, and brought forth fruit. . . .

   When any one heareth the word of the kingdom, and understandeth it not, then cometh the wicked one, and catcheth away that which was sown in his heart. This is he which received seed by the way side. But he that received the seed into stony places, the same is he that heareth the word . . . with joy receiveth it; yet hath not root in himself . . . for when tribulation or persecution ariseth because of the word . . . he is offended. He also that received seed among the thorns is he that heareth the word; and the care of this world, and the deceitfulness of riches, choke the word, and he becometh unfruitful. But he that received seed into the good ground is he that heareth the word, and understandeth it; which also beareth fruit . . . (Matthew 13:3–8, 19–23).

7. The kingdom of heaven is likened unto a man which sowed good seed in his field: but while men slept, his enemy came and sowed tares among the wheat. . . . But when the blade was sprung up, and brought forth fruit, then appeared the tares. So the servants

of the householder came and said . . . Sir, didst not thou sow good seed in thy field? . . . He said unto them, An enemy hath done this. The servants said unto him, Wilt thou then that we go and gather them up? But he said, Nay; lest while you gather up the tares, ye root up also the wheat with them. Let both grow together until the harvest: and in the time of harvest I will say to the reapers, Gather ye together first the tares, and bind them in bundles to burn them: but gather the wheat into my barn.

Then Jesus sent the multitude away, and went into the house: and his disciples came unto him saying, Declare unto us the parable of the tares of the field. He answered . . . He that soweth the good seed is the Son of man; The field is the world; the good seed are the children of the kingdom; but the tares are the children of the wicked one; the enemy that sowed them is the devil; the harvest is the end of the world; and reapers are the angels. As therefore the tares are gathered and burned in the fire; so shall it be in the end of this world. The Son of man shall send forth his angels, and they shall gather out of his kingdom all things that offend, and them which do iniquity; and shall cast them into a furnace of fire: there shall be wailing and gnashing of teeth. Then shall the righteous shine forth as the sun in the kingdom of their Father (Matthew 13:24–30, 36–43).

8. The kingdom of heaven is like to a grain of mustard seed, which a man took, and sowed in his field: which indeed is the least of all seeds: but when it is grown, it is the greatest among herbs, and becometh a tree, so that the birds of the air come and lodge in the branches thereof (Matthew 13:31–32).

9. The kingdom of heaven is like unto leaven, which a woman took, and hid in three measures of meal, till the whole was leavened (Matthew 13:33).

10. The kingdom of heaven is like unto treasure hid in a field; the which when a man hath found, he hideth, and for joy thereof goeth and selleth all that he hath, and buyeth that field (Matthew 13:44).

11. Again, the kingdom of heaven is like unto a merchant man, seeking goodly pearls: who, when he had found one pearl of great price, went and sold all that he had, and bought it (Matthew 13:45–46).

12. Again, the kingdom of heaven is like unto a net, that was cast into the sea, and gathered of every kind: which, when it was full,

they drew to shore, and sat down, and gathered the good into vessels, but cast the bad away. So shall it be at the end of the world: the angels shall come forth, and sever the wicked from among the just, and shall cast them into the furnace of fire: there shall be wailing and gnashing of teeth (Matthew 13:47–50).

13. If a man have an hundred sheep, and one of them be gone astray, doth he not leave the ninety and nine, and goeth into the mountains, and seeketh that which is gone astray? And if so be that he find it . . . he rejoiceth more of that sheep, than of the ninety and nine which went not astray. It is not the will of your Father which is in heaven, that one of these little ones should perish (Matthew 18:12–14).

14. The kingdom of heaven is likened unto a certain king, which would take account of his servants. . . . One was brought unto him, which owed him ten thousand talents. But forasmuch as he had not to pay, his lord commanded him to be sold, and his wife, and children, and all that he had, and payment to be made. The servant therefore fell down, and worshipped him, saying, Lord, have patience with me, and I will pay thee all. Then the lord of that servant was moved with compassion, and loosed him, and forgave him the debt.

But the same servant went out, and found one of his fellow-servants, which owed him an hundred pence: and he laid hands on him, and took him by the throat, saying. Pay me that thou owest. And his fellowservant fell down at his feet, and besought him, saying, Have patience with me, and I will pay thee all. . . . But he went and cast him into prison, till he should pay the debt. When his fellowservants saw what was done, they were very sorry, and . . . told unto their lord all that was done. Then his lord . . . said unto him, O thou wicked servant, I forgave thee all that debt, because thou desiredst me: shouldest not thou also have had compassion on thy fellowservant, even as I had pity on thee? And his lord was wroth, and delivered him to the tormentors, till he should pay all that was due unto him. So likewise shall my heavenly Father do also unto you, if ye from your hearts forgive not every one his brother their trespasses (Matthew 18:23–35).

15. The kingdom of heaven is like unto a man that is an householder, which went out early in the morning to hire labourers into his vineyard. And when he had agreed with the labourers for a penny

a day, he sent them into his vineyard. And he went out about the third hour, and saw others standing idle in the marketplace, and said unto them; Go ye also into the vineyard, and whatsoever is right I will give you. And they went their way. Again he went out about the sixth and ninth hour, and did likewise. And about the eleventh hour he went out, and found others standing idle, and saith unto them, Why stand ye here all the day idle? They say unto him, Because no man hath hired us. He saith unto them, Go ye also into the vineyard; and whatsoever is right, that shall ye receive.

So when even was come, the lord of the vineyard saith unto his steward, Call the labourers, and give them their hire, beginning from the last unto the first. And when they came that were hired about the eleventh hour, they received every man a penny. But when the first came, they supposed that they should have received more; and they likewise received every man a penny. . . . They murmured against the goodman of the house, saying, These last have wrought but one hour, and thou hast made them equal unto us, which have borne the burden and the heat of the day. But he answered one of them, and said, Friend, I do thee no wrong: didst not thou agree with me for a penny? Take that thine is, and go thy way: I will give unto this last, even as unto thee. Is it not lawful for me to do what I will with my own? . . . So the last shall be first, and the first last: for many be called, but few chosen (Matthew 20:1-16).

16. A certain man had two sons; and he came to the first, and said, Son, go work to day in my vineyard. He answered and said, I will not: but afterward he repented and went. And he came to the second, and said likewise. And he answered and said, I go, sir: and went not. [Which of them] did the will of his father? They say unto him, the first. Jesus saith . . . Verily I say unto you, that the publicans and the harlots go into the kingdom of God before you. For John came unto you in the way of righteousness, and ye believed him not: but the publicans and the harlots believed him: and ye . . . repented not . . . that ye might believe him (Matthew 21:28–32).

17. There was a certain householder, which planted a vineyard, and hedged it round about, and digged a winepress in it, and built a tower, and let it out to husbandmen, and went into a far country: and when the time of the fruit drew near, he sent his servants to the husbandmen, that they might receive the fruits

of it. And the husbandmen took his servants, and beat one, and killed another, and stoned another. Again, he sent other servants more than the first: and they did unto them likewise. But last of all he sent unto them his son, saying, They will reverence my son. But when the husbandmen saw the son, they said among themselves, This is the heir; come, let us kill him, and let us seize on his inheritance. And they caught him, and cast him out of the vineyard, and slew him.

When the lord therefore of the vineyard cometh, what will he do unto those husbandmen? They say unto him, He will miserably destroy those wicked men, and will let out his vineyard unto other husbandmen, which shall render him the fruits in their seasons. Jesus saith unto them, Did ye never read in the scriptures, The stone which the builders rejected, the same is become the head of the corner: this is the Lord's doing, and it is marvellous in our eyes? Therefore say I unto you, The kingdom of God shall be taken from you, and given to a nation bringing forth the fruits thereof. And whosoever shall fall on this stone shall be broken: but on whomsoever it shall fall, it will grind him to powder (Matthew 21:33–44).

18. The kingdom of heaven is like unto a certain king, which made a marriage for his son, and sent forth his servants to call them that were bidden to the wedding: and they would not come. Again, he sent forth other servants, saying, Tell them . . . Behold, I have prepared my dinner: my oxen and fatlings are killed, and all things are ready: come. . . . But they made light of it, and went their ways, one to his farm, another to his merchandise: and the remnant took his servants, and entreated them spitefully, and slew them. When the king heard thereof, he was wroth: and sent forth his armies, and destroyed those murderers, and burned up their city.

Then saith he to his servants, The wedding is ready, but they which were bidden were not worthy. Go ye therefore into the highways, and as many as ye shall find, bid to the marriage. So those servants went out into the highways, and gathered together . . . both bad and good: and the wedding was furnished with guests. And when the king came in to see the guests, he saw there a man which had not on a wedding garment: and he saith . . . Friend, how camest thou in not having a wedding garment? And he was speechless. Then said the king to the servants, Bind him hand and foot, and take him away, and cast him into outer darkness. . . . For many are called, but few are chosen (Matthew 22:2–14).

19. The kingdom of heaven [shall] be likened unto ten virgins, which took their lamps, and went forth to meet the bridegroom. Five of them were wise, and five were foolish. They that were foolish took their lamps, and took no oil with them. . . . While the bridegroom tarried, they all slept. At midnight there was a cry, Behold, the bridegroom cometh; go ye out to meet him. The virgins arose and trimmed their lamps. And the foolish said unto the wise, Give us of your oil; for our lamps are gone out. But the wise answered, Not so; lest there be not enough for us and you: but go ye to them that sell, and buy for yourselves. And while they went to buy, the bridegroom came; and they that were ready went in with him to the marriage: and the door was shut. Afterward came the other virgins, saying, Lord, Lord, open to us. But he answered and said, Verily, I say unto you, I know you not. Watch therefore, for ye know neither the day nor the hour wherein the Son of man cometh (Matthew 25:1–13).

20. The kingdom of heaven is as a man travelling into a far country, who called his own servants, and delivered unto them his goods. And unto one he gave five talents, to another two, and to another one; every man according to his ability; and straightway took his journey. Then he that had received the five talents went and traded with the same, and made them other five talents. And likewise he that had received two, gained two. But he that had received one digged in the earth and hid his lord's money. After a long time the lord of those servants cometh, and reckoneth with them. He that had received five talents came and brought other five talents, saying, Lord, thou deliveredst unto me five talents: behold, I have gained five talents more. His lord said unto him, Well done, thou good and faithful servant: thou hast been faithful over a few things, I will make thee ruler over many things: enter thou into the joy of thy lord. He also that had received two talents came and said, Lord, thou deliveredst unto me two talents: behold, I have gained two talents beside them. His lord said unto him, Well done, good and faithful servant. . . .

Then he which had received the one talent came and said, Lord, I knew thee, that thou art a hard man, reaping where thou hast not sown, and gathering where thou hast not strowed: and

I was afraid, and went and hid thy talent in the earth. . . . His lord answered and said unto him, Thou wicked and slothful servant, thou knewest that I reap where I sowed not, and gathered where I have not strowed: thou oughtest therefore to have put my money to the exchangers, and then at my coming I should have received mine own with usury. Take therefore the talent from him, and give it unto him which hath ten talents. For unto every one that hath shall be given . . . but from him that hath not shall be taken away even that which he hath. And cast ye the unprofitable servant into outer darkness: there shall be weeping and gnashing of teeth (Matthew 25:14–30).

21. When the Son of man shall come in his glory, and all the holy angels with him, then shall he sit upon the throne of his glory: and before him shall be gathered all nations: and he shall separate them . . . as a shepherd divideth his sheep from the goats: and he shall set the sheep on his right hand, the goats on the left. Then shall the King say unto them on his right hand, Come, ye blessed of my Father, inherit the kingdom prepared for you from the foundation of the world: for I was an hungred, and ye gave me meat: I was thirsty, and ye gave me drink: I was a stranger, and ye took me in: naked, and ye clothed me: I was sick, and ye visited me: I was in prison, and ye came unto me. Then shall the righteous answer him, saying, Lord, when saw we thee an hungred, and fed thee? or thirsty, and gave thee drink? When saw we thee a stranger, and took thee in? or naked and clothed thee? Or when saw we thee sick? or in prison, and came unto thee?

And the King shall answer and say unto them, Verily I say unto you, Inasmuch as ye have done it unto one of the least of these my brethren, ye have done it unto me. Then shall he say unto them on the left, Depart from me, ye cursed, into everlasting fire, prepared for the devil and his angels: for I was an hungred, and ye gave me no meat: I was thirsty, and ye gave me no drink: I was a stranger, and ye took me not in: naked, and ye clothed me not: sick, and in prison, and ye visited me not. Then shall they also answer him, Lord, when saw we thee an hungred, or athirst, or a stranger, or naked, or sick, or in prison, and did not minister unto thee? . . . Verily I say unto you, Inasmuch as ye did it not to one of the least of these, ye did it not to me. And these shall go away into everlasting punishment: but the righteous into life eternal (Matthew 25:31–46).

22. A certain man went down from Jerusalem to Jericho, and fell among thieves, which stripped him of his raiment, and wounded him, and departed, leaving him half dead. And there came down a certain priest that way: and when he saw him, he passed by on the other side. Likewise a Levite, when he was at the place, came and looked on him, and passed by on the other side. But a certain Samaritan, as he journeyed, came where he was: and when he saw him, he had compassion on him, and went to him, and bound up his wounds, pouring in oil and wine, and set him on his own beast, and brought him to an inn, and took care of him. And on the morrow when he departed, he took out two pence, and gave them to the host, and said, Take care of him; and whatsoever thou spendest more, when I come again, I will repay thee. Which of these three, thinkest thou, was neighbour unto him that fell among the thieves? And he said, He that shewed mercy on him. Then said Jesus unto him, Go, and do thou likewise (Luke 10:30–37).

23. He said unto them, Which of you shall have a friend, and shall go unto him at midnight, and say unto him, Friend, lend me three loaves; for a friend of mine in his journey is come to me, and I have nothing to set before him? And he from within shall answer and say, Trouble me not: the door is now shut, and my children are with me in bed; I cannot rise and give thee. I say unto you, Though he will not rise and give him, because he is his friend, yet because of his importunity he will rise and give him as many as he needeth.

    I say unto you, Ask, and it shall be given you; seek, and ye shall find; knock, and it shall be opened unto you. For every one that asketh receiveth; and he that seeketh findeth; and to him that knocketh it shall be opened. If a son shall ask bread of any of you that is a father, will he give him a stone? or if he ask a fish, will he give him a serpent? or if he ask an egg, will he give a scorpion? If ye, being evil, know how to give good gifts to your children: how much more shall your heavenly Father give the Holy Spirit to them that ask him? (Luke 11:5–13).

24. The ground of a certain rich man brought forth plentifully: and he thought within himself, What shall I do, because I have no room to bestow my fruits? And he said, I will pull down my barns,

and build greater; and there will I bestow all my fruits and my goods. And I will say to my soul, Soul, thou hast much goods laid up for many years; take thine ease, eat, drink, and be merry. But God said unto him, Thou fool, this night thy soul shall be required of thee: then whose shall those things be, which thou hast provided? So is he that layeth up treasure for himself, and is not rich toward God (Luke 12:16–21).

25. Let your loins be girded about, and your lights burning; and ye yourselves like unto men that wait for their lord, when he will return from the wedding; that when he cometh and knocketh, they may open to him immediately. Blessed are those servants, whom the lord when he cometh shall find watching: verily I say unto you, that he shall gird himself, and make them to sit down to meat, and will come forth and serve them. And if he shall come in the second watch, or come in the third watch, and find them so, blessed are those servants. And this know, that if the goodman of the house had known what hour the thief would come, he would have watched, and not have suffered his house to be broken through. Be ye therefore ready also: for the Son of man cometh at an hour when ye think not (Luke 12:35–40).

26. And he put forth a parable to those which were bidden, when he marked how they chose out the chief rooms; saying unto them, when thou art bidden of any man to a wedding, sit not down in the highest room; lest a more honourable man than thou be bidden of him; and he that bade thee and him come and say to thee, Give this man place; and thou begin with shame to take the lowest room. But when thou art bidden, go and sit down in the lowest room; that when he that badeth thee cometh, he may say unto thee, Friend, go up higher: then shalt thou have worship in the presence of them that sit at meat with thee. For whosoever exalteth himself shall be abased; and he that humbleth himself shall be exalted (Luke 14:7–11).

27. A certain man made a great supper, and bade many: and sent his servant at supper time to say to them that were bidden, Come; for all things are now ready. And they all . . . began to make excuse. The first said, I have bought a piece of ground, and I must needs go and see it: I pray thee have me excused. Another said, I have bought five yoke of oxen, and I go to prove them: I pray thee have

me excused. And another said, I have married a wife, and therefore I cannot come. So that servant came, and shewed his lord these things. Then the master of the house being angry said to his servant, Go out quickly into the streets and lanes of the city, and bring in hither the poor, and the maimed, and the halt, and the blind. And the servant said, Lord, it is done as thou hast commanded, and yet there is room. And the lord said unto the servant, Go out into the highways and hedges, and compel them to come in, that my house may be filled. For I say unto you, that none of those men which were bidden shall taste of my supper (Luke 14:16–24).

28. Which of you, intending to build a tower, sitteth not down first, and counteth the cost, whether he have sufficient to finish it? Lest after he hath laid the foundation, and is not able to finish it, all that behold it begin to mock him, saying, This man began to build, and was not able to finish. Or what king, going to make war against another king, sitteth not down first, and consulteth whether he be able with ten thousand to meet him that cometh against him with twenty thousand? Or else, while the other is yet a great way off, he sendeth an ambassage, and desireth conditions of peace. So likewise, whosoever he be of you that forsaketh not all that he hath, he cannot be my disciple (Luke 14:28–33).

29. What woman having ten pieces of silver, if she lose one piece, doth not light a candle, and sweep the house, and seek diligently till she find it? And when she hath found it, she calleth her friends and neighbours together, saying, Rejoice with me; for I have found the piece which I had lost. Likewise, I say unto you, there is joy in the presence of the angels of God over one sinner that repenteth (Luke 15:8–10).

30. A certain man had two sons: and the younger of them said, Father, give me the portion of goods that falleth to me. And he divided to them his living. And not many days after the younger son gathered all together, and took his journey into a far country, and there wasted his substance with riotous living. And when he had spent all, there arose a mighty famine in that land; and he began to be in want: And he went and joined himself to a citizen of that country; and he sent him into the fields to feed swine. And he would fain have filled his belly with the husks that the swine did eat: and no man gave unto him. And when he came to himself, he said,

How many hired servants of my father's have bread enough and to spare, and I perish with hunger! I will arise and go to my father, and will say unto him, Father, I have sinned against heaven and before thee, and am no more worthy to be called thy son: make me as one of thy hired servants. And he arose, and came to his father. But when he was yet a great way off, his father saw him, and had compassion, and ran, and fell on his neck, and kissed him. And the son said unto him, Father, I have sinned against heaven, and in thy sight, and am no more worthy to be called thy son. But the father said to his servants, Bring forth the best robe, and put it on him; and put a ring on his hand, and shoes on his feet: and bring hither the fatted calf, and kill it; and let us eat, and be merry: for this my son was dead, and is alive again; he was lost, and is found. And they began to be merry.

Now his elder son was in the field: and as he came and drew nigh to the house, he heard music and dancing. And he called one of the servants, and asked what these things meant. And he said, Thy brother is come; and thy father hath killed the fatted calf, because he hath received him safe and sound. And he was angry, and would not go in: therefore came his father out, and entreated him. And he answering said to his father, Lo, these many years do I serve thee, neither transgressed I at any time thy commandment: and yet thou never gavest me a kid, that I might make merry with my friends: but as soon as this thy son was come, which hath devoured thy living with harlots, thou hast killed for him the fatted calf. And he said unto him, Son, thou art ever with me, and all that I have is thine. It was meet that we should make merry, and be glad: for this thy brother was dead, and is alive again; was lost, and is found (Luke 15:11–32).

31. There was a certain rich man, which had a steward; and the same was accused that he had wasted his goods. And he called him and said, How is it that I hear this of thee? give an account of thy stewardship; for thou mayest be no longer steward. Then the steward said within himself, What shall I do? for my lord taketh away from me the stewardship: I cannot dig; to beg I am ashamed. I am resolved what to do, that, when I am put out of the stewardship, they may receive me into their houses. So he called every one of his lord's debtors unto him, and said unto the first, How much owest thou my lord? He said, An hundred

measures of oil. And he said unto him, Take thy bill, and sit down quickly, and write fifty. Then said he to another, And how much owest thou? He said, An hundred measures of wheat. And he said unto him, Take thy bill and write fourscore.

And the lord commended the unjust steward, because he had done wisely: for the children of the world are in their generation wiser than the children of light. Make to yourselves friends of the mammon of unrighteousness; that, when you fail, they may receive you into everlasting habitations. He that is faithful in that which is least is faithful also in much: and he that is unjust in the least is unjust also in much. If therefore ye have not been faithful in the unrighteous mammon, who will commit to your trust the true riches? And if you have not been faithful in that which is another man's, who shall give you that which is your own? No servant can serve two masters: for either he will hate the one, and love the other; or else he will hold to the one, and despise the other. Ye cannot serve God and mammon (Luke 16:1–13).

32. There was a certain rich man, which was clothed in purple and fine linen, and fared sumptuously every day: and there was a certain beggar named Lazarus, which was laid at his gate, full of sores, and desiring to be fed with the crumbs which fell from the rich man's table: moreover the dogs came and licked his sores. And it came to pass, that the beggar died, and was carried by the angels into Abraham's bosom: the rich man also died, and was buried; and in hell he lift up his eyes, being in torments, and seeth Abraham afar off, and Lazarus in his bosom. And he cried and said, Father Abraham, have mercy on me, and send Lazarus, that he may dip the tip of his finger in water, and cool my tongue; for I am tormented in this flame. But Abraham said, Son, remember that thou in thy lifetime receivedst thy good things, and likewise Lazarus evil things: but now he is comforted, and thou art tormented. And beside all this, between us and you there is a great gulf fixed: so that they which would pass from hence to you cannot; neither can they pass to us that would come from thence.

Then he said, I pray thee therefore, father, that thou wouldest send him to my father's house: for I have five brethren; that he may testify unto them, lest they also come into this place of torment. Abraham saith unto him, They have Moses and the prophets; let them hear them. And he said, Nay, father Abraham: but if one went unto them from the dead, they will repent. And he said unto him, If they hear not Moses and the prophets, neither will they be persuaded, though one rose from the dead (Luke 16:19–31).

33. Which of you, having a servant plowing or feeding cattle, will say unto him when he is come from the field, Go and sit down to meat? And will not rather say unto him, Make ready wherewith I may sup, and gird thyself, and serve me, till I have eaten and drunk; and afterward thou shalt eat and drink? Doth he thank that servant because he did the things commanded him? So likewise ye, when ye shall have done all those things commanded you, say, We are unprofitable servants: we have done what was our duty to do (Luke 17:7–10).

34. Men ought always to pray, and not to faint: There was in a city a judge, which feared not God, neither regarded man: and there was a widow in that city; and she came unto him, saying, Avenge me of mine adversary. And he would not for a while: but afterward he said within himself, Though I fear not God, nor regard man; yet because this widow troubleth me, I will avenge her, lest by her continual coming she weary me. And the Lord said, Hear what the unjust judge saith. And shall not God avenge his own elect, which cry day and night unto him? I tell you that he will avenge them speedily. Nevertheless when the Son of man cometh, shall he find faith on the earth? (Luke 18:1–18).

35. He spake this parable unto certain which trusted in themselves that they were righteous, and despised others: Two men went up into the temple to pray; the one a Pharisee, and the other a publican. The Pharisee stood and prayed thus, God, I thank thee, that I am not as other men are, extortioners, unjust, adulterers, or even as this publican. I fast twice a week, I give tithes of all that I possess. And the publican, standing afar off, would not lift up so much as his eyes unto heaven, but smote upon his breast, saying, God be merciful to me a sinner. I tell you, this man went down to his house justified: for every one that exalteth himself shall be abased; and he that humbleth himself shall be exalted (Luke 18:9–14).

36. He called the multitude, and said unto them, Hear, and understand: Not that which goeth into the mouth defileth a man; but that which cometh out of the mouth, this defileth a man. Then came his disciples, and said unto him, Knowest thou that the Pharisees

were offended, after they heard this saying? But he answered and said, Every plant, which my heavenly Father hath not planted, shall be rooted up. Let them alone: they be blind leaders of the blind. And if the blind lead the blind, both shall fall into the ditch. Then answered Peter and said unto him, Declare unto us this parable.

And Jesus said, Are ye also yet without understanding? Do not ye yet understand, that whatsoever entereth in at the mouth goeth into the belly, and is cast out into the draught? But those things which proceed out of the mouth come forth from the heart; and they defile the man. For out of the heart proceed evil thoughts, murders, adulteries, fornications, thefts, false witness, blasphemies: These are the things which defile a man: but to eat with unwashen hands defileth not a man (Matthew 15:10–20).

37. He spake a parable unto them, Can the blind lead the blind? shall they not both fall into the ditch? The disciple is not above his master: but every one that is perfect shall be as his master (Luke 6:39–40).

38. Verily, verily, I say unto you, He that entereth not by the door into the sheepfold, but climbeth up some other way, the same is a thief and a robber. But he that entereth in by the door is the shepherd of the sheep. To him the porter openeth; and the sheep hear his voice: and he calleth his own sheep by name, and leadeth them out. And when he putteth forth his own sheep, he goeth before them, and the sheep follow him: for they know his voice. And a stranger they will not follow, but will flee from him: for they know not the voice of strangers. This parable spake Jesus unto them: but they understood not what things they were which he spake unto them.

Then said Jesus unto them again, Verily, verily, I say unto you, I am the door of the sheep. All that ever came before me are thieves and robbers: but the sheep did not hear them. I am the door: by me if any man enter in, he shall be saved, and shall go in and out, and find pasture. The thief cometh not, but for to steal, and to kill, and to destroy: I am come that they might have life, and that they might have it more abundantly. I am the good shepherd: the good shepherd giveth his life for the sheep. But he that is an hireling, and not the shepherd, whose own the sheep are not, seeth the wolf coming, and leaveth the sheep, and fleeth: and the wolf catcheth them, and scattereth the sheep. The hireling fleeth, because he is an hireling, and careth not for the sheep.

I am the good shepherd, and know my sheep, and am known of mine. As the Father knoweth me, even so know I the Father: and I lay down my life for the sheep. And other sheep I have, which are not of this fold: them also I must bring, and there shall be one fold, and one shepherd. Therefore doth my Father love me, because I lay down my life, that I might take it again. No man taketh it from me, but I lay it down of myself. I have power to lay it down, and I have power to take it again. This commandment have I received of my Father (John 10:1–18).

### 373. Ten Mountaintop Experiences

1. Noah's ark came to rest upon the mountains of Ararat (Genesis 8:4).

2. Abraham offered up Isaac upon a mountain in the land of Moriah (Genesis 22:2).

3. The angel of the Lord appeared to Moses in the burning bush at Mount Horeb (Exodus 3:2).

4. Moses received the Ten Commandments atop Mount Sinai (Exodus 20).

5. Aaron died upon Mount Hor (Numbers 20:22–28).

6. The Lord showed Moses the Promised Land from the top of Mount Pisgah (Deuteronomy 34:1–4).

7. Satan took Jesus up into an exceeding high mountain, and sheweth him all the kingdoms of the world, and the glory of them; and saith unto him, All these things will I give thee, if thou wilt fall down and worship me. Then saith Jesus; Get thee hence, Satan: for it is written, Thou shalt worship the Lord thy God, and him only shalt thou serve (Matthew 4:8–10).

8. Jesus went up into a mountain and delivered the Sermon on the Mount (Matthew 5–7).

9. Jesus was transfigured in front of Peter, James, and John up in a high mountain (Matthew 17:1–9).

10. Jesus was betrayed and arrested on the Mount of Olives (Matthew 26:30–57).

## 374. The Fatherless and Motherless (Orphans in the Bible)

1. Benjamin and Joseph lost their natural mother when Rachel died while giving birth to Benjamin (Genesis 35:16–18).

2. About four hundred young virgins from Jabesh-gilead were orphaned all about the same time (Judges 21:1–12).

3. Ichabod was born a full-fledged orphan (1 Samuel 4:19–22).

4. Mephibosheth lost his father (Jonathan) when he was just a child (2 Samuel 4:4).

5. The nameless young son of a widow was raised from the dead by Elijah (1 Kings 17:8–23).

6. Joash was only one year old when his father, Ahaziah, was slain (2 Kings 11:1–21).

7. Azariah was left fatherless at age sixteen when his father, King Amaziah, was murdered (2 Kings 14:17–21).

8. Manasseh was twelve years old when his father, King Hezekiah, died (2 Kings 20:21; 21:1).

9. Josiah was only eight years old when his father was murdered (2 Kings 21:23–26; 22:1).

10. Jehoiachin was eighteen when his father died (2 Kings 24:6–8).

11. Esther was orphaned when she was a young girl and was raised by her cousin, Mordecai (Esther 2:5–7).

12. Daniel, Shadrach, Meshach, and Abednego were probably all orphans (Daniel 1:1–17).

# 42

## ENCOURAGEMENT

In formulating this list, I felt the reader would benefit from seeing these nuggets of truth pulled from the Scriptures and listed in a way that might encourage when each is read separately. Take in one stunning revelation at a time. Perhaps even single out favorites and place them in a prominent place for reminders of God's abundance.

*Note:* These quotations are taken from the *New King James Version of the Bible.*

### 375. Twenty-nine Positive Statements From Scripture

1. *You can do it!*
   "I can do all things through Christ who strengthens me" (Philippians 4:13).

2. *You are healed.*
   "Who Himself bore our sins . . . by whose stripes you were healed" (1 Peter 2:24).

3. *You can prosper.*
   "Beloved, I pray that you may prosper in all things" (3 John 1:2).

4. *Great things are in store for you.*
   "Eye has not seen, nor ear heard, nor have entered into the heart of man the things which God has prepared for those who love Him" (1 Corinthians 2:9).

5. *They cannot overcome you.*
   "No weapon formed against you shall prosper" (Isaiah 54:17).

6. *You can get over it!*
   "Forgetting those things which are behind . . . I press toward the goal for the prize of the upward call of God in Christ Jesus" (Philippians 3:13–14).

7. *You won't go hungry.*
   "I have been young, and now am old; yet I have not seen the righteous forsaken, nor his descendants begging bread" (Psalms 37:25).

8. *You have eternal life.*
   "For God so loved the world that He gave His only begotten Son, that whoever believes in Him should not perish but have everlasting life" (John 3:16).

9. *You are a king.*
   "Jesus Christ . . . has made us kings" (Revelation 1:5–6).

10. *You are a joint heir with Jesus.*
    "The Spirit Himself bears witness with our spirit that we are . . . joint heirs with Christ" (Romans 8:16–17).

11. *You can be courageous.*
    "Be strong and of good courage" (Joshua 1:6).

12. *You have the strongest defense.*
    "If God be for us, who can be against us?" (Romans 8:31).

13. *You are a child of God!*
    "As many as received Him [Jesus], to them He gave the right to become children of God" (John 1:12).

14. *You have the mind of Christ.*
    "We have the mind of Christ" (1 Corinthians 2:16).

15. *You have been given great and precious promises.*
    "His divine power has given to us . . . great and precious promises" (2 Peter 1:3–4).

16. *You have a sound mind.*
    "God has given us . . . a sound mind" (2 Timothy 1:7).

17. *All things are working toward your good.*
    "All things work together for good to those who love God" (Romans 8:28).

18. *You are privy to the secrets of God!*
    "We speak the wisdom of God in a mystery, the hidden wisdom

which God ordained before the ages for our glory" (1 Corinthians 2:7).

19. *You have angels ministering for you!*
"Are they [angels] not all ministering spirits sent forth to minister for those who will inherit salvation?" (Hebrews 1:14).

20. *You are an ambassador for Christ.*
"We are ambassadors for Christ" (2 Corinthians 5:20).

21. *You are seated in heavenly places in Christ Jesus.*
"God . . . [has] made us sit together in heavenly places in Christ Jesus" (Ephesians 2:4–6).

22. *You were made to be the righteousness of God.*
"For He [God] made Him who knew no sin to be sin for us, that we might become the righteousness of God in Him" (2 Corinthians 5:21).

23. *God the Father loves you even as He loved Jesus.*
"That the world may know that You have . . . loved them as You have loved Me" (John 17:23).

24. *You have passed from death to life if you love the brethren.*
"We know that we have passed from death to life, because we love the brethren" (1 John 3:14).

25. *You are sanctified.*
"We have been sanctified through the offering of the body of Jesus Christ once for all" (Hebrews 10:10).

26. *The Lord hears your prayers.*
"The eyes of the Lord are on the righteous, and His ears are open to their prayers" (1 Peter 3:12).

27. *You shall reign with Jesus.*
"If we endure, we shall also reign with Him" (2 Timothy 2:12).

28. *You are justified.*
"Man is not justified by the works of the law but by faith in Jesus Christ" (Galatians 2:16).

29. *You are more than a conqueror.*
"In all these things we are more than conquerors through Him who loved us" (Romans 8:37).

# BIBLIOGRAPHY

Bible Dictionary—Concordance to Holy Bible (Appendix to King James Version). Philadelphia: Holman Bible Publishers, 1942.

Buckland, A. R., ed., A. Lukyn Williams, asst. *The Universal Bible Dictionary*. New York: Fleming H. Revell Co., 1951.

Douglas, J. O., ed. *The New Bible Dictionary*. Grand Rapids: Eerdmans, 1962.

"For Today and Every Day" (Appendix to King James Version). Philadelphia: Holman Bible Publishers, 1947, 1949.

Halley, Henry H. *Halley's Bible Handbook*. Grand Rapids: Zondervan, 1965.

Lockyer, Herbert. *All the Kings and Queens of the Bible*. Grand Rapids: Zondervan, 1961.

_____. *All the Men of the Bible*. Grand Rapids: Zondervan, 1958, 1979.

_____. *All the Women of the Bible*. Grand Rapids: Zondervan, 1967, 1979.

Marshall, Rev. Alfred, D. Litt. *Interlinear Greek-English New Testament*. Grand Rapids: Zondervan, 1958, 1969.

McCary, James Leslie, and Mark McElhaney. *The Abbreviated Bible—with the Apocrypha*. New York: Van Nostrand Reinhold Co., 1971.

Nave, Orville J. *Nave's Topical Bible*. Chicago: Moody Press, 1921.

Pfeiffer, Charles F., ed. (O.T.), Everett F. Harrison, ed. (N.T.) *The Wycliffe Bible Commentary*. Chicago: Moody Press, 1962, 1972.

Rea, John, general ed. "Aids to Understanding the Holy Bible" (Appendix to *Family Bible*). Cleveland: The World Publishing Co., 1968.

Reese, Edward, ed. *The Reese Chronological Bible*. Minneapolis: Bethany House, 1977, 1980.

Robertson, A. T. *A Harmony of the Gospels*. New York: Harper & Row, 1950.

Strong, James. *Strong's Exhaustive Concordance of the Bible*. Nashville: Abingdon Press, 1890, 1963.

Unger, Merrill F. *Unger's Bible Dictionary*. Grand Rapids: Moody Press, 1957, 1961, 1966, 1981.

Wilkerson, David. *The Jesus Person Pocket Promise Book*. Ventura, CA: Gospel Light Publications, Regal Books, 1972, 1979.